THE STORY OF GREECE AND ROME

Tony Spawforth is emeritus professor of ancient history at Newcastle University, presenter of eight archaeological documentaries in the 'Ancient Voices' series on BBC2 and author of numerous books, including *Greece and the Augustan Cultural Revolution*. He lives in Brighton, UK.

THE
STORY OF
GREECE
AND
ROME

TONY SPAWFORTH

YALE UNIVERSITY PRESS
NEW HAVEN AND LONDON

For information about this and other Yale University Press publications, please contact:
U.S. Office: sales.press@yale.edu   yalebooks.com
Europe Office: sales@yaleup.co.uk   yalebooks.co.uk

Set in Minion Pro by IDSUK (DataConnection) Ltd
Printed in Great Britain by Hobbs the Printers Ltd, Totton, Hampshire

Library of Congress Control Number: 2018939477

ISBN 978-0-300-21711-7 (hbk)
ISBN 978-0-300-25164-7 (pbk)

A catalogue record for this book is available from the British Library.

10 9 8 7 6 5 4 3 2 1

CONTENTS

List of Maps and Plates   *vii*

Acknowledgements   *ix*

Prologue The Wild and the Tamed: Ancient Views   1
of Civilization

Part I The Greeks

1   The Dawn of Greek Civilization   15
2   The Rise of the Hellenes   32
3   New Things: The First Greek City-States   45
4   As Rich as Croesus: Early Greeks and the East   60
5   Great Greeks: The Greek Settlement of the West   75
6   Meet the (Western) Neighbours   90
7   'Lord of All Men'? The Threat of Persia   105
8   The Same but Different: Athens and Sparta   119
9   'Unprecedented Suffering'? The Peloponnesian War   134
10 Examined Lives and Golden Mouths   148
11 'A Brilliant Flash of Lightning': Alexander of Macedon   163
12 Game of Thrones, or the World after Alexander   177

Part II The Romans

13	'Senatus Populusque Romanus'	195
14	Boots on the Ground: Building the Roman Empire	210
15	Hail Caesar! The Advent of the Autocrats	225
16	'Fierce Rome, Captive'? The Lure of Greece	241
17	What Did the Romans Do for Their Empire?	257
18	'Barbarians' at the Gate	271
19	The 'Jesus Movement'	286
20	United We Stand: The Final Century	301
21	Divided We Fall: A Tale of Two Empires	316
	Epilogue	330
	Timeline	*334*
	Notes	*340*
	Further Reading	*354*
	Index	*356*

MAPS AND PLATES

Maps

1.	Greece and the Aegean World.	16–17
2.	The Eastern Mediterranean and the Near East.	62–3
3.	Italy.	76
4.	Central Asia.	178
5.	The West.	256

Plates

1. An Athenian vase depicting Demeter's gift of agriculture to mankind, c. 470 BC. Marie-Lan Nguyen.

2. A plaster cast of a marble statue of Hadrian. Reproduced by permission of the Museo della Civiltà Romana, Rome. Photo: John Williams.

3. A fragment of a wall painting from the excavation of an ancient Egyptian palace at modern Tell el-Dab'a, c. 1473–1458 BC. Colours digitally restored by Clairy Palyvou. © M. Bietak, N. Marinatos, C. Palyvou/graphic work M. Negrete-Martinez.

4. An Athenian wine jug, late 700s BC. National Archaeological Museum, Athens. Photo: Giannis Patrikianos. © Hellenic Ministry of Culture and Sports/Archaeological Receipts Fund.

5. A scene on a Corinthian pottery jug, c. 640 BC, depicting two Greek armies marching into battle. World History Archive/Alamy Stock Photo.

6. The remains of paved haulage across the Isthmus, built *c.* 600 BC. Erin Babnik/Alamy Stock Photo.

7. An unfinished Greek temple, Segesta, Sicily. Alec/Public Domain.

8. The Tomb of the Leopards at Tarquinii. Adam Eastland Art + Architecture/Alamy Stock Photo.

9. A depiction of Xerxes I on his tomb in Naqš-i Rustam. Erich Schmidt/CC-BY-SA-3.0.

10. A modern replica of an Athenian trireme, Piraeus, Greece. Templar52.

11. The Ear of Dionysius, ancient quarry, Sicily. Laurel Lodged/CC-BY-SA-3.0.

12. A depiction of two actors on an Athenian vase, *c.* 400 BC, Naples Archaeological Museum. © agefotostock.

13. A cast bronze spear butt and inscription, late 300s BC. Newcastle upon Tyne, Shefton Collection 111. Photo: Andrew Agate.

14. Stone water spout, early 100s BC, Ai-Khanoum, Afghanistan. © Livius.org.

15. A monumental altar at Pergamum depicting Athena fighting Giants, 197–158 BC. Gryffindor/Public Domain.

16. 'Tomb of Scipio Barbatus', engraving by Giovanni Battista Piranesi, *c.* 1756. Giovanni Battista Piranesi/Public Domain.

17. A scene from a monument celebrating the Roman victory over the Macedonians in 168 BC. © Bildarchiv Foto Marburg.

18. A marble statue of Livia Drusilla, Madrid Archaeological Museum. Adam Eastland Art + Architecture/Alamy Stock Photo.

19. A fragment of the Antikythera mechanism, National Archaeological Museum, Athens. Photo: Giannis Patrikianos. © Hellenic Ministry of Culture and Sports/Archaeological Receipts Fund.

20. The theatre at the Lycian city of Patara. Kamil Isik/Public Domain.

21. A sculpture of the head of Pompey the Great. Carole Raddato.

22. A scene from the Column of Marcus Aurelius, Rome, *c.* AD 185. Barosaurus Lentus.

23. The ruins of the Roman amphitheatre at Lyon. Pymouss.

24. The head of Constantine, from a colossal statue now in the Capitoline Museum, Rome. BibleLandPictures/Alamy Stock Photo.

25. The Mausoleum of Galla Placidia. imageBROKER/Alamy Stock Photo.

26. A painted ceiling at the château of Vaux-le-Vicomte, France, late 1650s. www.all-free-photos.com.

27. François Testory performing *Medea (Written in Rage)*, London, October 2017. Courtesy of François Testory, Neil Bartlett and Jean-René Lamoine. Photo: Manuel Vason.

ACKNOWLEDGEMENTS

For different kinds of help and opportunities which I have drawn on in writing this book I am grateful to many people and institutions over many years, and not least to: Carla Antonaccio; Josephine Balmer; Bob Barber; Richard Bidgood; Manfred Bietak; John Boardman; the British School at Athens (Chapter 11 is based on my research as a British School Visiting Fellow in 2014); the late Hector and Elizabeth Catling; Erica Davies; Esther Eidinow; Nelson Fernandez; Anastasia Gadolou; David Gill; Heinrich Hall; Paul Halstead; Andrew Hobson; Simon Hornblower; Monica Hughes; Lucia Iacono; the Joint Library of the Societies for Hellenic and Roman Studies, London, and its staff; Peter Jones; Nota Karamaouna; Marie-Christine Keith; Stephanie and Nigel Kennell; Maria Lagogianni; Jona Lendering; Chris Mann; the late Chris Mee; Michael Metcalfe; the late John Moles; Lyvia Morgan; Andrew Parkin; Derek Phillips; Chrysoula Saatsoglou-Paliadeli; Rowland Smith; Allaire Stallsmith; Ann Steiner; Lucrezia Ungaro; Manuel Vason; Rania Vassiliadou; Sally Waite; Susan Walker; Jennifer Webb; and John Wilkes.

I owe a special thanks to Paul Cartledge, not only for helpful conversations but also for his rigorous scrutiny of a first draft. I am grateful to the wise and careful comments by Yale's anonymous readers, which I have done my best to take on board. More broadly, I am indebted to the scholars whose writings and researches I have absorbed in my thinking and writing. They are many, many more than are identified by name in the limited references at the back of this book.

Shortcomings that remain, of whatever kind, are mine alone.

I was lucky to have had the chance to try out some ideas for how to write the book while a speaker on cultural tours run by the Cultural Travel Company; Martin Randall Travel; Peter Sommer Travels; and the UK Friends of the British School at Athens. I am grateful to the guests on these tours for their patience, their interest and their observations, which were more valuable than they sometimes seemed to think.

At Yale I am indebted to the book's editors, Marika Lysandrou, whose suggestions helped significantly to pull the book into better shape, and Rachael Lonsdale, who saw it through to publication. I am grateful to Heather McCallum, who invited me to write this book and who has encouraged me throughout.

I thank Andrew Lownie for his support, moral and practical. Finally, there is my deep gratitude, as always, to Lee Stannard.

Tony Spawforth
January 2018

PROLOGUE
THE WILD AND THE TAMED: ANCIENT VIEWS OF CIVILIZATION

Over two and a half thousand years ago, perhaps in the later 700s BC, a poet told of events which took place during a ten-year siege of the city of Troy. This poem – the *Iliad* – marked the start of one of the world's greatest and oldest storytelling traditions, still influential today. Like the word 'story' itself, this tradition is a gift to us from the ancient Greeks.

This book offers the reader a story of my own. Its ambition is to provide between one set of covers an accessible account of the enormous sweep of ancient history which has to be considered not only in order to appreciate the remote ancient society which gave us the poet Homer and so much else, but also the later centuries of antiquity when a new and seemingly unstoppable force – the Romans – embraced and perpetuated the cultural legacy of Classical Greece.

For centuries, well into the Christian era, the ancient Greeks, their way of life and their cultural traditions, took shelter behind the booted legionaries guarding the Roman Empire. Thanks to the Romans, all sorts of debris from ancient Greek culture survived into the mediaeval world. Some of it has come down to us.

This is a book that tells a story about a 'civilization'. In my view, two millennia or so later, when it comes to ancient Greece and Rome it is their civilization that is the real basis for wonder today. My story is about the building of this civilization by many hands, and, like all stories, it has a beginning.

In the years around 440 BC, an artisan at work in the potteries of Athens decorated a cup with the figure of a snake-man. Now in a Berlin museum, the pot depicts a bearded figure who holds a staff. So far so normal: but below the waist he has serpent-coils instead of legs. Greeks called this kind of supernatural creature a 'dragon', or *drakōn*: whence 'Draco' Malfoy, Harry Potter's Slytherin arch-foe. In decorating this cup, the pot painter had in mind a particular 'dragon'. He made this clear by adding in paint, for those who could read the Greek letters, the name 'Cecrops'.

Ancient writers called Cecrops a legendary king of Athens. In the stories they told, they credited him with civilizing the ancestors of the ancient Athenians by inventing the institution of marriage – earlier Athenians had indulged in free love, it was said. He also introduced them to writing, to burial of the dead and to city building. In gratitude for his gifts, Athenians founded a shrine of this serpent-king on the Acropolis. Here, a stone's throw from the Parthenon, their descendants still worshipped him with religious rites into the first Christian centuries.

But this was not the only way in which the Greeks imagined their journey from savagery to civilization. In the same period, some Greeks were telling a new and radical story. One spring day, also around 440 BC, an audience of up to twelve thousand Athenians crowded into a special building made of wood on the slopes of the Acropolis. They had come to enjoy a newish art form, one that, in a modern definition, 'repeated human experiences, with small changes': or as we say today, dramatic performances, plays.

At one point the audience heard a chorus of male performers impersonating old men sing out this verse: 'Wonders are many, and none is more formidable than humankind.' Even in translation from Ancient Greek, these words of the playwright, the Athenian Sophocles, seem extraordinary. In a world full of superhumans, the dramatist's line concedes nothing to the powers of legendary figures or to gods. Instead its author understands civilization as a human creation. As the chorus next explained, humans had taught themselves how to hunt and fish, how to tame wild animals and yoke them in order to till the soil and grow crops, how to sail the seas, communicate by speech, build homes, live in communities and ward off at least some diseases.

This Greek idea of a cultural ascent of man from primal beginnings achieved by human capacity alone may strike us as modern. It channelled the revolutionary new ways of thinking about human nature emerging in parts of the Greek world in the 500s and 400s BC.

Today we turn to archaeologists, along with various other experts of the kind whose disciplines start with the prefix 'palaeo-', to reconstruct humankind's early steps towards cultural complexity. The ancient Greeks never developed the tools, conceptual or practical, for this kind of investigation. For centuries they lived with two essentially incompatible explanations of cultural origins. One emphasized superhuman intervention, the other humankind's innate capacities.

The gifts of Cecrops to the primitive Athenians included two common criteria of what we mean by civilization today: city life and writing. The Greeks had a word for this state, *hēmerotēs*. 'Civilization' is a common translation. The core sense is 'tameness', closely allied to notions of 'gentle' or 'humane' behaviour. To Greeks, the opposite was 'wildness', of raw nature but also of humans. Unlike many city dwellers today, the ancient Greeks lived close to wild nature. This was more than a matter of, say, urban foxes and seagulls. In the 300s BC lions still roamed northern Greece.

On the cleverly conceived top floor of the Acropolis Museum in central Athens visitors can walk around the outside of the Parthenon – or rather, around a display of remnants of the marble figures once adorning the outside of this most accomplished of ancient Greek temples, begun in 447 BC. Viewing this display, you get a true sense of what, in terms of effort and cost, lies behind the textbook enumerations of the Parthenon's vital statistics.

A series of sculptured slabs ran right round the temple just below the guttering. Each measured roughly 4 by 4 feet and had figures carved in relief not far off a foot deep. There were ninety-two of these slabs alone – ninety-two – on the original building, quite apart from a continuous frieze of sculptured figures and massings of fully realized statues in both gables.

For the subject matter of these ninety-two slabs, the committee of democratic citizens in charge of the project approved a choice of four stories of warring and mayhem, all set in Greek legendary time. In one story, fantastic creatures – man above, horse below – are shown trampling and throttling nude, perfectly formed Greek men who fight back to victory with bare arms and legs. One slab shows a pointy-eared horse-man carrying off a Greek girl who tries to unhand herself from her captor's grasp. A vulnerable breast exposed by the ruffling of her dress leaves little of her predicament to the viewer's imagination.

To judge how ancient Athenians responded to this subject matter is hard. Possibilities range from pure visual delight to deeper reflection inspired by what they saw. Based on analysis of the larger cultural context, experts are more confident about the aims of the storytellers. Among other things, they probably meant the Athenian citizen to read a hidden meaning into these striking scenes. The popular legend of the wild horse-men served as an illustration, or symbol, of something more profound, namely, the danger to the delicate bloom of civilized Greek life from the forces of the untamed.

By the time the builders of the Parthenon had got to work, Greeks were rethinking their ideas about civilization and its enemies in the aftermath of a real and present threat to precisely their way of life: 'On, you men of Greece! Free your native land. Free your children, your wives, the temples of your fathers' gods, and the tombs of your ancestors. Now you are fighting for all you have.' This was how another, slightly earlier, Athenian play had imagined the Greek rallying call at the battle off the island of Salamis, near Athens, in which a fleet of chiefly Athenian allies won a decisive victory over a Persian armada bent on adding Greece proper to a vast empire already including the Greek settlements along the western coast of what is now Turkey.

Premiered in the Athenian theatre just eight years later (472 BC), *The Persians* was an Athenian playwright's triumphant dramatization of how the Persian court in faraway Iran received the totally unexpected news of this humiliating defeat. The playwright, called Aeschylus, offered his Athenian audience a crowd-pleasing Greek stereotype of the Persian enemy.

Ten times he makes Persians refer to themselves as 'barbarian' (*barbaros*). In origin this Greek word denoted a speaker of a non-Greek language. Aeschylus played with a more recent Greek tendency to use it in a negative way, in the modern sense of barbarous or barbaric, as Greeks found themselves threatened by a new and unfamiliar type of *non*-Greek, the aggressively imperialistic Persians.

In the course of the play actors assigned Persians a range of unenviable traits including cruelty, excessive luxury, over-emotionalism and servility, as shown by their autocratic king and his abject subjects from whom he demanded absolute obedience. As that rallying call implies, Aeschylus meant Greeks to see themselves as the opposites – and of course superiors – of the Persians. They were free: Persians were slaves. This idea of freedom also crops up in today's narratives and debates about what we mean by civilization. As well as (for instance) writing and cities, some commentators also see the presence of the idea of freedom as a 'criterion of civilized modernity'.

Among the ancient Greeks, 'barbarian' by the mid-400s BC was well on its way to acquiring the meanings of its modern derivatives, 'barbaric' and 'barbarism'. The Athenian builders of the Parthenon had in their minds this growing Greek sense of superiority to non-Greeks, especially Persians. They seem to have commissioned the temple partly as a victory trophy to celebrate Greek military successes against the Persians. They asked sculptors to depict not real battles but parables expressing the grand idea that victory over Persia was also victory over a barbarian threat to the (civilized) Greek way of life. Such narratives helped to promote a sense of sameness, not just among Athenians, but Greeks more generally: despite their myriad differences among themselves, victory over Persia brought them a shared sense of what they were not.

As masons and sculptors laboured on the Parthenon, another work of art, more than its equal in novelty and lasting impact, was taking shape in the mind of a Greek storyteller. The writer Herodotus hailed from the ancient Greek city of Halicarnassus. The port city of Bodrum on the south-western coast of Turkey now occupies the site. Herodotus lived through the middle 400s BC and he wrote a long work of historical narrative in continuous prose – the earliest of its kind to survive from anywhere in the world.

Herodotus described the cultural diversity of Greece's non-Greek neighbours with respect and dispassion. He recognized that every human society has a natural tendency to think its ways best.

> For if it were proposed to all peoples to choose which seemed best of all customs, each, after examination, would place its own first; so well is each convinced that its own are by far the best. It is not therefore to be supposed that anyone, except a madman, would turn such things to ridicule.

The cultural relativity and pluralism of this kind of thinking make Herodotus sound, once again, almost modern. He carefully recorded traditions asserting that Greeks were indebted to non-Greeks for features of their civilization. He states that the letters of the Greek alphabet were introduced to Greeks by a migrant from the world of the Phoenicians (Greeks gave this name to the population inhabiting the Mediterranean coastline from modern Syria into northern Israel). Language experts confirm the Phoenician origin of the Greek alphabet. Thus the Greek letter *beta* ('b') not only looks similar to but also derived its name from its Phoenician equivalent, *bēt*.

This openness to foreign cultures was a hallmark of the ancient Greeks, along with the technology transfers it allowed. Even during the wars between Greeks and Persians of the early 400s BC, Greek attitudes to 'barbarians' were more open-minded than might be expected. The British Museum displays another product of the Athenian potteries, a storage jar made around 480 BC. One side depicts a young man playing the pipes. Over his full-length tunic he wears a sleeveless jerkin intricately woven with a chequer pattern and bordering. This luxurious overgarment was of Persian inspiration. It seems that Athenian citizens accepted eastern fashions even as they fought their way to victory over the Persian invasion force.

It follows that how the ancient Athenians saw the world was not entirely consistent. Many people today are capable of this kind of doublethink, depending on where they are and who they are communicating with: on context, in other words. In that case, it might seem risky for historians to generalize about the characteristics, attitudes or values of 'ancient Greeks' as a whole. Yet the ancient Greeks themselves did: they came to see themselves as an ethnic group sharing certain cultural traits. Some Greeks had acquired this sense of a collective identity by the time of, once more, Herodotus. He preserves the earliest surviving definition of what he calls 'Greekness': 'the kinship of all Greeks in blood and speech, and the shrines of gods and the sacrifices that we have in common, and the likeness of our way of life.' Herodotus does not reveal what, in his view, gave rise to this sense of a broader community of Greekness. Nor does he claim that Greeks were Greeks because they belonged to a single political entity. In his day, the 400s BC, Greeks lived in hundreds of different, and usually warring, states. Greek civilization was not defined by large-scale political organization.

Even so, Greek civilization 'spread'. At the time of writing, a perpetually travelling exhibition is making its way around the world: Europe, North America, Australia, Japan . . . It keeps moving because to return the ancient objects which it showcases to their ultimate country of origin would be to expose them to Islamist vandalism.

Among these objects is a stone fitting once forming part of a public fountain. The sculptor has carved it in the form of a grotesque mask, of the characteristic kind – covering the whole head – worn by actors in ancient Greek comedies. In this case, out of the gaping mouth would once have sprung not words but a cooling jet of water.

This object must have served its intended function in an ancient community embracing two features of Greek civilization: a public water supply and an appetite for watching Greek-style plays. If this water jet came from Athens, it would be a rather commonplace find. Remarkably, French excavators dug it up on the northern frontier of what is now Afghanistan, at an archaeological site known locally as Ai-Khanoum.

Dating from the early 100s BC, the carved spout indicates that people living the ancient Greek way of life must once have inhabited this rugged part of central Asia. To judge from other finds, Greek settlers arrived here around 300 BC, in the wake of the Asian conquests of Alexander of Macedon (died 323 BC), bringing with them their own customs. Their descendants maintained themselves in this remote spot until nomads from the north destroyed their settlement around 150 BC.

Ancient Greeks, then, were migrants and emigrants. They celebrated this trait in their many stories (not always factually true) about ancestors leading expeditions to found cities in all three continents known to, and named by, Greeks: Europe, Asia and 'Libya', as they styled North Africa. They called these foundations 'settlements away from home'. Ai-Khanoum is one of the most far flung. They were one way in which Greek civilization 'spread'.

There was another way as well. In modern Sicily a favourite on the tourist trail is a well-preserved Greek-style temple serving an ancient city called Egesta or Segesta. Begun in the 400s BC and never finished, the temple's Doric colonnades now stand in splendid isolation amid a scenic landscape of hills and fields. Apart from its beauty, the ruin is remarkable because its builders were not ethnic Greeks but a native people.

The Egestans had become attracted to aspects of the Greek way of life because they had Greek settlers as neighbours in this part of Sicily. Some of what they saw they liked enough to adapt for their own purposes – like the earlier Greek takeover of Phoenician letters. Greek settlers in Sicily had not necessarily gone out of their way to 'spread' their way of life. The Egestans evidently opted to absorb those Greek cultural novelties because they found them appealing.

Nearby societies unrelated to the ancient Greeks by ethnicity or 'heritage' (as we might say today) ended up taking on board major aspects of the Greek way of life, including the Greek language. The 'spread' of Greek civilization in this way depended on choices made by non-Greek communities. In these choices, the originality and technological accomplishment of the ancient Greek brand of cultural creativity must have played a large part in its appeal.

Some academics see a degree of resemblance between the 'spread' of Greek civilization in this way and modern globalization, a word used to describe the way in which cultural exchanges promote a more interconnected world. Some also see the capacity to become a 'super-culture', with a geographical reach extending well beyond the originating people, as a marker of a true civilization.

The Sorbonne University in Paris is one of the oldest universities in the world. Among its offerings are courses on 'French civilization'. These include instruction in 'various aspects of French culture'. Given this identifying by French people of their national culture as a 'civilization', it is perhaps no surprise that the word itself is the fairly recent invention of a Frenchman. The eighteenth-century writer who coined *civilisation* had in mind a related group of words in Latin, the language of the ancient Romans. These hinged on the Roman concept of the citizen (*civis*) and his responsibility to society (*civilitas*).

The Romans conquered much of the Greek-speaking world in the last two centuries BC. In the process, they encountered the heartlands of Greek civilization. They absorbed, appropriated and adapted what they found. It was the Romans who did most to turn Greek civilization into an ancient 'super-culture', as just defined.

This process of cultural transfer was extraordinary in historical terms. After all, the Romans were the political masters of the Greeks and proud of what they saw as Roman military superiority, proved time and again on the battlefield. None of the other subject peoples of their multi-ethnic empire had cultural traditions that the Romans found even remotely as seductive, let alone that they wanted to emulate – or better. Without its fateful attraction to the Romans in the early centuries of the Christian era, the cultural legacy of Greece would not have been preserved and cultivated to anything like the extent that it was.

Unlike the Greeks, who explored their idea of *hēmerotēs* through the many stories they told, the Romans did not have a regular term equating to 'civilization'. So their attitudes to the subject are hard to pin down. A room in the archaeological museum in Istanbul offers a handle on the evolution of their thinking. It provides visitors with a visual statement of what important people within the ruling stratum of the Roman Empire, at a particular moment, thought civilization was, and its relationship to the Roman emperor.

A marble man, larger than life-size, kitted out in the dress armour of an imperial commander-in-chief, stands with one foot on a subdued enemy who wears trousers, sign of the barbarian. The intended meaning of the statue is linked to the scene that decorates this Roman emperor's breast-plate. In an archaic style suggesting great antiquity, it shows a figure of a standing goddess, herself armed. The snake on one side of her and the owl on the other were the attributes of Athena, the patron-goddess of Athens. It is she who must be shown here. This Athena's feet hover above more figures, a she-wolf who suckles two young children.

Here the unknown sculptor has created an image that, like the Parthenon sculptures, has a layer of meaning that is hidden, or at least veiled, from us. The wolf is the creature of Roman legend that suckled the infant twins Romulus and Remus. The twins were the mythical founders of Rome. Athena here seems to be a symbol of Athens. She stands for the Greek city that the Romans saw, above all others, as the originator of both the basics of civilized life such as agriculture and the rule of law, as well as the finest flowering of Greek civilization in what we would call the humanities and the sciences.

The cowed figure with trousers beneath the imperial foot shows that the Romans had also absorbed the negative Greek stereotype of the 'barbarian'. In this Roman imperial world of the early second century AD (the bearded emperor is Hadrian, who ruled AD 117–138), the threatening barbarians still lived beyond the edges of the Empire.

Modern narratives about civilization are reluctant to arrange peoples into a hierarchy of the more and the less 'civilized'. The Romans, following the Greeks, had no such qualms. Consciously or not, their rulers found in the idea of the barbarian a way of promoting a sense of identity among the multi-cultural subjects of Rome by emphasizing what all of them were not. The statue is a piece of propaganda. Its 'message' seems to have been aimed at the educated classes, especially those people who saw themselves as the cultural heirs of the Athens of the 400s and 300s BC.

The statue was meant to reassure such individuals that the Roman emperor identified with their cultural values. His aggressive posture insin-uated that he would use force to defend these values against external attack. This image offered a justification for taxes, legionaries and imperial rule. The statue type is perhaps the closest the Romans ever came to identifying the state with the defence of civilization. But the image itself is warlike, violent, even a touch 'barbaric'.

Hadrian himself came from a rich family of Italian migrants settled in Spain. As was the norm for his social class in Roman society, an expensive education had immersed him in Greek civilization. His personal enthusiasm for Greek culture and its values is conveyed by this passage from a much later Roman writer, presenting Hadrian in flattering terms as an intellectual and artistic prodigy:

> He immersed himself in the studies and customs of the Athenians, mastering not just their tongue, but also the other disciplines: singing, lyre-playing and medicine, music and geometry; he was a painter and sculptor in bronze or marble, almost equalling the Polyclituses and the Euphranors. Thus in all respects he had such accomplishment in these areas, that human nature had rarely managed to produce work of such distinction.

The reign of Hadrian belonged to a period of eighty-odd years (AD 98–180), which an eighteenth-century historian of the Roman Empire, the Englishman Edward Gibbon, considered the era in the history of the world when the human race was 'most happy and prosperous'. Nowadays many academics would want to sound more cautious. They might point to the near-absence in the Roman Empire of what today we would call 'social justice', not to mention the extensive presence of slavery. Gibbon's 'prosperity' was mainly the preserve of a small imperial elite. Even so, the Roman Empire lasted, from century to century.

> What is more precarious than the evils now surrounding the inhabited world? To see a barbarous, desert people overrunning another's land as their own, and our civilized way of life consumed by wild and untameable beasts, who have the mere appearance of human shape alone.

The author of this lament, written in Greek, was a Christian monk called Maximus. He was born in Roman territory, in what is now the Golan Heights, and wrote these words around AD 640: five centuries after Hadrian gave the name 'Palestine' to this part of the Roman Empire. Maximus alludes to a new power in the east, aggressive and militant, the Muslim caliphate, bent on conquering what was now left of the Roman Empire. When Arab armies captured Jerusalem in AD 637, Palestine, the homeland of Maximus, ceased to be Roman territory.

By this date the Roman Empire was no longer a pan-Mediterranean state. Its emperors now ruled from Constantinople, a new imperial capital founded on the Bosporus in AD 324. The Romans had been unable to preserve imperial rule in western Europe. Here large-scale migration from the AD 370s onwards was helping to lay the foundations of a new, 'mediaeval' world.

The focus of this book is the ancient world. It offers my personal story, unfolded in roughly chronological order, about the beginnings and the development of the two ancient and overlapping societies, Greek and Roman, which gave us 'classical civilization'. It is aimed at readers who are interested enough in the topic to start reading this book, but who have little or no background in the disciplines of Classics or Ancient History.

The story offered has to be selective since the subject is so vast. The book focuses on providing an up-to-date historical background to the cultural creations of classical antiquity which still matter to some of us today, from artworks, theatre and the so-called first computer (discussed in Chapter 16) on the Greek side, to the villas and towns of the Roman Empire, their remains suggesting a quality of daily life at which we can still marvel.

It also emphasizes the scale of the creative interaction with neighbours that, as often as not, stimulated cultural innovation. This included the eastern influences behind much of the cultural flowering of the first Greek city-states (seventh–sixth centuries BC) and the adoption, already touched on, of many aspects of Greek civilization by the Romans on a scale that invites comparison with, say, the Meiji 'westernization' of Japan (1868–1912).

It is hard to think of any great civilization in world history that does not offer the uneasy contradiction of high achievement in the field of culture married to state-condoned oppression of fellow humanity in some form or other. In these matters the societies of ancient Greece and Rome often behaved in ways that can seem harsh to us today. In addition they fought endless wars. This book avoids the rose-tinted lens through which, say, the Victorians liked to contemplate the 'glories' and 'grandeur' of ancient Greece and Rome. They were the heirs of a long-running tendency among Europeans, stretching back to the Renaissance, to accord the civilization of Greece and Rome an exaggerated respect and authority – to see it as 'classical', in other words.

In the end, though, writers (I believe) should nail their colours to the mast. This book is firmly on the side of wondering at the achievements of ancient Greece and Rome as it recounts the extraordinary story of these intermingled civilizations.

PART I

THE GREEKS

CHAPTER 1

THE DAWN OF GREEK CIVILIZATION

During the Stone Age, some human groups in different parts of the world learnt how to grow edible plants instead of foraging in the wild. They also began to tame and manage some of the wild animals that they hunted for food. As a result, they were no longer bound to the migrations of their prey, and could remain in one place. The first settled communities emerged. Because farming feeds more mouths than hunter-gathering, these groups of first farmers were more numerous. They needed to organize themselves in more complex ways.

This change in human behaviour was momentous: hence its modern name, the Neolithic Revolution. Traditionally historians see here a welcome change: a stage in a progress to a more civilized state. It was not a straight-forward advance. On the facts, archaeologists now think that the diet of the first farmers would have been less healthy. It turns out that a cereal-based diet is less diverse than the food of most hunter-gatherers and more likely to be deficient in some nutrients.

In truth, not everyone today embraces the idea of a 'progression' from 'savagery' to 'civilization' as humankind's obvious destiny. Stone Age societies survive in the modern world. Some people are squeamish about judging indigenous Amazonians or Australians as worse off or inferior because they have not 'advanced' to what others in the world are used to calling the civilized state. Others see moral merit in lifestyles seemingly less shaped by western values.

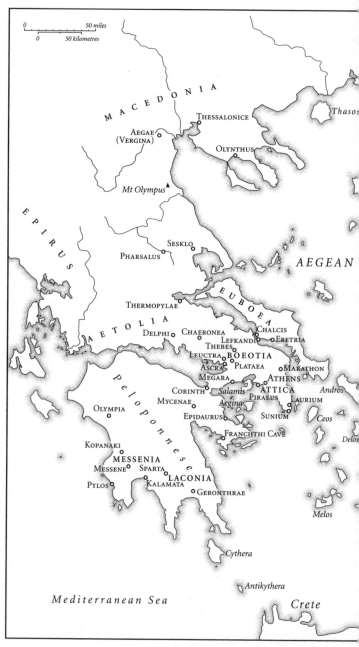

1. Greece and the Aegean World.

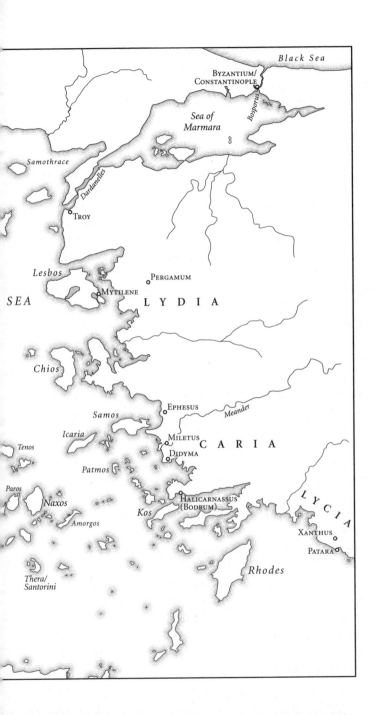

By and large the ancient Greeks saw matters more simply. Their view of agriculture as a great human blessing is clear from their tradition that a benevolent divinity had intervened in primal times to teach them its techniques. This was Demeter, the grain goddess. Athena did the same for the olive, Dionysus for the vine. As for what life was like before farming, one Greek writer in the second century AD described it as 'harsh, rustic, and little different from living on a mountain'.

In 1968, in a cave, not exactly on a mountain but on a seaside headland in southern Greece, American archaeologists found a caveman from the Stone Age. A male in his late twenties, he had apparently died from blows to his head. His group buried him in a simple grave in the cave floor. The archaeologists matched ash from burnt wood with information from tree rings – the technique known as carbon-14 dating – to produce a time for his death and burial in the late 7000s BC.

Nowadays, a visit to the Franchthi Cave is a civilized business. Inside there is a wooden walkway. Panels give information about the excavation. The finds indicate that the Stone Age band that camped here lived by hunting deer. They gathered wild plants such as pistachio nuts, oats and lentils. Personal possessions would have been few: a necklace of pierced seashells, say.

Among the finds, archaeologists discovered basic tools shaped from obsidian, a flint-like rock formed from volcanic glass. The best quality, with the fewest impurities such as flecks of trapped pumice, comes from the Aegean island of Melos, one of the Cyclades. What can be done with obsidian is the stuff of a modern flint-knapping course. On these courses, enthusiasts for ancient outdoors knowledge learn the correct technique for banging lumps of flint together. At the cost of cuts, bruises and significant fatigue, they aim, by chipping and flaking the stone, to shape it into, say, a primitive blade.

With obsidian, the fresh surface produced by such laborious methods attracts water trapped inside the stone. This forms a 'rind'. By measuring the thickness of the 'rind', archaeologists can date the tool-making moment that triggered its formation. By such means, archaeologists know that the hunter-gatherers of the Franchthi Cave were already using obsidian in around 8500 BC.

By implication, then, these cavemen were also mariners, or in touch with others who were braving the Aegean Sea in simple paddle boats. This rudimentary seafaring was encouraged by the way in which the Aegean islands cluster together, one in sight of another. On a calm day, they invite the adventurous to risk taking to the water. The cultural connectivity that the Mediterranean Sea enabled, with all its momentous consequences for the building of ancient Greek civilization, turns out to have had truly ancient beginnings.

Our Greek writer described human life before the invention of agriculture as 'life before Triptolemus'. Ancient Greek myth recounts how this legendary prince, son of a local king ruling what now is a satellite town of Athens, embarked on a kind of apostolic mission to spread knowledge of farming. His teacher was the goddess Demeter. The opulent Getty Museum in Malibu, California, possesses a clay vase from Athens which a craftsman decorated (about 470 BC) with a painting of this popular ancient story. The young Triptolemus sits in a winged chariot clutching grain stalks in both hands. Demeter and her daughter are standing by to bless his mission and watch him fly off.

Archaeologists are uncovering the real facts about how sowing and ploughs originated in Greece. Underlying them, some archaeologists think, was a basic human drive to seek an advance in the material conditions of life. Sesklo is a modern village in a large and fertile plain in the region of Thessaly, on the Aegean side of central Greece, north of Delphi. Today's visitor sees open countryside all around, well watered and not especially level. This means that the soil is well drained. So it was less difficult for the first farmers to cultivate. This was just as well: they had to work with implements of the basic variety, made from stone and bone.

On a man-made mound at Sesklo, archaeologists have found the remains of a long-lived settlement of these first farmers. They started by building themselves simple houses of wood and sundried mud. They grew wheat and barley on nearby hillsides. They kept sheep and goats. They knew how to shape clay. This community grew up in the 6000s BC. At its height it spread over some 32 acres of land – the size of the main campus of Columbia University in New York. But this was a low-density settlement, not a city. At most it is now thought to have numbered perhaps five hundred or so souls at any one time.

It is a mystery how these first farmers in Greece learnt the new technology. They husbanded sheep and goats from genetic lines that were not native to Greece. The same is true of the cereals that they planted. There is

DNA evidence to suggest that both livestock and crops could have come from what is now Turkey. Farmers from there, migrating westwards, might have arrived with animals and seeds in their baggage.

Working with these finds, archaeologists try to probe the minds of the first farmers in Greece. Psychological impacts on humans from the huge change in human lifestyle – from wandering hunter-gatherers to settled agriculturalists – might be predicted. Finds from Sesklo are on display in the archaeological museum of Athens. They show that life was still simple. There is early pottery. It looks rather crude to a modern eye, since the potter's wheel had yet to be invented.

There are also clay figurines. They, and many others like them, show that Greece's first farmers attached importance to representing the female form. These are naked, fleshy females. Hips, thighs and upper arms bulge unrealistically; so do bellies. Art historians would say that these 'Venus' figures served as symbols of a specific ideal of the feminine. Some academics use these enigmatic figures to claim that the 'Neolithic mind' honoured the feminine qualities in nature to an unusual degree. People might have worshipped great goddesses. Real women in these societies, they suggest, were accorded an unusual social prominence.

The social role of Neolithic males is not fully grasped. The community at Sesklo built stone walls around the top of its mound. Some archaeologists think that their purpose was defensive. On this view, Sesklo men could have been fighters and killers, using their tools for more than just hunting wild animals or butchering dead meat. Archaeologists have identified hundreds of other Neolithic communities sharing the same agricultural plain as Sesklo in this part of Greece. Perhaps they co-existed peacefully. Perhaps from time to time they fought with each other over what was a finite supply of local farmland.

Another find from Sesklo is a small clay model of a house. It is roughly square. It has crude rectangular openings on all four sides. They apparently stand for doors and windows. It has a slightly pitched roof with a central opening, as if to emit the smoke from a hearth. Many clay house models have been found in the Neolithic settlements of Greece. Their makers were not aiming at faithful depictions. It was the idea of a house that fascinated them.

Archaeologists see the Neolithic period in Greece as lasting for four millennia, from around 7000 BC to 3000 BC. The house models appear about halfway through this vast span of time. They show that the organization of human society at Sesklo evolved over time. Experts think that the pioneers who founded these communities saw themselves as working for a collective, not so unlike the original ethos of the Israeli kibbutz. The house models seem to mark a later turning away from this idea of working in the name of the community. Instead they emphasize the importance of the individual household.

The most impressive building at Sesklo has stone foundations, walls of sundried brick and (originally) a timber roof. The builders erected it in a central place on the highest point of the mound towards the end of the Neolithic, in the 3000s BC. People entered through a porch into a more or less square chamber with a rectangular clay hearth. There were holes in the clay floor for three poles once supporting the roof.

Archaeologists have revealed similar buildings from this period elsewhere in the plain. They could be communal meeting places. Another idea is that they might be residences of a top stratum in a society that had become more hierarchical. This would then be a pivotal moment in Greek prehistory. It would mark the emergence on a small scale of a society in which some people ranked higher than others. Some households might have achieved greater success as farmers, or had a bigger say in trade.

The finds from Sesklo include at least two axe-heads made from copper. They too date from the 3000s BC. By then Greece's early farmers knew that rock could contain metal and that metal had advantages over stone. There were craftsmen who knew how to melt such rock, or ore, in a furnace in order to extract the metal. They could make an axe-head – as here – by pouring the molten copper into a mould. The people of prehistoric Greece were entering the metal age.

How Greece's Neolithic farmers gained their first knowledge of metalworking is another prehistoric mystery. They went on to discover how to mix other elements with copper, notably tin. In this way they could make the much harder alloy that we call bronze. People could now make much stronger tools for key activities like farming, construction or warring. From around 3000 BC, bronze objects start to be found in Greece alongside copper ones.

As with obsidian, so with metals, prehistoric Aegean people must have risked paddling boats across the sea to connect with human groups who controlled metal resources. When I lived and worked in Athens in my late twenties, I sometimes used to have a day off on the Greek island of Andros, easily reachable by bus and ferry. Andros is a westerly outlier of the Cyclades, an archipelago in the central Aegean Sea. Here, on a coastal cape, archaeologists have discovered the earliest rock art in the Aegean area.

Alongside wolves, jackals and an octopus is a depiction – crude to modern eyes – of a longboat, essentially a large canoe, with a schematized row of oars. This kind of craft could carry a modest cargo. At the end of the Neolithic era – the date of this rock art – the pace of trading was picking up. A hierarchy of settlements was also emerging. Because these longboats needed manpower, only larger communities could have owned them.

At this time the islands of the Cyclades were home to some of the earliest sources of copper ore. Today's visitor to the Goulandris Museum of Cycladic Art in central Athens is led back in time to this dawning age of Greek metalworking. On the first floor, a space resembling a jeweller's shop show-cases the world's leading collection of so-called Cycladic figurines. A fairly typical specimen stands about 10 inches high. It is carved from the white marble so plentiful in the Cyclades. The figure depicts a naked female with an oval-shaped head who 'stands' with slanting feet, slightly bent knees, her arms crossed on the belly below pronounced breasts. The visitor can best appreciate the high level of technological accomplishment from the smoothness and polish of the hard marble surface.

These stark figurines nowadays enjoy a second life as prized icons of early Bronze Age Aegean 'art'. In today's museum showcases they mostly give an impression of pure white form. This appealed to Modernist artists like Brancusi or Giacometti. However, archaeologists have noticed traces of orig-inal paintwork on some figurines. Once they were decorated with tattoos and jewellery. For this, Cycladic craftsmen would have used natural pigments such as ochre, extracted from the rich mineral deposits of their islands.

The Goulandris Museum displays a Cycladic chisel made of the newfan-gled bronze. The tattooed people who fashioned these figurines were island farmers of Greece's early Bronze Age. The heyday of their way of life lasted for five or so centuries, from roughly 2800 to 2300 BC. Mostly the figurines depict the naked female form in the same pose. Their uniform style shows that the islanders had developed a shared sense of cultural community. Braving winds and currents, they used their crude paddle boats to visit each other.

These dangerous voyages were a matter of basic survival. Archaeologists systematically walk the island landscapes to examine surface finds – mainly pottery sherds – for signs of past settlement. The results suggest that the islands might have been too thinly inhabited in the early Bronze Age for local people to have reproduced themselves demographically. They could have taken to the water from the need to find mates. The original meaning of the figurines remains enigmatic today. One tempting suggestion is that the naked marble females symbolize, among other things, the high value that these islanders placed on women's fertility.

South of the Cyclades lay a hazardous expanse of open sea before the ancient seafarer, an island-hopper by preference, reached Greece's most southerly land mass. Traditionally, it is here, on the island of Crete, that archaeologists have begun their story of Europe's first 'states', that is, organized political communities under a centralized authority wielding power over a complex society no longer based solely on kinship and clan.

The ancient Greeks had many legends about Crete's former greatness. These centred on a king called Minos who lived at a place called Knossos:

Minos is the first to whom tradition ascribes the possession of a navy. He made himself master of a great part of what is now termed the Hellenic sea; he conquered the Cyclades, and was the first colonizer of most of them, expelling the Carians and appointing his own sons to govern in them.

These are the words of an Athenian historian, Thucydides, who set down his account of Greek history at the end of the 400s BC. To the educated elites of nineteenth-century Britain, this mention of an ancient empire based on sea-power and colonization had a familiar ring. Thucydides helped to inspire a British amateur archaeologist to go out to Crete and dig for evidence of Minos.

The British Museum's display of artefacts from prehistoric Crete includes a number of objects captioned as gifts from Sir Arthur Evans. This diminutive Victorian, a product of Harrow School and Oxford University, came from a family grown rich on the manufacture of paper. In 1900, in middle age, he used this money to buy the land and to start excavations at a site which earlier travellers had already identified as ancient Knossos.

He found remains of buildings one on top the other from a period of nearly six hundred years, from around 1900 to perhaps 1370 BC. They belonged to a huge multi-storey structure of the middle and late Bronze Age centred on a great courtyard and equipped with an elaborate drainage system of clay pipes and stone channels. The maze-like complex was subject to partial ruination and repeated rebuilding over its long life. Archaeologists lay much of the blame for this cycle of destruction and renewal on seismic activity, for which Crete and its neighbourhood are well known: there were forty-five earthquakes on Crete in 2014 alone – an average of almost one a week.

Evans found evidence for writing, as well as many refined artworks. These include wall paintings preserving glimpses of a courtly world of elegantly costumed, bare-breasted women. One painting shows athletic young men in mini-kilts jumping a bull. This hazardous sport recalls today's young *toreros* in the Gers region of south-west France who display their prowess by somersaulting off the backs of charging cows. The bull imagery of ancient Knossos hints at one possible source of local wealth: the management of cattle.

Evans combined the ancient Greek stories and assumptions based on the international politics of his own day to interpret his finds. He identified the large complex as a palace, seat of the political power of Minos and his dynasty. Inside he had found objects and features which he saw as evidence of goddess worship and of shrines. So he made Minos a ruler combining secular with religious authority: a priest king. He called these lost people 'Minoans'. He had no hesitation in labelling their way of life a 'civilization' – as he saw it, the earliest in Europe to merit this label. Mingling images of the Roman and British empires, he saw the Minoans in their unfortified centres like Knossos as benevolent seaborne imperialists presiding over a 'Pax Minoica', or 'Minoan peace'.

The Minoans raise basic questions of who they were and where they came from. Evans found earlier remains beneath the 'palaces'. These go as far back in time as the Neolithic farmers of this part of Crete in the 6000s BC. So Minoan civilization may have been home-grown, based on earlier developments. For instance, archaeologists have found offcuts of olive trees used as firewood on Crete some 300 years before the earliest 'palace'. This find points to olive-oil manufacture on Crete by this date, since the offcuts probably reflect the pruning of cultivated olive trees.

The stimuli prompting human culture on prehistoric Crete to give rise to Minoan civilization certainly included overseas contacts. At Knossos, the earlier levels produced a fragment of hippopotamus tooth. This ancient alternative to elephant ivory may have originated in Egypt's River Nile.

Even without the later traditions of the ancient Greeks regarding Minoan sea-power, it is probably significant that Crete in the early Bronze Age saw major developments in seafaring during the two or three centuries before Evans's first 'palace' at Knossos. Until then the hazardous business of paddling canoes over long distances must have sharply limited the range and frequency of Aegean Sea voyages. Late in the 2000s BC came a step change. Communities on Crete became familiar with the sailing ship.

The evidence comes from images of such vessels which now appear as designs on the small stones that Cretan craftsmen shaped into seals for their owners to wear as ornaments and to use for sealing. These early images of deep-hulled sailboats reflect a major gearing up of sea-craft. Cretans and their neighbours could now make faster sea journeys over longer distances, more often and carrying more cargo. The households or groups in island society who controlled this quickening pace of exchange with the outside world would also have gained in wealth and power.

Since the pioneering work of Evans, archaeologists have uncovered Minoan 'palaces', towns, 'villas', mountain sanctuaries and tombs all over Crete. Beyond Crete, on the Cycladic island of Santorini, they found a settlement buried, Pompeii-style, beneath the ash and pumice from a violent eruption of the island's volcano. The finds include Minoan-style houses and large numbers of a distinctive type of clay container made on Minoan Crete for the transport and storage of Cretan olive oil and wine. Minoan prosperity was also based on agriculture and the exploitation of a surplus.

In 1990, the Austrians unearthed thousands of fragments of wall paintings in the Minoan style at an archaeological site in northern Egypt. Long before this last discovery, archaeologists had identified the 'Keftiu' of Egyptian texts and art as Minoans. These were men with Minoan kilts and hairstyles who brought gifts to the pharaohs Hatshepsut (reigned about 1473–1458 BC) and her co-ruler Thutmose III. So the Minoans and their way of life in their heyday made an impression on much of the eastern Mediterranean, including Egypt, at this time the great power of the region.

Perhaps the most obvious sign that these Minoans were a relatively 'advanced' society is their use of writing. On display in the British Museum is a fine bronze axe-head with the hole for the haft flanked by two linguistic signs. This script is unique in the ancient world. Evans dubbed it Linear A because the signs – as here – are made up of conjoined lines rather than the stylized pictures of objects in, say, the hieroglyphs of the Egyptians. From human contacts made by vessels sailing between east and west, the Minoans had encountered writing, an older invention in the Near East. Someone saw the potential for Minoan Crete, and a transformation took place, with the Minoan side adapting foreign ideas to suit themselves.

Despite continuing efforts, experts have yet to decipher Linear A, let alone identify the underlying language. With more confidence archaeologists can comment on how the Minoans used this script. Incised on clay 'pages', the longest documents include numbers and lists and seem to be accounts, transaction records and so on. There are special signs for 'olive' and 'wine'. These products were stored in bulk in some Minoan 'palaces'. At Knossos, Evans found a series of 18 oblong magazines holding 150 or so massive clay storage jars, each roughly the height of an adult human.

One of the great riddles about Minoan Crete concerns the 'palaces' themselves. Today, many archaeologists question Evans's interpretation of Knossos as the seat of a monarchy. Among experts, 'palace' is going out of fashion in favour of 'court building'. This term gives proper prominence to the paved courtyards at the heart of these complexes, at Knossos and elsewhere on Crete.

The absence in Minoan art of depictions of a ruler does not support the notion of Minoan 'palaces'. In contemporary monarchies further east, craftsmen of major artworks mainly served the gods and the monarch. At Egypt's Deir el-Bahri in western Thebes, the great temple built by Queen Hatshepsut is full of statues with but one subject, the queen. At Knossos, Evans dubbed one space a 'Throne Room' because against a wall he found an elaborate seat with a high, carved back made of the alabaster-like mineral known as gypsum. Nowadays archaeologists reason that this room was used for religious ritual. Perhaps a Minoan priestess or priest sat on the 'throne'.

Clues to one important purpose of the palace at Knossos are displayed in the British Museum in the form of shelves of Minoan pots. Many are drinking cups. The finest cups have thin, delicate walls and are prettily decorated with a black slip on top of which the potter has added designs in red or white. These are examples of so-called Kamares ware, the superior product of a new invention on Crete, the potter's wheel, and mainly made for drinking. Such vessels were stored in the court buildings in large quantities. In one spot at Knossos, archaeologists found over 150 cups toppled to the ground. Some vessels were much grander than others.

One particularly lavish type takes the form of a bull's head carved in stone. Craftsmen hollowed out the head, then sealed the neck with a separately attached stone 'plate'. To heighten the impact, they might add eyes of rock crystal, or pick out nostrils with gold leaf. These heads were not just made to dazzle. They have holes at the top and bottom for holding and pouring liquids. What is more, they are only found in fragments, and the muzzle is usually missing. Archaeologists surmise that they were deliberately smashed after use with a blow to the nose.

The reader might be forgiven for thinking of the fading custom in today's Greece of smashing plates and glasses during celebrations. Archaeologists now imagine the central courts of the 'palaces' as spectacular settings for, among other things, great communal feasts. Here, they suggest, a social stratum of top people in Minoan society would periodically gather to bond over food and drink. The bull's head containers hint at rituals and ceremonial interactions. The mass banquets of London's livery companies, with their loving cups, speeches, music and processions, seem to offer a pale modern parallel for this ritualized style of commensality.

All this merrymaking may suggest a Minoan leadership in need of social glue to reduce the danger of inter-communal conflict. Since studying Minoan weaponry, archaeologists have largely ditched Evans's utopia of 'peaceful' Minoans. The quantity of Minoan bronze daggers, swords, arrowheads and so on seems too high if Minoans carried weapons only for ceremony or status, never to threaten, or enact, violence.

Another great riddle concerns the demise of Knossos as the centre of a prehistoric state. Around 1450 BC the buildings suffered damage at a time when other Minoan court buildings on the island were destroyed and never rebuilt. Yet Knossos continued to serve as a political hub. Archaeologists are uncertain when the end came – perhaps three generations later, around 1370 BC. Knossos suffered a final destruction. This time there was no rebuilding.

The wheels of power at Knossos turned to the very last moment. This is known because the destruction involved fire, which baked a last generation of over two thousand administrative tablets with linear script. But Evans, who found these tablets, saw that their script was different from, and later than, the linear script discussed above. He dubbed these scripts respectively Linear Class A and B. The second, unlike the first, has been deciphered.

In 1952 a former wartime pilot and keen linguist, the architect Michael Ventris, a Briton, dropped a bombshell. He established that the language of Linear B was a form – the earliest attested – of Ancient Greek. At a stroke it turned out that the earlier Minoans who used Linear A were not Greek-speakers, but the users of Linear B were. By Ventris's time, archaeologists had also found – and continue to find – Linear B tablets on Bronze Age sites in Greece proper. It followed that Knossos in its final phase was much closer to the mainland than previously, culturally and perhaps politically too.

As for what the mainland was like in the Bronze Age, the ancient Greeks of historical times told many stories about two feuding dynasties ruling in their remote past – the time leading up to the Trojan War. Surviving works of the imagination by Greek poets and playwrights have ensured immortality for King Oedipus of Thebes in central Greece, who unwittingly killed his father and married his mother, or Agamemnon of Mycenae in the Peloponnese, who led the Greeks to victory at Troy, only to be murdered on his return home by his wife as he was taking a bath.

These tales inspired another pioneering archaeologist, a rich German businessman called Heinrich Schliemann. In 1876, when he was in his mid-fifties, Schliemann began excavations in the north-east Peloponnese at ancient Mycenae. His finds were so sensational that when he published them in a book, William Gladstone himself, the four-times British prime minister, wrote the preface. Schliemann found astonishing treasures dating from around 1550 BC, the same period as the heyday of Minoan Knossos.

These finds, now the highlight of the National Archaeological Museum in Athens, include the gold mask of a moustachioed male which Schliemann over-excitedly claimed as the 'death mask of Agamemnon'. Like Evans at Knossos some twenty years later, he had discovered a new Bronze Age civilization. Since then archaeologists have shown that 'Mycenaean' civilization lasted for some four centuries, much longer than Schliemann realized.

In the 1950s a joint team of Americans and Greeks resumed excavations at a Mycenaean site discovered before the Second World War at ancient Pylos in the south-west Peloponnese. This showcases the culminating phase of Mycenaean culture in the 1200s BC. Under a protective roof of corrugated iron, today's visitor sees a somewhat unprepossessing complex of rooms and outbuildings delineated by stubs of walls. At the centre is a rectangular suite of porch, vestibule and hall with a huge circular hearth where people gathered to consume wine, judging from finds of drinking cups. On the other side of the Peloponnese, visitors to Mycenae and nearby Tiryns encounter less well-preserved examples of a central suite of identical plan. This striking display of Mycenaean cultural uniformity might seem to hint at central planning. Most archaeologists see these elite buildings as the palaces of Mycenaean rulers in the 1300s and 1200s BC.

Unlike the court buildings of the Minoan heyday, these later Mycenaean palaces have left written records which linguists can read. As at Knossos, at Pylos a final conflagration roasted an archive of Linear B tablets, over a thousand of them. Ventris's decipherment of Linear B has unlocked the content of these documents in Mycenaean Greek. The work of palace scribes, they mainly detail day-to-day economic oversight, the commanding and redistributing of goods, and the management of manpower in the service of the palace. In so doing, the tablets reveal the Pylos establishment as the political centre of this south-western quadrant of the Peloponnese.

They also mention a supreme official called the *wa-na-ka*. This is an archaic form of the Ancient Greek word *anax*, meaning a lord or master. So it turns out that king-like figures in Greece's remote past had a historical reality outside the stories of classical Greek writers. More tantalizing is whether there was more than one *wa-na-ka*, each ruling his own territory, or a single *wa-na-ka* presiding over all the palace-centres of a Mycenaean super-state, as hinted at five centuries later in Homer's poem, the *Iliad*. This presents Agamemnon of Mycenae as supreme leader of the Greeks, 'master [*anax*] of men'.

Some Mycenaean scribe seems to have created Linear B by adapting the linear script of Minoan Crete to his own language. Many of the signs are very similar. Archaeologists have found many other witnesses to close cultural contact between the Mycenaean mainland and Crete. A bird in the 'Orpheus' fresco from Pylos could easily have flown off a Minoan wall painting. There must have been a lively criss-crossing of the Aegean Sea.

A startling discovery in Turkey now provides a glimpse of the risky journeys underpinning the Mycenaean way of life. In 1993, lecturing on a cruise along Turkey's south-western coast, I passed a diving support vessel bobbing on deceptively placid seas near the tip of Cape Uluburun, 5 miles east of the holiday town of Kaş. This was the last-but-one season of a ten-year campaign by underwater archaeologists. They were laboriously exploring the wreck of an ancient trader that met a violent end while trying to round the headland sometime in the very early 1300s BC.

The main cargo was bulk copper – a staggering 10 tons' worth of ingots tidily arranged in rows across the hold. There was also a ton or so of tin, the other essential ingredient for bronze-making. Tests show that the copper almost certainly came from Cyprus – by then the main source of this metal in the eastern Mediterranean. A much longer journey must be envisaged for the tin, perhaps brought to the Mediterranean by donkey trains from remote Afghanistan.

Other discoveries suggest a home port for the vessel in what is now southern Lebanon and Israel. Here archaeologists place a society of merchant seafarers whom they call 'Syro-Canaanites' and see as the Bronze-Age ancestors of the later Phoenicians. Finds of seemingly personal items of Mycenaean pottery and weapons indicate that Mycenaean Greeks were also on board the doomed ship – mercenaries, maybe, or emissaries. Luxury objects such as ostrich eggs, ivory and a golden scarab inscribed in Egyptian hieroglyphics with the name of the beautiful Egyptian queen, Nefertiti (about 1340 BC), hint that this was no ordinary assortment of goods, but rather a gift from one ruler to another.

Not that these were peaceful times. The world of the Mycenaean palaces grew out of an earlier society of warriors in Bronze Age Greece. In 2015 archaeologists at Pylos found the near-intact tomb of one of these fighters, a well-to-do male in his early thirties buried with a splendid bronze sword – the hilt was made of gilded ivory – and with a mirror and combs, accoutrements of a warring coxcomb, proud of his appearance.

Two centuries or so later, by the 1200s BC, at least some of the later palaces were massively fortified. The ancient Greeks of classical times were much impressed by the great blocks of the prehistoric defences of Mycenae, hailing them as the work of giants. One of Schliemann's more famous finds at Mycenae was a ceramic vase about 16 inches high, made at this time and also now in the National Archaeological Museum, Athens. The painted decoration shows a march of bearded men, armed and armoured to the teeth. They may indeed be taking part in a funeral, as has been suggested. Even so, these figures clearly represent a class of fighters in the society that built the Mycenaean palaces.

Why the end came when it did, and how, no one really knows. Fire engulfed the palaces around 1200 BC in a general catastrophe devastating Mycenae, Tiryns, Pylos and Thebes. There was a larger instability at this time – the capital of the Hittite Empire, ancient Hattusa, some 200 miles east of modern Ankara, was also destroyed. Giving these far-off events a modern resonance, some experts have proposed climate change as an underlying factor. Core samples from the bed of Lake Galilee show a sudden rise in the types of plants found in desert terrain in the years between around 1250 and 1100 BC, as if there was a severe drought event in the eastern Mediterranean.

On the Greek mainland, whatever else it may have been, the Mycenaean collapse was definitely political. The state system that built the palaces vanished, along with the record keeping, the luxury goods and other signs of a complex society. Judging from the archaeological record, survivors now lived a much simpler life for two to three centuries.

During these centuries, ironworking slowly spread in Greece, with important economic implications. Deposits of iron ore are common in Greece. Over time this domestic abundance of such a strategic raw material would undermine the old system of long-distance trade in copper and tin. Oral traditions kept alive by survivors slowly turned the increasingly dimly remembered world of the Mycenaeans into the stuff of legend.

As well as this wealth of stories, the legacy of the Mycenaeans to subsequent centuries included abandoned monuments, some of the Greek gods and, in places, a population of Greek-speakers. Prehistoric times had laid a cultural base on which later Greeks built. Yet the shape of what emerged in the centuries after the palaces fell would be startlingly different from what had gone before, as the next chapters will show.

CHAPTER 2

THE RISE OF THE HELLENES

The classical Greeks knew nothing about the catastrophic end of Mycenaean civilization as revealed by modern archaeology. They had their sacred stories about cosmic origins and the earliest times. These myths – as we would call them – told of catastrophes marking major boundaries in the beginnings of time, including wars between gods and a great flood.

For the Greeks contemplating their remote past, the watershed separating legend from fact was the Trojan War, fought between their ancestors and the people of Troy. Later Greeks located Troy on the north-west coast of Turkey, near the Dardanelles. In later times noble families in ancient Greece claimed to descend from warriors who fought in this conflict, such as Ajax or Achilles. In classical times, Greek scholars produced dates for the war. One of these dates placed the fall of Troy precisely 407 years before another event for which the history-minded Greeks had also worked out a precise year. This was the first celebration of the Olympic games on record, supposedly in 776 BC. By such reckoning, Troy fell in 1183 BC.

Archaeologists from Schliemann onwards have excavated an archaeological site at Turkish Hissarlık in the belief that this was ancient Troy. They have found the remains of an important city of the late Bronze Age, one repeatedly destroyed and rebuilt. They date two of these destructions on either side of the archaeological date for the collapse of the Mycenaean palaces, around 1200 BC. This approximate coincidence of archaeological dates with ancient Greek dates for the Trojan War abets the long line of eminent scholars who believe that this war was a real war fought by Mycenaean Greeks against an Asiatic enemy.

Whether this view is correct remains an open question. The later Greeks also saw migration as an important part of the story of how their world came into being, and here the corroborating evidence is more reliable. Our words 'Greece' and 'Greeks' derive from 'Graecia' and 'Graeci', diminishing names that the condescending Romans bestowed. Late in the 400s BC, the Athenian historian Thucydides wrote about the beginnings of the land he knew by its Greek name: 'it is evident that the country now called Hellas had in ancient times no settled population; on the contrary, migrations were of frequent occurrence, the several tribes readily abandoning their homes under the pressure of superior numbers'. Thucydides thought that the first migrations fell before the Trojan War. Eighty years later, he writes, 'the Dorians and the descendants of Heracles became masters of the Peloponnese'. These Dorian Greeks were the supposed invaders from whom the later Spartans proudly claimed descent.

Experts in two different fields, historical linguistics and historical genetics, are helping to flesh out these dim traditions repeated by the later Greeks. Linguists long ago showed that the language of the ancient Greeks descended from the same lost proto-language as a raft of modern languages in both Europe and Asia. These include both Welsh and Hindi, the majority language of modern India. So it has always seemed likely that the prehistoric language that evolved into the Linear B of the Mycenaeans and, centuries later, into the dialect of Greek spoken and written by Thucydides, entered prehistoric Greece from elsewhere.

Some archaeologists think that the first farmers of Neolithic Greece were outsiders who brought with them a proto-Greek language around 8000 BC. The growing field of ancient DNA points provisionally in another direction. Recent studies of genomic information taken from prehistoric human remains identify a seemingly large-scale migration into Europe from the Eurasian Steppe to the north of the Black Sea. This would have taken place around 2500 BC. More tests on Mycenaean DNA may show whether it was this migratory movement that could have brought the ancestors of the Mycenaean Greeks into the southern Balkans.

That different Greek-speaking groups arrived in Greece at different times is borne out by the fact that Greece in historic times was a land of regional dialects. Thucydides stigmatized one Greek-speaking subgroup in the central Greece of his own day (later 400s BC) as 'speaking a dialect more unintelligible than any of their neighbours'. These dialects emerge into the light of history after the return of writing to Greece in the 700s BC, about which more shortly. They can be studied from inscriptions on stone, potsherds and so on. Linguists discern five major 'families' of these dialects, each based on its own geographical region.

Generally speaking, when different dialects of the same language co-exist, this is because their speakers live isolated lives in tight-knit communities. Much of north-east England, where I used to teach, is a region rich in living dialects. Academics who study them assign their formation to centuries of migratory movements, Angles, Scandinavians and so on, stretching back to Roman times. Movements of this kind are the usual explanation given for the regional dialect families of Ancient Greek.

So experts can say that the evidence of language does not flatly contradict the later traditions of the Greeks themselves about ancient migrations into their land. The ancient Greeks did not have the concept of 'dialect families'. Still, they knew that among themselves they spoke different varieties of Greek. Thucydides wrote of the 'Doric dialect' spoken in his day by descendants of the 'Dorian' incomers.

The second of the five major dialect families identified by modern scholars, so-called 'Attic-Ionic', was common to both the Athenians living on the Greek mainland and the Ionians. In historical times Ionian Greeks were settled in the region south of modern Izmir on Turkey's west coast. They gave this area their name, 'Ionia'. Dorian Greeks pronounced the '*e*' of Attic-Ionic as '*a*', Attic-Ionic final '*s*' as '*r*', and so on.

After the fall of the Mycenaean palaces, archaeologists mainly rely on pottery to chart the conditions of human existence in Greece. For the next century and a half pot-making slumped, literally: the shapes seem to sag. They look homemade. In those impoverished times, makers and users of pots no longer lived in a human environment demanding well-crafted objects. The catastrophic events of around 1200 BC had triggered nothing less than a societal collapse. Conditions in Greece then perhaps can be likened to the seventeenth-century English philosopher Thomas Hobbes's harsh vision of humanity bereft of any form of political community or commonwealth: 'No arts, no letters, no society; and which is worst of all, continual fear, and the danger of violent death: and the life of man, solitary, poor, nasty, brutish, and short.'

After the Mycenaean breakdown, archaeologists infer from such finds – and the fact that suddenly there are so few of them – the crumbling of pre-existing political communities. A dark age in other words. There were fewer people and many fewer communities. The survivors were poorer. There were migrations. Then, from around 1050 BC, the humble clay pot starts to tell a more hopeful story.

In the archaeological museums of Greece one omnipresent artefact from these times is a distinctive way of decorating pottery known as Geometric. The potter painted the surface with concentric circles, key patterns, zigzags, lozenges, dots and so on. Just by looking at them you can see that many of these pots show great technical virtuosity. The style originated around 1050 BC. Its advent marks an unmistakable, if modest, sign of a return of more settled conditions in some parts of Greece, allowing cultural ambitions slowly to rise.

Over the next three centuries the style became common to the whole Aegean region and defines a shared culture: 'Geometric Greece', as some archaeologists label the period. It is a shame that nothing certain can be said about the symbolism of the style, assuming that it was not purely decorative. There has been no shortage of modern speculation – that the concentric circles and pointy discs represent the sun, for instance, or that the tidy patterns channel a yearning for order.

Another corner of Greece around 1000 BC has lit up the kind of Greek society that used this pottery. My first proper academic job was as assistant director of the British School at Athens, a research centre. I well remember great consternation in the office one morning in August 1981. Reports had come in of major vandalism at an archaeological site where Greek and British archaeologists had been excavating together for some time. It turned out that a local landowner had taken a bulldozer overnight to a plot of land on which he planned to build a summer house. Before he was stopped he had managed to erase the middle portion of a huge ancient building.

As a direct result, the Greek authorities confiscated the land, and Greek and British archaeologists carefully excavated what was left. The place was modern Lefkandi to the north-east of Athens, on the coast of the large offshore island known in ancient times as Euboea. Nowadays visitors to the site enter a modern shed where they confront unglamorous remnants of mud-brick walls and not a great deal else.

What they cannot miss is the scale of this hairpin-shaped structure. This was a big building. It measured 164 feet long – about half the length of a modern football field – and 46 feet wide. Archaeologists estimate that its ancient builders would have used up many hundreds of days of human labour. It was a building that was meant to impress people. What really surprised archaeologists was the early date, as revealed by the finds of Geometric pottery – around 1000 BC.

The architecture is like nothing of earlier date in Greece. Recent research suggests that a wooden fence may have surrounded the structure, not the wooden veranda usually posited. Finds included a pottery creature, man above, horse below: one of the earliest known images of a centaur, a fantasy figure of the legends which later Greeks recorded in writing. The biggest discoveries were two burials inside the building.

Excavators found a subterranean shaft shared by an inhumed female and her companion, a cremated male. They were clearly of high status to judge from the grave goods. These included a dagger with a handle of ivory imported from the Near East. There were also 'antiques'. One was a Mycenaean bronze bowl originally made on Cyprus, the other a solid-gold throat piece, or gorget, apparently made by Babylonian craftsmen a thousand years earlier.

Academics are still discussing these startling finds. In this part of Greece, around 1000 BC, once again society had grown more complex. There was a stratum of wealthy aristocrats. They enjoyed the power to command the labour of their inferiors and had access to exotic materials like ivory. Seemingly, vessels used the island's nearby shoreline to offload, and perhaps on-load, objects of long-distance trade. Socially these leaders distinguished themselves by owning rare heirlooms, and by celebrating elaborate funerals. Some archaeologists believe that the deceased pair had previously lived in the hairpin building and that this was ritually 'killed' by being pulled down over their graves.

The finds at Lefkandi offer a link to the two poems which stand today as the lasting legacy of Geometric Greece. The university department where I used to teach displays a plaster bust of a bearded old man with lifeless eyes. Somehow he has survived years of rag days and student parties unscathed. This modern cast, one of thousands, replicates an ancient Greek sculptor's imagining of Homer as a blind, philosopher-like sage. Already in ancient times he had become a figure of myth. Whether a Homer ever actually existed is something which the experts debate.

The two poems ascribed to him by the ancients are the earliest surviving literature of the ancient Greeks, and so of the whole Western tradition. The *Iliad* explores a dramatic moment in the ten-year Trojan War. The *Odyssey* tracks the adventures of a Greek warrior as he makes his way home over ten years from Troy. One only has to think of Hollywood's retelling of these poems, most recently in 2004 with the feature film *Troy*, to be reminded of their place in world culture.

I myself inherited a translation of Homer once belonging to my grandfather's grandfather. Published in 1801, its three volumes are pocket-sized, literal companions. My ancestor possessively signed his name in flowing copperplate to each volume. The translation was once a popular one, by the English poet Alexander Pope, who died in 1744. When he took on Homer, Pope was still in his twenties.

Pope's rather free translation gives the general sense of the original. His stately English now has an additionally eighteenth-century ring. It captures something of the archaic sound of Homer for the Greeks of later antiquity themselves:

> Achilles' wrath, to Greece the direful spring,
> Of woes unnumber'd, heav'nly Goddess sing!
> That wrath which hurl'd to Pluto's gloomy reign
> The souls of mighty chiefs untimely slain;
> Whose limbs unbury'd on the naked shore,
> Devouring dogs and hungry vultures tore:
> Since great Achilles and Atrides strove,
> Such was the sov'reign doom, and such the will of Jove!

Homer portrays a legendary world which faintly resembles that of the Norse sagas. Divinities and supernatural creatures share a stage with human heroes who excel at fighting. There is poignant humanity in the recognition of our common destiny:

> Like leaves on trees the race of man is found,
> Now green in youth, now with'ring on the ground;
> Another race the following spring supplies.

As well as poetry that has proved timeless and universal, Homer also offers demonstrable touches of archaeological reality. He describes a helmet given to the hero Odysseus:

> A well-prov'd casque, with leather braces bound
> (Thy gift Meriones) his temples crown'd;
> Soft wool within, without, in order spread,
> A boar's white teeth grinn'd horrid o'er his head.

Archaeologists have found several of these boar's-tooth helmets in Mycenaean graves. Also in the *Iliad*, Homer describes the funeral of a Greek warrior, Patroclus, who has fallen before the walls of Troy. The description shows similarities to the burials at Lefkandi. It includes the cremation of the dead man; placing his bones in a special jar (gold in the *Iliad*, a bronze heirloom at Lefkandi); wrapping the relics in a special fabric (Lefkandi's is the earliest find from Greece of ancient cloth); and the accompanying sacrifice of horses (four in the *Iliad*, the same number at Lefkandi).

Modern insights suggest an explanation for Homer's curious referencing of cultural goods and practices separated, as in these examples, by three centuries or so. In the 1930s, a young American scholar, Milman Parry, argued that the Homeric poems were the cumulative outcome of generations of oral performance. Bards would have sung earlier versions during a lengthy phase in which the Greeks had no writing, only speech. These performances would have been fluid, combining memory with improvisation. Bards would use a repertoire of fixed expressions. This made it easier for them to fit their spontaneous additions to the pattern of beats which runs through all the poetry.

Different generations of oral bards would have introduced contemporary colour to make a core legend about a war long ago, and its aftermath, more realistic for their audience. One of these formative performances perhaps took place at funeral games at Lefkandi around 1000 BC. A bard might have flattered his aristocratic listeners gathered in the hall of the hairpin building by matching local rites for a princely couple with the funeral of Patroclus.

In the centuries to come, the poems of Homer achieved a fundamental importance for the ancient world. Known to all, their portrayal of gods and mortal men and women, of divine power and human fortunes, profoundly shaped how the Greeks imagined the world, both seen and unseen. Quotations from Homer's poems seeped into ancient discourse in much the same way that phrases from the King James Bible have enriched spoken and written English in more recent times. Later Greek literati wrote with Homer's verses ringing in their heads.

All this culturally momentous future was possible because, at some point, the oral poetry of Homer was committed to writing. There had been no writing in Greece since the ruination of the Mycenaean palaces. Recent researchers push the origins of the new writing into the late 800s BC. This may well be the date of three copper plaques found in Egypt and now in European collections. Tested for authenticity in the Getty Conservation Laboratory in Malibu, California, each is covered on both sides with the type of Greek inscription known as an abecedary, letters of the alphabet.

Whoever wrote these abecedaries was pioneering a very different type of Ancient Greek script from Linear B. Greeks had become aware of the alphabet used by the people they knew as Phoenicians, seagoing folk based in the ports of the Levant, met with already. The abecedaries were found in Egypt, an indicator of a Greek world in later Geometric times that was increasingly connected once more with a larger Mediterranean world by seafarers and trade.

By this date Greeks had managed without writing for the best part of five centuries. The Phoenician alphabet was not fully alphabetic in our sense, since it contained signs only for consonants. For some reason Greeks vastly extended the versatility of what they took over by borrowing Phoenician signs for Greek vowel sounds as well. The end result was a script of the 'one letter, one sound' type.

The earliest examples of the new script do not suggest that dry accounting, Linear B-style, was the priority. The National Archaeological Museum in Athens displays in a special case a wine jug found in a grave in 1871. An Athenian potter made it around 740 BC, painting the surface in the Geometric style, now nearing the end of its popularity. On the shoulder someone scratched a rather unskilled run of letters in the new script: 'He who of all the dancers now performs most daintily . . .' A second line, hard to decipher, is often rendered as 'the [jug] is his' – a prize in other words. The first line is fitted to the same rhythmic pattern of beats as Homeric poetry. The early date of this scrap of verse makes it important. It shows that Greeks wasted no time in exploring the expressive potential of the new writing. Some authorities believe that the much greater undertaking of converting Homeric epics into written form belongs to this same period, the later 700s BC. Perhaps there was a poet who shaped and polished the great inheritance of oral material. He might even have been called Homer.

The world conjured up in Homeric poetry was not one in which writing seems to have been a commonplace activity. This suggests that the new Greek alphabet and the new literacy among Greeks to which it gave rise could still have been novelties when the poems were written down. Whether the Homeric aspic captured other realities from the moment in time when the poems were set down in writing is a matter of learned debate.

For instance, one vignette seems to hint at the Greek politics of the future. The *Iliad*'s King Agamemnon, the Greek commander-in-chief, has summoned the Greek army besieging Troy to an assembly. He has staff-wielding aristocrats steward the assembly, making sure that everyone is sitting quietly. He makes his speech. Then a common soldier, well known for his habit of criticizing his betters, dares to speak out. He reminds Agamemnon that it is thanks to the men that their leader's royal tent is filled with Trojan booty.

To be sure, this is a society in which the king and the aristocrats dominate the commoners, who normally know their place. Yet in this scene, Homer seems to imagine for his audience of aristocrats and their retainers the possibility of a more collective politics, in which the many, not just the one or the few, have their say. Cooperative communities, anchored geographically to a particular locality and valuing a communal life, were in fact the hallmark of a new political map of ancient Greece as it starts to come into focus from the 700s BC onwards.

To this century belong the earliest reasonably reliable dates and events of their history recorded by the Greeks themselves. Because experts today can now start to draw on the historical traditions of the ancient Greeks themselves, the 700s BC mark a new phase in the way they conventionally divide up Greek history into periods. The Archaic Period is held to start in 776 BC, supposedly the first celebration of the athletic games at ancient Olympia to be officially recorded.

Archaeologists have found some of the best evidence for the emergence of these collective communities in Archaic Greece at places of religious activity. A case in point is the large offshore island of Euboea, today's Evvia. Fifteen miles or so south-east from the archaeological site of Lefkandi, the modern coast road reaches Eretria, a nineteenth-century town superposed on an ancient predecessor. Everywhere, ancient remains litter the modern streets and poke out of building plots. Through a wire fence the visitor can look at a particularly complicated jumble of foundations, a series of structures one on top of another. The topmost foundations belong to a Greek temple erected around 525 BC. Two sets of foundations below are remains of a building shaped like a hairpin with one end curved.

People erected this some two centuries earlier, around 725 BC. Of flimsier materials, the walls being simple bricks of sundried mud, this earlier building even so must have been eye-catching, if only for its length, roughly the equivalent of, say, the forty-yard dash, a popular speed test for American footballers. It must have dominated its surroundings when it was built.

Archaeologists see this hairpin building as serving the same essential purpose as the Doric-style temple built on top of it two centuries later. It was dedicated, that is, to a Greek divinity, Apollo. In its architectural ambition it served as an impressive expression of local religious feeling. On the practical level, it provided a shelter for an important focus of ancient Greek worship, a representation of the god. Like many sacred sites in many cultures, it would be rebuilt more than once on the same spot.

In general plan this temple looks like a slightly smaller version of the hairpin building at nearby Lefkandi encountered earlier in this chapter. As we have seen, this predecessor from around 1000 BC obviously served the two notables buried inside. It could have been their former home.

It is possible that the aristocrats of these earlier times also exercised priestly authority, guarding the sacred objects of the local divinity in their residences. Some archaeologists think that the Eretrian hairpin and other 'first temples' of the 700s BC point to a religious restructuring. A communal new building, mimicking the aristocratic architecture of the time, was now erected to protect the property of the god, offering access to a wider group. It was as if the protests of Homer's curmudgeonly plebeian were inching, ever so slowly, towards greater political realization.

The religious customs of the time offered the political communities emerging in Archaic Greece a potent form of social glue. When individuals came together as groups to worship at a shared sacred site, they were engaged in what modern sociologists call community building. It follows that Archaic Greek society as a whole must have been predisposed to believe in its gods, and that a – basically – uniform pattern of rituals and, indeed, pantheon of gods was developing. Another sacred site shows vividly how the levers of Greek religion operated at this time to bring people together to mix socially.

Olympia was one of the chief Greek shrines of the god Zeus. In the 700s and 600s BC, the sacred site was a leafy, riverside spot where visitors passed the time in outdoor activities. The modern museum on site gives some clues to what these were. The display includes case after case of metalwork from this period, much of it in the form of bits of bronze cauldrons – bowls, that is, designed to stand on three legs so that a fire could burn underneath, while something cooked inside.

On websites today, if you are so disposed, you can order a modern witches' cauldron. It looks ordinary enough but becomes magical, apparently, if the owner applies a special paste to it, conveniently supplied by the manufacturer. Those ancient cauldrons from Olympia are not entirely remote in spirit. By this date such cauldrons had been around for a long time in Greece: 'three legs' or *ti-ri-po-de*, tripods in other words, turn up in the Linear B tablets of the Mycenaean Bronze Age. So here too an originally mundane form – a cooking utensil – has been turned into something special and sacred. On one particularly massive specimen at Olympia, its bowl over two feet wide, you can see ancient Greek lettering on the rim, in what at the time was the local dialect here. It reads simply, 'Sacred to Zeus'.

These ancient cauldrons communicated an air of manliness. Many have metal attachments, which are sometimes all that survives: a horned bull, or a male warrior with uplifted spear-arm. These extras raised the prestige of the object, transforming it into something finely wrought and therefore costly. Homer's *Iliad* also talks about tripods. They feature in the Homeric description of preparations for athletic games to mark the funeral of the dead Greek hero Patroclus:

> The swarming populace the chief detains,
> And leads amidst a wide extent of plains;
> There placed 'em round: then from the ships proceeds
> A train of oxen, mules, and stately steeds,
> Vases and Tripods, for the fun'ral games . . .

Some experts believe that all these dedications of cauldrons celebrated victorious contestants in the all-male running races of the earliest Olympics.

This ancient athletic meet began life at Olympia as a gathering for Greece's social stratum of 'sceptre-wielding' aristocrats. The objects never quit the sanctuary because the winners left them behind as 'sacred to Zeus': offerings to the god. As an attendant, in Homer's words, 'to his wrists the gloves of death bound' for a bout of tooth-and-claw wrestling, a real-life Greek blue-blood could become for a moment 'great Ajax' and fancy himself competing in Homer's games.

Olympia lies a short distance inland from the west coast of the Peloponnese. Today the archaeological site has its own port for visiting cruise ships and seems far from remote. In the 700s and 600s BC the region was not exactly a Greek hub, but rather out of the way. This might have encouraged aristocrats from different parts of Greece to meet here at what became regular, fixed intervals. At Olympia they could socialize without being beholden to some overweening local power.

As the inscribed cauldron shows, these aristocratic athletes competed in honour of Zeus, but also for honour among men. With its contests, its ritual feasting on the meat of sacrificed animals cooked in cauldrons, and its acts of offering, the four-yearly gathering at Olympia was a religious event. Competitive athletics is one of the best-known legacies of the ancient Greeks. The ancient Egyptians had also developed sporting activities such as running, throwing and wrestling out of the primitive need for men to fight and to hunt. The Archaic Greeks likewise fought and hunted and were as competitive as any neighbouring ancient people, if not more so. Where they were culturally distinctive was in conceiving athletic contests as a form of pious offering aimed at pleasing their deities.

In turn they could think in this way only because, helped along by the art of the line of bards culminating in Homer, they had come to imagine their gods as resembling themselves not only in looks but also in passions. So Greeks took for granted that these human-like gods would welcome as a gift the human excellence brought out in competitive sport, as much as they would a finely wrought object made by the best of human craftsmen.

At religious events like Olympia, Greek aristocrats of Archaic times who had come together from different communities perhaps dwelt more than they normally did on what far-flung Greek-speakers had in common. An aristocratic outlook is usually one that sets great store on superior lineage. Homer's Greek paladins leave no doubt that pride of birth was a hallmark of their society. A good example is a warrior called Glaucus, who openly vaunted his five generations of male forebears, all of them kings and great warriors. When Archaic Greeks thought about a larger Greek identity, it was natural for them to imagine Greeks as different branches of a genealogical family.

'And from Hellen the war-loving king sprang Dorus and Xuthus and Aeolus delighting in horses.' This is an ancient quotation from a lost Greek poem composed in the Archaic Period, perhaps around 700 BC. In it the poet, who was called Hesiod, tidied up existing genealogies of gods and heroes. He livened up his material by emphasizing the alluring females thanks to whose fertility and childbearing labours these lineages were perpetuated.

It turns out that Archaic Greeks thought of themselves as a modern plant family: a single race divided into subgroups, with a common ancestor. This was Hellen, as in the quotation, from whom had sprung Dorus, the ancestor of the Dorian Greeks. Another ancient quotation from this lost poem gives a son to Xuthus called Ion, the ancestor of the Ionian Greeks.

Genealogies sprung from figures whom many people might be inclined to think of as mythical are far from being a uniquely Greek way of imagining ethnic identity – one only has to think of Adam and Eve. For ancient Greeks, or 'Hellenes', their legendary family trees likewise had sacred authority. The father of Hellen was Zeus himself.

All those cauldrons at Olympia are one sign that in early Archaic times the Greek world was becoming richer. As well as undergoing economic developments, it was also becoming more complex politically. Although powerful aristocrats abounded, many Archaic Greeks lived in local communities in which pressure seems to have been building to enlarge the decision-making group. At the same time, many of these Greek settlements were forging identities as self-governing republics, passing laws, waging wars and behaving in other ways like mini-states.

Geographically the heartland of this settlement pattern came to resemble a political patchwork spread across the valleys and uplands of mainland Greece, the Ionian and Aegean islands, and the shores of western Turkey. The ancient Greeks had a word for this type of settlement. The most common translations in English are 'city-state' or 'citizen-state'. This is the Ancient Greek word which gives us our word 'politics'. It is time to say more about the *polis*, the crucible of Greek civilization.

CHAPTER 3

NEW THINGS
THE FIRST GREEK CITY-STATES

In my twenties I was a volunteer on an archaeological dig near ancient Sparta. Every morning at the crack of dawn the director drove a jeep-load of postgraduates halfway up a rural hillside. This was as far as a vehicle could go. Then we walked up to the archaeological site through a riot of yellow euphorbias harbouring large caterpillars with stinging hairs.

On arrival, I think none of us, not even the most bleary-eyed, ever tired of what we saw. The dig was perched on the summit of one of a range of foothills lining the side of a great valley. Immediately beneath us stretched a sea of silvery-green olive trees. Closing the far side of the valley reared a snow-capped range of majestic mountains. I was not the only digger who habitually daydreamed while contemplating all this natural splendour when I should have been bagging up the small finds.

On the summit stands ancient masonry enclosing a pimple of natural rock, the object of our efforts. We were digging the ruins of a Spartan shrine. For six or so centuries from the 700s BC, ancient Spartans clambered up here to worship at what they believed to be the tombs of a famous married couple, leading players in Homer's Trojan War. In the 600s BC a worshipper left an offering inscribed in the local alphabet for 'Menelaus' Helen' – a dainty bronze flask suited to holding perfume. For the Spartans this was the tomb of beautiful Helen, wife of the king of Sparta, snatched by a Trojan prince, the act justifying Greek aggression in Homer's Trojan War.

For the Spartans, Helen and Menelaus were more than a pretty story. The finds of archaeologists suggest that locals across a wide swathe of Archaic Greece were making offerings at places that they believed marked the graves of figures from remote times. As well as their gods, the Greeks also believed in the existence of demi-gods – the glorious dead of ancient days, with the power to assist mortals from the grave if they were properly worshipped with gifts and sacrifices. So this activity had religious overtones. Their generic name for one of these male demi-gods was the Greek word we translate as 'hero'. There were also 'heroines'.

Scholars see here a desire of fledgling Greek communities in Archaic times to claim kinship with earlier inhabitants of their land. These communities might have had one or more villages as their focal point. The villagers were mainly farmers. The surrounding land fed, clothed and housed the community by means of its crops, its livestock, its wildlife and its natural resources.

Some experts think that the population had been rapidly rising in Greece in the 800s and 700s BC. One of the arguments is an apparent increase in the number of child burials found by archaeologists in some parts of Greece at this time, as if more infants and children were dying as a proportion of a rising population. This is a complex debate that cannot be discussed here in detail.

If population growth was putting pressure on the resources of the land, this would have given added impetus to a community to stake out its territory. Through acts of worship at supposed tombs of supposed ancestors, its members might 'perform' their traditions of alleged common descent from an older population once working the same land – land now also claimed by neighbours. The message would be: 'We were here first.'

Alternatively, a group of violent incomers might try to soften its domination of a region's prior inhabitants by paying honours to the master of the place in former times. This scenario could fit the Spartans. They claimed to descend from the Dorian Greeks who, so the Greeks believed, migrated into the Peloponnese after the Trojan War. Later Greeks remembered these Dorians for using force against the existing inhabitants. By finding a spot visible for miles around at which to honour Menelaus and Helen, pre-Dorian rulers of the area in the days of the Trojan War, the incomers could also have tried to build bridges to this older population – a 'carrot and stick' approach, you could say.

An inscription on stone in Ancient Greek dating from about 650 BC records for the first time a particular *polis* and the workings of local politics there. Typically of most of these hundreds of Greek city-states, ancient Dreros on the island of Crete was small and unimportant in the larger scheme of Greek history. It was more like a large village, controlling the nearby valley, now an olive grove.

In time, Dreros was dignified with some public buildings and a plaza for meetings, but it was never anything like a 'city' in the modern urban sense, nor in terms of population. A place like Dreros probably never had more than a few hundred freemen, of whom perhaps one or two score counted locally as rich and aristocratic. Archaeologists have been drawn to the site mainly because it is relatively well preserved, thanks to its location up a rocky hillside in the mountainous interior of eastern Crete.

Clearing an ancient cistern here, archaeologists found an inscribed block of grey stone. It records a decision of the local body politic:

> May God be kind [?]. The Polis has thus decided; when a man has been Kosmos, the same man shall not be Kosmos again for ten years. If he does act as Kosmos, whatever judgments he gives, he shall owe double, and he shall lose his rights to office, as long as he lives, and whatever he does as Kosmos shall be nothing. The swearers shall be the Kosmos and the Damioi, and the Twenty of the Polis.

This inscription uses writing in a different way from the literate poets of Archaic Greece. Here the words are in prose rather than in the rhythmic verses that transported listeners to a supernatural world. The plain and matter-of-fact register suits the here-and-now character of the inscription. This is a written law, one of the earliest to survive from the ancient Greeks.

The inscription shows that Dreros around 650 BC was a self-governing little commonwealth making its own rules. It had established regular arrangements for the peaceful settlement of disputes and appointed a public official, called the Kosmos, who sat as a judge for a fixed term. Some abuse of power could have prompted this law. Perhaps an aristocratic Kosmos had not handed over to a successor as he should have, but had hung on to judicial power.

The law would have aimed to deter such behaviour in future with threats of fines and disqualification from public office. The people of Dreros might have supported this law as a way of discouraging local aristocrats from getting above themselves. Aristocrats themselves might have welcomed it because it assured the orderly passing round of office, satisfying their political ambitions. Writing allowed this tiny republic to give a communal ruling an air of greater permanence and solemnity by publishing it – for anyone to read who could – on imperishable stone.

Warfare looms large in any history of ancient Greece. It is not by chance that the earliest ancient tradition about relations between the Archaic city-states is about going to war with each other. Greek writings record a great war fought long ago on the offshore island of Euboea. The earliest mention, helping to date this event, is an ancient quotation from a lost Greek poet of the seventh century BC. The quotation mentions aristocratic swordplay, not plebeian archery or slings, as 'the warfare in which those spear-famed lords of Euboea are skilled'. Two centuries later, the Athenian historian Thucydides wrote of an earlier age: 'All wars were fought individually between neighbours. The main exception was the war fought long ago between Chalcis and Eretria, when alliance with one side or the other split the rest of Greece.' Here the ancient historian hints how smaller Greek states, ones comparable in size to Cretan Dreros, had little choice except to align themselves with one or other of the two powerful protagonists – a pattern which would repeat itself in Greek history. He implies that the cause of the war between Chalcidians and the neighbouring Eretrians was a dispute over land ownership. The local wars between neighbours that preceded this first 'great war' of the Greeks presumably were also disputes about land. Modern ideas about population rise and the territorial symbolism of tomb cults at the dawn of Archaic Greece, such as that of Helen and Menelaus at Sparta, fit with this picture of a mainly agricultural society under pressure, fighting over limited amounts of good farmland.

A Greek geographer writing around the time of the birth of Jesus gives more details about the aristocratic character of this war. In his researches he had read of a great gathering of poets at this same place, Chalcis, 'to attend the funeral of Amphidamas. Now Amphidamas was a warrior who had given much trouble to the Eretrians, and had fallen in one of the battles for the possession of the Lelantine plain.' This plain can still be visited. We met with the large island of Euboea – nowadays an hour's journey from Athens – in the last chapter. This was an important area in early Greek history. Driving north from Eretria up the island's long west coast for 19 miles or so, the visitor crosses a rich plain before arriving at today's Chalkida. The blocks of flats and commercial buildings of this, the modern island's largest town, sit on top of the remains of ancient Chalcis.

As for the plain, today it is covered with vineyards, olive trees, fields of corn and market gardens. No one seriously doubts that this was the ancient Lelantine plain. It would have been able to support a large population for ancient times, and was well worth fighting over.

The ancient writings hint at the style of fighting. There was hand-to-hand swordplay between warriors battling on foot. Mighty Amphidamas of Chalcis sounds like a noble champion from the world of Homer, receiving a magnificent funeral with games in his memory, like Patroclus. The impression given is that the two chief states of Euboea at the time of this war – sometime in the seventh century BC – were aristocratic. Lords fought to protect the community; in Homer at least, the locals gave these lords land and food in return.

In human history war has a well-known tendency to speed up innovation. A museum in Rome displays a painted ceramic pitcher made in the potteries of Corinth, a prosperous Greek state commanding the isthmus joining the Peloponnese to central Greece. Around 640 BC a painter there chose to show in exquisite detail the front files of two Greek armies about to collide. Each side fields rows of warriors marching in close formation to the tune of a piper. The warriors hold their large circular shields by putting the shield arm inside a grip held at the elbow. Each row of warriors presents a 'wall' of overlapping shields to the enemy.

Many historians – not all – believe that what is depicted here is a new style of fighting which grew up in Greek lands in the 600s BC. It would have gradually supplanted the older, aristocratic, style of individual heroics as exemplified by the war over the Lelantine plain. Its key novelty was the heavily armed infantryman, who came from a less exalted background than the likes of Amphidamas. By protecting the exposed right side of his neighbour with the left side of his shield, the new-style warrior expressed a solidarity with his fellows that could be a real life saver in combat. Men who fought in unison on the battlefield could also become a new, united voice in the body politic back home.

Social tensions certainly developed inside some Archaic Greek states, even if the best-documented instance might not have been typical. Born roughly when the Corinthian potter was perfecting his pitcher, an Athenian called Solon grew up to become both a statesman and a poet. In some verses of his that have survived as quotations in other ancient authors, Solon boasts of his success in mediating social unrest in the city – possibly when he was chief magistrate in 594/3 BC:

> For I gave the common folk such privilege as is sufficient for them, neither taking away nor adding to their honour; and such as had power and were splendid in their riches, I provided that they too should not suffer undue wrong. Nay, I stood throwing a mighty shield over both sorts, and would have neither to prevail over the other unjustly.

Much later Athenians remembered Solon for land reform in a society so remote that they no longer understood what it was that he had achieved. They knew of a mysterious 'shaking off of burdens'. This alleviated the distress of a no less enigmatic group, 'those who have to pay a sixth part'. It may be that Solon abolished gifts by peasant farmers to local lords for protection, this practice having hardened in recent generations into a grinding tax of one-sixth of the year's produce. Whatever the case exactly, with Solon we sense the importance – and prior rigidity – of property classes in Archaic Athens, and how their loosening might have fed into the gradual extension of some political rights down the social scale.

The internal politics of the Archaic Greek states gave us another word, one destined for a long life. A Greek 'tyrant' (*tyrannos*) was an unconstitutional ruler. Some experts make the analogy with modern dictators. Ancient writers suggest that tyrants were common in Archaic Greece. Athens after Solon was ruled for half a century by one of these tyrants.

Typically of what passed for politics in Archaic Greece, this Athenian tyrant rose to power against a background of rivalries between noble magnates and their supporters. One of these ambitious lords, a war hero, was able to persuade the Athenian people to give him a personal bodyguard for his own protection. Pisistratus, as he was called, then used these men of the people to capture the Athenian Acropolis. He made this rocky outcrop his tyrannical seat, before being hounded into exile by his enemies, only to return for a second spell as tyrant.

As so often in history where powerful individuals are concerned, tyrants were larger-than-life figures to whom colourful stories got attached. In one ancient anecdote, Pisistratus and a political ally dressed up a particularly handsome and tall Athenian woman as the armoured goddess Athena. This impersonator of the deity then stood beside him in the chariot in which he drove back into Athens – as if his return to power had the goddess's blessing: '. . . heralds ran before them, and when they came into town proclaimed as they were instructed: "Athenians, give a hearty welcome to Pisistratus, whom Athena herself honours above all men and is bringing back to her own acropolis." '

Athena was the patron divinity of the Athenians and at this time, around 560 BC, her sanctuary on the Acropolis was already rich with monuments and offerings. The story sheds light on religious attitudes at the time. Pisistratus neither involved any religious authority at Athens in his plan nor thought that his action showed disrespect for the goddess. This was a society in which religious rites could be present at almost all aspects of public life. Yet the story also presents religious culture as something that political leaders could try to manipulate. Pisistratus could be pragmatic about religion, as an aspect of everyday life useful for helping Athenians adapt to the changing world around them.

Creative thinking, leading to innovation, was a hallmark of the society of the Archaic Greek states. A generation after the escapade of Pisistratus, a different kind of new thinking was producing spectacular results in another Greek city-state which, like Athens, was one of the thirty or so that were sizeable and important enough to count for something in the larger world. The later ancients remembered Archaic Samos for its engineering novelties. One of these was a great tunnel. Starting on either side of a mountain and meeting in the middle, workmen successfully dug an artificial underground passage over half a mile long in order to channel water from a spring down to the ancient settlement.

Sitting in a taverna on the East Aegean island of Samos in 2015, I chatted to the proprietor, a former engineer, about this ancient project. With more than a touch of local pride, he explained how the ancient Samians, working down from the summit, could have used water as a level so as to establish the two starting points. They would have gone on to dig bores into the mountain to make checks on the slope and straightness of the tunnel as it progressed. His point was that this was relatively simple engineering if you already knew how. The genius of the Samians was that this was a first. Someone had made it up.

A short drive from the modern town of Pythagoreio takes you to the remains of the chief shrine of the ancient Samians. For centuries locals and foreigners came here to worship the goddess Hera. Flattened by time and by later quarrying of the ancient masonry, the ruins conceal traces of another man-made wonder. In the foundations of Hera's last temple its ancient builders reused stone column-drums from a predecessor on the same site. Because it was built on the marshy terrain which Greeks associated with the worship of Hera, this earlier temple, built around 575 to 550 BC, failed structurally soon after.

The visitor can still contemplate the crisp perfection of the horizontal fluting around one of these reused drums. This precision was achieved by machine engineering. A Samian architect had invented a lathe. In the workshop, this mechanism would have rotated the work-piece – a drum, say – while a sharp tool cut into its side. This new invention became an object of lasting wonder. According to a Roman author, clearly fascinated, the mechanism was so finely balanced that a child could turn a stone held on this lathe with his hand.

The earlier Samian temple collapsed because it was an ambitious experiment that had gone wrong. It was to be vast, with a footprint roughly the size of a football pitch. Each of its forest of 132 columns reached twice the height of a giraffe. To raise this structure, unparalleled for its time, Greek architects and masons had to find solutions to problems never encountered before. The novelty of the project turned the building site into a laboratory.

The earliest Greek philosophers lived close to Samos. In recent times the narrow channel between the island and Turkey has offered a short if precarious crossing into Europe for migrants. In the 500s BC, the coast of what we think of as western Turkey was home to the Greeks of Ionia. Their prosperous cities, especially one called Miletus, produced the earliest thinkers in the western tradition.

Of ancient Greek thought, the twentieth-century English philosopher Bertrand Russell had this to say:

> They [the Greeks] invented mathematics and science and philosophy; they first wrote history as opposed to mere annals; they speculated freely about the nature of the world and the ends of life, without being bound in the fetters of any inherited orthodoxy. What occurred was so

astonishing that, until very recent times, men were content to gape and talk mystically about the Greek genius.

Russell was charting the foundational place of the ancient Greeks in the history of western philosophy. He was also thinking about the long-term fruits of an initial turning away from seeing supernatural beings and forces as the explanation for all things. It is not straightforward today to make sense of these pioneering ideas by a handful of contemplative Greeks. A Dutch scholar has recently offered this translation of all that survives of the first written work of Greek philosophy:

Whence things have their origin
Thence also their destruction happens,
As is the order of things;
For they execute the sentence upon one another
– the condemnation for the crime –
In conformance with the ordinance of Time.

The author of this utterance, Anaximander, was a man of Miletus. In 546 BC he was in his mid-sixties. As to what Anaximander might have reasoned about the nature of the cosmos, Russell thought that here he was expressing 'a conception of justice – of not overstepping eternally fixed bounds'. Another interesting question, almost as hard to answer, is why Anaximander and the other first philosophers launched their scientific and rationalistic speculations in the first place. Since older civilizations nearby had not taken this philosophical turn, experts have sought to pinpoint triggers in the culture and society of Archaic Greece.

The inscribed law from Dreros, or the reforms of Solon: these were not authoritarian measures, but ones that the mini-republics of Archaic Greece adopted after some kind of public debate. If speakers had to speak out in support of their proposals, they might also have had to work out arguments based on reason in the face of possible opposition, from fellow aristocrats, for instance.

The practical inventiveness of Archaic Greek architects and engineers might also have been a stimulus to thinking 'outside the box'. Were philosophizing Milesians inspired by visits to the great building sites of the eastern Aegean? Among these early Greek thinkers, 'pure' and applied problem solving could go hand in hand, as in this story from Herodotus about how one of them engineered a river crossing for a king and his army:

> Thales, who was in the encampment, made the river, which flowed on the left of the army, also flow on the right, in the following way. Starting from a point on the river upstream from the camp, he dug a deep semi-circular trench, so that the stream, turned from its ancient course, would flow in the trench to the rear of the camp and, passing it, would issue into its former bed, with the result that as soon as the river was thus divided into two, both channels could be forded.

In Anaximander's day another invention was taking hold of the Greek world. The British Museum displays examples of the first Greek coins. On one of them, a lump of precious metal the size of a thumbnail, reclines a fierce lion. This example was minted around 550 BC in Anaximander's home city of Miletus. The Greek city-states of Ionia borrowed this invention from eastern neighbours, the Lydians, of whom more in the next chapter. Once they had done so, the Ionian cities seem to have moved rapidly to production of relatively small denominations in huge quantities, as if coins were already coming into everyday use.

The new coins required their users to commit to a belief in the coin as a measure of a value that was notional only – even if in those days the piece of metal from which the coin was made came closer to replicating the coin's stated value than with today's coins. The users of these first Greek coins would have had to recognize the difference between something 'being' (the coin) and something 'seeming' (its supposed value).

As a result, it has been suggested, the adoption of coin had an impact on the cognitive development of the early Greeks, since it required them to recognize a different kind of underlying reality, one that was abstract and invisible. This in turn influenced the unconscious of those first philosophers who groped for new explanations of the universe based on a single, invisible, principle.

Others have sought a link between the first Greek philosophizing and the nature of Archaic Greek religion. Greek religion was not a religion of the book. The ancient Greeks never believed that their misbehaving gods had laid down rules for the regulation of mortal behaviour. No divinity either had dictated, as might be said today, a 'creationist' account of natural origins. In fact, once people went beyond the myths, Greek religion did not have a great deal to say about the nature of the world. Their religious system left Greeks relatively free to speculate about life and the universe.

Here we might briefly return to the competitive temperament of the Greeks, already touched on in connection with their love of athletics. The temple-building Samians had rivals a short distance across the water. As described just now, their first great temple to Hera foundered. They promptly started to rebuild it on an even larger scale. Assuredly not by chance, this rebuilt temple, of which a solitary column still stands, fractionally outdid in size a recent super-temple raised by the city-state of Ephesus across the water on the nearby Ionian shore.

The Samians and Ephesians were part of a frenzy of temple building in Archaic Greece. In 2014 a Republican senator from Illinois complained that Chicago was no longer a world-class city, since not one of its skyscrapers was in the top ten tallest in the world. Fanning the frenetic spread of the first wave of major Greek temples seems to have been an ancient version of today's skyscraper envy.

On the face of things, each Archaic state was culturally similar to its neighbours – broadly the same ethnicity, language and so on. For one community's collective identity to stand out, to assert that 'we are Samians, not Ephesians', the same things had to be done differently and – obviously – better. What is indeed striking about these communities when looked at more closely is the diversity of their local identities. For example, the Archaic Corinthians used their own version of the Greek alphabet, they worshipped their own local version of the Greek pantheon of gods, evolved their own laws and so on. The political fragmentation of Archaic Greece into a mosaic of small states was itself a force for creativity and innovation.

The British Museum devotes a large room to the rich material culture of Archaic Greece. By grouping objects geographically the display brings out this character of diversity in sameness. It also shows off a very visual expression of this same spirit of inquiry which was a trait of Archaic Greeks. If one material dominates the room it is clay, mainly in the form of products from local potteries all over the Archaic Greek world.

Each production centre seems to have developed a distinct style, within a broad framework of similar techniques, shapes and decorative subject matter. Centuries later, a Roman writer opined that 'Choræbus, the

Athenian, was the first who made earthen vessels'. The display does indeed bring out the undoubted superiority in this ancient Greek industry of one particular cluster of potteries, those of Athens.

In the 1980s a furore fired up the tight-knit world of experts in ancient Greek pottery studies. Two British academics claimed that the Athenian potteries producing these fine pieces were merely imitating the lost gold and silver vessels made by metalworkers for a 'high end' stratum of aristocratic Greeks. Feelings ran high over what for some was an assault on the artistic originality of the makers and decorators of Athenian crocks. I remember a tense London seminar at which an academic from one side of the argument arrived with a conspicuous tape recorder to record what the speaker from the other side was about to say, rather like a police interview.

Even so, visitors to any of the world's great collections of Athenian pots confront a strange and exuberant aesthetic distinctly of its time and place: black figures on a red background, or the other way round; painted stories covering bellies, shoulders, lips and feet. The subjects can be gods and legends, or illustrations of the societal norms of those times – men arming, women weaving textiles and so on.

Perusing this material, the spectator may well be struck by the evident fascination of the pot painters with the human body and, more specifically, the young male body, often shown scantily clad or naked. As a trait of ancient Greek culture, this open admiration for male looks seems less exceptional today than a generation ago. We ourselves live in a world of male beauty contests, of advertising that exploits the male body beautiful and, increasingly, of male body-image anxiety.

The display in the British Museum shows how – for commercial reasons – the pot painters of Archaic Athens were keen to improve their technique. One side of a water jar dated around 510 BC depicts a group of near naked males in black silhouette, the other, four males shown more naturalistically to a modern eye as reddish-brown figures with black hair. This 'red-figure' technique was a new invention.

Another interesting thing is how much better the pot painters became over time at depicting the human body. In the 500s BC some painters, somewhere, must have been curious enough to start observing bodies from life, and naked ones at that. These red-figure males are shown filling up water jars at one of the public fountain houses that Pisistratus provided for the Athenians. Three of them are young males, nude. The painter uses their manhandling of the jars, hoisted on a shoulder, or being filled, to show off his treatment of musculature in different action poses.

It is possible to see in this little scene a small expression of a larger trait of ancient Greek culture. Sometimes this is called 'humanism'. By this is meant the great interest the Greeks took in exploring and expressing human experience. Caution is needed here. A positive generalization about a whole people amounts to idealization, a negative one to stereotyping. It would be absurd to claim that the ancient Greeks were collectively more 'humane' than, say, the ancient Egyptians or Babylonians. What it seems safe to say is that Greek culture was more human-centred or 'anthropocentric': more inclined, that is, to see human beings as the most significant entity in the cosmos.

The Greeks could behave in ways that many people in today's world of human rights would class as barbarous. Slavery was a universal fact of ancient Greek society. For their time and place the ancient Greeks were perhaps unusual in developing a cultural mindset facilitating in its thinkers, writers and artists an intense engagement with human nature and culture, not just the world of divinity. It was to the latter that the cultural efforts of neighbours like the ancient Egyptians were so much more orientated.

The chapter is not quite finished with these pottery products. Captions label them as cups, bowls, jugs, storage jars and so on. In other words, this is ancient crockery, and it gives clues about Archaic Greek social life. The shapes just named were made to contain potables for guests at a particular type of Greek social gathering, the drinking party, or 'symposium'. By the 500s BC the Athenian potters were turning out forms for what had evolved into a social ritual with a central place in the aristocratic circles of Archaic Greece.

There were conventions regarding how strong the drink was (the bowls were for diluting wine with water), and a lord of revels who ensured they were observed. Passing round the drinking cup was important, and it had to go from left to right, unlike the port decanter, which people in London's gentlemen's clubs consider good form to pass to the left. These drinking sessions could last well into the night. Wives and daughters were excluded. Female courtesans and comely boys were welcomed.

Many images painted on this drinking equipment focus on raucous group misrule ranging from drunkenness to orgies (museums do not always put these latter images on display). Here the society of Archaic Greece looks very much a man's world. Media headlines over today's sagas of the 'lads' night out' might almost caption some of these vivid ancient images: 'boozed-up youngsters fight in the streets', 'rowdy students mob house', 'graphic sex act'.

And yet there were differences: the symposium was by no means all about male hopes of debauchery with girls, or boys. Talk was important, although this seems to have been both structured and competitive, perhaps not so unlike the verbal performances which made conversation in the salons of eighteenth-century Paris so dazzling and, for the new arrival, so formidable. For young nobles, the symposium, like the salon, was also formative, an education. A poet called Xenophanes composed edifying verses especially for performance at these events:

Now is the floor clean, and the hands and cups of all . . .
The mixing bowl stands ready, full of gladness,
and there is more wine at hand . . .
But first it is meet that men should hymn the god with joy,
with holy tales and pure words.
Then after libation and prayer made that we may have strength to do
right – for that is in truth the first thing to do –
no sin is it to drink as much as allows any but an aged man
to get home without an attendant.
And of all men is he to be praised who after drinking brings noble
deeds to light,
as memory and strength will serve him.
Let him not sing of Titans and Giants – those fictions of the men
of old –
nor of turbulent civil broils in which is no good thing at all;
but to give heedful reverence to the gods is ever good.

This poem from the 500s BC offers rules for proper behaviour at a drinking party. Guests should drink moderately, respect the gods and recite poetry about noble deeds and not about monstrous gods like the Titan Cronus, who ate his children. For green young men listening in this way to their elders and betters, partying might have been not only pleasurable but also improving.

To the east of Archaic Greece lay a much older, non-Greek, world. Hearsay about its banqueting practices probably gave the Greeks ideas about how to organize a drinking party. They may have taken over the Near Eastern custom of reclining to eat and drink. More broadly, the innovative world of the Archaic Greeks makes no sense unless they are pictured as a people who had fallen under the spell of foreign travel and alien cultures, just like the Minoans and Mycenaeans before them. It is time to explore this interconnected Archaic world of neighbours more fully.

CHAPTER 4

AS RICH AS CROESUS
EARLY GREEKS AND THE EAST

All ancient Greeks knew the poet who authored these lines:

> You yourself wait until the season for sailing is come, and then haul your swift ship down to the sea and stow a convenient cargo in it, so that you may bring home profit, even as your father and mine, foolish Perses, used to sail on shipboard because he lacked sufficient livelihood. And one day he came to this very place, crossing over a great stretch of sea . . . and he settled near Helicon in a miserable hamlet, Ascra, which is bad in winter, sultry in summer, and good at no time.

Hesiod is usually thought to have been active around 700 BC. Here the poet portrays himself as the son of a migrant from a Greek state on what is now the coast of north-western Turkey. Poverty drove the father to start a risky journey that ended with him settling with his sons as a farmer in the backwoods of the Greek mainland.

Nowadays the site of the ancient village of Ascra can be reached from Athens by car in under two hours. Once the furthest outskirts of the capital have been shaken off, travellers find themselves in a different Greece, deeply rural. As you start to drive through Boeotia, the region to the north of Athens, the soil changes to a rich brown, fertile enough to grow cotton in modern times.

Boeotian Ascra today is a landlocked hill in a near-empty valley over which towers Helicon, a real mountain. From here the brother to whom Hesiod addresses himself would not have had an easy job transporting a cargo of farm produce on stony tracks down to the nearest port. This haven was itself little more than the seaside mouth of a torrent bed.

As to the trade which Hesiod imagines his brother conducting, questions come more easily than answers. Was it short-haul, to a neighbouring community, or long-distance, venturing further out into the Mediterranean? Did he take his goods as a part-load on someone else's boat, Phoenician-owned for instance, or did he have his own vessel? Was he a market-oriented farmer producing an annual surplus, or was he a self-sufficient peasant who made just the occasional foray in order to trade some grain for, say, a new metal tool?

Despite these unknowns, the poem does depict rustic Ascrans going down to the sea in ships. One or more vessels had brought the young migrant father from Asia Minor to Ascra in the first place. No part of Greece is more than 60 miles from the Mediterranean Sea. Except in the direst of times, its ancient inhabitants always had this chance to make connections with the outside world, to meet foreigners, to travel, to see and touch alien artefacts.

As well as complete vases, the British Museum curates heaps of sherds from broken Greek pots. On one such sherd, just over 3 inches long, a row of birds in flight is painted. This attractive fragment comes from one of the most debated archaeological sites in the eastern Mediterranean. In the 1930s the museum sponsored a dig near the mouth of the River Orontes in what is now south-east Turkey, close to the Syrian border. There is not much to see at the site today, just a low mound in a sea of orange trees.

The excavators dubbed this man-made feature 'Al-Mina' in Arabic, 'the Port'. They found ancient warehouses. To their surprise, they also recovered large amounts of ancient Greek pottery. Much of it turns out to have been made in the late 800s and the 700s BC on a Greek island already familiar to the reader, Euboea. The hand of a Euboean potter probably painted that flight of geese-like fowl.

All these Greek pots arrived by sea. So Al-Mina and the ancient Greeks of the time of the Geometric style formed part of a long-distance network. Vessels must have plied routes that linked the Aegean with the coasts of southern Turkey, Cyprus and the Levant. By this time, parts of Greece were once more embedded in a linked world of long-distance trade.

2. The Eastern Mediterranean and the Near East.

Archaeologists nowadays see Al-Mina as a trading station with a population of varied ethnic backgrounds: an *emporion* in Ancient Greek. It seems likely that there were Greeks residing there, using their own potter. The non-Greek pottery points to the presence of other groups, including traders from a major seafaring people a short way south along the same coast.

We have already met more than once with the Phoenicians, as the Greeks called them, the Canaanites of the Old Testament. To build their ships they enjoyed the huge advantage of the strong, straight timbers of the local cedar forests in what is now Lebanon. Phoenicians were an enterprising society of experienced seafarers prepared to risk sailing far from home. The reach of their voyages extended the length and breadth of the Mediterranean, leaving tangible traces.

At the ancient site now known by its modern name of Kommos, on the south coast of Crete, archaeologists have found a religious shrine of Near Eastern type, and much Phoenician pottery. With its sandy coastline, now favoured by nudists and well suited to beaching ancient ships, Kommos was once a stopping place welcomed by Phoenician seafarers plying the high seas. They planted friendly settlements at key points further afield, such as Carthage in modern Tunisia and Gadir (Cadiz) in southern Spain. They specialized in long-distance trade in costly commodities like silver, with a high value compensating for the risks involved.

It has been seen that the Phoenicians were the ultimate source of the new alphabetical script which Greeks created at just the same time as their pottery started to travel to Al-Mina. This trading station is one possible locality for cultural exchanges between Greeks and easterners. These went way beyond the Greek adaptation of Phoenician script. Scholars have learnt to use the term 'orientalizing' to describe the way in which Greek craftsmen encountered eastern styles of art decorating imported objects – metalwork for instance. From the later 700s BC fascination with some of these motifs prompted Greek artisans to adopt and adapt them for their own craft products.

The British Museum displays a miniature clay perfume container with the spout moulded in the form of the bared teeth of a lion, with a shaggy mane achieved in painted lines. A Corinthian made this little pot around 640 BC. The idea for the unusual form of the spout ultimately came from the animal heads attached to metal bowls imported from the Near East.

These were a sought-after display item for Greek aristocrats in early Archaic times. Following an immutable law of consumption, local manufacturers of cheaper ceramics imitated the decoration of these exotic bowls for a less exalted Greek market.

There is no doubt that the goods and ideas of the ancient Near East had a deep impact on the developing cultural life of Archaic Greece and that they had already done so in earlier centuries of Greek prehistory. Because the hard evidence is very patchy, with new finds and new insights always around the corner, scholars have learnt to take a provisional line on just how profound these influences were. The Greek rite of animal sacrifice is one example of these difficulties.

'Thus saith the Lord of hosts, the God of Israel: Add your burnt offerings to your sacrifices and eat ye the flesh.' Taken from the Book of Jeremiah, this quotation from the Old Testament is one of many passages in the Hebrew Bible showing the central place of animal sacrifice in ancient Jewish worship. The following is a translation from an inscription in ancient Greek found on the Cycladic island of Kea, ancient Ceos:

> The chief magistrates who are in office are to pay the person who has undertaken the duties, 150 drachmas for sacrificial victims. Whoever takes on the duty is to provide a surety acceptable to the magistrates that he will give the feast as prescribed by law. He must sacrifice one mature ox and one mature sheep. If he sacrifices a pig it must not be older than 18 months. A feast is to be provided for the citizens, for those invited by the city-state, for resident foreigners and freedmen and for all that pay taxes to the city-state of the Coressians. Supper, wine, fruit and nuts, and all the rest are to be well provided along with an amount of meat not less than 2 minas in raw weight, and a part of the entrails which the sacrificial beasts have. The chief magistrates and the financial officer must examine the beasts and weigh the meat and preside at the sacrifice [etc.].

In ancient times this Greek island of roughly 50 square miles was divided between no fewer than four tiny city-states, of which Coressia was one. The Coressians like all Greek city-states organized sacred killings of animals on a regular annual basis. As here, a public feast might follow, when meat from the butchered carcasses could be shared out equably among citizens and other invitees.

Broad similarities between the ancient Jewish and Greek rites include the role of an outside altar on which a fire could be lit, victims mainly selected from domesticated species, burning of some parts of the carcass as an offering to the divinity, and human consumption of the meaty parts. In Greek sanctuaries, the importance of the rite is shown by the standard practice of aligning the main doors of a temple with an open-air altar. This allowed the statue of the divinity inside to become a spectator at the fate of the victim offered on the altar outside.

Animal sacrifice already had a long human history. Archaeologists find it hard to distinguish between slaughter and sacrifice as the cause of death of the animals whose bones they find in excavations. Still, there is a growing consensus that the deposits of animal bones providing evidence for human feasting from Neolithic settlements in what is now eastern Turkey and Syria probably derived from a rite of sacrifice. The practice could then have spread. The Mycenaean Greeks certainly engaged in animal sacrifice. Linear B inscriptions include lists of animals intended for sacrifice and, probably, feasts.

The burning of parts of the carcass for the god is a distinctive part of the later Greek ritual. Archaeologists are still debating whether this was a feature inherited from Mycenaean religion or a more recent development. A tradition found in an ancient Cypriot Greek writer of uncertain date, perhaps the first century BC, records how a burnt sacrifice accidentally introduced a taste for cooked flesh among his compatriots in the time of Pygmalion, a legendary king of Cyprus:

> ... afterwards, when the victim was burnt, a portion of the flesh fell on the earth, which was taken by the priest, who, in so doing, having burnt his fingers, involuntarily moved them to his mouth, as a remedy for the pain which the burning produced. Having, therefore, thus tasted of the roasted flesh, he also desired to eat abundantly of it.

This ancient Greek tradition describes an event set in mythical times and tells a tale that sounds too good to be true. It would not be sound historical method to rely on it as a source of historical fact, even if the story fits with the modern idea of animal sacrifice as a Near Eastern practice rippling westwards in prehistoric times.

That said, if burnt offerings were indeed a later addition to prehistoric Greece's sacrificial repertoire, the island of Cyprus, some 62 miles from the

Syrian coast, was certainly in the right place. Many archaeologists working on Cyprus infer from their finds that migrant Greeks from the Aegean as well as people from the Levant settled on the island in the times following the collapse of the Mycenaean palaces. This would have made the island a classic zone of contact between cultures.

East of Al-Mina lay the peoples of Mesopotamia, a fertile country watered by its two great rivers and the seat of ancient civilizations including the Sumerians and then the Babylonians, centred on the great city of Babylon, 50 miles south of modern Baghdad. A Greek poet from the Aegean island of Lesbos, some 3 miles from the Turkish shore, shows that Archaic Greeks were visiting the Middle East in the 600s BC. This poet hymns the warlike exploits of his brother in Mesopotamia, where he killed a warrior of great height 'while fighting as an ally of the Babylonians'. What the poet shies away from saying is 'as a mercenary'.

This scrap of evidence offers a glimpse of a largely lost horizon of culturally momentous contact between Greeks and Mesopotamians. Thales of Miletus has already been encountered as an inventive Greek engineer at the start of the 500s BC. According to the historian Herodotus, Thales also foretold when 'the day was suddenly turned to night . . . fixing it within the year in which it did indeed happen'. The historical and astronomical data point to the eclipse of 28 May 585 BC.

Whatever the truth behind this story, many experts see the ultimate source of the observations, techniques and mathematics enabling Greeks to predict astronomical phenomena to be the Babylonians. Babylonian interest in the motion of the heavenly bodies was deep and ancient. By this date, their scholars had developed skills of analysis and reasoning. Archaic Greek encounters with these ways of thinking might have contributed more broadly to the rise of the first Greek philosophers.

Some experts believe that, long before, it was Babylonian storytelling that influenced the earliest Greek poetry to be written down, that of Homer. The great epic of ancient Mesopotamia was a poem about a male hero called Gilgamesh. At one point this hero, who is mourning the death of his friend Enkidu, is said to behave like a distressed lioness who has lost her cubs:

Like a lioness who has been deprived of [her c]ubs,
he kept pacing about, hence [and forth].

With the difference that the lioness has become a lion, Homer applies a similar comparison to the hero Achilles, grieving for his friend Patroclus:

> The lion thus, with dreadful anger stung,
> Roars through the desert, and demands his young . . .
> So grieves Achilles . . .

The coincidence between the Mesopotamian and the Greek poems is striking, and experts see others – too many to set out here. Is it far-fetched to imagine a fireside encounter at Al-Mina, or on Cyprus, when polyglot merchants exchanged stories, some of them drinking from Euboean cups? In such ways in the 800s or 700s BC, an ancient tale from the Middle East might have entered the food chain of Greek storytelling.

Once in the era of Archaic Greece proper, the evidence for cultural exchange between Greeks and easterners improves. The conservation miracle that is Abu Simbel is famous throughout the world. In 1968, workers dismantled this ancient Egyptian temple and rebuilt it further upstream on the River Nile, on a site safe from the floodwaters of the new Aswan dam. On the shin of a giant statue of Ramesses II, builder of the temple seven centuries earlier, someone around 593 BC incised this graffito in five wavy lines of Ancient Greek:

> When King Psammetichus came to Elephantine, those who sailed with Psammetichus the son of Theocles wrote this; and they came above Kerkis as far as the river allowed; and Potasimto led those of foreign speech and Amasis the Egyptians etc.

The graffito commemorates Greeks serving as mercenaries in an army commanded by a much later pharaoh called Psammetichus. The Greek leader of this band sounds like an expatriate living in Egypt, since his parents gave him an Egyptian name, the same as that of the pharaoh he later served. At this time Egypt remained a powerful state as well as an ancient one – the pharaoh Psammetichus belonged to the twenty-sixth dynasty of native rulers.

The Nile valley was also wealthy, and it was these riches that attracted Archaic Greece's long-distance traders. The British Museum's display on Archaic Greece includes a clay storage jar which a restorer has deftly pieced together from fragments. The style is obviously Greek – a meander-pattern here, an Ionic capital there.

So it is a surprise to see, on the neck, Egyptian hieroglyphics spelling out the name of a second pharaoh of Egypt's twenty-sixth dynasty, Apries, who ruled from 589 to 570 BC. British archaeologists found this Egyptianizing product of a Greek pottery over a century ago on the site of an ancient settlement of Greek merchants some 50 miles inland from the Mediterranean mouth of the Nile.

The Greek name for this place, Naucratis, meant 'ship power'. This maritime prowess belonged to a twelve-strong group of Archaic Greek states allowed by the pharaoh to set up a trading concession here – Egyptian goods in exchange for Greek ones. Prominent among the Greek imports welcomed by the Egyptians, so the Greek historian Herodotus writes, was wine.

In turn this suggests a sophisticated winemaking business in some parts of Archaic Greece. Two likely sources of this wine were the eastern Greek islands of Samos and Chios. These islanders, who had helped to found Naucratis, made their own long-distance storage jars, each capable of transporting several gallons' worth of liquid in a vessel's hold.

The family of the ancient world's most famous female poet was involved in this long-distance trade. Sappho, a native of the Greek island of Lesbos, lived at this time. In 2014 an Oxford scholar published an enigmatic fragment of a new poem by Sappho found on an Egyptian papyrus, where she references her brother's trading:

> But you keep babbling that Charaxus is coming [*or* has come],
> His ship full of cargo . . .

This Charaxus crops up in a piquant story of Herodotus shedding a sidelight on how money was both made and spent in Naucratis during the trading station's sixth-century BC heyday. According to the Greek historian, a smitten Charaxus once spent heavily to buy the freedom of a 'sexually irresistible' slave whose sex-trafficking master had brought her to Naucratis to work – so the historian's euphemistic Greek puts it – as a 'woman companion'. Once freed, Rhodopis, as Herodotus names her, stayed on in the emporium, achieving renown in her calling and financial success.

Sex workers and sex trafficking were as embedded in ancient society as they are in ours, as were the same double standards. Cocking a snook at Greek prejudices against working women, Rhodopis decided to spend a tenth of her fortune on 'preserving her memory' by making an offering to the god Apollo at Delphi. The historian later claimed to have seen this gift – a great heap of iron roasting spits – with his own eyes.

Plying the Mediterranean, ships like those of Charaxus also spread ideas. At much the same time as the establishment of Naucratis, the Archaic Greeks started to produce monumental sculpture in stone. These statues were a symptom of how Archaic Greeks were becoming richer and also more confident in the permanence of their world, since the chief quality of stone is its durability.

The Metropolitan Museum in New York displays one of the first Archaic Greek statues on a new, much larger, scale. This marble figure of a naked youth is over 6 feet high. He has long beaded hair falling over the shoulders. To create this stone giant, its unknown sculptor might well have been indebted to Egyptian know-how. The ancient Greeks believed that the Egyptians invented the technique of releasing such figures from a block of stone, by laying out a grid on the surface with which to plan out the intended figure before carving began. Later Greeks thought that their own sculptors then borrowed this technique.

Many experts think that Archaic Greeks could not have made the transition from wooden to stone architecture without Egyptian technology, or the inspiration provided by the sight of Egypt's great architectural monuments lining the banks of the Nile. In the centre of modern Syracuse's old town the visitor can see behind modern railings what is left of the earliest known example of this new type of Greek building.

Each column in this Sicilian Greek temple of Apollo is carved from a single block of stone weighing some 35 tons. It is as if the architect worried that only monoliths on this scale could hold the stone superstructure aloft. In a Greek inscription still visible on the riser of one of the steps, as if amazed at what he had achieved, one of the construction team boasted of how he had 'executed columns – fine works'. It is likely enough that Archaic temple-builders ultimately drew on Egyptian techniques for cutting, lifting and fitting large stone blocks.

It has been seen that the Greeks began to make coins somewhere around 600 BC. The historian Herodotus linked this invention with a neighbouring people from inland Asia Minor, known to Greeks as the Lydians: 'The Lydians ... were the first men whom we know who coined and used gold and silver currency; and they were the first to sell by retail.'

There are indeed early coins inscribed in the Lydian script with the name 'Walwet'. The bearer of this name is usually identified as the Lydian king whom the Greeks called Alyattes. He reigned from about 610 to 560 BC. Although Herodotus implies that Lydian coins were used in small retail transactions, the value of the only known denominations seems too high. Possibly Alyattes and other Lydian kings minted their coins to pay for the armies with which they aggressively conquered a large land empire of tribute-paying subjects in western Turkey. These subjects came to include the Greeks of Ionia.

From this empire building, the Lydian kings grew hugely rich. In the British Museum's display on Archaic Greece, a case of finds from the Ionian Greek city of Ephesus on Turkey's west coast includes a fragment from a temple column inscribed with two Greek letters. These are a *kappa* ('k') followed by a *rho* ('r'), the first two letters of a proper name, ΚΡΟΙΣΟΣ. Croesus, as he is best known today, was the last Lydian king, coming to the throne in the late 580s BC. Here he used his imperial funds to sponsor the cost of individual columns in the great temple of the goddess Artemis that the Ephesians built in the 550s BC.

From this distance in time it is no longer possible to say exactly how the Lydians and the Greeks each contributed to the invention of coinage. In other ways too, Lydian riches made a deep mark on the way of life of their nearest Greek neighbours. A Greek poet of Late Archaic times portrays a Greek musician from Sappho's island, Lesbos, as cutting a figure in the high society of the Lydians on the nearby mainland of Asia Minor. As a result, this musician is said to have invented a type of lyre on an Asian model, 'after hearing at Lydian feasts the plucked strings that answer to it from the lofty harp'.

Aristocratic Greeks of Archaic times copied the luxurious customs of the Lydians rather as the nobility of eighteenth-century Europe aped the manners of France. Another Archaic Greek poet describes the 'dainty ways learnt from the Lydians' of the rich citizens of another Ionian city, his home town, also on the west coast of Turkey. 'They went to the central plaza with cloaks of purple dye, not less than a thousand of them all told, vainglorious and proud of their comely tresses, reeking of perfume ...'

Berlin's Altes Museum provides a clue to the appearance of these dainty gentlemen. On display is a headless marble statue of a young man which German archaeologists found near the great Ionian centre of Miletus. It has been seen that Archaic Greek sculptors often represented young men as nude. This particular Archaic youth of about 530 BC is emphatically not naked, nor is he lean and well-muscled. On the contrary, he is plump and fussily dressed in a sleeved outfit reaching to the feet. This ample drapery bears traces of dark red paint meant to signify the expensive dye that the Greeks and Phoenicians extracted from certain kinds of Mediterranean shellfish. Greeks called this dye *porphyra*, or 'purple'. In this figure, rich clothing combined with corpulence as a sign of wealth and status, of a superior being with access to the 'Lydian' pleasures making life worth living.

Greeks also made Lydian customs scapegoats for the commodification of sex. Several centuries later a Greek author preserved the following story about an Archaic Greek tyrant ruling the island of Samos:

> Clearchus says that Polycrates, the tyrant of dainty Samos, was ruined by his reckless personal behaviour, because he aspired to Lydian soft-ness. He accordingly constructed the alley in the city of Samos that imitates the area in Sardis [*the Lydian capital*] known as Sweet Embrace, and wove the notorious 'Samian flowers' to match the 'Lydian flowers' . . . the Samian alley was a narrow street filled with working women, and it literally filled Greece with everything that promotes hedonism and excess, while the 'Samian flowers' were exceptionally beautiful women and men.

This chapter ends as it began by pondering the extent and the impor-tance of trade in the economic life of the Archaic Greeks. I once found myself one of a fortunate party permitted by the kindness of the Greek army to enter the pine-scented grounds of a military school built right next to the modern Isthmus canal cutting through the neck of land linking the Peloponnese to central Greece.

After a colonel had ordered the reluctant guards to open the gate for us, Greek conscript soldiers escorted us to an open-air classroom. A young officer gave us a military-style briefing, standing at a lectern, barking commands to an even younger subordinate wielding a pointer. In passable

English the yellow lettering on a huge noticeboard next to him had this to say:

> Technical work of paved road, which was used to avoid circumnaviga-
> tion of Peloponnese. The boats were transferred with the use of the slide
> from the Saronikos Gulf into the Corinthian Gulf. Manufactured in 600
> BC from the tyrant of Corinthus and ancient wise man, Periandros.

Over the officer's shoulder we could see, curving out of sight, the well-preserved stretch of ancient paved road that was the object of our visit. While the officer expounded his subject with a military certainty, I heard murmured doubts from our group. Could the Archaic Corinthians really have devised a means, on a regular basis, of lifting a whole ship out of the water and dragging it a distance of just under 4 miles over an isthmus rising some 260 feet above sea level? Put into some kind of wheeled cradle, each wooden ship would have risked major stress in transit even if it avoided actual mishap, quite apart from the huge cost in animals and men of each operation.

Even so, the Archaic Corinthians must have had pressing reasons for investing in the technical challenge of building the sweeping gradients of this stone roadway. Nowadays experts think that it was meant chiefly to serve as a porterage. Men would unload a cargo on one side of the Isthmus and use oxen to drag it on wheeled carts for reloading onto another vessel on the other side. The Corinthians probably built this grooved roadway because they hoped to attract merchants who could afford to pay the toll moving high-value, low-bulk commodities.

Today's sailors still respect the strong and contrary winds around the capes of the southern Peloponnese. 'Stay ten miles off Cape Malea, and off Cape Grosso ten and another ten', as one Greek proverb goes. As seen with Cape Uluburun, promontories posed problems for ancient navigators in the Bronze Age. In Archaic Greece vessels usually hugged the shore still. The painstaking building of the Corinthian haulage suggests how much was at stake for vessels with valuable cargoes in avoiding such lethal headlands.

The haulage also highlights the economic importance of long-distance trade at this time. The ancient Greeks believed that the riches of the Corinthians derived in large part from seaborne commerce. Astride the

Isthmus, this city-state faced in two directions. As an ancient writer put it, 'The one leads straight to Asia, and the other to Italy.' It is time to turn to the activities of Archaic Greeks in the west. Here migrants from the Greek homelands created their own versions of the Greek way of life, amid close encounters, sometimes peaceful, but often not, with their non-Greek neighbours.

CHAPTER 5

GREAT GREEKS
THE GREEK SETTLEMENT OF THE WEST

By the entrance to the archaeological museum at Sparta when I worked there in the 1970s there stood an ancient stone carving of Heracles. The demi-god was easily recognizable by his attributes, a manly beard, a knotty wooden club and the skin of the lion that he killed as one of his Labours. Artistically the sculpture is nothing special. Still, it would have reminded ancient Spartans that their community had been founded in the remote past by wandering descendants of Heracles, the so-called Heraclidae.

Many Greek states told stories of origin about distant founders who had led migrant ancestors to settle their city. It was seen that prehistoric Greece was a land of migration, of groups coming and groups going. Greek migration was also a fixture of Archaic times. Later Greek tradition produced dates for some of the settlements far from home founded in this period, with 734 BC for the first. In this period Greek migrants settled around the Black Sea, on France's Côte d'Azur, on Spain's Costa Brava and in what is now Libya.

Of these frontier settlements, the most prosperous concentration, where early Greek civilization most obviously flourished, was in southern Italy and Sicily. The ancient Greeks thought of these two areas of Greek settlement, separated by the modern Strait of Messina, as related in kind. One Greek geographer from the time of Christ called the whole area 'Great Hellas', 'Magna Graecia' in Latin, in the sense of not 'better than', but an extension of, the original Greece.

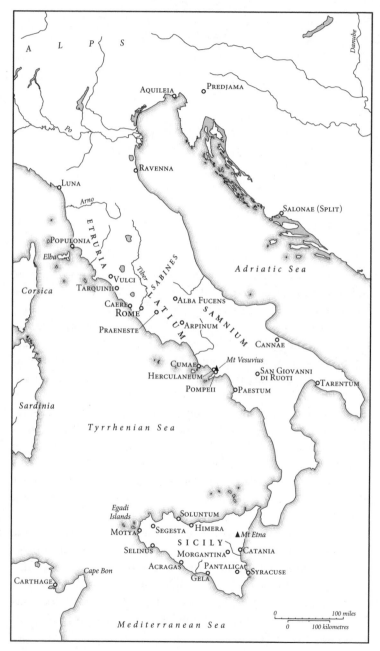

3. Italy.

Trade was one reason why Greeks sailed west. Modern Ischia is an island in the Bay of Naples, about two-thirds the size of Guernsey. That same geographer calls the island by its ancient Greek name, Pithecusae. He adds that these Greek settlers were eventually driven away 'by earthquakes, and by eruptions of fire, sea, and hot waters'. Today this volcanic island is full of thermal springs, and its fertile soils support lush gardens and tropical plants. Ancient settlers here could have been self-supporting in food while they got on with the main business of trade.

Archaeologists have used the finds dug up from nearly 500 ancient graves here to build a picture of a mongrel population that ran into the thousands in the 700s BC. There were Greeks from the island of Euboea and from Corinth, as well as people who placed Near Eastern inscriptions and religious symbols on their pottery, and yet others, mainlanders perhaps, who used Italian-style brooches. So Pithecusae, like Al-Mina, could also have hosted cultural exchanges between Greeks and non-Greeks.

One find, smashed into many pieces when discovered and now glued back together and displayed in the local museum, is a ceramic cup from around 720 BC. On one modern interpretation, the vessel calls itself 'the delicious cup of Nestor' in a poem scratched on the side, one of the oldest examples of the Greek alphabet. It seems to be making a knowing allusion to the gold cup belonging to King Nestor of Pylos which Homer's *Iliad* describes.

Since its discovery in 1954, many scholars (not all) have come to see here a convivial joke of the kind that Greek revellers would later make as they lolled on cushioned beds in an Archaic drinking party. A bolder idea is that it was thanks to socializing between Greeks and easterners on eighth-century BC Pithecusae that Greeks first came across – and then adopted – the distinctive Near Eastern custom of reclining, not sitting, to eat and drink.

Between modern Catania and Syracuse in Sicily, the main road passes an industrial zone to the east. Beyond this is a little-visited archaeological site. It sits on a flat promontory looking out to sea and is flanked by the mouth of a river and a beach which would have been suitable for drawing up ancient ships. The excavations should not be visited before the spring flush of high grass has received its annual strimming. This verdancy is a corrective to the parched images of a Sicilian summer evoked by Sicily's Giuseppe di Lampedusa (died 1957), author of *The Leopard*: 'bare hillsides flaming yellow under the sun' with 'never a tree, never a drop of water'.

Compared with much of Greece, Sicily looks rather fertile. Today the rich brown soils covering the rolling hills of the interior grow acre upon acre of grain. They support orchards, vineyards and olive groves. Ancient Greeks saw rural Sicily as much more productive than southern Greece. Athenians envied the fact that, unlike them, Sicilian Greeks were self-sufficient in grain and could breed many horses on their well-watered lands. Ownership of a horse for ancient Greeks had something of the cachet of driving a Rolls-Royce today.

On this particular promontory archaeologists found an ancient Greek settlement enclosed by a defensive wall. This was not a haphazard habitat of narrow winding streets like one of the modern island's country towns. Here building plots and thoroughfares were laid out on a series of man-made grids in turn grouped around a central trapezoid of land reserved for use as a public plaza.

The date produced by the pottery finds for the creation of this planned community was somewhere in the late 700s BC. Later Greek writers mentioned this place. They knew it as Megara, the original expedition of founding fathers having named the outpost after the homeland they had set out from, an older Megara, a neighbour of Athens.

Ancient writers gave as triggers back home for this type of expedition strife within the community, resolved by the expulsion of troublemakers. They also mention natural causes, such as drought and hunger, and a surplus of people, forcing some to look for new lands. The targeting of Sicily's landed potential fits well with these environmental and economic pressures. So does the likelihood that mainland Greece's population rose rapidly, as was seen, in the 700s BC.

The people of mainland Megara in the later 700s BC were probably still in the formative stage of becoming a 'city-state': working out political institutions, building a corporate identity and so on. It cannot be said for sure, in fact, that at this date they would have been politically capable of organizing this kind of expedition. Would-be migrants could have taken the initiative themselves. Not much is known about the ancient mainland city of Megara buried beneath its modern namesake, but archaeologists believe that its neighbour to the west, Corinth, was still a collection of villages in the 700s BC. So the expedition from here probably arrived in Sicily not just without a blueprint for how to create a political community, but with no inherited knowledge of how to lay out a new settlement or divide up farmland among themselves.

The members of this expedition, it was said in antiquity, had set out under a leader. They met with various misadventures once the group arrived in Sicily before they found a suitable place to settle. At one point they joined an older community of Greek settlers further north, but relations broke down and the Megarans were thrown out. After further wanderings, eventually an indigenous ruler of those parts led the migrants to the promontory site and gave up some of his lands for them to live off.

Later Greeks created these written accounts generations after the event and we cannot assume their historical accuracy. Take the seemingly obliging local potentate: did the newcomers, presumably young, well-armed Greek males, perform some service for him, or rather the opposite – threaten him with force? Yet the details do hint credibly at the problems that these enterprising groups of migrants faced on arrival: identifying a suitable place to settle with little or nothing in the way of accurate local knowledge; cooperation with, and then hostility from, rival settler groups; and negotiation with indigenous landholders.

The archaeological museum in Syracuse now houses the most spectacular find from the excavations at Megara Hyblaea, as the Sicilian offshoot was called. This is a limestone statue of a seated female, which has lost its head. Through circular holes in her garment she breastfeeds two infants, whom she envelops with her arms and cloak. Conservators have reassembled the figure from hundreds of fragments found in one of Megara's cemeteries, where it must have acted as the marker of a grave. As for date, it was commissioned some two centuries after the founding of the settlement, judging from the style of the carving. This relates it to Greek sculpture of the later 500s BC.

This celebration of female fertility – smoothing over, perhaps, the challenges of suckling two babies at once – is rather unusual for Greek art. On the Greek mainland, sculptors generally preferred to depict females as young maids, warring Amazons, women under threat of rape, or goddesses in all their perfection. It is quite likely that this unusual choice of subject matter reflected the social values of the indigenous culture of Sicily, as well as the concerns for reproduction in this enclave of frontier Greekness. Based on the size of excavated houses and other factors, archaeologists estimate that in the hundred years or so after its foundation, the population might have risen from an initial group of two hundred or so to around two thousand or more.

So there is also an interesting question to ask about the part played by migrant Greek females on the one hand, and local women on the other, in ensuring the early settlement's demographic future. There are various possibilities here, from family-based 'chain' migration to what in more recent times has been called 'libidinous colonization', when settlers would deliberately marry their offspring to indigenous partners, so that the newcomers would not be disadvantaged as foreigners. Experts weigh up the particular case of Greek migrants to Sicily and southern Italy. Biological mixing of the newer arrivals with the older population is likely. The extent to which this happened remains entirely up in the air.

The ancient Greek tradition about the helping hand offered to the newly arrived migrants by a local ruler – Hyblon was his name – has an analogue in the archaeology of this part of Sicily. The scenic hill country to the west of the Greek settlement is a haven today for walkers and lovers of fauna and flora. This last includes a plant known locally as 'seddaredde' with a powerful attraction for bees. It contributed, perhaps, to the area's ancient reputation for the excellence of its honey.

Here – Pantalica as the place is called – archaeologists have found a vast area of limestone cliff-faces pitted with rock-cut chambers, some four thousand of them according to a survey in 2007 and 2008: a mixture of tombs and dwellings. They occupy an obviously defensive position on a plateau flanked by river valleys. The ancient Greeks called the pre-Greek people living up here 'Sicels'. One tradition claimed that they were migrants themselves, arriving before the Greeks in rafts from Italy.

Morgantina is the ancient name for an inland settlement on the eastern side of Sicily, some 37 miles from the coast. The well-tended archaeological site is worth visiting, and not just for its spectacular view of Mount Etna. This was also the findspot for some objects of great interest now kept in the nearby hill town of Aidone. A highlight of a visit to the museum here are the marble heads, hands and feet of two seated statues of females, divinities in all likelihood from a local shrine, whose lost bodies would have been made from some less expensive material. These are works in the Greek sculptural style of the 500s BC as is clear from the faces, carved with the so-called Archaic smile, an enigmatic expression of seeming joy typical of statues from Athens at this time.

Sculptures such as these might seem to indicate that Morgantina was another settlement of migrant Greeks (despite being far from the coast, their preferred habitat). Another find hints at a more blurred reality. Archaeologists from the American excavations here have published four letters in the Greek alphabet reading 'ΠΙΒΕ', or 'pibe'. They had been scratched on the foot of a clay drinking cup imported from Athens.

There is no such word in Ancient Greek. Experts think that the language must be that of the indigenous Sicels, written down in lettering borrowed from the Greeks. It is thought to give a command: 'Drink!' If this were the same word in Ancient Greek and painted, not incised, it would be just the sort of playful instruction that vase painters in Athens at this time put on pottery intended for the wine-drinking party. Whoever the local user of this cup might have been, the conclusion is well-nigh unavoidable that with its graffito it provides evidence for native Sicilians embracing for their own use the trappings of a foreign – Greek – form of sociability.

Other finds include an unplanned grouping of elongated huts or long-houses with wattle-and-daub walls and thatched roofs from the 900s and 800s BC. These confirm the origins of Morgantina as an indigenous settlement. Then, in the 500s BC, new cultural leanings came into play, including the examples just discussed. Inhabitants also started to use more sophisticated Greek-style building techniques, such as dried mud brick for walls, clay roof tiles and so on.

'Hybridity' is one of the words that academics use to describe when different ethnic groups interact to produce 'transcultural' forms. The reality at Morgantina underlying the cross-cultural contact is hard to grasp without historical documents. Even if there was peaceful interaction between non-Greek Sicilians and Greek newcomers, the experience could still have been disruptive for the older ethnic group. Not all its members would have had equal chances to display the 'hybrid' form of identity. Greek pottery, for instance, and any Greek wine drunk from it were imports that were not likely to be cheap.

Relations between Greek settlers and the older population varied enormously. Greek writers record traditions of fighting between the two groups, although there is little sense that these struggles were great obstacles to the flourishing of the Greek settlements in Sicily. In Archaic times warfare with the non-Greek population was the experience of three of the richest Greek settlements in Sicily, strung out on the long south coast. Their ancient Greek names (working westwards) were Gela, Acragas and Selinus.

Today, the last two are big tourist attractions thanks mainly to eye-catching groups of Greek-style temples from the 500s and 400s BC. These ruins are the most obvious manifestation of great riches and large populations in Greek times, as well as the urge of the settlers to draw attention to themselves. Selinus commanded a coastal plain of well over 1,000 square miles according to one scholar's estimate, about two times the area of modern Los Angeles. Neighbouring Acragas was the Argentine of Greek Sicily, its fertile lowlands famous for its rich horse-breeders, as well as supporting export trades in olive oil and wine.

The *Lebensraum* aggressively sought by Greek settlers in this part of Sicily seems to have been a factor in their armed clashes with the pre-Greek population. This much later story from a Greek writer of Roman times concerns the men of Acragas in the 500s BC, their tyrant leader at the time, Phalaris, and an indigenous people in this part of the island whom the Greeks called 'Sicani':

> When the men of Acragas attacked the Sicanians, Phalaris found it impossible to capture their city by siege, because they had laid aside a great quantity of corn, and therefore he entered into a treaty of peace with them. He had in his camp some corn, which he agreed to leave for them, on condition that he received from them an equal quantity after their harvest. The Sicanians readily complied with these terms, and received the provisions. Phalaris then contrived to bribe the superintendents of the granaries secretly to remove their roofs in some places; as a result, the rain came in through the holes, and rotted the corn. As soon as the harvest was over, Phalaris received his quantity of new corn, according to their agreement; but when the old corn was found to be rotten, the Sicanians were reduced by hunger, and after giving up their provisions to him, were forced to surrender their liberty as well.

Some readers may puzzle over the obvious inconsistency of this ancient Greek tale, as I do. If the besieged Sicanians already had plentiful stores of corn, why should they have wanted yet more from the departing men of Acragas? This Phalaris attracted more than his share of what to modern readers seem rather tall stories. Of these the most notorious in ancient times concerned his bronze bull. This hollow animal was equipped with a door, as well as pipes in the nostrils to emit sound. With a fire lit beneath and a victim trapped inside, the bull became an instrument of punishment, and this was how Phalaris was said to employ it. Yet a credible witness, a Sicilian Greek, claimed that the very same bull could still be seen in Acragas in his own day, the 40s BC.

What both stories channel was a perception that Phalaris was both clever and cruel. He is the earliest example from Sicily (his rough dates were around 570–550 BC) of the type of Greek ruler met with in an earlier chapter, the tyrant. In Greek Sicily this kind of military dictator was a common phenomenon, not just in Archaic times, but right down to the Roman conquest in 211 BC.

Phalaris was said to have seized power in a coup by means of another ruse while serving as a local magistrate. He was able to capture the citadel of Acragas, arm a force of slaves and take advantage of a religious festival to massacre many of the free men and take women and children as hostages. He then seems to have embarked on warfare to enlarge the lands of Acragas, in part at the expense of indigenous neighbours in the interior.

It is a different matter to judge any local factors aiding his rise to power. The fact that he was a magistrate at the time of his coup suggests – at this early date – that Phalaris was an aristocrat. He was evidently ambitious. He could have found the chances for individuals from his class to rise to prominence in public office frustrated by the fact that they were relatively many in number, as follows from the likelihood that the population of Acragas was large by ancient Greek standards.

Some of these Greek settlements in Sicily came to harbour significant disparities in wealth and these gave rise to social tensions. Phalaris might have found political supporters among the poorer Greeks of settler stock who looked to him to take care of them – by conquering more land, for instance. As for terror as a weapon for holding on to power, today's dictators have shown that this can work, at least for a time. The bronze monster might have been more than a load of bull.

Next-door Selinus was the westernmost of the Greek settlements. Perhaps the most astonishing sight to greet today's visitor are the imploded ruins of a giant temple just outside the ancient urban centre. The vast field of debris testifies to the planned scale of this monument, so large that it was never finished. Italian archaeologists found more evidence for the riches of the settlers here.

A Greek inscription once adorning an interior doorway of the temple records how the men of Selinus thanked the gods for a victory in an unknown war with an offering incorporating sixty talents of gold. If a talent in Selinus was a measure of weight roughly the same as an Athenian talent, this would have been the equivalent of over a ton's worth of the precious metal.

The Greek temples in Sicily ostentatiously reflect religious practices shared by the settlers with the homeland. A museum in the modern town of Castelvetrano near the site of Selinus displays a strip of lead telling a similar story about the religious ideas of the settlers here, although it reveals religious thinking of a different kind. The metal is inscribed, incised rather, and the Ancient Greek is hard to read and in fact indecipherable in places. In the 1980s this find from the ancient site was housed in the Getty Museum at Malibu. Realizing the importance of the inscription for the history of Greek religion, in 1991 the museum voluntarily returned the tablet to Italy.

In the most interesting lines the lead strip prescribes how murderers can be purified from vengeful demons who act on behalf of the wronged victim – ghosts in other words. To appease these revenants, haunted individuals had to revere them with animal sacrifices, then use salt to mark a boundary round the altar, sprinkle water and step away. Since we are in Greek Sicily, political strife might have caused the internal violence which seems to have troubled Selinus in this way. More surprising is the matter-of-fact belief in ghosts in an official document as this clearly was, promulgated by the civic body. The kind of ritual behaviour prescribed here would not be out of place in one of the English author Dennis Wheatley's fantasy novels about the modern occult.

That said, the religious beliefs and practices look Greek. The people of Selinus still upheld their Greek religious culture at this time – some five generations after migrants founded the city in the late 600s BC. Prominent in the inscription is the cultic surname 'Meilichius'. Despite its Greekness, some experts believe that in its origins this cultic surname conceals an association with Molek, a divinity of the ancient Levant who appears in the Bible as the Moloch of the Canaanites. The matter cannot be gone into here, although – as it happens – the people of Selinus had as neighbours in western Sicily not only other Greek settlers and indigenous people but also communities of the Levantine population dubbed *Phoinikes*, Phoenicians, by the ancient Greeks.

West of Selinus the modern autostrada in this part of Sicily stops some 20 miles before a pungent zone of salt-beds fringing a placid coastal lagoon. The small island of just over a hundred acres in the middle of the lagoon is ancient Motya. The site offered the Phoenicians just the sort of offshore protection they favoured for their trading settlements. For their merchantmen plying the western Mediterranean, sailing via Motya reduced the time they had to spend risking the open sea. The enclave that Phoenicians founded here around 700 BC grew in size to the point that the population eventually had to cram itself into tower blocks several stories high. The place came to resemble, if not Manhattan, then, as one historian has suggested, an Italian city of the Renaissance.

In the 500s BC, the shadow of a very different Phoenician enclave had started to fall over Sicily. From high ground in the west of the island it is possible to see the tip of Cape Bon in Tunisia, some 90 miles south. Before Phoenicians established themselves at Motya they had already settled a peninsula just to the west of this cape, in what is now the Bay of Tunis. Greeks called this place 'Karchedon'. Romans later knew it as 'Carthago', its population as 'Poeni', or Punes. By the mid-500s BC the Carthaginians were becoming a force to be reckoned with in this part of the Mediterranean.

The seafaring peoples of the Levant were interested in trade, not empire-building. Despite modern denials, their Carthaginian offshoot, however, does seem to have wanted to dominate territory as well as shipping routes. Writers in Roman times recorded the Carthaginian invasion and conquest of 'a portion' of Sicily as early as the mid-500s BC. These later traditions of Carthaginian aggression should not be accepted uncritically. As will be seen in a later chapter, the Romans went on to fight three epic wars against Carthage. A 'national' enemy with a long history of military aggression suited the Roman narrative.

That said, one Greek historian knew of a battle between Carthaginians and the Greeks of Selinus, when many soldiers on the Greek side fell before the city's walls. This undated event may well belong to the 500s BC. As we shall see in a later chapter, when the Carthaginians made a treaty with a fledgling Italian power at this time (508 BC), the wording – preserved by an ancient writer – mentioned 'the part of Sicily which the Carthaginians control'. By the time of this agreement with the Romans, Carthage saw the western part of the island as firmly under its hegemony.

In the archaeological museum at Delphi the visitor can see one of the greatest works of Greek sculpture. I once stood in front of this bronze statue with an artist friend who was viewing it for the first time. He was completely lost in admiration for the sculptor's extraordinary attention to such details as the veins in the feet, and the serene beauty somehow imparted to the young man's face, complete with individual metal eyelashes.

The super-rich patron who gifted this figure of a charioteer was a Greek from Sicily who wanted to mark the victory of his team in the four-horse chariot race, highlight of Apollo's four-yearly games at Delphi. The Greek inscription on the base of the monument preserves the donor's name. He turns out to belong to the most powerful family in Sicily in the 480s and 470s BC.

For a generation four brothers ruled like a dynasty over a web of alliances knitting together the Greek settlements of the island. The dominant sibling, Gelon, first seized power as a military dictator or tyrant in Gela. He went on to capture the Greek city of Syracuse on the east coast, which he then made his main base, assigning the rule of Gela to a brother. In the generations before Gelon the Corinthian settlers at Syracuse had already made themselves masters of a large hinterland and divided it up into parcels from which the local aristocrats took their collective name, 'sharers in land plots'. The site also made an excellent natural port. From here a coast-hugging route linked shipping with the sole of Italy and the dash across open sea between what is now Puglia and the offshore islands of western Greece.

The regal behaviour of these brothers extended to dynastic marriages with other Sicilian tyrants, as well as spending their wealth to build an ambitious image of cultural excellence which they projected onto a larger Greek stage, as the Delphic Charioteer shows. In turn these tyrants attracted to Sicily significant cultural figures from the Greek world to the east.

The whole interlude makes clear the continuing cultural orientation towards the Greek motherland of the aristocratic class in the Sicilian Greek settlements from which this family was sprung. It also shows how the aristocratic culture of Greek Sicily could compete on something like equal terms with that of Greeks elsewhere at this time, especially when political power and cultural leadership on the island became concentrated on an ambitious tyrant and his court.

How innovative Archaic Sicily's Greek culture was, as opposed to having a reputation for spending from a deep purse that naturally attracted Greeks in search of patronage, is a large and difficult question that could make the subject of a book itself. Here it is possible only to paint a few brush-strokes. What one can say is that Greek culture in Sicily certainly had its moments.

In the sixth century BC home-grown wordsmiths included a Greek poet, one Stesichorus. He wrote long poems retelling Greek myths in an original way and his influence is suspected on the mythical plots of the far more famous Athenian playwrights of the following century, Aeschylus and Euripides. Like these authors of tragedies, Greek writers of comic plays were poets who (as with Shakespeare) composed dialogue in lines of scanning verse. In the fourth century BC the Athenian philosopher Plato hailed another elusive Sicilian writer as the 'chief poet of comedy'. This Epicharmus (the 'ch' pronounced as in chorus) is also a suspected influence on Athenian comic theatre of the fifth century BC, discussed in a later chapter.

In the visual arts, just to take Greek temples, no Sicilian example has satisfied modern aesthetes as the Parthenon does. The ancient Greeks themselves marvelled far more at the size than the architectural refinement of their temples, and here Greek Sicily certainly did compete. The temple of Olympian Zeus begun by the Greeks of Acragas in the late 500s BC was praised by a writer from the mainland three centuries later as 'in plan and size second to no other in Hellas'. This concedes not only its superiority in size but also in design.

The museum at modern Agrigento includes a vast hall devoted to this extraordinary building and displays reassembled remnants of its most startling design feature. This was a series of naked male figures some 25 feet high, each so large that it had to be made up of lots of small blocks. Somehow these figures had been incorporated into the (long toppled) structure. However, such is their originality that modern archaeologists cannot agree on exactly where they might have gone.

Before Gelon's time there were no outside powers with designs on Sicily that risked checking the prosperity of its Greek incomers. Under Gelon, Sicilian Greeks for the first time faced an existential threat from a seaborne enemy. A dramatic find in the north of the island has brought this moment vividly to life. Early this century Italian archaeologists uncovered a series of mass graves of adult males, a total of at least sixty-five bodies, laid out respectfully in rows. They showed signs of violent wounds, including one skeleton with the blade of a spear still buried in its side.

The small finds indicate a date in the early 400s BC. This made the Italians think of a great battle here in 480 BC. The site is about 25 miles east of Palermo, just off the autostrada. Here, on a bluff looking out to sea, migrant Greeks had established their only outpost in this part of the island. The battle of Himera, named after the Greek settlement, took place at the foot of this bluff, where the findspot of the mass graves must mark the scene of some of the most intense fighting.

On one side of this battle was a large Carthaginian army that arrived by sea after sailing up the west coast of the island. The strategic concern of the Carthaginians seems to have been the expansionist tendencies in western Sicily of the Greek power bloc led by Gelon, whose father-in-law, the tyrant of Acragas, had seized control of Himera in 483 BC. On the other side was the army of this father-in-law, reinforced by a Syracusan army led by his kinsman. During a battle lasting all day, the Greeks burnt the Carthaginian ships drawn up on the nearby beach and routed the disheartened troops of the enemy, slaughtering or capturing them in great numbers. As a result, Carthage now shelved its ambitions in Sicily, for the time being.

Gelon and his family were not slow to advertise to a larger Greek world their defeat of this assault on Greeks by a non-Greek power. At Delphi, once more, French archaeologists have found the base for a victory monument set up by Gelon. Ancient writers mention the offerings it supported: a golden tripod and statue of the Greek goddess of victory, resting, it seems, on a tall column.

Allegedly on the same day, in the straits of Salamis near Athens, an allied Greek fleet won a decisive victory over a Persian armada led by the 'Great King', Xerxes. A year later, an allied Greek army defeated the remnants of this Persian invasion force at Plataea in central Greece. To mark this victory the allied Greeks also offered a golden tripod at Delphi, it too held high for all to see by a slender column. Gelon's gift for self-publicity is one reason for thinking that he set up his own tripod *after* the mainlander offering. He wanted to offer a visual parallel between the Greek defeat of the Persians and his own great achievement, vanquishing the Carthaginians.

Among Greeks, Gelon had an additional motive for talking up this achievement. According to the historian Herodotus, the Greek mainlanders had sent envoys to Gelon asking for armed assistance, against Xerxes, addressing him flatteringly as 'lord of Sicily'. Supposedly Gelon replied that he was willing to help, but on condition that he took personal command of the allied Greek forces. This proved too much for the proud Spartans, and so the envoys left empty-handed.

Herodotus goes on to tell another story that gives an insight into Gelon the hard-nosed political operator and shows why he might have gone on the 'PR offensive' in the wake of Persia's defeat. When he heard that a Persian army had indeed crossed into Greece, Gelon sent three fast ships loaded with money to Delphi. Here they were to await the outcome of the invasion, with orders to bring the treasure back home if the Greeks won, but to gift it to the other side if the Persians were the victors. So much for the unity of Hellas.

With the booty from Himera, including a captive labour force, Gelon's family network embarked on a spree of new public works in the Greek cities of Sicily. For much of the ensuing fifth century BC the island's inhabitants were left to themselves, until outsiders once again set covetous eyes on the island's riches.

Greek Sicily is the highlight in any account of early Greek settlement overseas. Historians do not rate the originality of the settler culture on the island that highly, but are impressed by the material remains. In the wealth to which they attest these remains outstrip any traces to be seen nowadays of other Greek outposts founded at this time, with the exception of what is now Libya.

Here, on the fertile coastal strip some 130 miles east of Benghazi, at the place they called Cyrene, Dorian Greek immigrants from what is now the island of Santorini, ancient Thera, prospered and built their Greek-style temples, relatively untroubled, it seems, by the previous occupants of the land.

In the end the Sicilian Greeks would be less fortunate at the hands of their neighbours and near-neighbours in North Africa and Italy. Three of these nearby societies would interact both with the Greeks and with each other in ways decisive for ancient Mediterranean civilization. It is time to look at this trio more closely.

CHAPTER 6

MEET THE (WESTERN) NEIGHBOURS

Over in North Africa, the descendants of Phoenician migrants settled at Carthage developed into an advanced society. They had a written language and some kind of literature. The practical Romans rated highly enough one of their books, an agricultural manual, to commission a translation from the Phoenician into their own language, Latin. Apart from mainly short inscriptions, Carthaginian writings do not survive: the Carthaginians join other ancient cultures that have left no written account of themselves. Instead we are left with a kind of mirage, the Carthage of Greek and Roman writers.

As seen, already in Archaic times western Greeks had cause to fear the Carthaginians. Not only did the Carthaginians not go away, but, over six or so centuries, their power grew, until it would menace Rome, as a later chapter will show. The stories of Greek and Roman writers have significantly shaped how the Carthaginians are remembered today.

Because in the end the societies of Greece and Rome lived on until well into the Christian centuries, whereas the Romans annihilated the original Carthage in 146 BC, these stories might seem suspect as 'victors' history'. In the nineteenth century, the most controversial claim these classical authors made about the Carthaginians gave the French writer Gustave Flaubert the material for a fictitious moment in his novel set in ancient Carthage called *Salambô*, published in 1862.

> Presently a man who staggered, a man pale and hideous from terror, pushed forward a child; then could be distinguished between the hands of the Colossus a little black mass – it sank into the opening. The priests leaned over . . . and a new chant burst out, celebrating the joys of death and the renascence of eternity.

Flaubert here imagines the sacrifice of the first of a batch of children, 'enveloped in black veils'. The colossus is the statue of a Phoenician divinity whom Greeks identified with the god in their own pantheon with a similar appetite for human infants, Cronus, who ate all his children except Zeus. Flaubert's description seems to have been inspired by an ancient writer from Greek Sicily called Diodorus. This source recounts the pose of this Carthaginian statue, its hands extended and sloping downwards, 'so that each of the children placed thereon rolled down and fell into a sort of gaping pit filled with fire'.

Other Greek and Roman writers refer to this practice of the Carthaginians, which was evidently well known to their Mediterranean neighbours. Despite its sounding like so much hostile propaganda, the basic truthfulness of this ancient tradition is confirmed by the finds of archaeologists. In 1925, on the site of Carthage, they discovered a sacred enclosure with many stones inscribed with dedications in the Carthaginian version of Phoenician script and marking the location of ceramic urns containing the ashes of cremated infants. The bones of sheep and other animals, also recovered, suggest that the archaeologists had found in general the remains of sacrifices, not burials.

There has been a lively modern debate about the finds from here and from another ten enclosures thought to be of this same type on Phoenician settlement sites in the Mediterranean, including Motya in Sicily. The case is strong for taking the burnt bones and the accompanying inscriptions mentioning 'mlk', a Phoenician word apparently meaning a sacrificial offering, as a corroboration of the tradition recorded by Greek and Roman writers.

Judging from the inscriptions, those who made these offerings, mainly men but occasionally women, sacrificed a child of their own as a vow or in thanks to the divinity and perhaps only in an emergency. At Motya, Italian archaeologists have estimated from the cremated bones that in any year only a couple of sacrificed children were buried. As for the origin of the practice, migrating Phoenicians of the early Iron Age presumably brought it with them from the Levant. Here the Old Testament ascribes similar rites to the Canaanites and, indeed, to Abraham.

The vast majority of people would see the deliberate burning alive of fellow humans in today's world as barbaric. Yet it seems futile to judge the Carthaginians of remote times by contemporary standards. The custom was part of a religion, and therefore of a morality. The practice did not mean that Greeks and Romans withheld their admiration for other aspects of Phoenician Carthage.

There was praise for Carthaginian political stability. In the later 300s BC the Greek philosopher Aristotle thought it worthy of note that the ordinary people of Carthage seemed to be satisfied with their system of government, judging from the fact, as he claimed, that they had never resorted to mob violence or supported a tyrant. A Roman statesman, Cicero, recognized the 'judgment and training' of the ruling classes that steered the nearly six centuries of Carthaginian power. At all times, the influence of aristocratic dynasties seems to have been strong, not least in appointments to the command of Carthage's military. This type of political leadership was to the liking of the upper orders in Greek and Roman society too.

The main business of the Phoenicians who migrated westwards from their homeland was always trade. As seen, the Greeks believed that they chose places to settle for that reason – promontories and offshore islands like Motya in Sicily or Carthage itself, sites well suited to act as trading stations with local people and as stopping points for long-haul shipping. For Greeks, Carthage became a byword for riches. Much of this wealth came from the profits of commerce, whether this was the actual business of shipping and marketing goods or the land-based production of merchandise for export on territory dominated by the Carthaginians.

Not necessarily the most valuable of the commodities traded, but certainly one of the more tangible today, was farm produce. Archaeologists find traces of this trade in the form of amphorae – those ancient clay containers mass-manufactured by hand for transporting goods by sea – and the biological remains inside them. Analysis of these shows that amphorae made in Carthage from the 600s BC onwards might carry olive oil and wine, as well as preserved fish and meat. Carthaginian amphorae have been found on the west coast of Spain, in southern France, Sardinia,

Sicily and southern Italy, as well as elsewhere in North Africa. An underwater dig from the time of the Carthaginian domination of Sardinia has produced evidence for amphorae packed with cuts of sheep, goat and cattle small enough to fit into the containers.

Archaeologists now think that the Phoenician settlers at Carthage gained control of the fertile hinterland surrounding their settlement – the countryside of modern Tunis – as early as the 600s and 500s BC. An ancient Greek writer preserves a unique description of this farmland as it looked to an invading army three centuries later (310 BC):

> The intervening country through which it was necessary for them to march was divided into gardens and plantations of every kind, since many streams of water were led in small channels and irrigated every part. There were also country houses one after another, constructed in luxurious fashion and covered with stucco, which gave evidence of the wealth of the people who possessed them. The farm buildings were filled with everything that was needful for enjoyment, seeing that the inhabitants in a long period of peace had stored up an abundant variety of products. Part of the land was planted with vines, and part yielded olives and was also planted thickly with other varieties of fruit-bearing trees. On each side herds of cattle and flocks of sheep pastured on the plain, and the neighbouring meadows were filled with grazing horses.

The description makes clear that by this date rich Carthaginians were not only merchants but also landowners – ones who enjoyed life in their country houses. It was the agricultural wisdom driving this idyll of fertility and prosperity that the Romans sought to capture when they had the twenty-eight volumes of that Carthaginian agricultural expert translated into Latin, as seen.

As it happens, the above description neatly matches the farm products from Carthage's rural hinterland in 310 BC with those foodstuffs which have left biological traces in Carthaginian transport amphorae. Much of this produce must have been destined to feed the Carthaginians themselves. It was also needed to feed Carthage's armies.

We catch a glimpse of this aspect in 480 BC. A Greek historian relates that the Carthaginians supplied the invasion force which Gelon of Syracuse defeated at the battle of Himera with grain shipped by merchantmen, not from the mother city, but from Sardinia. The same text shows that this island by now was a Carthaginian dominion.

The ancient Greeks believed that Carthage intervened to direct the activities of farmers in lands under its sway. Scholars know this only thanks to an anonymous Greek writer in much later antiquity who compiled a collection of 'marvellous things heard'. Meant to entertain as much as to inform, this unlikely format preserves the following scrap of information:

> At the present day, [Sardinia] is no longer fertile, because when ruled by the Carthaginians it had all its fruits that were useful for food destroyed, and death was fixed as the penalty for the inhabitants if anyone should plant anything of the kind.

Were this a reliable ancient source, it might suggest that Carthage had once tried to promote grain production in Sardinia at the expense of other crops – and with a heavy hand. However, archaeologists who survey the surface of modern Sardinia's countryside for signs of human activity in ancient times – mostly in the form of potsherds – have not been able to corroborate this picture.

The distribution of ancient sherds on the ground points to diversity, not sameness, in the agricultural regime – a more manorial set-up in one part of the island, centred on a 'big house'; elsewhere, lots of middling and small freeholders. So the idea that Carthage went in for Soviet-style central planning of the farming economy so as to obtain the resources it needed – remarkable if true – as yet remains unproven.

To protect their trading interests, the Carthaginians made formal agreements with other Mediterranean powers. The Latin text of an early example (508 BC) of this kind of diplomacy could still be seen at Rome in the 100s BC, when 'the difference between [its] ancient language and that of the Romans today' was a potential obstacle to comprehension according to a Greek writer called Polybius.

His history preserves a paraphrase of this treaty of friendship which shows that the Carthaginians wanted to protect the places in which they traded from foreign – Roman in this case – encroachment. Among other stipulations, they banned Roman navigation further west along the African coast than an enigmatic 'Fair Promontory' – perhaps Cape Bon, some 75 miles north-east of Carthage.

The other weapon the Carthaginians developed was a navy. The Greek historian Herodotus describes an early appearance of one of their war fleets in a battle fought off the island of Corsica. The Carthaginians had been provoked by Greeks who had settled on the island and then used their ships to 'harass and plunder' the Carthaginian merchantmen plying this part of the Mediterranean. As a result of this action, the Greek settlers and their families abandoned Corsica, falling back on the toe of Italy.

Historians see this battle, thought to have taken place around 535 BC, as an important step in the creation of a Carthaginian sea empire in the western Mediterranean. The Carthaginians had not acted alone, however. Showing again their early aptitude for 'international' relations, they had made common cause with another seafaring people with a grievance against the Greek pirates of Corsica. These people fought alongside the Carthaginians with sixty ships of their own. It is time to turn to the Italic people best known today by their Roman name: *Etrusci*, or Etruscans.

From where I write on the south coast of England, the nearest 'Etruscans' are about 220 miles away – and to the north. Before being swallowed up by the suburbs of the city of Stoke-on-Trent, there once was a village in Staffordshire called Etruria. On the spot there is still an Etruscan Primary School, an Etruria Hall and even an Etruscan Street. This outbreak of 'Etruscomania' in the heart of the Midlands resulted from the fashionable enthusiasms of an English manufacturer of earthenware, Joseph Wedgwood. He built his new manufactory here and housed its workers in the new model village.

This was in 1770, just as an Italian antiquarian was publishing, tome by tome, a great learned work called (in Latin) 'Etruscan Vase Painting'. These ancient wares with their painted images were being found in large numbers by eighteenth-century investigators of archaeological sites in what was now Tuscany, the region extending roughly from Rome to Florence, once the homeland of the ancient Etruscans. For Europeans who could afford them, these vases became hugely collectible. For those who could not, Wedgwood's factory offered modern versions imitating the ancient shapes and decoration. His business model was summed up by the Latin motto of the new works, which translates as 'The Arts of Etruria are Reborn'.

For the student of the ancient world, this episode in the more recent history of European taste is chiefly interesting for capturing the cultural proclivities of ancient Etruscan grandees of the 500s and 400s BC. Discerning scholars in the eighteenth century were already starting to question the assumption that, because these ancient earthenware vases were found in the rich tombs of ancient Etruria, the ancient Etruscans must therefore have made them.

By the mid-nineteenth century, experts had shown beyond any real doubt that the vases were ancient imports to Etruria. Their style and technique meant that they had to have been made in the potteries of ancient Greece. The aristocrats of Archaic Etruria could not get enough of these black and orange wares.

To understand why outsiders like the Greeks wanted to trade with the ancient Etruscans, today's historically inclined visitor to Tuscany could do worse than visit the scenic Tuscan Mining Park. This conservation area of some 420 square miles protects a mineral-rich Italian landscape of metal-bearing hills yielding a whole list of different ores including lead, zinc, copper, silver and iron. There are many traces of mining activity, recent and less so.

The ancient Etruscans are the earliest inhabitants of this part of Italy to have entered history as miners, as is recounted by that same ancient writer 'on marvellous things heard':

> In Etruria there is said to be a certain island called Aethalia [modern Elba], in which out of a certain mine in former days copper was dug, from which they say that all the copper vessels among them have been wrought; that afterwards it could no longer be found: but, when a long interval of time had elapsed, from the same mine iron was produced, which the Etrurians, who inhabit the town called Populonium, still use.

In actual fact, there are only hints at best as to what foreign merchants exchanged for the products of Greece once they reached the Etruscan coast. As seen, the early Greeks established a settlement much further south on the island of Ischia, ancient Pithecusae. Here archaeologists have found traces of imported iron ore in the Greek settlement.

The just-mentioned Populonia (the usual ancient spelling) was an Etruscan port city in what is now north-west Tuscany. Today the archaeological park here, set in rolling fields reaching down to a wooded bay, allows visitors to contemplate an ancient metalworkers' quarter. That Archaic Greek traders visited this coastline received confirmation from a startling find at another Etruscan emporium.

In 1970 archaeologists were digging a sanctuary area at the port of the most important of the Etruscan cities, ancient Tarquinii. Here they found a tapering lump of stone which turned out to be an ancient anchor, left by its owner as an offering in the sanctuary after he had added an inscription. The Greek letters of around 500 BC say 'I belong to Apollo of Aegina. Sostratus son of [—] had me made'.

It was natural for experts to identify this Archaic Greek shipowner with a successful trader of the same name hailing precisely from Aegina, a Greek island on the doorstep of Piraeus, the port of Athens. The historian Herodotus, the source for this man, records that he made the greatest profit on his merchandise of all Greeks of that time: 'no one could compete with him'.

Control of access to minerals seems to have played a large part in the economic system producing the wealth of the Etruscans. The detailed picture is a case of seeing through a glass darkly, as so often with the economic life of ancient peoples. How the Etruscans spent their riches is easier to track, thanks mainly to their burial customs, which produced the elaborate grave-goods now displayed in a number of museums around the world.

A highlight of Berlin's Altes Museum are the cases of finds from what archaeologists have come to call the Tomb of the Warrior at Tarquinii. These include a splendid panoply of arms and armour. Taken together, the objects show that the dead man enjoyed a high rank in a militaristic society topped by figures such as this, members of a fighting elite. One suggestion is that such 'warrior-princes' at this time – the later 700s BC – grew rich from 'protection money' paid by foreigners seeking out the metal sources of the region.

In the 600s and 500s BC the stimulus of overseas contact, along with wealth from metals, seems somehow to have galvanized the Etruscans into developing proper civic communities comparable in some ways to the young city-states of the Archaic Greeks – from whom the Etruscan leaders conceivably took the idea. Experts read the social changes marking this transformation once more from burial customs.

On the ground, the most impressive remains of the Etruscans are the cemeteries of the rich oligarchies dominating most aspects of life in these Etruscan cities. At modern Cerveteri, the ancient Etruscan city of Caere, the visitor can walk down streets of the dead past mausolea built to accommodate several generations of the same family. The atmosphere here put me in mind of the socially exclusive cemetery of Picpus in modern-day Paris. Here the paths are lined with the family tombs of the high French aristocracy.

Two aspects of Etruscan society which the tombs highlight are the luxurious living of these great families and the 'freedoms' of their womenfolk. The ancient Greeks, whose social values were far more conservative, condemned this relative licence by the familiar device of exaggerating it. Here one (male) Greek author cites an earlier Greek author (fourth century BC, also male) as his authority:

> [so-and-so states that] it is a law among the Etruscans that all their women should be in common: and that the women pay the greatest attention to their persons, and often practise gymnastic exercises, naked, among the men, and sometimes with one another; for that it is not accounted shameful for them to be seen naked. And that they sup not with their own husbands, but with any one who happens to be present; and they pledge whoever they please in their cups: and that they are wonderful women to drink, and very handsome.

Some of the truth can be retrieved from the tombs. The creators of the Etruscan necropolis of Tarquinii went in for wall paintings reminiscent of the tombs of ancient Egypt, in that they too depict images informative of Etruscan lifestyles. One, dubbed the Tomb of the Leopards, dating from around 480 BC, is a gorgeous affair, with bright paintwork covering all the surfaces of the main chamber. Around the walls runs a frieze which shows couples sharing couches as they recline at a banquet.

With its accompanying musicians and naked serving boys, this scene superficially resembles a Greek drinking party. Yet these are not male couples, as they would be if this were the work of an Athenian vase painter on a piece of pottery destined for use in a Greek symposium. The Etruscan couples are male and female. The women are fully clothed – so not obviously prostitutes by the canons of Greek art at least – and they seem to partake equally in the pleasure of the moment. The modern viewer is left guessing as to who exactly they are: the wives of the men, or free women 'supping not with their own husbands'?

As this example suggests, the Etruscans interacted with foreign cultures, but what they took they adapted to suit themselves, whether a social practice or an art form. The same was true of their alphabet. Another Etruscan item on display in the Altes Museum looks a bit like a clay roof tile, except that it is covered with incised writing. This is one of the longest preserved examples of the Etruscan language written in a script which the Etruscans took over from one of the early local alphabets of the Greeks, who in turn, as seen, had adapted the alphabet of the Phoenicians. Scholars have partly deciphered Etruscan. They know that this text on clay, dating from around 470 BC, records the annual calendar of rituals to be performed by the priests of an Etruscan sanctuary.

Etruscan religion with its pantheon of divinities, its sanctuaries with their temples reminiscent of (but not identical to) those of the Greeks, and with its routines of animal sacrifice, bears resemblances to the religious cultures of the Greeks and Romans. Ideas, practices and divinities certainly changed hands between neighbours over the centuries. However, a chance find from 1877 near Piacenza in northern Italy, and now in the town's archaeological museum, leads the puzzled viewer directly into a weird and wonderful aspect of ancient religious ritual for which the Etruscans became renowned.

This strange object is a bronze sheep's liver, and it does indeed resemble the real thing, complete with protruding gall bladder. Divided up by incised lines into forty sections, each inscribed in Etruscan, it provided a soothsayer with an initial guide to the interpretation of anomalies on an actual liver. This was an internal organ that an Etruscan diviner would be confronted with when reading the signs of the god in the entrails of a sacrificed animal. The diviner would also prepare himself by immersion in the Etruscan books of sacred lore which the old families in charge of these matters were still compiling in the decades before the birth of Christ.

I mention here the ancient skill today known as extispicy (from the Latin for the inspection of *exta*, entrails) because it was one of the most obvious legacies of the Etruscans to their immediate neighbours, the Romans. For centuries, the Roman state used Etruscan-style diviners called haruspices, whether actual Etruscans or Romans trained up in the knowledge, to help interpret worrisome omens. In general the Romans remembered the Etruscans as a great Italian power:

> Before the Roman supremacy, the power of the Etruscans was widely extended both by sea and land. How far it extended over the two seas by

which Italy is surrounded like an island is proved by the names, for the nations of Italy call the one the 'Tuscan Sea', from the general designation of the people, and the other the 'Atriatic', from Atria, a Tuscan colony.

These are the words of the Roman historian Livy, whose writings date from late in the first century BC. The nature of this Etruscan hegemony is hazy to say the least. It was certainly not an empire as such, since the Etruscans themselves were never a centralized power. They remained a federation of twelve small states, albeit one capable of concerted decision-making in 'foreign affairs'.

Even if there was no Etruscan 'empire' as such, Etruscan warships based on the coastal centres such as Tarquinii were a real threat, and not just to those Greek settlers on Corsica. A bronze helmet found among the ruins of Olympia in 1817 and now on display in the British Museum turns out to be Etruscan-made. The three-line inscription on one side, however, is in Ancient Greek: 'Hieron [son] of Deinomenes and the Syracusans, [dedicated me] to Zeus, [spoils] of the Tyrrheni [Etruscans] from Cumae.' Cumae was a Greek settlement on the Bay of Naples. Harassed by Etruscan warships, its people sent envoys appealing for help to the most powerful man in Greek Sicily at this time, Hieron of Syracuse, a brother of Gelon. Hieron agreed, sailed north with his fleet and defeated the Etruscans in a sea-battle off Cumae. This placing of the captured helmet before Greek eyes at Olympia was all of a piece with his family's other acts of self-advertisement in the religious centres of the Greek mainland. The exact year is known thanks to a later Greek historian: 474 BC.

With historical hindsight Hieron's helmet offering signals one of the moments when the candlelight of Etruscan power began to flicker. The River Tiber separated the Etruscans from another people in the patchwork of pre-Greek populations in ancient Italy. Like the Etruscans, these Italic *Latini*, or Latins, had archaeological roots in the early Iron Age and by the 500s BC had come to see themselves as sharing a common ethnicity. Unlike the Etruscans, however, one of these Latin settlements, some 15 miles upstream, was already lording it over others at the time of Hieron's helmet offering.

The jumbled ruins of ancient Rome can dazzle the modern visitor to the Eternal City. They can also baffle, as might be expected of structures piled one on top of another over the twelve centuries or so of classical antiquity. One of the most bewildering corners of the ancient site is the hill that evolved into the Park Avenue of the ancient city, where Roman aristocrats, followed by the emperors, built their residences. Just to look at a modern plan of the ruins is almost to induce dizziness, nowhere more so than on the side of this so-called Palatine Hill – the south-east – overlooking the Colosseum.

An unassuming modern shelter now protects what archaeologists found here in 1946. The find itself is not even a structure, just a set of man-made holes for wooden posts dug into the bedrock. This is all that is left of a dwelling hut built of twigs and clay, architecturally the diametrical opposite of the much later palaces and temples high above it. It dates from the 700s BC and it excites archaeologists because the much later Romans are known to have carefully preserved several huts like this as tangible links to the stories they told about the origins of their community.

According to a Greek writer living in Rome shortly before the birth of Christ, he saw one of these huts in what would have been the same general vicinity as the findspot of the post-holes:

> Romulus and Remus lived the life of herdsmen and earned their living with their hands. They lived for the most part on the hills, building huts entirely out of wooden poles and reeds. One of these huts survives even to my own day, preserved on the slope of the Palatine facing the Circus and called the Hut of Romulus. Those in charge of its care preserve its sanctity and resist improvements that would make it more stately. When the hut gets damaged by storm or routine wear, they replicate its earlier appearance as closely as possible.

Archaeologically the actual hut in question did not survive the 600s BC. But the Romans seem to have retained a memory that their earliest ancestors settled this spot. It is not inconceivable that another such Iron Age abode, patched up so often as to be more a replica than the real thing, was remembered by later Romans as the 'hut of Romulus' himself.

It emerges from this early exercise in heritage management that the Romans cared deeply about their origins. So the particular form taken by the legend of Romulus can come as a surprise. The exposure of Romulus and his twin at birth, and their suckling by a she-wolf: these episodes might

seem to have a fittingly legendary flavour. Less so the fratricide and base-
ness that were to follow.

After Romulus kills his own brother Remus and founds his new city on
the Tiber, he peoples his settlement by proclaiming it an inviolate refuge for
anyone on the run. In this way he attracts all the 'obscure and lowly' types
of the neighbourhood, 'whether free man or slave'. The Spartan upper crust
claimed descent from Heracles, the Athenians from Apollo. The Roman
statesman Cicero could characterize the Romans en masse as the 'dregs of
Romulus'. The story is significant because it hard-wired Romans into associating their origins with a tradition of embracing outsiders, as well as
giving these origins a populist tinge.

Another foundation story has a disturbing topicality in the early twenty-
first century, since it involved a mass abduction of unmarried girls.
Romulus, having attracted males to people Rome, now needed females to
ensure the settlement's biological future. At his instigation, the young males
took advantage of the presence in Rome for a religious festival of many
families of Sabini, a neighbouring people, to seize their maidens. The girls
were then subjected to forced marriage. Once more the Roman historian
Livy gives details. Their 'husbands', he writes, sought to mitigate this act of
mass rape by 'pleading the irresistible force of their passion – a plea effective beyond all others in appealing to a woman's nature'.

Today's historian needs to ask what purpose was served when Livy
chose to dwell on this episode. To a modern mind it might seem to portend
the violence and, indeed, misogyny of ancient Roman society. To later
Romans themselves listening to Livy's account read aloud, the treatment of
the Sabine girls might have offered another example of how open Romans
were to sharing the benefits of their way of life with foreigners. Livy relates
how the Roman husbands sought to win over their brides by promising that
they would share Roman 'citizenship'. And more: 'dearest of all to human
nature, they would be the mothers of free men'.

Not all was ignoble about Rome's self-confessed origins. Romulus himself
was of royal birth, with an ancestry giving the first Romans a very different
kind of pedigree. When his forebear – yet again an outsider – arrived on
Latin soil with his men, the local ruler was 'filled with wonder at the renown
of the race and the hero'. This was because the newcomer, who settles
in Italy, was Aeneas of Troy, an illustrious figure in Homer's *Iliad* where
he appears as a valiant warrior and a prince of Troy's ruling house. The

Romans, then, could also present themselves as Trojan stock. This lineage shows that the Romans imagined ancient Italy as always having had eastern connections.

The Romans came to writing their own history late. Livy wrote in the late first century BC, and his Latin narrative is the earliest surviving account by a Roman of Rome's elder days. The actual first Roman historian, his account now lost, wrote only two centuries earlier. Scholars cannot really say what the Romans knew about their own history when they first cobbled it together: how much they drew on their own oral traditions, how much they borrowed from ancient Greek writers – who had been taking an interest in the Romans since the fifth century BC – and how much they simply made up.

Some of the earliest details have folkloric elements, such as the exposure of Romulus in a floating basket, Moses-style, and his being suckled by a female animal (a common ancient Near Eastern tale). Others point to the later creation of a backstory against a dearth of actual fact, such as the founder figure ('Romulus') whose name is given to the city that he founds ('Rome').

The later Romans also believed that at first they elected kings to rule them, starting with Romulus, who was followed by a further six. Two of these kings were said to be, again, outsiders, this time Etruscans from nearby Tarquinii. The last, Tarquin the Proud, was banished after his son's rape of a Roman matron triggered a popular uprising.

The Romans now opted for republican rule and replaced the king, a monarch, with two annually elected officials, the consuls. In the first century BC the Romans got round to putting dates on these founding events, working backwards from the records of the annual consuls to date Tarquin's fall, and then guessing – the only word for it – the chronology of the kings and Romulus's foundation of Rome. The dates arrived at translate into our time-reckoning as 509 BC for the end of Tarquin and 753 BC for the city's founding.

The Etruscan connection is interesting. Tarquinii was only 56 miles away. Whatever the truth behind these traditions about Etruscan kings of Rome, it is safe to assume political and cultural contact between the Etruscans in their glory days (the 500s BC) and their Roman neighbours, mediated by the muddy waters of the Tiber.

A further 12 miles north of Tarquinii are the ruins of Vulci, another Etruscan city. This was the findspot of an imported Athenian pottery jar now in a Munich museum. Dating from the later 500s BC, it shows the Trojan Aeneas in flight from Troy. Archaeologists also find Archaic Greek potsherds, if not complete pots, in Rome's subsoil. So the Archaic Romans, like their Etruscan neighbours, were exposed to Greek goods and perhaps to Greek ideas.

As seen, the Romans were important enough by 508 BC for the powerful Carthaginians far away in Africa to bother making a treaty with them. On their side, the Romans aimed to protect what was already a regional dominance. The Carthaginians were to do 'no wrong' to the 'Latins who are [Roman] subjects'. Looking far ahead, here is the germ of the future Roman Empire. Long before, the political self-determination of the Aegean Greek world was threatened by an earlier empire, to which I now turn.

CHAPTER 7

'LORD OF ALL MEN'?
THE THREAT OF PERSIA

Walking in Sultan Ahmet Square, today's visitor to Istanbul can still admire a monument that was already an antique when Constantine I transferred it from the Greek sanctuary of Delphi to Constantinople, as Istanbul was formerly called. Surviving the city's long and tumultuous history since, this dusty bronze pillar has remained ever since exactly where the first Christian emperor of Rome placed it seventeen centuries ago.

When it was first erected at Delphi in about 479 BC, the column was associated with a boastful Greek inscription probably added, illicitly, to the base. This was so self-aggrandizing, in fact, that Greeks of the time erased it almost at once:

Leader of the Greeks when he conquered the Medes,
Pausanias set up this monument to Phoebus [Apollo].

Who were these 'Medes'? In the Jewish Bible, the 'real' ancient Medes turn up in a prophecy as terrifying agents of God's wrath against the Babylonians:

Behold, I will stir up the Medes against them, which shall not regard silver; and as for gold, they shall not delight in it. Their bows also shall dash the young men to pieces; and they shall have no pity on the fruit of the womb, their eye shall not spare children. And Babylon, the glory of kingdoms . . . shall be as when God overthrew Sodom and Gomorrah.

These Medes of the Bible inhabited lands in what is now north-west Iran. Perhaps their fearsome reputation had reached Greeks in early Archaic times. This might explain why ancient Greeks generally tended to merge the Medes with a neighbouring Iranian people who supplanted them in the mid-500s BC as the chief military threat to the Greek world from the east. Greeks knew perfectly well who these Persian newcomers were, but they persisted in diminishing them by calling them 'Medes', as in the inscription above.

In doing so, the Greeks launched a long tradition of viewing the ancient Persians through a veil of unreality. The Hollywood movie *300*, released in 2006, portrayed King Xerxes of Persia as beardless, effeminate and decadent, while turning his Spartan adversaries into brawny (and bearded) studs. Here the film-maker's adaptation of the facts is more than just a matter of names. It denies modern beard-lovers some particularly splendid precursors. Xerxes and other kings of his dynasty sported strikingly long, luxuriant and well-groomed beards in Persian art.

Ultimately the film channels a negative image of the Persian enemy which the Greeks themselves created after the Persian Wars – or, as they called this conflict, 'the Median things'. One reason why this great contest between Greeks and Persians deserves its own chapter is because it triggered a 'Western' way of seeing 'the East' that is still influential today.

From around 540 BC the Persians under their first three kings, Cyrus the Great, Cambyses and Darius I, built up a huge land empire. The first Chinese emperor would not solder together the unitary state of 'Chin' for another three centuries. Stretching from modern Bulgaria to today's Pakistan, in its heyday the new Persian state had no territorial peer. To create it the Persians used naked aggression. Their aim, to put it bluntly, was to take by force what belonged to others – not just movable property, but the profits that accrued from the permanent subjection of peoples and lands.

In central Asia, on an ancient and modern route linking the Mesopotamian plain with the highlands of western Iran, the third of these kings, Darius, created a monument to his own glory. Cut into the face of a cliff, for all to see, there was a large relief sculpture of bound captives being either paraded before, or in one case trodden on by, the monarch. Not everyone could have read the long inscription captioning the image, if only because the script is over 300 feet above ground level.

Although these writings are in three ancient languages of the region, as if communication mattered, this high-up monument has more the feel of a proclamation to eternity. Here is the opening:

> I am Darius, the Great King, king of kings, king of Persia, king of lands, the son of Hystaspes, the grandson of Arsames, an Achaemenid.
>
> Darius the King says: 'My father is Hystaspes; the father of Hystaspes is Arsames; the father of Arsames is Ariaramnes; the father of Ariaramnes is Teispes, the father of Teispes is Achaemenes.'
>
> Darius the King says: 'For that reason we are called Achaemenids. From ancient times we are noble men. From ancient times our family has been royal.'

Darius, one of the greatest of ancient Persia's kings (ruled 522–486 BC), here emphatically justified his right to the kingship in terms of his membership of a long-established sovereign house with a collective name derived from its notional ancestor: the 'Achaemenids'. The inscription is an early instance in history of an individual claiming one-man rule on the basis of belonging to a very special family – a dynasty, in modern terms.

Experts debate whether Darius was in actual fact a born Achaemenid, or whether this vaunted ancestry was a fictional cover-up of what might in fact have been his usurpation of power in the murky years after the death of Cambyses, who had been the legitimate son and heir of Cyrus. Be that as it may, only his male-line descendants, also 'Achaemenids', would succeed him. They did so for another 150 years, down to the fall of the empire. So the effort of Darius to ram home the dynastic principle seems to have helped to give stability to the Persian Empire.

The Persian kings had their own way of imagining this empire. This way was alien to the political thinking of the ancient Greeks. It is on display in the royal burial ground of the Achaemenids in the south-west of modern Iran. At a place called Naqš-i Rustam, three Achaemenid kings commissioned tombs cut into, once more, a steep cliff-face. Each has a sculptured façade repeating the same image, copied from the earliest of these tombs, that of Darius himself.

Each king stands on a piece of furniture with legs, a platform-like throne. Underneath, as if lifting and moving the throne with the monarch on top, are two rows of human figures, with a further two supporting the legs. Each figure is identified by an inscription in Old Persian: 'This is the Persian', 'This is the Armenian', and so on. Each figure represented a whole people over whom the king claimed to rule.

Another caption reads: 'This is the Yauna'. The Persians derived their word for 'Greeks' from 'Ionians', meaning the Greeks of Asia Minor, who were now Persian subjects. It is hard to imagine a more explicit image of the relationship of dominance claimed by an absolute ruler over his subjects. No wonder that the Greeks thought of the Persian king's subjects as his 'slaves'.

A little over 7 miles south of his eventual resting place, the same Darius started to build a great palace, around which grew up a city. One ancient Greek writer called this city 'the richest under the sun'. Since excavations on the site and the partial restoration of the palace in modern times, this place has become emblematic of the greatness of ancient Persia.

When the ill-fated shah of Iran chose to throw a lavish party in 1971, he summoned his guests to a specially constructed tent city here at ruined Persepolis, this being its ancient Greek name: 'City of the Persians'. Heads of state were wined and dined by a culinary team from Maxim's, a top Parisian restaurant of the time, and entertained by a pageant comprising thousands of modern Iranian troops dressed up as members of the Achaemenid Empire.

This ancient royal centre offered ancient visitors further displays of what is best described as a Persian ideology of royal power. Sculptured panels showing bearers of gifts from the peoples of the empire to their ruler adorn processional staircases leading up to what must have been a focal point of the palace. A computer-generated visualization in the British Museum's Iranian gallery conjures up this palace hub in its ancient pomp: gilded rafters supported by elaborately worked capitals in turn held up by a lofty forest of columns brightly painted in pink and blue.

When the king was in residence, it was here that he seems to have conducted much of the routine business of ruling. This consisted – rather surprisingly, perhaps, after so much talk of Persians conquering – of sitting enthroned to give audience. The hall was grand and meant to impress. Its actual functioning might not have been so different from the traditional *majlis* – or audience – of more recent Arab potentates: 'an arena for media-tion, dispute settlement, the renewal of allegiance, but most importantly the representation of power. Attending the *majlis* of a local emir gave subjects the opportunity to assess the magnitude of this power.' In the case of the Achaemenid kings, the mightiest of such subjects, ones who might need reminding of their place, were the families of the Persian aristocracy. The male members of these families provided the king with his provincial governors, his generals, and sometimes with husbands for his daughters.

A system of royal gifts and rewards redistributed the profits of empire to these magnates and sought to keep them in line. Much later in the history of the Persian Empire, a glimpse of this system comes in the eyewitness account (400 BC) of a Greek soldier involved in raiding Persian targets in what is now western Turkey. He took part in a Greek attack on a rich property belonging to a certain Asidates (a Persian name in Greek form). This man lived there with his wife and children like a feudal lord:

> When they reached the place, about midnight, the slaves that were round about the tower and most of the animals ran away, the Greeks leaving them unheeded in order to capture Asidates himself and his belongings. And when they found themselves unable to take the tower by storm (for it was high and large, and furnished with battlements and a considerable force of warlike defenders), they attempted to dig through the tower-wall. Now the wall had a thickness of eight earthen bricks. At daybreak, however, a breach had been made; and just as soon as the light showed through, some one from within struck with an ox-spit clean through the thigh of the man who was nearest the hole; and from that time on they kept shooting out arrows.

How this Persian notable came to own a fortified estate close to the Aegean Sea, well over 1,500 miles from his homeland, is unknown. Ultimately his title must have derived from the Persian conquest of this region under Cyrus the Great (around 550 BC): his land was Persian booty, in other words. Grants of conquered territory were not just rewards. By encouraging a diaspora of ethnic Persians, the kings in Iran tried to build up a loyal network among the subject populations in their remoter provinces.

To their Greek neighbours the Persian kings were fabulously rich. Their wealth is best grasped by an ancient Greek total for the treasure amassed by Alexander of Macedon when he in turn conquered Persia: '. . . the whole treasure, collected from all quarters . . . amounted to 180,000 talents [of silver]'. Scholars accept this figure as plausible. Since a talent weighed roughly 57 pounds, Alexander's treasure amounted to over 4,600 tons of silver. Exact comparisons with today's values are hard to make. To give a very rough indication, at 2011 values in the USA, this haul would have been worth some $3.7 billion.

As for the origins of this treasure, the Persian kings grew so rich mainly by demanding an annual tribute from their subjects in return for military protection. What Alexander plundered was the (relatively small) amount lying around unspent in the storerooms of the royal palaces at that moment. Collecting the tribute was a task the Persian kings delegated to their provincial governors. The Greek historian Herodotus claimed that it was Darius who introduced this system of taxation. As a result of this reform, Herodotus says, the Persians called Darius 'the retail merchant'.

The pause button must now be pressed in order to consider Herodotus for a moment. Although he has already occurred frequently as a source in this book, it must be admitted that as a historian he was, and remains, controversial. His is the major written account from ancient times for the early phase of Persian empire building. It is true that the Persians were a literate society. The kings commissioned inscriptions in Near Eastern languages, as seen. There is no known literature in Old Persian, however. As with the Carthaginians and Etruscans, Greeks and Romans wrote the ancient accounts of the Persians that still exist.

Without Persia Herodotus might not have written his history, since Persia provided him with his subject, specifically the wars of 490–479 BC fought between the mainland Greeks and the armies of Darius and Xerxes, father and son – the so-called Persian Wars, as modern historians call them. So the ancient Persians should take some credit for indirectly stimulating a new type of ancient Greek cultural activity still in its infancy when Herodotus wrote. He called this activity 'learning by inquiry,' *historiē* in Herodotean Greek. As his subject for this kind of investigation he took, not the remote age of Greek myths and legends, but an event of great magnitude, as he saw it, in the recent past of the Greeks.

Almost as soon as he made his work available to Greek booksellers to copy and sell in a papyrus-roll format (around 420 BC), fellow Greek writers attacked him for untruthfulness. The later ancients recognized his place in the development of history-writing. By the first century BC a distinguished Roman could hail him as the 'father of history'. But that did not prevent them from claiming that he was a bad historian.

This was partly because ancient historians were a quarrelsome, back-stabbing lot. In mitigation, Herodotus lived at a time when written records were few and far between. Ancient societies, including Greece, still depended heavily on word of mouth. So Herodotus relied on the interview technique certainly for much, if not most, of his information.

On the plus side, he wrote at a time when stories about the Persian Wars could still have been circulating at second or even first hand. Alarm bells might ring at his obvious relish of a good story, although this is one reason why he remains such an entertaining read today. On the other hand, he can hardly be blamed, as he has been, for his belief in supernatural influences on human affairs. In his world, most people really thought that the gods were everywhere and were active interveners in human affairs.

There is a more serious charge against Herodotus than a naïve faith in his informants, or failures in seriousness, or 'superstition'. In the late twentieth century some experts became convinced that Herodotus deliberately invented stories and passed them off as true. This heated debate cannot be gone into here, and anyway many scholars are unconvinced by this approach. It is true that Herodotus was limited in his pioneering inquiry after historical truth by ways of ancient thinking different from today's, as he was by the nature of human memory – its capacity to misremember past events, even ones at which the informant was supposedly present.

Although Herodotus can hardly be blamed for not knowing it, when he relied as he often says he did on information supplied by 'the locals', he also had to deal with what academics now call 'social memory'. By this they mean the popular stories of past times that a traditional society hands down by word of mouth. These tales do not pass through the scrupulous filter of the sceptical historian. Their purpose is less to preserve historical truth than, say, to give a social group a shared identity. Over time such 'old wives' tales' can take on the dimensions of legend. The stories about King Arthur might be an example of this.

This 'health warning' about Herodotus may seem all the more needed, because his history is the only detailed narrative of the Persian Wars that now exists. It must always have been one of the closest in time to its subject matter, since Herodotus seems to have been born at around the period of the conflict. He was able – so he says, or so his writings imply – to access information from survivors, or people who had known them. His account is a blessing in another way: it preserves for posterity the names and actions of individuals. These bring the war vividly to life.

As for reliability, I respect the view of a former university colleague of mine, and an expert on the subject, who wrote:

> the more one studies him [Herodotus], the more one comes to the conclusion that there is very little that he says about the two Persian invasions of Greece which can be proved to be wrong, and one is continually struck by the realisation that there is a lot more acute observation and analysis in what he says than one at first thinks.

In 2015 I led a group of enthusiasts up an overgrown farm track behind the archaeological museum at modern Marathon some 25 miles north-east of Athens. After a short but steep climb, we had an excellent view of the modern plain of Marathon below us. In the middle distance we could just make out a brown pimple. This was the ancient earth mound under which the Athenians buried the remains of their 192 casualties after a day's fighting with a Persian force, probably thickest at that very spot.

Herodotus describes how battle had been joined:

> The Persians saw [the Athenians] running to attack and prepared to receive them, thinking the Athenians absolutely crazy, since they saw how few of them there were and that they ran up so fast without either cavalry or archers. So the barbarians imagined, but when the Athenians all together fell upon the barbarians they fought in a way worthy of record. These are the first Greeks whom we know of to use running against the enemy. They are also the first to endure looking at Median dress and men wearing it, for up until then just hearing the name of the Medes caused the Greeks to panic.

Further away from us, at the far end of the plain, we could see the promontory which protected the stretch of beach on which the Persian ships landed their troops. Herodotus says that they fled back there pursued by the Athenians, who tried to set fire to the enemy vessels. One was a man whom Herodotus turned into a hero, as he liked to do in his storytelling: 'Cynegirus son of Euphorion fell there, his hand cut off with an axe as he grabbed a ship's figurehead.'

At our end of the plain, in the gap between the foothills on which we were standing and the modern shoreline, once wended the ancient road back to Athens. Along it, too late, came reinforcements sent by the Spartans in tardy response to an Athenian messenger who had run the 140 miles from Athens to Sparta with an Athenian plea for help. By the same road a later messenger ran the much shorter distance back to Athens, with news of the Athenian victory. This is the run commemorated in today's marathon races.

The battle of Marathon (490 BC) had come about because two mainland Greek cities, one of them Athens, had earlier given military support to a coordinated revolt against Persian rule by the Greeks in western Turkey – their kin, as both sides believed, since the Athenians too belonged to the Ionian 'branch' of the Greek people. To the Persians, however, the Athenian intervention in Asia Minor probably looked like unprovoked aggression.

This revolt had broken out under Darius, a generation or so after the conquest of Greek Ionia under Cyrus. Persian forces finally crushed the Greeks in a naval battle (494 BC) outside the harbour of Miletus. On this occasion Persia's war galleys were mainly built and crewed by Phoenicians, themselves now Persian subjects. Persian troops then razed to the ground Miletus, home of the first Greek philosophers. This was the Ionian city whose leaders, Herodotus says, had prompted the revolt.

After Marathon, the Persians put back to sea. Soon after, they sailed away. Darius died, and his son and heir, Xerxes, in effect inherited Persia's unfinished business with Greece. Herodotus reports a council at which two Persian princes, an uncle and a cousin, gave the king their advice. Apart from anything else, this vignette conveys a vivid impression of Achaemenid Persia being run as a kind of family firm, rather like the ruling clans of today's Gulf states.

The first reason that Xerxes – according to Herodotus – gave for wanting to invade Greece matches what can be inferred about Persian royal thinking from the inscriptions in Old Persian that Darius, the father of Xerxes, placed on his Iranian monuments – retribution for injuries to the Persians: 'I do not wish that a man should do harm; nor do I wish it that, if he should do harm, he should not be punished.' Thus spake Darius in words engraved on, once again, his tomb. Herodotus might have had informants who told him about these Persian ethics of kingship. There were other reasons too according to Herodotus: further expansion of the Persian Empire, and the greater glory of the monarch. The bombastic presentation of Achaemenid rule in the royal inscriptions from Iran makes these motives eminently believable too.

So the wheels of war began to turn once more, this time on a larger scale. Xerxes was planning to come in person at the head of a great host. Advance reports of Persian preparations inevitably reached Greece, where reaction was mixed among the city-states. Herodotus reports individual states consulting oracles – the customary ancient Greek means of assessing or managing risk.

He claims to reproduce a rambling, riddling response by Apollo's prophetess at Delphi to the Athenian emissaries. Athens should put her trust in a 'wood-built wall', 'withdraw from the foe' (that is, retreat), but also be aware that 'a day will come when you will meet him face to face'. The oracle ended:

Divine Salamis, you will bring death to women's sons
When the corn is scattered, or the harvest gathered in.

Understandably Athenians were divided as to what all this meant. Then a political leader with an interest in the Athenian navy – his name was Themistocles – persuaded them that the wooden wall was a reference to their warships. Fortified by this reading of the oracle, the assembled citizens resolved to stand and fight. The representatives of Athens and of other like-minded states, including the chief land power on the Greek mainland at this time, Sparta, then met in a congress. They vowed to put aside their quarrels and make a military and naval alliance.

In spring 480 BC Xerxes and his army crossed the Dardanelles on a specially made pontoon bridge into Europe. The Greek allies decided to see if they could prevent the Persians from entering central Greece from the north by holding a land pass which they knew as the 'Hot Gates' (Thermopylae) from its thermal springs. At the same time they would use a fleet of allied warships to block the Persian armada at the entrance to a nearby sea channel. Xerxes would need to use this channel if his fleet, which included supply ships, was to continue to shadow the land army.

Nowadays the site of Thermopylae is a two-hour drive north from Athens. In 480 BC this was a defensible pass, 50 or so feet wide at its narrowest point, with mountains on one side and marsh and sea on the other. The sea has since receded here, making the strategic significance of the place in Xerxes' time harder to grasp today.

Herodotus relates how a small allied army of 5,300 men under the overall command of a Spartan king, Leonidas, took up positions. Although numerically a fraction of the Persian army, they could take advantage of the confined space which prevented Xerxes from deploying his superior strength. What happened next, as Herodotus tells the story, did much in ancient times to confer a near-mythic status on the Spartans as warriors.

First a Persian scout came up to the Greek position. He was astonished to see the Spartan men calmly exercising naked and dressing their long locks. A renegade Spartan explained to an equally disbelieving Xerxes that Spartan soldiers always combed their hair when about to risk their lives. After the Greeks beat off successive Persian attacks, a local Greek in hope of a reward guided the Persians by night over a mountain path which would allow them to surprise the Greeks in their rear.

The next morning, hearing this news, Leonidas sent home all but 1,200 of the Greek contingent. With them and his fellow Spartans, he made a last stand, since it was 'unfitting' that he should abandon his command. They fought to the death, 'with swords, hands and teeth'. After the war, the Greeks set up memorials here. A short poem was inscribed (there is now a modern replica) to commemorate the Spartans, all but two of whom had fallen: 'Stranger, go tell the Spartans that here we lie, obedient to their commands.' The Greek ships pulled back on hearing what had happened. The Persians were now free to continue their southward march, plundering Greek sanctuaries and, according to Herodotus, raping women. The Athenians completed a (probably pre-planned) evacuation of their city and country villages, sending the women and children to take refuge in the Peloponnese. The Persians captured and burnt the Athenian Acropolis.

The allied fleet had regrouped in the waters of the offshore island of Salamis, just outside what is now Piraeus, and separated from the mainland by a narrow and sinuous channel. Encamped on the island with their galleys beached on its shore, the Greek allies were all for falling back on the nearby isthmus connecting the Peloponnese to central Greece. Themistocles, cast by Herodotus as a wily and honey-tongued strategist, managed to convince his fellow Greeks that this was a bad plan because in doing so the allied fleet would 'lead' the Persian army towards the Peloponnese. Not without difficulty, the allied naval contingents were persuaded to stay united and await the Persian fleet.

Xerxes' fleet sailed round Cape Sunium and up the west coast of the Athenian land mass. At night Persian ships took up positions at either end of the channel between Salamis and the mainland, trapping the Greek galleys. The next morning the encamped Greeks took to the water. Xerxes watched the battle from a vantage point on the mainland, expecting of course a great victory. In fact the Persians suffered a decisive defeat.

Herodotus says that this was chiefly because Persian ships in front tried to turn and flee the attacking Greek ships. Then they ran into a new wave of their own galleys going forward 'so that they too could display some feat to the king'. Greeks must have liked the idea that the very presence of Xerxes contributed to his misfortune. The Greeks had made effective use of the narrow channel. It had trapped them, but had also prevented the Persians from making the most of their superior numbers.

According to Herodotus, Xerxes was undecided at first what to do next. He was worried that the Greeks might now sail to the Dardanelles, cutting the pontoon bridge and leaving him stranded in Europe. He was also persuaded that he had achieved his chief objective, the punishment of Athens, now a smouldering ruin. He departed with what was left of his fleet, but not before taking up the offer of a Persian general, also a nephew, to finish off the job if the king allowed him to choose the best troops from the, as yet undefeated, Persian land army. This the nephew, Mardonius, did, wintering in northern Greece among friendly, pro-Persian Greeks.

Over that winter the Macedonians made an early appearance in Greek affairs. At this time, Macedon, an ancient state located in what is now northern Greece, was a Persian dependency. Its hereditary ruler had paid homage in the time of Darius, then sealed his status as the king's vassal by marrying a daughter to a prince of the Achaemenid blood. Mardonius now sent the son and successor of this Persian client ruler to negotiate terms with the Athenians, choosing him 'partly because the Persians were akin to him'. The Athenians rejected the overture. This took courage. Needless to say they were reminded that Persia was the Goliath in this conflict and was bound to prevail in the end.

At this point the Greek alliance looked in danger of unravelling. The Peloponnesian Greeks wanted to barricade themselves behind a wall across the Isthmus. The Spartans seemed more interested in celebrating their annual festival for Apollo. Eventually, however, they did honour their alliance, sending five thousand of their young men to war, under the command of a Spartan royal, the vainglorious Pausanias, encountered at the start of this chapter.

Hearing this, Mardonius pulled back from Athens, which the Persians had occupied for a second time, but not before once again setting the city alight

Today the drive from Athens to ancient Plataea takes about seventy-five minutes. After leaving the modern highway to the Isthmus, an old road meanders northwards through what once were the borderlands of ancient Athens, negotiates a mountain pass, then descends into rolling farmland. Plataea was the name of the ancient city-state of these parts, and it was here that Mardonius encamped, in terrain suited to his cavalry. Few tourists come here, but local Greeks well remember what happened here. I have seen their elaborate wreaths left by the ancient city-walls to commemorate the battle of 479 BC.

The Peloponnesians, led by the Spartans and joined by the Athenians, took the route I have just mentioned. As Herodotus describes the battle, it was chaotic, the Greeks disunited, harried by the Persian horsemen, praying, sacrificing, awaiting their soothsayers to declare the entrails propitious. Herodotus believed that the fact that the easterners did not wear heavy body armour, whereas the Greek infantrymen did, put them at a crucial disadvantage.

So did the success of the Spartan troops in making a beeline for Mardonius himself and killing him. This prompted the Persians to turn tail, some for the long road back to the Dardanelles, most taking shelter behind the palisade of their fortified camp. The Athenians 'by courage and constant effort' were the first to scale this. The camp then became an abattoir, the Greeks cutting down tens of thousands of the enemy.

The Spartans lost ninety-one men, the Athenians fifty-two. From the loot, the Greek allies set up the bronze pillar at Delphi supporting a gold tripod for Apollo bearing on the base that inscription of Pausanias with which this chapter started. When the Spartans back home got wind of this, it was they who had it erased.

For centuries the ancient Greeks could not stop talking about their astounding success against Persian arms in 490 BC and again against Xerxes. Until Marathon, Salamis and Plataea, Greeks saw the Persians as invincible. In numbers alone they were terrifying. Herodotus puts Xerxes' invasion force in 480 BC at well over two and a half million men. Experts doubt this figure, with reason. But no one questions the overwhelming numerical superiority of his host.

Herodotus makes clear that the prospect of Xerxes' attack divided the Greeks, as well it might have. As he says, some Greek states sided with the

Persians from necessity. Others, he makes clear, were happy to do so. When he recounts what motivated the states minded to resist, he highlights the huge importance which they attached to a word which around now started to appear in the works of ancient Greek writers: 'freedom'. This meant independence from foreign rule, for which the city-states seem to have had a particular passion. Xerxes found this startling: 'that freedom of theirs', Herodotus has him say with disdain.

Herodotus thought that the Spartans and Athenians played pivotal parts. As the main Greek powers on land and sea respectively, they arguably had the most 'freedom' to lose. Still, their defiance was remarkable. The force led by Leonidas knew the risk of death before it set out: Leonidas selected only men who already had sons. Everyone looked to the Spartans to set an example. In 479 BC, only after Pausanias had set out against Mardonius did the other Peloponnesian Greeks send forces of their own.

As for the Athenians, their warships – and the lower-class rowers who propelled them – were so crucial that the threat of their coming to terms with Persia worked as glue holding the Greek alliance together. When Herodotus wrote, many Greeks had since come to dislike Athens, as a later chapter will show. So Herodotus knew he was sticking his neck out when he gave as his opinion that, in the Persian Wars, it had been the Athenians with their fleet who had really won the day:

> As it is, to say that the Athenians were the saviours of Greece is to hit the truth. It was the Athenians who held the balance; whichever side they joined was sure to prevail. Choosing that Greece should preserve her freedom, the Athenians roused to battle the other Greek states which had not yet gone over to the Persians and, after the gods, were responsible for driving the king off.

The Persian conquest had ended the cultural flowering of the eastern Greek cities in Archaic times. The victory over Persia now crowned mainland Greece as the centre of Greek political power. In Athens itself, defeat of the Persians would act as an electrifying catalyst both in its politics and in its culture. It is time to look more closely at the Athenians and Spartans, the chief protagonists on the Greek side, and their divergent destinies in the aftermath of victory.

CHAPTER 8

THE SAME BUT DIFFERENT
ATHENS AND SPARTA

In the centre of modern Athens American archaeologists in the 1950s
rebuilt a ruined antiquity, the so-called Colonnade or Stoa of Attalus.
Nowadays they use its basement to store and study the finds from their
next-door excavations on the site of the agora, or civic centre, of ancient
Athens. The ground floor, familiar to tourists from all over the world,
houses a museum of the choicest discoveries.

This restored monument is the one that the British writer and humorist
Nancy Mitford targeted for her derision in 1955: 'in a ghastly graveyard
marble, the Stoa, said to be "of Attalos", but really of Mr Homer A. Thompson'.
Homer Thompson, the Canadian specialist in ancient architecture who
guided the precision-led restoration, was a scholar of huge learning. The
marble in question, white with a honey tinge, was also used to build the
Parthenon.

On an Athenian summer's day in 2014 American friends, Ann and
Richard, an archaeologist and her assisting husband, took me down into
the Stoa basement, an oasis of cool air, to show me their current work. They
were carefully measuring sherds of broken crockery dug up in association
with what must have been one of the ancient agora's most distinctive
structures, its only perfectly circular building.

This Tholos, as the ancients called it, was somewhere between the crow's
nest and the ship's bridge of the Athenian democratic style of government.
It was where the fifty officials responsible for the routine business of the

state ate their staff meals, which were funded by the public purse. A third of them at any one time slept here as well, on call in an emergency.

These fifty officials were selected according to rules with particular ends in mind. First, the hands that rested on the levers of power were many, not few. Nor did they rest for long. These officials only served for a month before a different set of fifty replaced them, and so on throughout the ten months of the ancient Athenian year. All of them came from the same body, a state council of five hundred citizens. In turn council members served for one year only. They too were then replaced with new faces, five hundred of them.

Second, the selecting of councillors was done by a citizen lottery. This is extraordinary in one way, given the political responsibilities of the councillors. The whole point of a lottery is its randomness – chance alone decides who is selected. Its widespread use by the Athenian democracy shows how seriously the Athenians took the idea that all eligible citizens must have an equal chance to serve the city. Merit was all very well, but in practice this might favour citizens whose merit was, or seemed to others to be, the result of privilege – wealth, a private education, social connections and so on.

As to how this Athenian democracy had come about, its earliest stirrings were doubtless older than the first firm date pinpointed by ancient writers, 508/7 BC. At this time, against a background of political rivalry between Archaic Athenian aristocrats, one of them, called Cleisthenes, hit on the ploy of boosting his support by 'taking the people into his *hetaireia*'. As used here by Herodotus, 'faction' and 'party' are among suggested translations of this word. It had some of the sense of the French word *nébuleuse* when applied to the concentric social circles surrounding great lords in pre-Revolutionary France: 'people gathered around a leading personality in complicated relationships of dominance and dependence'.

For details of what Cleisthenes did next experts rely on an ancient Greek book preserved on a papyrus from Egypt describing the Athenian democracy of the 330s BC and its earlier history. According to this account, Cleisthenes introduced a wholesale reorganization of the way the Athenians did politics.

In outline, he now created a formal citizen body, based on registration of all Athenians in registration centres centred on localities – mainly pre-existing villages – in the 930 square miles of surrounding countryside controlled by Athens. As if to cut across the old landed interest and its local clienteles, he then mixed up these citizens geographically by grouping far-flung local registration centres into ten new citizen-tribes. Each of these tribes in turn sent 50 councillors to sit on a pre-existing government council, its membership now expanded to 500.

Another procedural innovation of Cleisthenes is worth mentioning, not least because the finds of archaeologists vividly illustrate its workings, in the form of hundreds of humble potsherds with names scratched on them. 'Cimon, son of Miltiades, take Elpinice and go.' This Athenian's background was impeccably aristocratic. His father had led the Athenians to victory at Marathon. Cimon himself was a leading Athenian naval commander and politician in the quarter-century or so after the battle of Plataea. The journey wished on Cimon by this graffito, however, was one into exile from Athens.

He had fallen foul of the institution of 'ostracism', from the ancient Greek for a potsherd. Athenians would assemble to vote by means of a name scratched on an *ostrakon* for the banishment of a particular politician. He would have to go abroad for ten years if a minimum of six thousand votes had been cast and his name was in the majority. According to that papyrus, Cleisthenes saw ostracism in the first instance as a way of enabling Athenians to rid themselves of would-be tyrants. But soon 'it was also used to remove any other person who seemed to be too great'. In other words, it had become a tool of rival politicians.

In Cimon's case, the 'graffitist' had added a personal insult. Elpinice was Cimon's devoted sister – too devoted. At any rate, there was talk, recorded centuries later by a writer of Roman times, that her relations with her brother were incestuous. This graffito, from the 460s BC, suggests that these rumours of sexual impropriety already circulated in Elpinice's lifetime. In the best traditions of democratic cut-and-thrust, sexual innuendo provided ammunition for her brother's political enemies.

The democracy put in place by Cleisthenes was a work in progress. The old aristocratic structures of power could not be dismantled overnight. Going back to the broken crocks that my friends were examining, detective work on this kind of evidence provides new insights into the very different kinds of Athenian holding office in the democratic system.

In the case of these particular pots, made in the years around 460 to 450 BC, their ancient users were Athenian citizens holding democratic office thanks to a lottery. They would have represented a mix of social backgrounds, including Athenians who had to work for a living. Piecing together as much as they could of at least twenty-two clay cups used for drinking, my friends discovered a striking common feature. Most if not all these cups were about the same size, with a likely capacity of around half a pint.

This was not the only egalitarian note. The officials who drank equal measures from these standard cups did so at meals which they took, not sprawled on cushioned couches like Greek aristocrats but, it is thought, sitting upright on a bench around the inside wall of the Tholos, facing each other in a big circle.

To grasp the import of this apparently deliberate symbolism, another style of official dining in the same vicinity is revealing. A few hundred yards to the north, American archaeologists have found crockery discarded as rubbish after being broken during, once more, shared meals. This locale, however, had distinctly upper-class associations, specifically with another group of annual officials who dined at public expense in democratic Athens, the ten archons.

The archons had been the senior officers of Archaic Athens. In those days elected aristocrats dominated the posts. Once it came to power, the Athenian democracy whittled away the powers of the archons. However, at the time that this crockery was made, around 460 to 450 BC, the position was still a preserve of the richest Athenians.

These diners literally speak to us, because they scratched graffiti on their earthenware. The graffiti are a revelation. They praise and insult individuals in the style of the homoerotic banter of – precisely – aristocrats reclining at a private symposium. 'Alcaeus is beautiful' runs one. Another, as if in reply, asserts to the contrary: 'Alcaeus is a lewd fellow'. This Greek word for 'lewd' is related to the Greek word for 'buttocks'. These might have been Athenian 'toffs' using the word, but it was not a polite one.

More than that, these graffiti are incised on the undersides and feet of vessels, and so most easily read if these vessels were already broken into pieces. It may well be that the upper-crust diners who scratched these graffiti amused themselves by making fun of the democratic procedure of ostracism. As seen, this too involved citizens scratching names on bits of broken pot.

The reason for dwelling on these fragments of ancient Athenian mealtimes is that they vividly suggest the social differences underlying the achievement of ancient Athenian democracy. The word for democracy in Ancient Greek, *dēmokratia*, means 'people power'. Yet Athenian democrats had to take constant account of the continued existence of an Athenian upper crust with inherited wealth and aristocratic attitudes.

A walk through the sculpture galleries of the National Archaeological Museum in modern Athens is almost a stroll through the cemeteries of the landed families of Archaic Athens. Standing on their bases are expensive statues of strapping youths honed by hours of leisure spent in the gymnasium, and richly dressed maidens, destined for socially advantageous matches.

In Athens there had been no social revolution as in Russia in 1917. The descendants of these families lived on under the democracy, rich, entitled. Left to themselves, they took time to abandon the outward signs of their old status. These were the sort of noble Athenians who 'not long ago, laid aside the fashion of wearing linen tunics and golden brooches shaped like cicadas, which they used to fasten their hair bun', according to the Athenian historian Thucydides, writing around 400 BC.

These people were not just potential opponents of the democracy. They also needed to be on side for the positive reason that Athens needed their financial clout. With no system of direct income tax (unknown in antiquity), the Athenians looked to their richest citizens to 'volunteer' to pay for certain public services from their own pocket.

An elegant structure in the Plaka district of modern Athens gives an insight into how this system worked. A marble cylinder on a square podium, topped by a conical roof, the Lysicrates Monument was erected by a rich Athenian to commemorate, not to say flaunt, his role as the producer of successful plays performed for the benefit of the citizenry at the city's annual festival of drama.

Relatively few tourists find their way to the barren hillside not far from the Acropolis known as the Pnyx to the ancient Athenians. Thanks to erosion the site is now a puzzle. In front of a stepped platform cut into the natural rock the ground slopes downwards. In ancient times it sloped upwards instead, so as to form an auditorium. Here in the open air, citizens sat comfortably to hear fellow citizens addressing them from the platform. Then they voted with a show of hands. This was the bridge of the democracy: the citizens meeting as a sovereign assembly and voting directly on matters of state, not relying on representatives to do so on their behalf, as in today's parliamentary systems.

This referendum-like mode of popular sovereignty was feasible thanks to the relatively small numbers of citizen-voters in ancient Athens. Their total number in the 400s and 300s BC probably fluctuated in the region of thirty to forty thousand. Many lived, not in Athens proper, but in the surrounding townships and villages. Some of these can still be visited. At Sunium, for instance, famous for its temple of Poseidon, tourists can also walk ancient streets, passing remnants of ancient houses belonging to the 'men of Sunium'.

Up on the Pnyx, the auditorium could never have accommodated the full citizen body. Modern archaeologists put the seating capacity at around six thousand. This meant that the Athenian assembly habitually made its sovereign decisions on the basis of a maximum of perhaps around one-fifth of all eligible voters. As in the low turnouts in popular elections in western democracies, this paradoxical state of affairs does not seem to have been a cause of undue concern for the Athenians – who were, admittedly, a far smaller and more homogeneous body.

An Athenian philosopher writing in the early to mid-300s BC, when Athens was still very much a democracy, claimed a remarkably egalitarian ethos for these meetings. When the assembled citizenry needed expert advice, Plato says, they summoned an architect, say, or a shipwright. However,

> if anyone else, whom the people do not regard as a technical specialist, attempts to advise them, no matter how handsome and rich and well-born he may be, not one of these things induces them to accept him; they merely laugh him to scorn and shout him down ... Such is their procedure in matters which they consider professional. But when they have to deliberate on something connected with the administration of the state, anyone may stand up and offer advice, whether he be a carpenter, a blacksmith, a shoemaker, a merchant, a ship-captain, wealthy, poor, noble, or base-born.

In practice, there was always a tendency for the assembled citizens to allow themselves to be led by speakers from the upper echelons of Athenian society who had the leisure to devote themselves to public life. Thucydides thought that the Athenians in effect submitted to 'one-man rule' under the greatest of these leaders, who dominated his city through the middle decades of the 400s BC.

A Roman-period marble bust of this man on display in the British Museum copies a lost statue from his own time. It shows a mature, bearded, male. Greek letters spell out his name: 'Perikles'. Contemplating the idealized features of this handsome yet authoritative personage, one might well believe, as Thucydides claimed, that Pericles owed his political influence not just to 'ability' but also to 'personal repute' – charisma, in other words.

In a paradox familiar in modern democracies, Pericles, far from being a man of the people, was by background an aristocrat from a rich and distinguished Athenian family. The ancients looked back on him as one of the main architects of the great flowering of Athens in the fifth century BC. Under his ascendancy Athens became a dominant – not to say domineering – power in the Aegean, as the next chapter shows.

Later writers also credited him with pursuing greatness for Athens through cultural excellence. One Roman-period writer went so far as to describe the architectural marvels erected on the Acropolis during his leadership – including the Parthenon – as 'works of Pericles'. He had a cultured entourage which included the artist Pheidias, entrusted with oversight of the Parthenon; the philosopher Socrates; and a live-in partner called Aspasia, who was said to give political advice to Pericles while acting as the madam of a brothel – rather like King Louis XV's mistress Madame de Pompadour in eighteenth-century France.

Thucydides bestowed a kind of immortality on Pericles by putting into his mouth a speech to his fellow citizens presenting a solemn and elevated picture of Athens in 431/430 BC. It is known nowadays as the Funeral Oration because the occasion on which the historical Pericles pronounced something like this speech before an Athenian audience was a public funeral for fallen citizen-soldiers.

The reader at this point can be told a bit more about Thucydides. Experts regard him as the greatest of the Greek and Roman history-writers who have come down to us. This is because he was not just highly intelligent. He also approached his task – the history of the great war of his lifetime between Athens and Sparta – with a concern for truth and with a rational and analytical approach. He saw humankind, not the hand of gods, as the driver of human fortunes. Unlike modern critics of the value of studying the past, he believed that history could teach lessons for the future. The same or similar events would happen again 'in all human probability'.

He was also explicit about his methods – unlike some history-writers even today, and a great novelty for a Greek writing two and a half millennia ago. He says that for the events of the war he interviewed eyewitnesses, but freely admits that accounts of the same events would vary, making it 'hard work' to establish the facts. He found it difficult, he wrote, to recall the actual words of speeches, even ones that he had heard himself.

His method when it came to composing the speeches he puts into the mouths of his historical actors – generals haranguing troops, or debaters before political assemblies in various Greek cities – poses a problem for modern admirers of his stated commitment to accuracy. As well as his own memory, he drew on informants who reported on speeches which he had not himself heard. He then says that in general with speeches in his history, he composed them so as to convey both the truth of what was said, and also what was 'appropriate' in the circumstances.

The last criterion hints that Thucydides might have made up parts of speeches despite what he knew, or thought he knew, had actually been said. This makes for an insoluble difficulty, not least when assessing the Funeral Oration as evidence for what the historical Pericles actually said and thought. I proceed on the assumption that Thucydides would have avoided flatly contradicting the memories of those Athenians who had been present at the actual event.

In eulogizing the city for which the Athenian soldiers gave their lives, the Pericles of Thucydides praises its democratic features, including the city's law courts which 'treat everyone equally in the settlement of private disputes'. The Athenians went to great lengths to ensure that juries in their legal system were immune from tampering by the rich and influential. They paid citizens to serve as jurors and they developed an elaborate system for randomizing the assigning of jurors to particular courts by means of the jurors' 'tickets' – bronze strips with an individual citizen's name punched on it. There are numerous examples of these in museums today.

Thucydides' Pericles drew attention to the political opportunities for everyone in the democracy. 'Poverty' was not a bar to serving the city in public office – this was thanks to measures such as the lottery system, as stated earlier. On the other hand, the democracy enabled elitism of the right sort, since 'excellence' in a citizen conferred promotion in the state on merit.

In all this, indeed throughout the speech, Thucydides' Pericles had in mind citizen-males like himself. Athens in the 400s and 300s BC was the

ancient society that probably came closest to having a general considera-
tion for its (citizen) members. However, there were significant groups of
disenfranchised residents, starting with the womenfolk of the citizenry.
Thucydides' Pericles mentions them only once, when addressing the
mothers and widows of the fallen who were present in the audience: 'Great
is your glory if you fall not below the standard which nature has set for your
sex, and great also is hers of whom there is least talk among men whether
for good or bad.' Exactly what is 'Pericles' saying here? A Roman-period
writer, so a lot closer in time to the age of Pericles than us, glossed the
passage as follows: 'the name of the good woman, like her person, ought
to be shut up indoors and never go out'. Even if it is not certain what
'Pericles' – let alone Pericles – thought on this point, it remains a fact that
the Athenians, like other male-dominated Greek societies in this period,
deemed their womenfolk unfit for political decision-making by virtue of
their supposed inherent nature. This way of thinking was universal among
ancient Greeks. At about this time Greek medical writers started to
construct a cod physiology which seemed to justify it. Women's bodies
were wet and spongy. They were fundamentally different from and inferior
to those of men, conceived as hard and dry.

Naturally the slaves owned by many Athenian citizens, and as much
their private property as their livestock, had no political rights. As in
modern democracies, foreign residents in Athens were also excluded from
political participation. The many registered migrants living in Athens at
this time – Greeks called such people 'metics' – were often traders and artisans attracted by the economic opportunities of a flourishing city. Native-
born Athenians tended to think of them as self-interested rather than
civic-minded, although this was certainly not true of all of them. The
Athenians jealously guarded the status of Athenian citizen, which Pericles
had restricted to men born of two Athenian parents. It must be said that
this meanness of the democracy with Athenian citizenship and its perks
hardly encouraged migrants to place the public welfare above their private
interests.

Roughly 140 miles south-west of Athens, the motorway from the
Isthmus, having smashed its way through the mountainous centre of the
Peloponnese, starts to descend into a green valley edged by hills and mountains. This natural setting is so scenic that the stark contrast with the harsh
way of life of the Greeks who once lived here is a historian's commonplace.

This was the home of the Spartans, in the fifth century BC first the rivals, and later the open foes, of Athens.

The most spectacular of these mountains towers to the west: Mount Taygetus (pronounced 'Ty-*ee*-getus'), a range of peaks retaining their snow cap most years until well into May. In antiquity bears roamed the heights. To understand the ancient Spartans, the mind's eye must cross these redoubtable mountains into the region on the far side.

This region is now centred on Kalamata. As the juicy olives named after this modern town suggest, the farmland of the south-western quarter of the Peloponnese is extremely productive. Some 24 miles to the north-west of the town, near today's olive-growing village of Kopanaki, Greek archaeologists in the early 1980s discovered the remains of an ancient farmstead from the 500s and 400s BC. This had been a sizeable building, a rectangle 100 feet long, with an upper storey. The site has since disappeared, although the museum in Kalamata keeps some of the finds. These include parts of large clay storage jars for agricultural produce.

If this all sounds rather unexciting, the identification by experts of the type of farm is anything but. They think that this could have been the centre of a large estate worked by slaves, rather like the plantations of the antebellum American South. In this case the 'planter' would have been a Spartan, the slaves the so-called Helots. Of the miserable lot of these Helots a Spartan poet of the 600s BC had this to say: 'Like donkeys worn out with huge burdens, compelled by a terrible necessity, they bring to their masters a half of all the fruits of the earth.'

Sparta was not the only Greek state to exploit an agricultural underclass who were forced to work the land. Where the Spartans do seem to have been unusual, and probably unique, is in the harshness of their treatment of these serf-like workers. Even in a slave-owning society like ancient Greece, Spartan cruelty was well known enough to attract the notice of fellow Greeks.

Thucydides describes an exceptional episode in 424 BC when the Spartans 'disappeared' some two thousand Helot men, selected because 'they were the most high-spirited and the most apt to revolt'. In the 300s BC, if not earlier, Greeks were aware of a Spartan custom whereby nocturnal bands of young Spartan warriors went around randomly killing Helots. Sometimes they did so in broad daylight too, when they could easily identify and pick off the physically fittest of the Helots labouring in the fields.

The ancients themselves were not sure whether the Spartans had always treated the Helots like this. As with many aspects of ancient Sparta, scholars are uncertain too, although these debates cannot be gone into here. Thucydides records a revolt by the Helots on both sides of Taygetus in 464 BC. In ancient times such slave revolts were uncommon, if only because slaves were usually of mixed origin, arriving in their place of servitude thanks to the workings of the slave market and not necessarily even sharing a common language.

However, Thucydides says that the rebellious Helots had a collective name, 'Messenians'. They descended from the original inhabitants of the region beyond Taygetus, who, supposedly, had already been calling themselves 'Messenians' before the Spartans conquered them. If the Helots over the mountains had shared stories about a common ancestry and a violent subjugation in far-off times, and so come to build a common identity out of adversity, this could have motivated them to unite to throw off the Spartan yoke.

The risk of revolt by Helots frightened their Spartan masters. Thucydides had personal knowledge of the Peloponnese, the region of southern Greece that Sparta dominated. He thought that policy at Sparta 'was governed at all times by need to take precautions against the Helots'. The Spartans were constantly worried, not just because they depended on Helot labour to free them from working the land themselves, but also because the Helots outnumbered them.

Greeks thought that Sparta was thinly populated by normal standards. They meant chiefly the fighting population of able-bodied Spartan males. This was small when compared to Sparta's military clout in the larger world. It was also getting smaller. Herodotus has a Spartan informant in 480 BC describe Sparta to the Persians as 'a city of about eight thousand men'. By the middle decades of the 300s BC, this number had dwindled to 'not even a thousand' according to the well-informed Aristotle.

An ancient writer describes Spartan customs which would make sense if designed to encourage procreation:

> For among the Spartans it was a hereditary custom and quite usual for three or four men to have one wife or even more if they were brothers, the offspring being the common property of all, and when a man had begotten enough children, it was honourable and quite usual for him to give his wife to one of his friends.

Such customs help to explain why fellow Greeks saw the Spartan way of life as more or less the opposite of that of most Greek states. Long after Spartan greatness was just a historical memory, the ancient Greeks and Romans remembered one thing above all.

They called it the Spartan 'discipline'. By this they meant the barracks lifestyle of all Spartan warriors. In the 400s BC this made Spartan soldiering seem far more rigorous when compared with the relatively amateur armies of citizen-farmers fielded by most other Greek states, Athens included. Thucydides has Pericles praise the Athenians for – in effect – the amateur quality of their soldiering. As fighting material, he says, Athenian men were blessed with their courage. This in turn was a by-product of the Athenian way of life, which was morally superior to that of their Greek opponents. When 'Pericles' refers to an unnamed enemy that 'from early childhood pursues courage by a laborious training', his Athenian audience would have known at once whom he had in mind. In ancient Greece, only one city trained children to fight.

Other distinctive features of this way of life included the all-male dining clubs where Spartan men took their meals. As a condition of his citizenship, each clubman had to contribute to his own upkeep from the produce of his Helot-farmed land. But increasingly there were Spartans without enough land to maintain their contributions. As to why this was so, the philosopher Aristotle thought that the declining number of Spartan citizens arose from the way in which Spartan laws of inheritance had concentrated landed property in the hands of the few. 'It has come about that some of the Spartans own too much property and some extremely little.' When the wealth gap poses such problems in today's world, perhaps the Spartans should not be unduly censured for failing to solve the economic disparities which caused their citizen numbers to decline. Meanwhile, with an eye on the Helots, the Spartan citizens kept up their 'discipline'. The truly remarkable feature of this state regimen was the military-style training of youths, beginning at the age of seven, when boys were taken from home for this purpose.

One archaeological site in particular is associated with this training. Today's motorway from Athens into Sparti, the modern town overlying ancient Sparta, crosses the gravel banks of the River Eurotas and heads through the outskirts towards the central square. Doing so it passes one of Greece's brown and yellow archaeological signs, which directs the visitor down a track to an old excavation on the river's right bank.

As with most remnants of ancient Sparta, the human imagination has to work here with poor materials. An ancient Greek inscription on a toppled block references 'the customs of Lycurgus'. He was the lawgiver in the remote past to whose wise dispositions the Spartans attributed their way of life. For the rest, battered bits of ancient buildings do little to bring to life what was once a major centre for Spartan religion – except, that is, the substantial remains of an open-air altar.

Here took place one of the more peculiar tests in the training of the Spartan youth:

He [Lycurgus] made it a point of honour to steal as many cheeses as possible from the altar of Orthia, but appointed others to scourge the thieves, meaning to show thereby that by enduring pain for a short time one may win lasting fame and felicity. It is shown herein that where there is need of swiftness, the slothful, as usual, gets little profit and many troubles.

This description comes from a Greek author writing in the early 300s BC who knew Sparta well and was probably an eyewitness to this cheese-stealing from the altar of the goddess Orthia. In this trial the Spartan lads had to be nimble so as to snatch cheeses while avoiding the lash. Some of the aims of what passed for a Spartan education can be glimpsed here: the promotion of not just manly courage but also stealth and cunning – the sort of qualities one might expect from so-called special forces in the modern military. Since they were under orders, the boys also learnt obedience – not to mention, once it was all over, the sense of solidarity that comes from an ordeal shared and survived.

Ancient writers disagreed about whether active homosexuality formed part of this education. An Athenian admirer of Sparta who knew the city first hand states that the Spartans considered touching the boys as 'most shameful'. On the other hand, a prominent Roman of the first century BC thought that Spartan custom permitted 'embraces and lying together' with 'cloaks [or covers] in between', the equivalent of sex with your clothes on. Cicero, the Roman in question, was probably told this detail on one of his visits to the Sparta of his own day. It is odd enough perhaps to be true.

Sparta was not just a boot camp – at least, not always. In the British Museum a showcase displays objects found by archaeologists who excavated

Orthia's shrine at the start of the twentieth century. They include examples from the thousands of parts of clay face masks which Spartans of the 500s and 400s BC had left as offerings to the goddess.

These masks often have strong facial expressions – heavy wrinkles, for instance – and fall into a number of types, such as old women, youths and warriors. Since they are mostly too small to have ever been worn, scholars think that their donors left them to Orthia as permanent mementoes of performance masks made of a perishable material such as linen. Experts debate the nature of the Spartan performances that these masks commemorated.

Their most recent student thinks that the Spartans used the hypothetical originals in a form of comic theatre akin to farce: masked performers who enacted slapstick, exaggerated characters and improbable plots. In this way the Spartan worship of Orthia might even have played its part in the hazy evolution of the masked performances in sanctuaries in Archaic Greece into fully fledged theatre. But this final transformation took place in fifth-century BC Athens, as we shall see, and certainly not in Sparta.

There are other traces of an early atmosphere of artistry and creativity at Sparta. A papyrus in the Louvre preserves the comparison by a Spartan poet living in the 600s BC of two beautiful maidens of Sparta:

> Don't you see? One is a racehorse
> from Paphlagonia. But the mane
> of the other one, my kinswoman
> Hagesichora, blossoms on her head
> like imperishable gold.
> And the silver look of her face –
> what can I tell you openly?
> She is Hagesichora.

The ancient evidence does not tell exactly when and how – perhaps under pressure from Helot revolts – the Spartans turned towards the harsh and rigid life of military routines which their name evokes today. It seems to have happened by the time of their great war with the Athenians, which broke out in 431 BC.

The cultural similarities between Athenians and Spartans arising from their shared Greekness can be overlooked. The Spartans also had an acropolis, if not a lofty one like that of Athens, and they erected on theirs a temple to the same divine protectress, whom they called in their dialect 'Athana'. But it was as a clash of opposites that the ancients preferred to look back on the disastrous conflict between the two powers, which we examine next.

CHAPTER 9

'UNPRECEDENTED SUFFERING'?
THE PELOPONNESIAN WAR

Most visitors to the National Archaeological Museum in Athens are unaware of another museum next door. Little visited except by specialists, the Epigraphical Museum houses a sensational collection of inscriptions from ancient Greece.

Among experts, the acknowledged queen of this collection is a monolithic block some 18 feet high. It almost reaches the ceiling, and a ladder is needed to read the letters at the top. When you look closer, you see that the material is modern plaster. Into this are set many fragments of a single ancient inscription.

American experts created this wonder of modern scholarship in 1927 by fitting together over 180 fragments, all originally from the same giant block of marble, perhaps a leftover from an abandoned building project. The Athenians of the age of Pericles had set up the original on the Acropolis. The document records annual payments to Athena, the goddess of the Acropolis. Each year an ancient mason climbed up a ladder to add a new record of these payments.

What makes this shattered monument so important is the identity of the payers. As seen, the Greek allies inflicted a decisive defeat on the remnants of Xerxes' Persian army of invasion at the battle of Plataea in 479 BC. After this victory, the allies looked to Sparta, the senior power on the Greek mainland, to spearhead the continuing struggle against the Persians, still a formidable threat to Greek settlements east of the mainland, thanks to their warships.

But the allied Greeks felt that the Spartan regent Pausanias, the Spartan general at Plataea, had started to behave more like a tyrant than a commander-in-chief. As seen already, it was he who placed a self-promoting inscription on the victory monument at Delphi, later removed. The allies asked the Athenians to take over the leadership instead, seeing how well they and their navy had performed in the struggle against the Persians.

Sensing their opportunity, the Athenians obliged. To fund the war-effort, they organized a system whereby the Greek allies contributed either money based on an assessment of their resources or, at the beginning, ships. Twenty-five years later, in 454 BC, the Athenians moved the allied treasury from the relatively neutral location of the Cycladic island of Delos to the sanctuary of Athena on their Acropolis. To appease the new protectress of the fund, the allies agreed to set aside a portion of their annual payments – a sixtieth – as an offering to the goddess.

It was for the inscription and advertisement of these annual amounts that the Athenians now erected the freestanding slab of stone somewhere on the Acropolis and put the masons to work. These lines from the first record of the payments to be inscribed on the block, 454/3 BC, show the format of the inscription:

Mecypernians
Stolians,
Polichnitans: 231 drachmae 2 obols.
Singians: 2[?]2 drachmae 2 obols.
Thasians: 300 drachmae.
Mysians: 33 drachmae 2 obols.
Picres the Syangelian: [50 drachmae] etc.

The location of the paying communities tracks the growing scope of the Greek alliance. Picres was a local ruler based to the east of Bodrum in south-west Turkey; he was not even an ethnic Greek, but a Carian. In the quarter-century since the Athenians had taken over, and under the leader-ship of their generals, the forces of the Greek allies had effectively turned the Aegean Sea and the littoral of western Asia Minor into a no-go zone for the Persian Empire – a feat of arms scarcely less remarkable than the earlier victories over Persia on the Greek mainland.

The greatest victory belonged to the mid-460s BC, when an Athenian general led a fleet of two hundred war galleys along the south coast of Turkey in search of a rumoured Persian force. This he located not far from modern Antalya, at the mouth of a river which the Greeks called the Eurymedon, a fast-moving torrent in its upper reaches, nowadays popular with white-water rafters. Here the Greeks landed their infantry and inflicted a crushing defeat on the enemy, who had abandoned their ships in the hope of finding safety on land.

The strategic aim of the Greek allies by this stage was to keep Persian sea-power well away from Greek lands by bringing the king to agree to a frontier, beyond which his warships were no longer to sail. Not far west of the River Eurymedon the coast of Turkey's southern mainland turns an abrupt corner at a promontory marked by a chain of five offshore islets. The ancient Greeks knew them as 'Swallow Islands'. I have cruised past this picturesque spot more than once in recent years, but probably at the wrong time of year for migrating swallows, although I did see dolphins. The Greeks are said to have chosen these islands as the boundary markers. There is a knotty problem for historians of whether they negotiated a formal peace with the Persians on these terms. But both sides stopped fighting each other at about this time.

Even so, the Athenians did not dissolve the Greek alliance against Persia. When they raised that great monolith on the Acropolis in 454 or 453 BC, sight of the expanse of blank stone beneath the first record to be inscribed might have caused a Greek from an allied state disquiet about future Athenian intentions. He will have known, too, that leaving the alliance was no easy matter, as the Thasians had found out.

In the quoted extract above, the 'Thasians' of line 5 are the citizens of Thasos, a rich Greek island in the northern Aegean. Thucydides describes how they tried to leave the alliance in 465 BC or thereabouts, despite, like the other allies, having sworn to remain in it 'for ever', meaning as long as the Persian Empire should exist. The Athenians promptly sent warships, landed on the island and determinedly besieged the Thasians behind their walls for three years. When the besieged eventually surrendered, the Athenians forced them back into the alliance on humiliating terms, including – salt in the wound – payment of recent arrears in their annual contributions.

There were other signs that the Athenians were starting to treat their allies more like subjects of an empire of which they alone were the masters. A century later, an Athenian writer recalled how the Athenians used to parade the allied payments 'on the stage, when the theatre was full, at the festival of Dionysus'. He was referring to the contributions in precious metal which allied representatives brought to Athens every spring. To some onlookers, this annual parade before the Athenian citizenry might have resembled more a show of Athenian power.

To those Greeks who had knowledge of the internal workings of the Persian Empire, this kind of Athenian behaviour smacked of the imperialistic ways of the very empire that the alliance was set up to resist. The Persians too went in for parades of contributions. As seen, the great palace of the Persian kings at Persepolis in south-west Iran was adorned with sculptured images of great processions. These gift bearers were the subjects of the king, organized by ethnicity and bearing the produce of their lands to lay before 'the Great King, King of Kings'.

Later writers record traditions that the Athenians started to divert the allied payments from the war chest – their raison d'être – to purely Athenian ends. In effect they treated them as part of the revenues of the city of Athens. It was in the mid-400s BC, under the leadership of Pericles, that the Athenians started to beautify their city in earnest. This striving for 'soft power' through cultural works has a modern ring. Pericles was creative, a builder as well as an imperialist.

The outcomes – notably the beautiful buildings of the Periclean Acropolis – occupy a central place in modern judgements about the brilliance of Greek civilization. The economic enterprise of individual Athenian citizens, as farmers, traders or anything else, was by no means the sole, or even the main, source of the wealth that made this achievement possible.

The policy of Pericles divided the Athenians. An ancient writer records that voices were raised in the citizen assembly opposing, on grounds that today would be called 'ethical', the misuse of allied funds for these purposes:

> And surely Greece is insulted with a dire insult and manifestly subjected to tyranny when she sees that, with her own enforced contributions for the war, we are gilding and bedizening our city, which, for all the world like a wanton woman, adds to her wardrobe costly marbles and sacred statues and temples worth their millions.

These later traditions were more than the echoes of smears against Pericles by rival politicians inside the hothouse of the Athenian democracy. The Athenians began building the Parthenon in 447 BC. Athenian inscriptions recording the annual accounts of the work indicate that the bulk of the funds for the new temple were transfers of monies by the Athenian officials who received the annual payments of the allies.

Apparently done without consultation of the allies, this misspending of allied treasure was supposedly defended by Pericles himself in forthright terms:

> For his part, Pericles would instruct the people that it owed no account of their moneys to the allies provided it carried on the war for them and kept off the barbarians; 'not a horse do they furnish,' said he, 'not a ship, not a heavily-armed infantryman, but money simply; and this belongs, not to those who give it, but to those who take it, if only they furnish that for which they take it in pay.'

This policy of spending on public works enlarged further the pool of Athenian stakeholders in maintaining Athenian domination of the Greek alliance. These included military personnel, notably the lower-class rowers – not always citizens admittedly – who received pay for their uncomfortable exertions at the oars of the Athenian war galleys, known today by their Latin name of trireme.

A trireme was a one-masted wooden vessel, its prow tipped by a bronze ram, propelled by three banks of oars per side. Like many others I once clambered aboard the modern reconstruction of a trireme, at the time in dry dock down at Piraeus, also the war harbour of the ancient Athenians. Despite the best effort of its young crew of rowers, in sea trials during the 1980s this minutely researched replica failed to keep up the fastest speeds recorded for the ancient Athenian originals – 10 or so miles an hour – for more than a few minutes.

This suggests that, like all naval powers, ancient and more recent, the Athenian fleet relied on the fine honing of skills through continuous service at sea, season after season, year after year. This enabled the crews not just to perform routine actions such as embarking and beaching, going ahead and going astern, using the sail and so on, but also a demanding manoeuvre like the – a literal translation of the Ancient Greek – 'sailing through and out', in which a line of galleys would attempt to sail through a line of enemy vessels and then to ram them with their bronze-sheathed tips from their exposed sides.

Poorer Athenians were stakeholders in the democracy more broadly. Pericles introduced pay for citizens who served on the juries in Athenian courts. These juries were large – 501 members was typical – in part to ensure a fairer trial by obstructing the use of bribes by the accused. In doing this, Pericles may thereby have deepened the Athenian sense at the time of a link between their democracy and their rule of the allies, given the increasing confusion of the city's different strands of revenue and the lack of accountability to the allies of how their payments were spent.

By launching into public works, Pericles expanded local stakeholders in the sea empire yet further. An inscription on display in the British Museum records wages to workmen on one of the new temples on the fifth-century-BC Acropolis – architects, masons, sculptors, carpenters and so on. As seen, all were potential beneficiaries of the Athenian diversion of allied funds for public works. These workers included citizen-artisans, foreign residents or metics, and Athenian slave-owners, who probably received the wages paid to the slaves working on these building sites.

As for the rest of Greece, the Athenians seem to have turned a blind eye to Athens's growing unpopularity abroad. Down in the Peloponnese, the Spartans and their friends looked on at Athenian ambitions with mounting unease. They too had a military alliance, a much older one. In the course of the 500s BC Sparta had created a permanent agreement between the Greek communities of the Peloponnese to fight together under Spartan leadership against a common enemy.

The historian Thucydides offers his version of how one Peloponnesian city presented the Athenians as a threat to a meeting of Sparta's citizen assembly in 432 BC. Envoys from the Corinthians, who had various grievances against Athens, contrasted the temperament of the Spartans to their face with that of the Athenians:

> And you have never considered what manner of men are these Athenians with whom you will have to fight, and how utterly unlike yourselves. They are revolutionary, equally quick in the conception and in the execution of every new plan; while you are conservative – careful only to keep what you have, originating nothing, and not acting even when

action is most urgent. They are bold beyond their strength; they run risks which prudence would condemn; and in the midst of misfortune they are full of hope ... They are impetuous, and you are slow to act; they are always abroad, and you are always at home.

This reluctance of the Spartans to venture outside their frontiers was probably driven by fear of a Helot revolt behind their backs. In the end the Spartans decided to go to war. Thucydides says that it was less the speeches of their allies that persuaded them and more their real fear of the Athenians 'and their increasing power'. So began a struggle that dragged on for a generation, and involved most of the Greek states on one side or the other. The ancients came to call this the Peloponnesian War.

Like the Trojan War, this was a war that owes its modern renown to works of ancient Greek literature. In Homer and Thucydides respectively, later centuries have found true greatness, both of artistry and of the human spirit, and additionally, especially in the case of Thucydides, of insight into the verities of statecraft and military command. To describe the Peloponnesian War is – more or less – to paraphrase Thucydides, by far the most important ancient source.

Thucydides relates how, for the first ten years, the Spartans and their allies staged an annual invasion of the farmlands surrounding the walled city of Athens so as to disrupt Athenian agriculture. A character in an Athenian comedy of this time voices the feelings of Athenian farmers about this enemy strategy: 'I detest the Spartans with all my heart, and may Poseidon ... cause an earthquake and overturn their dwellings! My vines also have been cut.' The Athenians in response crowded behind their city walls. They had prudently extended these a generation earlier so as to unite both the city proper and its harbour of Piraeus in a single fortification. The link between the two was a pair of parallel walls of sundried mud bricks some 4 miles long and 200 yards apart. Access to their harbour secured, the Athenians could rely if need be on their navy to provide supplies of imported food.

Given the rudimentary state of Greek ideas about disease at this time, no one, including Pericles, who had led Athens into what he considered a survivable war, foresaw the health risks posed by the concentration of all Athenians inside the walls. Here the country Athenians had to camp in shanty dwellings, stiflingly hot in the Athenian summer. Thucydides describes in detail a lethal epidemic which spread from the harbour to the whole city in the second year of the war. This caused, he wrote, 'men to die like sheep'. He carefully described the symptoms, which years of debate have failed to match conclusively to any modern disease.

He noted that animals could contract the disease from humans and humans from each other – by contagion, in other words. This observation contradicted what passed for Greek medical theorizing of the time, which blamed bad air for spreading illness – an explanation erroneously linked to geography. Thucydides used his historian's eye to observe a medical truth about the transmission of infectious diseases that western medicine did not fully accept before the nineteenth century. By the time the plague had spent itself, most inhabitants of the city must have been either dead or become immune – Thucydides says that the disease could revisit a victim, but far less severely. Pericles was struck down in 429 BC.

Safe inside their long walls, the Athenians even so showed resilience. In 415 BC, during a short-lived cessation of hostilities that gave both sides some recovery time, they revealed just how far they were from mending their imperialistic ways. Out in the central Aegean lay the small Cycladic island of Melos, inhabited by Greeks of the Dorian branch who looked on the Spartans as their cousins. These men of Melos had never joined the Athenian alliance and still held out, despite harassment by the allied fleet. The Athenians now sent a naval force in the name of the alliance. In a pow-wow the Athenian envoys sat down with the magistrates and oligarchs who ran the island and tried to persuade them to join the alliance – or else.

Thucydides gives his version of this debate, with the Athenians encouraging the Melians to interrupt and ask questions as they spoke. The envoys explained that the Athenians could not tolerate Melian neutrality, since this made them look weak in the eyes of their allies (an admission of allied malcontent with Athenian dominance), especially as Melos was just one small island. They made this argument as well: 'You know as well as we do that right, as the world goes, is only in question between equals in power, while the strong do what they can and the weak suffer what they must.' This ancient doctrine that might just 'is' – power rules OK, as it were – is liable to disturb liberal thinkers today on any number of levels. Still, it heedlessly continues its long run in the world's history where the behaviour of states is concerned. In the telling of Thucydides, the Athenians assumed that self-preservation would make the Melians submit. If so, they cannot have been pleased when the Melian oligarchs replied that they would feel shame in giving in without a fight. They would rather hope for the best, put their trust in the gods, and defend their freedom.

Thucydides, who probably saw in this Melian attitude a baleful lesson for his readers in the triumph of emotion over reason, describes what happened next. The Athenians and their allies laid siege to the town of Melos, forcing the islanders to surrender, and then 'put to death all the grown men whom they took, and sold the women and children for slaves, and subsequently sent out five hundred settlers and inhabited the place themselves.'

Elsewhere Thucydides presents the Athenians too as victims of faulty reasoning in war and suggests how the utterances of politicians could delude them. The most spectacular man-made cavern in modern Syracuse is a good place to introduce the Athenian expedition to Sicily. This cavern beguiles tourists with a feature prompting some of them to break into song: an echo. This so-called Ear of Dionysius is a lofty cave created by years of ancient masons quarrying down from the top for building stone.

In one of their local quarries the Syracusans corralled at least seven thousand soldiers, captives from an Athenian armada that had gone spectacularly wrong. This was in 413 BC. Thucydides emphasizes what he seems to have considered the unusual cruelty of this incarceration – the heat of the sun, lack of air, thin rations doled out by the Syracusans, leading to hunger and thirst, and the stink from the bodies of dead comrades. This episode closes his account of what he calls 'the most important action' of the whole war. He meant the military expedition from Athens which had set out for Sicily two years earlier.

Thucydides had the highest opinion of Pericles as a statesman. His own view was that the lesser quality of the Athenian leaders who succeeded him was to blame for what he called this 'blunder'. His analysis is hard to prove or disprove in the absence of alternative accounts. On its own terms, what turned out to be a disaster for Athens offered another lesson, this time about the unintended consequences of public speeches by politicians.

What seems to have attracted the Athenians to attack the rich island of Sicily in the first place was the hope of material gain. They dressed this up as the need to answer a call for help from their allies in Sicily, the non-Greek people of Egesta, against an enemy neighbour. Thucydides adds that, alongside the profit motive, the young Athenian men felt 'a longing for foreign sights and travel abroad'. Similar reasons are given by men and women who enlist today.

In the version of Thucydides the Athenians sit in assembly and listen to prominent Athenians giving speeches for or against this bold plan. There is the young Alcibiades, a glamorous member of the Athenian social elite whom Thucydides wants his readers to view with suspicion: someone 'exceedingly ambitious of a command by which he hoped to reduce Sicily and Carthage, and to gain in wealth and celebrity by means of his successes'. Whether or not the judgement was fair, this is arguably a recognizable type in western politics today.

Before Alcibiades spoke, an older politician called Nicias had attempted to dissuade the Athenians from the idea because he feared that his countrymen harboured the overambitious aim of conquering the whole island. He saw the plan as a distraction from the real enemy, the Spartans, and attacked without naming him the plan's advocate, a young man 'who seeks to be admired for his stud of horses', and 'to maintain his private opulence at his country's risk'.

Alcibiades then got up to rebut these criticisms and to speak in favour of the expedition, so eloquently that he left the Athenians keener than ever to go ahead. Nicias felt obliged to rise for a second time at the same meeting. Thucydides says that he now aimed to dissuade the Athenians by using a rhetorical trick. He talked up the military risks and argued that if the expedition were to go ahead it needed to be much bigger and more expensive. He hoped that the Athenians would give up the whole idea when they weighed these greater costs against an uncertain outcome.

In fact, his rhetoric achieved the opposite effect. He persuaded the Athenians that a much bigger force would make success a certainty. So the expedition went ahead, thanks to 'the enthusiasm of the majority', while 'the few who liked it not, feared to appear unpatriotic by holding up their hands (and voting) against it, and so kept quiet'. Here Thucydides shows his grasp of group psychology.

The Athenians arrived in Sicily and laid siege to the city of the Syracusans, who were fellow Greeks but – like the men of Melos – of Dorian ethnicity. With help from their kinsmen, the Spartans, the Syracusans proved a more formidable foe than the Athenians had reckoned with. As things went from bad to worse militarily, the Athenian general, none other than the same Nicias, missed a crucial last chance to sail home – he and the men alike were deterred by what Greeks generally at this date saw as a bad omen, an eclipse of the moon. When the force finally retreated by land, demoralized and short of water, order broke down when they reached a river. The Syracusans slaughtered the desperately thirsty men as they tried to drink, and enslaved the survivors.

The Athenian disaster in Sicily made a great impression on the Greeks. Every state was reconsidering its position in the face of a weakened Athens. The Spartans scented a decisive victory in the offing. They changed strategy. Instead of the old annual raids on Athenian territory, they fortified a stronghold a mere 11 miles north-east of Athens and kept it permanently garrisoned. The Athenians took heavy losses in the countryside, including, Thucydides says, all their farm animals.

There was more. Under cover of the Spartan occupation, 'more than twenty thousand slaves, the greater part of them skilled workers, deserted' their Athenian masters. At this time skilled slaves in the territory of Athens were mainly concentrated in the south. Here visitors venturing into the peaceful, pine-scented hill country near the modern town of Lavrion encounter a side of ancient Athens contrasting starkly with the aesthetic ruins on the Acropolis.

There are fenced-off entrances to ancient tunnels; slag heaps; great cisterns for collecting industrial quantities of rainwater; and ruined installations where workers once washed lumps of mined ore before heating them in a furnace to separate the noble metal from the base. In the nearby archaeological museum, teachers show throngs of Athenian schoolchildren a display of crude inscriptions found locally: the Ancient Greek word for 'boundary' features prominently. These stones once marked mining concessions granted by Athens to private individuals.

An Athenian writer called Xenophon, who as a boy might have seen Nicias in person, records how this hapless commander of the Sicilian expedition once owned a thousand slaves 'in the mines'. He made his profit by hiring out this workforce and its know-how to fellow citizens operating concessions. So, going back to the Spartans, their garrison now disrupted not just agriculture but another major source of Athenian wealth, the city's silver mines.

The Spartans had a more astonishing card up their sleeve. In its early years the Athenian alliance had successfully liberated and then recruited the Greek settlements of western Turkey previously under Persian rule. This constituted a loss of face to a hereditary monarchy that based its legitimacy on claims to rule over multiple 'lands' and 'peoples'. The current Persian king, Darius II, a grandson of Xerxes, felt the time was now right to put pressure on his chief governor in the region to have these Greeks resume their tribute payments – bring them back, in other words, under Persian rule.

The upshot was that the Spartans, in order to defeat Athens, made a treaty with the non-Greek foe against whom Spartans and Athenians had once fought side by side. In this deal, Sparta agreed to hand back the Ionian Greeks to Persia once Athens was defeated. In return, Persia gave military aid and enough treasure for Sparta to build and maintain a fleet to take on that of Athens.

The final blow to the dwindling resources of the Athenians came in 405 BC, when a Spartan admiral, Lysander, captured an Athenian fleet beached on the European side of the Dardanelles. After this disaster, the Spartans were able to prevent supplies of grain being shipped to Piraeus from what is now the Crimea and Ukraine. Most of what was left of the Athenian alliance now melted away. Lysander sailed for Athens. Inside their walls, the starving Athenians, mindful not least of the fate at Athenian hands of the people of Melos, braced for the worst.

To the sound of women playing flutes, the Spartans and their allies demolished the fortifications of Athens and imposed victors' terms. But they did not destroy Athens. Somewhat ironically in the circumstances, they said that they could not forget the city's great services in the Greek cause during the Persian Wars. Shorn of their imperial power, the Athenians survived.

For a generation, with ups and downs, including another major inter-Greek war, the victorious Spartans with Persian support dominated mainland Greece politically and militarily. This period seems to have seen, or hastened, social change at Sparta. During the Peloponnesian War the previously insular Spartans had become accustomed to serving abroad. They had seen wealthy Syracuse, the great rivers of northern Greece, and the opulent entourages of Persian officials. The leadership now had more connections and experience of the world.

In the view of our best source of information about Sparta in the decades following the defeat of Athens, the Athenian writer Xenophon, power now went to the head of the Spartans. Leading Spartans were no longer content to live modestly at home, but sought out trips abroad on state business. Some started to flaunt their riches. In positions of authority they let themselves be 'corrupted by flattery' while serving overseas – a roundabout reference, probably, to bribery.

This moralizing indictment is not necessarily way off the mark. Xenophon had Spartan friends in high places and knew Sparta well. He disapproved of the changes he records and saw a decline in Spartan values. That said, a moralizing judgement about a whole society is always difficult to evaluate objectively. Xenophon might have echoed the disapproving conservatism of some Spartan friends. A modern historian might ask whether competition for status among richer Spartans had taken new forms as they became more 'worldly'.

An achievement by a Spartan woman at around this time highlights the ostentation of rich Spartans and also – maybe – a conservative reaction to this phenomenon. Various ancient writings record that a daughter and sister of Spartan kings called Cynisca twice won the prestigious four-horse chariot race at Olympia in the 390s BC.

She went on to boast in a victory monument there that she was 'the only woman in all Greece who won this crown'. Owning and racing chariot teams, like the equestrianism of Queen Elizabeth II in modern times, was a sport for the rich, and Cynisca had serious wealth at her disposal.

Her inscription at Olympia makes Cynisca sound almost like a proto-feminist. It plays on an ancient Greek view that Spartan females enjoyed more social freedoms than their counterparts in other Greek cities. But a later Greek tradition claimed that Cynisca was put up to this venture by her royal brother, King Agesilaus II:

> Seeing that some of the citizens thought themselves to be somebody and gave themselves great airs because they kept a racing stud, he persuaded his sister Cynisca to enter a chariot in the races at Olympia, for he wished to demonstrate to the Greeks that this sort of thing was no sign of manly excellence, but only of having money and being willing to spend it.

This tradition cannot just be dismissed. If correct, Cynisca merely did her brother's bidding. The aim of the conservative Agesilaus was to try to check the costly appetite for horse-racing among his rich fellow Spartans by using Cynisca to show that a victory – achieved at second hand by a driver – did not make you any more of a man.

Spartan society was not just divided at the top. Thanks to Xenophon, who drew on his insider's knowledge, history records a failed plot among members of Sparta's – numerically far superior – underclass to take up arms against the diminishing elite of Spartan citizens with full rights. Xenophon reels off a list of categories of disadvantaged groups in Spartan society who were united in the view that they 'would be glad to eat the full citizens even raw'.

As seen in the last chapter, these full citizens, those who went through the military training and who were now benefiting economically from the Spartan hegemony, had no appetite to reform the unequal distribution of wealth which kept them on top. Yet the inheritance laws that seem to have helped a few families to become very rich were shrinking the patrimony of other Spartans.

Unable to pay their mess dues, these Spartans were being forced out of the citizen body altogether into a simmering state of social exclusion. It seems that the grip of the authorities was fierce enough to avoid civil conflict. Another danger was that Sparta's citizen army would shrink in numbers to the point where recovery from a decisive defeat in battle would no longer be possible.

This is exactly what happened in 371 BC. A Spartan army had marched out of the Peloponnese to assert Sparta's hegemony against the Greeks of Boeotia, the region to the north of Athens. This army was now decisively beaten. It was rare enough for Greeks to defeat Spartans on the battlefield. Greek onlookers were even more amazed by the disintegration that followed. Sparta was unable militarily to recover from the blow. She failed to prevent the Helots of Messenia or the cities of her Peloponnesian alliance from now seizing the chance to throw off Spartan domination.

The future philosopher Aristotle, aged thirteen at the time, later gave this analysis: 'The impact of one single battle was too much for Sparta; she succumbed owing to the shortage of manpower.' The insuperable rigidities of Spartan society may help to explain why the Spartan victory in the Peloponnesian War and the Spartan dominion in Greece that followed did not prompt a second flowering of Spartan culture. Both before and after her defeat, the cultural atmosphere of Athens was very different. In the next chapter I consider examples of the achievements of the Athenians and those other Greeks drawn to reside there at this time, and the local conditions encouraging individual geniuses to shine.

CHAPTER 10

EXAMINED LIVES AND GOLDEN MOUTHS

After the brilliance of Homer, modern critics traditionally identify a creative peak in Greek culture in the period from the first Greek victory over Persia (490 BC) to the rise of the Macedonian overlords (from 336 BC). A list of famous, even household, names living in these times (such as Sophocles and Socrates) would make the point about the widespread perception today of the high achievements of those two centuries.

The period is sometimes called 'Classical' with a capital 'c'. The denomination 'Classical' is more than a modern way of dividing up time. It conveys today's standard judgement about the near perfection of aspects of Greek culture in this period, compared with what went before and what came after.

This subjective rating owes some of its authority to the opinions of the ancients in the post-Classical centuries, and some to classical enthusiasts since the Renaissance. These last include all the creative people who have consciously taken inspiration for writing literature, for philosophizing, carving statues, designing buildings and so on from ancient models. The modest aim of this chapter is to sample some of what it is about 'Classical' Greece that (traditionally) has justified its high rating in the culture stakes.

Classical Greece by and large means Classical Athens. From the late fifth century BC, the signs start to mount showing how ancient neighbours of the Athenians, Greek and non-Greek, were embracing the innovations hosted, and occasionally promoted, in the 'revolutionary' cultural atmosphere of the fifth-century BC Athenian democracy. The British Museum offers one small example which visitors today can easily appreciate.

I was once told a true story about a visit to this museum by a distinguished advocate for the return to Greece of the Elgin Marbles. Arriving in a cavernous gallery before the Parthenon display, but also full of Greek sculpture, the personage mistook these statues for the more famous ones next door. An entertaining story maybe, but the mistake is almost understandable when you look at the clinging drapery of a row of freestanding female figures in this ante-gallery: they could almost have stepped off the Parthenon.

This specific idea for carving female drapery had occurred to the sculptors of the Parthenon half a century before. The visitor who turns left on entering the Duveen Gallery where the Parthenon sculptures are displayed will see at the far end the battered torso of a female figure. Close up she too has been carved as if the folds of her dress were stuck to her.

This 'wet look', which first appeared here on the Parthenon, was an Athenian sculptor's clever way of revealing the form almost more effectively than if the figure were nude – thus sidestepping the Greek cultural taboo of those times against the public depiction of naked goddesses. The ancient reputation of the Athenian artist Pheidias, who supervised the Parthenon sculpture, came to resemble Michelangelo's today. He might have been the creative genius here.

As with other aspects of ancient Greece, this approach to drapery effects is now so familiar, whether from ancient sculpture in modern museums or from neo-Greek statuary of more recent times, that it is easy to forget that it was something stunningly new at its first appearance.

In the following generation, lesser sculptors working in the Greek style copied this Athenian novelty. In the case of those figures in the previous gallery, they once adorned the so-called Nereid Monument. This was a tomb built in the 390s BC in south-west Turkey for a non-Greek ruler who loved Greek art.

Two ancient anecdotes illustrate a widespread enthusiasm for a Greek art form which fifth-century Athens developed to the point of more or less inventing it. After the Syracusans in 413 BC decisively defeated the Athenian expedition to Sicily,

> many Athenians who reached home safely greeted Euripides with affectionate hearts, and recounted to him, some that they had been set free

from slavery for rehearsing what they remembered of his works; and some that when they were roaming about after the final battle they had received food and drink for singing his songs . . .

By now in his late sixties, Euripides was a highly successful Athenian playwright. The story shows that the culturally up-to-date Syracusans must have seen Sicilian performances of his plays – written like all Greek drama of the time to be both spoken and sung. A generation later, in the 360s BC, a Greek tyrant of a city in central Greece 'left the theatre abruptly' during a performance of extracts from a tragedy by the same Euripides that had moved him to tears. He didn't want this display of emotion to dent his 'strong man' image.

This particular theatre in central Greece was one of many built in the 300s BC as the Athenian appetite for theatrical performances took hold among ordinary people across a large swathe of the Greek world. Cities demanded a new architecture in stone to dignify what was now a performance art able to attract audiences of ten or fifteen thousand at a time. Nowadays the theatre of Epidaurus built in the later 300s BC is the most famous of this first wave of monumental Greek theatres.

In the late fourth century BC the philosopher Aristotle, based in Athens, wrote down what he had found out about the origins of Athenian drama. It had developed, he thought, out of folk rituals that the Athenians performed to honour Dionysus, god of wine and ecstasy: tragic plays had grown out of group song and dance in praise of the god, and comedy from the carrying in bawdy procession of an image of an erect penis.

Other Greek civic communities, including the Spartans in the 500s BC, as seen, staged religious performances involving the use of a key element in Athenian drama of the fifth century BC, the mask. Where the Athenians differed from other Greek communities was in the development from such beginnings of the genre of the theatrical play in the recognizably modern sense. That is, a form of literature consisting of characters delivering dialogue, written by a playwright for live performance, not just for reading.

Early on, the Athenians had the bright idea of holding competitions for the best of these dramas at their annual festival for Dionysus in the city centre. They introduced contests for what became the two chief classes of ancient Greek drama: for the best 'tragedy' around 534 BC, and for the best 'comedy' in 486 BC. Then as now, competition was a stimulus to innovation.

A scrap of an ancient writing roll now in Vienna, made in the usual way from the stem of the papyrus plant, preserves a few lines of poetry from a fifth-century BC Athenian play:

> I grieve, I grieve – your mother's blood that drives you wild. Great prosperity among mortals is not lasting: upsetting it like the sail of some swift sloop some high power swamps it in the rough doom-waves of fearful toils, as of the sea.

The verses – also from Euripides – suggest the lofty solemnity of tragic language. But the great rarity of this fragment, dating from about 200 BC, is that along with the verses is written the musical score. For this the scribe used an established system of notation based on letters of the alphabet, placed above the words. So fifth-century BC audiences in the Theatre of Dionysus at Athens experienced a kind of musical theatre.

Experts infer from the way that the rhythmic pattern of beats of the lines – their metre – changes in surviving fifth-century plays that audiences at that time could have experienced performances as a mixture of sung choruses; arias and duets; passages of chanting or recitative; and rhythmic poetry delivered in a speaking voice.

There was also spectacle. In one of its storerooms the Naples Archaeological Museum guards an impressive product of the Athenian potteries – a vase, nearly 2.5 feet high. Around its middle runs a band painted with figures engaged in a theatrical performance. The painting dates from around 400 BC.

Some of the actors, all men, wear lifelike masks; others hold theirs. They are dressed in theatrical costume: 'Heracles', with his props of lion skin and club, is clearly recognizable. Others in the painting are chorus members, always citizen amateurs at this date, here dressed up with animal tails, hairy loincloths and drooping phalluses as 'satyrs,' fantasy creatures, wild followers of Dionysus. Some are practising their dance moves. The playwright is there, holding a copy of the text on a scroll. In central place sits the piper, playing his double flute, the usual instrument in fifth-century Athenian theatre.

At my school we studied for the exam in Ancient Greek the *Agamemnon* of Aeschylus. At that age I didn't particularly relish this high-minded and deeply moral tragedy about the relentless exaction by the gods of 'debts of justice' owed by sinning mortals, be they ever so high and mighty. Now I recognize its grandeur.

Agamemnon, the glory-seeking commander-in-chief of the Greek expedition against Troy, must suffer for the impious act of sacrificing his own daughter to obtain a fair wind for the Greek fleet. For being the instrument of divine justice his wife must suffer in turn – in the play it is she who avenges her daughter's death by killing her husband on his triumphant return home ten years later.

Aeschylus wrote the play as the first of three, the other two continuing the story, and all for performance at one festival. In the second play he serves the come-uppance now due to the wife. But the horror only worsens – it is her son who, on the orders of Apollo, avenges his father's death. In the third play Aeschylus redeems this awful cycle of familial bloodletting with a modern ending. With gods as advocates, the cast-off son is tried and acquitted for his mother's murder in an Athenian court before a jury of democratic citizens.

In this trilogy Aeschylus offered dramatic actions meant to inspire in the audience fear and pity. Like other tragedians, he found some of his plots in traditional stories about the bloody family dramas of the Greek ruling houses of mythical times. For his audience of Athenian citizens, Aeschylus ended the drama with a lesson in civics: the difficult ethical choices facing the conscientious citizen juror.

At the university where I used to teach in the north of England, the Classics department held annual open days at which lecturers gave talks to school sixth-formers studying classical subjects for university entrance exams. For years the most popular talk was invariably the one on Aristophanes, the only writer of comedies in fifth-century Athens whose plays have survived.

Sometimes there was standing room only, such was the demand of coach parties from schools all over the country to see the two lecturers – a male double act – imitate the comic turns of the ancient actors. Their party trick was to improvise with balloons of various shapes and sizes the item of ancient costume which did so much to set the tone for the humour of Aristophanes – dangling male genitals, in ancient times made of leather.

As a comparison shows, not all translators do justice to the obscene innuendo of Aristophanes, some of it homosexual in theme, as here:

That being agreed, an easy chair I've brought, a page too, young and strong, to carry it. Sit on him too, if ever he calls for it.

Now that that's settled, here's a folding stool for you, and a boy (he's no eunuch) who'll carry it for you. And if you feel like it sometimes, make a folding stool of him!

Apart from the bawdiness of some of the humour, another feature of the surviving plays that may strike a modern reader is how blatantly political they are. Not only did Aristophanes invent plots based on current affairs, notably the Peloponnesian War; he also introduced real-life politicians as characters in plots, made biting attacks on ones he disliked, and poked fun at the Athenian democracy itself – his audience, basically:

[FIRST SLAVE]: We two have a master with a farmer's temperament, a bean chewer, prickly in the extreme, known as Mr Demos of Pnyx Hill, a cranky, half-dead little codger. Last market day he bought a slave, Paphlagon, a tanner, an arch criminal, and a slanderer. He sized up the old man's character, this rawhide Paphlagon did, so he crouched before the master and started flattering and fawning and toadying and swindling him with odd tidbits of waste leather . . .

Here the character 'Demos', meaning 'People', stands for the citizen body. As seen, its place of assembly at this time was the Athenian hill of the Pnyx. The character of 'Paphlagon', a slave and leather tanner who fawns over, so as to take advantage of, his complacent master Demos, is a thinly veiled allegory for a populist politician of the post-Pericles era called Cleon, the son of a rich tanner, who used eloquent speeches to persuade the citizen assembly in favour of his policies.

In this play, *Knights* (424 BC), the plot follows two other slaves of Demos who successfully scheme against Paphlagon. He ends up losing his master's favour and is demoted to selling sausages at the city gates. At the end of the play, having been shown the error of his ways, old man Demos experiences a transformation, losing his ugliness to become beautiful.

The playwright exercised this freedom of expression against political leaders in the highly public arena of the theatre, where the audience comprised not only male citizens but also (probably) their womenfolk, as well as foreigners. The Athenians liked this play so much that Aristophanes won first prize at its first performance. But the play did not prevent the Athenians from going on to elect Cleon the real-life politician to a senior military command.

Not all modern leaders of western democracies would happily tolerate such public ridicule before the whole civic community. Although Cleon's response is unknown, sometimes the comic playwright's waspishness certainly seems to have stung. In another comedy, Aristophanes made fun of the intellectuals who had become a conspicuous feature of Athenian life in the second half of the fifth century BC. His target in one play was Socrates, an Athenian citizen in his mid-forties at the play's premiere in 423 BC.

Aristophanes presents Socrates as an eccentric, who walks barefoot in the city streets. His pallor betrays long hours indoors, unlike the suntanned norm for the active outdoorsy citizen male of those times. He is headmaster of a school where the teachers 'train you, if you give them money, to win any argument whether it's right or wrong'. That is, this school offered training in public speaking – rhetoric, as the Greeks called what at this time was a new discipline.

Aristophanes ridicules Socrates as a free thinker who rejected conventional religion. He is made to say that the gods are 'rubbish', with the exception of a new god called Dinos, who has ousted Zeus, and of the clouds (the play's title). These shape-shifting entities are goddesses, he tells a doubting pupil, who not unreasonably thinks they look more like fluffy sheep fleeces. The character Socrates then uses a teaching technique – question-and-answer, essentially – to lead this pupil into reversing his opinion. The young man even starts praying to the clouds.

The entertainment value for the audience seems to have lain in the way that Aristophanes had channelled a popular view of not so much the real-life Socrates as the general milieu in which his fellow citizens placed him, that of the nonconformist intellectual. The type held novel ideas verging on impiety, gained a hold over impressionable youth and took fees in return for classes in public speaking. To some this last kind of teaching wasn't entirely ethical. An unscrupulous citizen could enter public life and use deceptive arguments to win over an audience, even if he was not in the right.

The real Socrates, who must have been an extraordinary figure, did not teach for money. His philosophizing style seems to have been to go out in public, frequenting the streets and civic spaces of Athens, and to chat with people who fell in with him. It was partly in this way that he attracted friends and followers, including the young and the well born. These followers were usually men. Social norms discouraged respectable Athenian women from being seen to join in talk on street corners with groups of unrelated men.

These conversations were the essence of Socrates the philosopher. In them he would explore high-minded questions preying on his own mind, questions that today would be called 'ethical'. Essentially, they hinged on the morally serious business of how best to live one's life. His conversational technique for this purpose was, indeed, a kind of gentle cross-examination – as parodied by Aristophanes.

The ancient Greeks called this type of exchange 'dialectic', from the Greek verb 'to converse'. The idea was that the conversers would come to an acceptable definition of righteous living by speculating, for instance, on the exact meaning of common Greek notions of goodness. What was it, really, to be 'just', or 'moderate'? If he knew what these behaviours amounted to, a man had no excuse for not leading an ethical life.

Socrates ran up against the limits of Athenian tolerance for maverick thinking, when some fellow citizens brought charges against him of corrupting the young and impiety. This was in 399 BC, five years after the resounding defeat of Athens by the Spartans, years when the self-confidence of the Athenians was badly shaken. The democracy seemed fragile, and the oligarchic connections of some of Socrates' friends perhaps put him under suspicion.

This was where Aristophanes might have stung. Addressing the jury at his trial, Socrates was said to have decried the 'slanders' which had put him in the dock, pointing his finger specifically at the Theatre of Dionysus:

> For you yourselves saw these things in the comedy of Aristophanes, a Socrates being carried about there, proclaiming that he was treading on air and uttering a vast deal of other nonsense, about which I know nothing, either much or little.

One of the large juries of democratic Athens, numbering 501 citizens, found him guilty by a small majority of thirty. His accuser proposed the death penalty. By law the accused would propose a counter-penalty. With rich friends willing to put up money, the impecunious Socrates asked for a fine instead, but proposed a meagre one. The jury opted for death. Socrates duly drank a cup of poison.

Socrates owed his posthumous fame to the later writings of his disciples, who included a rich young Athenian called Plato. Plato's surviving writings feature a number of pieces formatted as conversations between Socrates and his followers. There is also what purports to be the defence which Socrates gave at his trial, known after the Ancient Greek word for this type of courtroom speech as *The Apology*.

Written twenty years after the event, this noble speech, from which the above quotation comes, seems to idealize the speaker. Like the entire presentation of Socrates in the writings of Plato, much of it may be, to put it bluntly, creative fiction. Plato's writings likewise obscure the difference between the philosophical beliefs of the teacher and those of the pupil.

One of these was the deeply moral idea that the philosophical life confers the hope of life after death – immortality in other words. Awaiting death in his cell, Plato has Socrates at this final crisis of his life converse with followers about his attitude to death.

'For if I did not believe,' he said, 'that I was going to other wise and good gods, and, moreover, to men who have died, men who are better men than those here, I should be wrong in not grieving at death. But as it is, you may rest assured that I expect to go to good men, though I should not care to assert this positively; but I would assert as positively as anything about such matters that I am going to gods who are good masters.'

Plato's Socrates then explores his idea that at death the body parts company from its partner in life, what he calls its *psyche*. If the *psyche* has kept itself as untainted as possible by the pleasures of the flesh, and the life led has been 'pure' and 'moderate' according to the ethical tenets of the lover of wisdom or philosopher, the reward after death is separation of the *psyche* from the body, its release from the underground realm of the dead and its journey upwards to a heavenly abode. In English the usual translation of this word *psyche* is 'soul', something that resides in the body in life, but is not *of* the body.

Another of Plato's dialogues gave rise to the modern idea of Platonic love. It is called the *Symposium* because it is set in a drinking party, albeit one where guests make the novel choice of conversing instead of the usual quaffing. It centres on Socrates once more. The subject of conversation is *erōs*, the Ancient Greek word for sexual love or desire.

Plato's Socrates presents his own views on this topic as the wisdom he learnt from a wise woman. She had reasoned to him that there were two kinds of pregnancy. One gave birth to human children in a relationship between a man and a woman. The other, which was superior, began with a man whose soul was pregnant 'with things that it is fitting for the soul to conceive and to bring to birth', namely wisdom and the other virtues. Its fruit came from the encounter with a beautiful body and soul worthy of impregnation with this wisdom:

For I imagine it's by contact with what is beautiful, and associating with it, that he brings to birth and procreates the things with which he was for so long pregnant, both when he is present with him and when he is away from him but remembering him; and he joins with the other person in nurturing what is born.

The wise woman goes on to claim that this is the 'correct kind of boy-loving'. Plato does not seem to allow for the possibility of this kind of chaste, educative relationship between a man and a woman. He himself never married.

He then uses an anecdote to illustrate the self-control of his hero Socrates in these matters. The handsomest of the young male guests at the Athenian party where this conversation supposedly took place relates with an air of disbelief how Socrates had once resisted his advances. Socrates had fended him off with the philosophical retort that his fine admirer was 'trying to get hold of truly beautiful things (Socrates' mind) in return for only apparently beautiful ones (the young man's body)'.

Plato's writings include the first surviving attempt to imagine an ideal society, a utopia. This was needed, the work explains, because existing types of Greek state, including democracy, were faulty. Plato's ideal society practised eugenics to ensure the reproduction of the fittest, abolished the family, and separated mothers from their children. Governing was to be entrusted to a class of philosophers, the Guardians, rigorously trained for the purpose. How serious Plato was about the achievability of this totalitarian vision is a debate among experts which we cannot go into here.

Unlike Socrates, Plato founded a private community of like-minded people, both students and other teachers, at a particular Athenian address, where it outlived its founder (who died in 347 BC) to become a long-lived institution of higher learning, one of the first of its kind in Athens.

An ancient life of Plato records that he did his teaching 'in the Academy, and that is a suburban place of exercise planted like a grove, so named from an ancient hero called Hecademus'. Greek archaeologists have located the site of this gymnasium, beneath the streets of the modern city to the north-west of the ancient agora.

In this vicinity Plato carried on with his philosophizing inquiries. The chief format seems to have been the conversation, Socrates-style, although one lecture by Plato survives. A comic playwright of the time mocks these inquiries, but at the same time reveals how varied they were. Here they included what we would call sciences, zoology and botany, as well as prac-tical researches:

> I saw a group of boys in the gymnasia of the Academy, and I heard strange talk that I can't describe. They were defining and classifying the natural world: the way that animals live, the nature of trees, and the species of vegetables. And in the middle of this they had a pumpkin and were investigating the species that it belonged to.

An ancient list survives of Plato's pupils. It is interesting for including, as well as Athenians, Greeks from all over the Aegean, in addition to Sicily and the Black Sea. Like his reputation, his community was 'international'. These young males must have had financial means to study away from home. So presumably did the two women on the list, both from the Peloponnese.

According to an ancient story, one of these women sought out Plato after reading one of his political works. She joined the community, 'disguising for some considerable time the fact that she was a woman' by dressing as a man. So it was not impossible for a woman of independent character in mid-fourth-century Greece to pursue the life of the mind. If nothing else, the fact that Axiothea – her name – felt obliged to cross-dress suggests strong social disapproval for Greek females spending time in the company of unrelated men.

Another of the 'international' pupils, hailing from northern Greece, was a young Aristotle. An ancient life labels him the most eminent of Plato's pupils and adds some personal details which may or may not be true: 'he had a lisping voice . . . He also had very thin legs, they say, and small eyes; but he used to indulge in fashionable dress, and rings, and used to shave.'

In the mid-1990s archaeologists digging near the Athenian residence of Greece's head of state found an ancient building. Its focus was a very large rectangular courtyard, some 25 yards across. The court was edged by colonnaded walkways, and behind these were various rooms. This is the classic layout for an ancient Greek exercise space or gymnasium.

Given the location, the archaeologists were confident that they had discovered the Lyceum, an Athenian gymnasium like the Academy. After Plato's death, this public place of exercise on the other side of town was where the mature Aristotle preferred to teach. It was here that he founded his own centre of higher studies. Like Plato's, this private institution lived on long after its founder's death.

Aristotle owes his greatness in antiquity and ever since in part to the encyclopaedic breadth of his inquiries. According to his ancient biographer he wrote around 550 books, which the biographer lists. They cover topics that span today's disciplinary divides between science, arts and humanities. Aristotle was equally at home inquiring about friendship, the workings of plants and animals, meteorology, deductive reasoning or logic, optics, Homer, astronomy, law, theatre – the list goes on. It makes the point that philosophers were the research-led academics of antiquity, although none repeated Aristotle's extraordinary range.

This taster comes from his factual survey of the animal kingdom and concerns the type of shellfish known today as molluscs:

> And generally, the molluscs are observed to be carrying their so-called eggs in spring and late autumn, except the edible sea-urchin, which, though it carries its so-called eggs most abundantly at these times, always has some, and most plentifully at the times of full moon and when the days are warm and sunny. This does not apply to the sea-urchins in the strait of Pyrrha, which are at their best in winter.

This 'strait of Pyrrha' can still be visited today. It is Aristotle's name for the funnel-like entrance from the open sea to the seawater lagoon of Kalloni on the Aegean island of Lesvos, ancient Lesbos, where Aristotle spent time in his forties. Altogether he makes five observations based on the waters of

Kalloni. Presumably he used to make expeditions there during his time on the island, seeing the catch of the fishermen for himself. Practical research in the modern sense, as here in the form of personal observation, was certainly one, if not his only, method of study.

Any supervisor of postgraduate students knows that pupils do not always agree with their teachers. Aristotle did not agree with Plato that skill in public speaking was merely a knack. Aristotle believed that there was a system to it. This made it a teachable skill, and as such worthy of a philosopher's attention. Aristotle wrote down his system, or a version of it. It included wisdom on how to prepare a not very educated audience by means other than the actual merits of the case:

> Things do not appear the same to a friendly and to a hostile hearer, or to an angry and to a calm hearer ... For if the juryman is friendly to the accused, he thinks the accused has done no injustice at all or only a slight injustice; but if he is hostile, quite the contrary is true ... Feelings are all those conditions that cause us to change and alter our attitude to judgments, conditions that imply pain or pleasure – for instance, anger, pity, fear, and all other such things.

Here Aristotle had in mind not least the need of a speaker to mould his audience in the law courts. In the ancient world this was one of the chief arenas for oratory. In fourth-century Athens there were speech-makers who specialized in producing expert speeches for the defence for a fee. In Athenian law the accused defended himself by delivering the bought speech in his own voice.

Copenhagen's superb museum of classical antiquities houses a full-length ancient statue of one of these speech-makers. A bearded man stands with his head bowed, his forehead creased in thought, his stage of life betokened by the sagging flesh of his arms and chest. This statue is a Roman copy. So are the many ancient busts which replicated the head alone of the same original figure. They all portray Demosthenes.

An exact contemporary of Aristotle, Demosthenes was a citizen of Athens and an orator politician of a common type in fourth-century Athens. He also took work as a writer of legal speeches. As seen in a later chapter, the Romans admired Demosthenes first and foremost as an orator. We are told that his oratory did not come naturally to him. He burnt the midnight oil composing his speeches. In old age he told a fellow Athenian about his voice exercises. They included correcting his lisp by reciting with a mouth full of pebbles, and, as a breathing exercise, talking while running or climbing. He practised expression and gesture in front of a mirror.

But Demosthenes owed his place in history to the political use to which he put his speaking skills. In speech after speech before the Athenian assembly, for years Demosthenes warned his city about a growing foreign threat. Two modern museums take up this story.

There is nothing unusual about archaeological museums housing human remains from ancient burials. However, tucked away in a storeroom in the Athens archaeological museum are boxes containing human bones of a special sort. Once (but no longer) on public display, these bones show clear evidence of wound marks. One sign of trauma has a special interest for me. The collection of antiquities in the north-east of England which I looked after as part of my former university job has an example of the weapon that might have caused it.

This particular wound is a small puncture to a skull, caused by a powerful blow to the head. It could have come from a weapon like the bronze butt of an ancient spear now displayed in Newcastle upon Tyne's Great North Museum. This butt is tipped with a small spike which made the butt a weapon in its own right if the shaft broke in battle. Its diameter almost matches the hole in the skull – the difference is one of a millimetre.

What makes this connection more than wild coincidence is, first, the Greek lettering embedded into this spike: 'MAK', in fourth-century BC forms. This must be an abbreviation of the word 'Mac[edonian]', as if the butt were government issue from the Macedonian state. Second, the skull belongs to one of the Greek victims of a battle in central Greece against the Macedonians – the threatening foreigners of many civic speeches by Demosthenes.

This battle, at a place called Chaeronea, where the skull was found, could have been Demosthenes' finest hour. In 338 BC a Macedonian army marched south. The news caused panic in Athens. Demosthenes gave a speech in the assembly which put courage into Athenian hearts. He then went as ambassador to the Thebans, in central Greece, and made them allies of Athens. His oratory roused them and their neighbours to armed resistance. Demosthenes himself fought on the allied Greek side in the ensuing battle.

Unfortunately, the Macedonians defeated the Greeks decisively. Their commander was their king, Philip, aided by his son and heir, the eighteen-year-old Alexander, in charge of the cavalry. Continuing military success would go on to bring Macedon to the top of the hard-power table. Macedonian might would also facilitate a dramatic spread of the soft power of Greek civilization – as far east as what is now Afghanistan. It is time to look more closely at the northern superpower whose rapid rise to hegemony conventionally closes the Classical phase of Greek history.

CHAPTER 11

'A BRILLIANT FLASH OF LIGHTNING'
ALEXANDER OF MACEDON

Once I came face to face not quite with Alexander the Great, but with what may be his oldest ancient likeness. I had received permission to mount wooden scaffolding in front of Tomb II at Vergina in northern Greece, erected so that archaeologists could get to grips with an ancient painting decorating the tomb's façade.

Anyone who has visited this tomb will know that it is a site of great sanctity for the modern Greeks. Wardens hush noisy Greek schoolchildren as if they are misbehaving in church. Close up the painting had been damaged by burial under a man-made mound of earth for twenty-three centuries. I knew what I was looking for, there in the centre: a splodge of pink – the garb of a young man on foot. Somewhere to his right, too abraded for me to see him clearly, was a rider on a horse.

For me this was a moment of great privilege: few people before or since have been this close to these two figures. Many experts believe that the tomb belonged to King Philip II of Macedon. This would make the two huntsmen featured in the centre of this painting, itself occupying such a prominent position above the tomb's entrance, most likely Philip himself, the older man on the horse, alongside young Alexander, his son and heir, going in for a kill on foot.

At that time I also saw, laid out in a showcase in the museum at nearby Thessaloniki, the cremated bones of the tomb's occupant – since put away from respect for a man regarded as a national hero by many Greeks today. Specialists have argued that these are Philip's bones.

They belong to a mature male in the right age range, who had a nick in the bone above the right eye-socket. This fits with an ancient description of Philip's war wounds: a lost eye, as well as a broken collar bone and a maimed hand and leg. If nothing else, this list shows what sort of monarchy based in northern Greece Philip headed for some twenty years (360/59 BC–336 BC): one where the king was first and foremost a war leader, a warrior who fought himself in the thick of the fray.

Well, there are archaeologists and historians who believe with a quasi-religious fervour that this is indeed the tomb of Philip. Others are not so sure. Unlike, say, the grave goods from Tutankhamun's burial place, those from Vergina, lavish and golden though many are, do not name the deceased. There are other troubling details – the dating of certain pots imported from Athens doesn't quite fit. This is a debate likely to rumble on.

On higher ground near the royal tomb archaeologists have found an ancient palace. It was organized Greek-style around two open courts. It once had an upper storey, commanding views over the Macedonian plain. The larger, monumental, court was framed by dining rooms for feasting. Some archaeologists now think that the builder of this palace was Philip II. Ancient writers show that Philip was a tremendous giver of parties. A famed diplomat as well as fighter, he knew all about the power of hospitality to soften up guests. His dinners dismayed some Greeks, being notorious for drunkenness, with the king himself leading the foolery.

Below the palace is a theatre. Alongside hunts and parties, the royal court had its cultured side. Among other skills for which Macedon's kings sought out Greek specialists, they had long liked Athenian-style theatricals. It may have been in this very theatre, two years after his victory at Chaeronea, that Philip, like a king in a Greek tragedy, met a sudden, violent and scandalous death, stabbed by a discarded male lover. Philip was an active bisexual, as we would say today; so, probably, was his son.

At the time, Philip was celebrating a festival attended by envoys of many foreign states, Greek but also non-Greek, since Macedonia was geographically on the cusp of Balkan regions that some southern Greeks considered 'barbarian'. Onlookers had just been treated to an extraordinary procession of statues – the twelve gods of Mount Olympus, to which Philip had added a thirteenth, of himself.

A century or so earlier, the Athenians had depicted themselves in the company of the gods on the sculptured frieze that ran round the outside of the Parthenon. Experts normally see this presumption as the vainglory of Athens in its pomp under Pericles: even the gods waited on the city. If Philip in 336 BC was bursting with regal pride when he approved this theatrical gesture, he had reason.

Philip's was one of those reigns in which a kingdom is transformed – like the rule of China's First Emperor, or Russia's Peter the Great. Hereditary royalty allows this chance. Philip's lineage claimed to be outsiders – Greeks of divine origin, in fact, since they alleged Heracles as their ancestor. Legend told of distant forebears who had gone north and won rule over non-Greek barbarians.

The story may or may not have been true. In any case, this lofty gene-alogy probably aimed at enhancing royal prestige among the Macedonians – and the (other) Greeks. In more recent times the Russian tsars claimed a Roman imperial origin. This outlandish ancestry aimed at setting them above the home-grown Russian noblesse, and to make the exotic Russian ruler more palatable to the more advanced states of the west – where early-modern Russians could be mocked as barbaric, as some Greeks mocked the Macedonians.

As Thucydides tells the story, the early Macedonians were essentially a band of warriors who used force to take over the lands of others. They had been European vassals of King Xerxes and, as seen, a Macedonian princess had wed a Persian prince. When Philip came to power in 360/359 BC, the kingdom was enfeebled, overrun by Balkan enemies, the Macedonians them-selves disunited. By a fluke of heredity, the ancient royal lineage produced a capable strongman to meet this crisis.

Inside the kingdom, Philip was the architect of two policies that did more than any other to reposition Macedon as a major power. First, ancient writers link him to the creation of a new army. Its key components were novel weapons and battlefield tactics, as well as a cutting-edge siege-train. It was probably Philip too who introduced the pay structure which we first hear of under his son Alexander. This incentivized poor Macedonian agriculturalists to commit full-time to military service. There was more:

> Philip used to train the Macedonians before battles, making them take their arms and march for three hundred stades [about 30 miles], carrying their helmets, shields, greaves, pikes, plus – in addition to

their arms – a stock of provisions and all the utensils necessary for daily life.

Apart from Sparta, citizen armies in Greek states did not usually train in this sort of way, which sounds almost modern. Nor did they fight all year round. Down in Athens, Demosthenes warned his fellow citizens about Philip's new way of fighting, that 'he draws no distinction between summer and winter, and that he has no season set apart for suspending operations'. What Philip had done was to create a lethal new combination: not only a militarized society traditionally primed for wars, but now a revolutionary new capability to win them.

Philip's second policy was to create an officer class based on talent. From this pool the king could not only command in battles but also had a supply of educated 'gentlemen' to serve as diplomats and proconsuls, once there were conquered territories to govern. The interesting thing about Philip is that he happily recruited non-Macedonians, including qualified Greeks, for this new meritocracy.

What was in it for such people? History is littered with royal servants hoping for self-advancement from a ruler offering gifts. An ancient inscription in handsome Greek letters found on the three-pronged peninsula east of modern Thessaloniki shows what rewards Philip distributed.

It gives details of Philip's allocation of landed estates in this area to a member of his officer class. 'Sine' was the name of one; 'Trapezus' another. The inscription dates from half a century later, when this man's grandson needed a later Macedonian king to reconfirm his title. This was required because the monarchy withheld complete security of tenure. Ultimately the land remained crown property. For each descendant of the original grantee to inherit, a new royal assent was needed. The system was a clever way of putting pressure on this class to serve well, not just now but also in the future.

As to how Philip came by these lands in the first place, the case of a Greek city called Olynthus is instructive. This city was an eastern neighbour of the Macedonians, sited on that same peninsula. When I visited the archaeological site, I was struck by the richness of the rolling farmland surrounding it. Americans dug here between the world wars. They uncovered the remains of neatly laid-out streets lined with terraced houses in which Greek citizen families lived lives of relative comfort – there was drainage; there were bathrooms.

They also found arrowheads. These were – once more – Macedonian state issue. In this case letters in Ancient Greek read 'Belonging to Philip'. In 348 BC Philip captured Olynthus and wiped it out. By right of conquest its farmland was now his, to be divided up into lots as gifts for his officers.

If some Greek bystanders aspired to join these robber barons, others were appalled: '[c]areless of what they had, they itched for what they had not, though they owned a whole section of Europe,' as one wrote sourly. So there was now, in Philip's reformed Macedon, a 'systemic' propensity for warmongering. Troopers needing pay, officers hungry for land, a kingship nurtured by military success: they all had a stake in identifying a new campaign.

After his victory at Chaeronea (338 BC), Philip was effectively master of a Balkan empire extending east to the Dardanelles and southwards to include most of mainland Greece. Some of this territory he ruled directly or through a viceroy, some of it, including the Greek states, through friendly regimes or at any rate (as at Athens) prudently cooperative politicians. In his appetite for further aggression, he now looked east.

In the fourth century BC the Persian Empire endured. There were no great new conquests, but the empire survived a revolt by provincial governors and recovered a long-insurgent province, Egypt. The ruling family kept its tight grip on the throne, and kings still displayed fortitude in war. Artaxerxes II must have been a successful ruler, managing to keep his throne for some forty-five years (from 405/4 to 359/8 BC). Once, returning home from campaigning in northern Iran,

> he dispensed with his horse and, with his quiver strapped to his back and shield in hand, personally led the column on foot as it marched through mountainous and precipitous country. This had such an effect on the rest of the army that they felt as if they had grown wings and had their burdens lifted, seeing as they did his determination and strength.

This kind of inspiring leadership of men was just what ancient writers repeatedly attributed to Alexander of Macedon. Still, Greek observers saw an underlying military decadence in Persia. Their view has to be accorded some credence, given what was to happen next.

When he was stabbed to death in 336 BC, Philip had already sent an advance force across the Dardanelles into Persian imperial territory in what is now north-western Turkey. He had also persuaded the cowed Greek states to supply troops for the army that was to follow, led by himself. A politician as well as a general, he had told them that now was the time to avenge Greece's gods for the destruction of their shrines by the impious Persians back in 480 and 479 BC.

After the Persians withdrew from Greece, the Athenians had built shattered blocks from the Persian burning of the Acropolis into its defensive wall – they are still visible today – as a memorial to the 'barbarian' sacrilege. Despite the passage of time, it would be wrong to think that the prospect of revenge had no traction among fourth-century Greeks.

The assassin's dagger brought an already-seasoned Alexander to the throne at the age of twenty. Within two years he had shown himself to be his father's son by a ferocious act of destruction. The Thebans to the north of Athens, misjudging the neophyte, decided to revolt. Alexander and his well-drilled men marched south like the wind: over 300 miles in twelve days. Theban stubbornness left him no choice, some said, but to lay siege to the city. It was 'stormed, plundered and razed to the ground'. The usual modern view of this ruthlessness was that Alexander needed a submissive Greece behind him if he were to pursue his father's Persian project.

The twenty-two-year-old Alexander's expedition against Persia joins the Trojan and Peloponnesian Wars as a creation, in the only form in which we can follow it today, of ancient men of letters. Of all the paraphernalia of ancient warfare – the archaeological evidence of arms and armour, encampments, victory monuments and so on, original documents such as troop dispositions or battlefield orders – little or nothing survives. The short-lived reign of Alexander – thirteen years – was, as one Roman historian wrote much later, 'a brilliant flash of lightning'.

It was in Roman times that the only ancient writers whose accounts of Alexander survive were writing. If they did not exactly stand on the shoulders of giants, they certainly sat in libraries surrounded by the works of predecessors. These in turn built on their predecessors, in a chain of armchair historians that reached back to the first writings of people alive in Alexander's day.

These first writers did include participants or, if not, writers who at least spoke to survivors, which is important, obviously. They wrote in Ancient Greek, whether because they were ethnic Greeks or Greek-educated Macedonians. Alexander's new subjects in Asia and Egypt left no accounts in their own languages of their experience of invasion and conquest.

On the other hand, since Macedonian power divided the Greek world bitterly, these first Greek writings – now lost – offered wildly varied versions of Alexander. We enter here, long before an American political commentator coined the expression, a smoky world of 'alternative facts'. Wherever Alexander comes out either too well or too badly in the surviving ancient writers, modern historians are not wrong to suspect the distant echoes of either the king's partisans or his enemies.

Scholars expend all the considerable ingenuity of their profession to get at the historical truth about Alexander. Even so, much depends, now as in ancient times, on where you stand in the first place. Already in the eighteenth century, learned Europeans wrestled with whether Alexander's prodigious career of conquest was a good or a bad thing – whether it was mainly about glory and plunder; whether in exchange for the undeniable violence he gave concrete benefits to the conquered; whether his treatment of Asiatics had anything to teach the Europeans in Mughal India, and so on.

The basic facts are agreed. Aged twenty-two, Alexander crossed the Dardanelles with an army of Macedonians and some Greek allies. At once resisted by a large Persian army, he achieved a decisive victory near Troy. Fighting his way through the interior, he reached south-east Turkey in November of the following year (333 BC). Here, near the ancient town of Issus, he was confronted for the first time by the Persian king himself, Darius III, at the head of an army larger than his own. As usual in his battles, Alexander led the cavalry charge; this broke the enemy line. Darius had his chariot turned and fled.

A cool-headed Alexander resisted the temptation to pursue Darius. To secure his territorial gains and protect his rear, he sought to neutralize Persian sea-power, based in the ports of the Phoenicians in what is now Lebanon. After successfully fighting his way down this coast, he then invaded Egypt, where Persian rule was unpopular.

Having made clear his empire-building intentions by leaving governors, tax collectors and garrisons among his new subjects in Asia, from Egypt Alexander retraced his steps through modern Syria and then turned east, into what is now northern Iraq. Here, in October 331 BC, on the dusty Mesopotamian plain, he met Darius with a new Persian army near Mosul, at ancient Gaugamela. For a third time Alexander won decisively, and for a second time Darius abandoned his chariot and fled.

Some specialists argue that by tradition the Persian king was perhaps more a bystander at his own battles, and that the uniqueness of his person required his withdrawal if the battle went ill. Inevitably, the Macedonians trumpeted this regal behaviour as cowardice. Whatever the case, Darius was the commander-in-chief of his army: to many on his own side, abandoning the field to save himself looked like poor generalship then – as it still does. His predecessor Artaxerxes II, the leader of men encountered just now, might have behaved differently.

With Darius on the run, Alexander was now in the heartlands of the Persian Empire. Glittering prizes were within reach – the rich royal cities of Babylon, Susa, Persepolis and Ecbatana. Alexander occupied them one by one, stripping the royal treasuries and eventually centralizing his vast haul of bullion in a Smaug-like trove at Ecbatana, in what is now north-west Iran.

After setting fire to the palace of Xerxes at Persepolis so as to back up his public claim that Greece had now been avenged, in 330 BC Alexander sent his Greek troops home. He himself was far from ready to admit 'mission accomplished'. The refugee Darius having been killed in a coup by his entourage, Alexander now set off to pursue the Persian royal kinsman who had claimed the Persian throne.

The next four years saw tough campaigning in Iran, Afghanistan and up into what is now Tajikistan, where he finally captured the Persian claimant. Afghanistan – the Greeks called it Bactria – was hard to pacify, then as now. To help matters, Alexander made a diplomatic marriage to Roxane, daughter of a local baron. He also founded a handful of Greek-style fortified cities in the region, settled with European veterans and indigenes. The point of these seems to have been above all strategic: a combination of bridgehead and bastion.

All these lands had belonged to Darius or his ancestors. In 326 BC Alexander invaded Pakistan, 'India' to the ancient Greeks, long lost to the Persian Empire. Based on the errors of Greek geographers, Alexander hoped to reach the ocean encircling, as he and they believed, the world.

Instead his men mutinied. They found a spokesperson in a Macedonian officer – the then holder, as it happens, of those estates of Sine and Trapezus. A furious Alexander was unable to budge his long-suffering men and had to turn back. He opted to sail down the River Indus and march back across southern Iran, with dreadful privations suffered by his troops in the deserts of that region.

In 324 BC a relentless Alexander was back in the old imperial heartlands. Discharging disgruntled Macedonian veterans and enlisting troops levied from his new Asian subjects, he had a new plan – an invasion of the Arabian peninsula.

Oil was not the attraction in those days, and the modern reader might wonder what had caught Alexander's eye – or rather, those of his scouts. The best ancient account, not untypically, gives both irrational and rational motives. The former was his 'insatiable thirst for extending his possessions'. The latter gives a glimpse for once of the calculated economic thinking behind Macedonian imperialism:

> The wealth of their [i.e. the Arabs'] country was an additional incitement – the cassia in the oases, the trees which bore frankincense and myrrh, the shrubs which yielded cinnamon, the meadows where nard grew wild . . . there were harbours everywhere fit for his fleet to ride in and to provide sites for new settlements to grow to great wealth and prosperity.

It was this lucrative luxury trade in spices and aromatics that Alexander and his entourage now eyed covetously. However, with plans well under way, shortly before his thirty-third birthday, in 323 BC, Alexander fell sick. Despite an ox-like constitution, this time he did not recover. Naturally, this being the court of a spectacularly successful ruler with many enemies, rumours of poison circulated.

I remember years ago being invited to listen to a fascinating presentation by trainee medics in a USA armed services hospital in Baltimore. By way of light entertainment they had an occasional lunchtime seminar for which they would be given in advance all the details (except the identity) of a famous person's death, and be asked to come up with a diagnosis.

This time it was Alexander, whose symptoms the ancient writers recorded in detail. Among the trainees there was no unanimity. One wondered about poison. Others leaned more towards a waterborne illness. Since he died at ancient Babylon, sandwiched between the sluggish waters of the Tigris and the Euphrates rivers, this does indeed seem quite a plausible cause of death, especially if the heavy drinking that ancient writers record had lowered his immune system.

When Alexander expired, his vast conquest-state stretched from today's northern Greece to today's Pakistan and Kashmir. Classicists can still be found who think that he had a long-term aim to advance Greek civilization in these lands. He would have used Graeco-Macedonian settlers to take the Greek way of urban living to the plains of Mesopotamia, the valleys of Afghanistan and so on.

In truth these new civic settlements seem to have been far fewer than ancient figures suggest – as few as nine, according to a recent study. As seen, in Alexander's lifetime these fortified outposts were tellingly concentrated among the belligerent peoples of the eastern frontier.

It is true that Alexander had had a Greek education. Philip had hired Aristotle, no less, to tutor his son. Alexander had a cultural outlook that in many ways was Greek. He loved the Greek theatre – actors followed his campaign. He staged Greek athletic contests for the army. He had Greek philosophers in tow. He kept a copy of Homer under his pillow supposedly – some scholars question this anecdote, which does indeed sound almost too good to be true. His official historian was a Greek, a kinsman and protégé of Aristotle, to whom the historian is said to have sent back 'observations from Babylon' for Aristotle's astronomical research – evidence for the continuing absorption by Greek culture of the older wisdom of the East, in this instance with the direct sanction of Alexander himself.

The young Alexander also acquired what seems to have been a personal fondness for the trappings and pastimes of the Persian royal court. To be sure, in part he was playing at what today would be called identity politics. This revealed itself in his sustained attempt to 'Persianize' his royal image. He used Persian culture to reach out to his Asian subjects and, among these, to one key group in particular – the high Persian aristocracy at the core of the fallen empire's governing elite. The support of these people could do much to build a new political consensus around the Macedonian conqueror.

Before his premature death, Alexander does not seem to have tried to learn Persian, but he took to wearing items of Persian regal dress, and started to hold court and give audiences in the Asiatic style of the vanquished Darius. Eventually he took two additional wives, both Persian royal princesses, and required eighty or so members of his officer class likewise to marry high-born Persians.

The classical writers detailed with horrified relish this apparent slide into Persian 'decadence'. It is hard to think of a historical parallel – perhaps as if the Spanish conquistador Pizarro, after having the pagan Inca emperor garrotted in 1533, had adopted his tasselled crown and expected people to approach him as well with gestures as if he were the divine Sun. According to one Greek contemporary of Alexander, 'myrrh was burnt before him, and other kinds of incense; and all the bystanders kept silent, or spoke only words of good omen, out of fear. For he was a very violent man, with no regard for human life.'

In fact, the burning of aromatics before the enthroned Persian king and a respectful silence seem to have been part of the normal procedure of Persian royal audiences. Here the ill-meant comment that follows suggests that this passage has something in common with modern 'fake news'.

How personally committed Alexander was to the Persian royal lifestyle is suggested by another cryptic passage from the same Greek writer, whose name was Ephippus. He claims that at his dinner parties Alexander was in the habit of dressing up as the Greek goddess of the hunt, Artemis. Like Artemis in Greek art, he would appear on a chariot as a feminine bow-hunter.

The Macedonian court went in for festive junkets, and Greeks dressing up as their gods was not unheard of at this time, both on and off the theatre stage. This ancient writer gives himself away, however, by adding the detail that Alexander on these occasions was dressed in his version of Persian regal costume. This involved flowing robes, of the kind that on men Greek writers derided as womanly.

Another Greek writer gives a clue to what lay behind this malicious tease. He tells of Alexander taking up chariotry and archery while in Asia – neither of them a traditional pursuit of Macedonian royalty. So the reality behind this alleged impersonation of Artemis may have been that Alexander, a keen huntsman himself, had decided to take his 'Persianizing' to a new level by learning to hunt in the traditional style of Persian kings, dressed, not as Artemis, but, even so, in the Persian regal dress that Greeks found effeminate.

The Persian kings were bow-hunters. They hunted in game parks from a moving chariot, which they would need to be able to get on and off during the chase, since they seem to have gone in for the kill on foot. The most prestigious prey was the king's opposite number in the animal kingdom, the Asian lion, now extinct in the wild, but which European travellers still saw prowling the outskirts of Baghdad in the seventeenth century.

In this second item of fake news about Alexander, that same writer – Ephippus – seems to have twisted a truth so as to present him as an upper-class Greek playboy whose behaviour at parties included cross-dressing and disrespecting the Greek gods. The story was credible to some Greeks because, on occasion, their upper classes really did behave in this way. As for the writer, there is an explanation for his malice. He was a refugee from the fall of Olynthus and therefore had good reason to hate the Macedonian royals.

Alexander might have had a personal liking for the customs of the Persian ruling class. In the Aegean world he was not alone if he felt some cultural sympathy for Persian ways. Ancient Greek writers liked to stereotype an opposition between 'good' Greeks and 'bad' Persians. Real-life Greek behaviour reveals a more cross-cultural reality. Rather surprisingly, Athenian vases show that fifth-century BC Athenians, the great victors of the Persian Wars, liked to wear items of Persian-style clothing, and to drink from vessels inspired by Persian designs. This bi-cultural approach by Alexander to ruling his empire lifts his imperialism somewhat above the run of ancient conquistadors.

The classical writers present Alexander as breaking new ground in another way – demanding worship as a god. Among political leaders of more recent times this kind of behaviour has a tin-pot aspect. One thinks of Turkmenistan's former president Saparmurat Niyazov, with his gold statue in the capital that revolved so that it always faced the sun, and who in 1999 renamed the months of the year after members of his family. Classicists who have accepted the ancient traditions about Alexander's quest for divinity have usually seen it as something shocking, a black mark against the historical figure and, more broadly, as a symptom of failings in Greek paganism which only the rise of a true faith, in the form of Christianity, could solve.

The actual facts where Alexander is concerned hinge on a handful of passages of Ancient Greek ceaselessly debated by the experts. Beyond these, there is the larger interpretation of a religious phenomenon. Did young Alexander personally believe in his divinity? Did he manipulate religious attitudes to enhance his political authority? Or did the initiative lie mainly with those doing the worshipping? Here the evidence is perhaps clearest. Asiatics were not involved. Instead, some Greek cities, including Athens, took formal decisions to venerate Alexander in his lifetime with the usual paraphernalia of Greek cult – the altar, the sacrifice, the prayers and so on.

Since readers might like to know why it is so tricky to establish the actual facts, here is an example. In winter quarters at Balkh in northern Afghanistan, in 327 BC Alexander experimented anew with the protocol of how he was to be approached when holding court. He tried to introduce into his Macedonian court Persian-style obeisance before the ruler. Some members of the entourage obliged; others balked; one laughed out loud watching others perform the gesture; Aristotle's kinsman refused the gesture altogether when his turn came. It was said that Alexander at the time tactfully chose not to notice.

The classical literati to whom we owe our portrait of Alexander were fascinated by this episode. In the Greek world, this act of obeisance, on your knees, head to the ground, was a gesture of mortal humility before a divine image. So it is clear that, at Balkh, resistance among the European entourage could have been on religious grounds.

The portrayal by ancient Greek writers, as we have it today, went further. It presented the episode as a significant step in a morality tale of Alexander's corruption by power and success. His head was now so turned that he sought worship as a god. This version was the one which, thousands of miles away in the Aegean, many Greeks chose to believe. Greek cities, including Athens, were now primed to offer Alexander what they had come to believe that he wanted.

They might have been right about what Alexander desired. An alternative is that this interpretation of the Balkh episode was circulated by Greek ill-wishers as, once more, a fake news story. Modern historians have long pointed out that the historical Alexander's motives could have been entirely secular. He sought further to conciliate the high Persian aristocracy by assuaging their sense of honour. He sought to do this by creating a semblance of greater equality between them and his European officer class (mostly Macedonians). When in the royal presence, Alexander wanted a level playing field. Elites of both groups were to perform the Persian-style obeisance – which was not an act of divine worship for Persians.

All this might seem remote from today's world. But there is an aspect to the debate about Alexander that is of more general human interest. In Alexander's day the religious outlook of the ancient Greeks blurred the line between humans and gods. An Athenian intellectual could tell King Philip that, if he conquered the Persians, 'there is nothing left for the king than to become a god'. Was this just flattery? Or did the Greek concept of what it was to be a 'god' have an elastic quality foreign to world religions today?

There again, some experts have wondered if there are modern-day behaviours which, if not exact analogies, might at least be suggestive. As well as the petty tyrannies of central Asia, the modern world has seen mass cults of living leaders, such as Chairman Mao.

Closer in time, at Donald Trump's election in 2016, commentators noted the quasi-religious character of the cult of personality around him. I myself saw TV interviews in which his American supporters made clear that for them the leader could do no wrong. Nor was the leader a remote and invisible force. Mr Trump was a tangible presence who might answer, if not your prayer, then your tweet.

Fuelling the suspension of disbelief among these Trump-enthusiasts was the conviction that the leader would deliver salvation from economic woes. In ancient times it was precisely the ability of powerful kings to offer practical protection – from human enemies, from forces of nature such as bad harvests and consequent famine – that allowed Greek communities to place them on the same level as gods. Greeks in the new world that Alexander ushered in bestowed on some of the Graeco-Macedonian rulers who followed him the same byname that they conferred on some Greek gods: 'Saviour'.

How much Alexander actively encouraged Greeks to worship him and how much he had this worship thrust upon him by Greeks themselves will continue to be debated by his modern historians. As for his legacy, since his reign was cut short, Alexander's version of an imperial state was at best a work in progress. It is slightly unfair to claim, as some scholars try to do, that his bold experiment with 'Persianizing' was a failure.

What is true, as the next chapter tries to show, is that his real legacy lay elsewhere.

CHAPTER 12

GAME OF THRONES, OR THE WORLD
AFTER ALEXANDER

A small-screen event of the early twenty-first century was an award-winning adaptation of a series of fantasy novels called *Game of Thrones*. Set in an imaginary land curiously similar to mainland Britain in the map adorning the opening titles of the TV series, the plot hinges on the violent competition for an overarching kingship among an interrelated group of noble lords and ladies ruling regional strongholds at varying removes from the royal capital.

Many historians, and indeed members of the public, will relate easily to this world. A basic principle of its organization is the lineage of hereditary rulers – 'House Stark', 'House Lannister' and so on. These lineages embody common stereotypes or aberrations of family life – the scheming mother-in-law, the dysfunctional teenager, incestuous siblings.

If the social and political context of the series looks superficially familiar, this is not only because dynasties are in some sense family life writ large, but also because much of the world has been organized into states ruled by hereditary families for much of history. So in the TV series many of us feel a certain conversancy with the world of palaces and thrones, the finery and ceremonial that display the hierarchy of social ranking in the so-called Seven Kingdoms.

With the swords but minus the sorcery, the upheavals in the ancient world following Alexander's death would not seem alien to fans of *Game of Thrones*. For a quarter-century or more different warlords, mainly the late

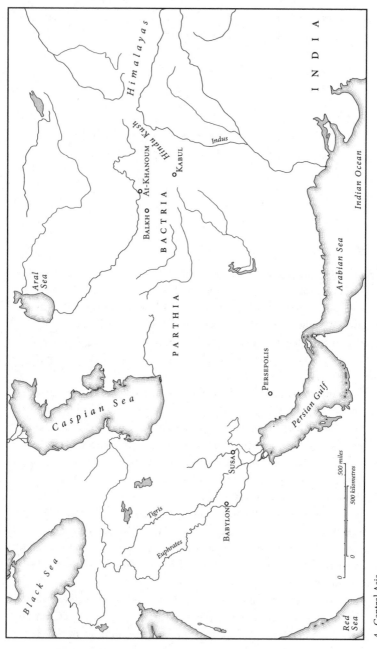

4. Central Asia.

king's Macedonian officers, fight each other all over the map of the ancient Near East. At stake for the most ambitious is the supreme kingship of Alexander's whole empire, for others the lesser project of carving off a slice of territory fit for a king for themselves.

The warlords form alliances and intermarry. Naturally they also kill each other, on and off the battlefield. Little mercy is shown the weak. Alexander's failure to secure the hereditary succession lay at the heart of this drama. His vulnerable widow and posthumous son, as well as the half-brother with a mental disorder who briefly succeeded him, are all slaughtered.

Out of this bewildering succession of marching armies and encampments, battles on land and sea, sieges of cities and so on, a post-Alexander political map started to emerge in the first decades of the 200s BC – well over a generation after the 'brilliant flash of lightning' had vanished.

This new world – conventionally called 'Hellenistic' – was inherently unstable. If there was constancy, it did not reside in unchanging rule over a given territory. The need for prestige and for booty meant that royal armies never really stopped fighting over this land or that. For the next two centuries, in what is now Turkey, the Levant and the Middle East, regions repeatedly changed rulers.

Permanence, such as it was, came from the new ruling families. Instead of a supreme king, the Hellenistic world got used to several kings. The male progeny of three of Alexander's officers turned out to be particularly good at transmitting this regal power from one generation to the next. From Ptolemy, Alexander's childhood friend, descended nine generations of rulers. Descendants of another officer, Seleucus, held on to power for ten generations. A third, Antigonus, founded only five generations of kings. Their rulership was the first of the three to be snuffed out by the Romans.

These military lineages each managed to retain a territorial core, a splinter of Alexander's imperial state won by a dynastic ancestor in the so-called Successor wars triggered by Alexander's death. For the Ptolemies this core was Egypt; it was Syria and, at first, Mesopotamia as well, for the Seleucids; and Macedon for the Antigonids.

The families held on to power with the help of other groups of stakeholders. Before the Soviets invaded Afghanistan, French archaeologists were busy uncovering an ancient fortified city on the country's northern frontier. One immediately striking feature of the published plans and photographs is the emphasis on protection from attack. On two sides flowed important rivers at their confluence. As well as water, all round the settlement ran a massive fortification of thick walls and towers of baked mud brick. Inside, finally, there was higher ground and a citadel as well as a lower town.

Some of the inhabitants of this place – known as Ai-Khanoum from today's nearby village – were clearly Greek. I mentioned in the prologue a travelling exhibition of 'treasures' from Ai-Khanoum doing the global rounds in the early twenty-first century. At the time of writing it is in Tokyo; I saw it in Amsterdam. Two finds stood out for me.

One was that waterspout shaped like a Greek theatrical mask, which I talked about earlier. The other remarkable find was an inscription, in proper Ancient Greek, carved in letters of the early third century BC on a block of local stone. On Afghanistan's border with Tajikistan that is remarkable enough. No less striking is the content: a copy for these faraway Greek settlers of a list, inscribed back home on the Temple of Apollo at Delphi, of famous advice from Greek sages: 'When a child show yourself well-behaved; when a young man, self-controlled; in middle age, just; as an old man, a good counsellor; at the end of your life, free from sorrow.' This ancient life coaching has aged well. Did fathers, or teachers, once stand before this stone to improve the Greek-speaking youngsters in their charge? On the site itself, another building which you have to pinch yourself to remember has been found in Afghanistan, not in Greece, is a Greek-style gymnasium of the typical plan, as seen in the last chapter: a large square courtyard for physical exercise, framed by buildings.

By the 200s BC, the gymnasium in a Greek city had become a standard institution of secondary education for the sons of better-off citizens who could pay the fees. Wherever it existed, as here, it is fairly safe to assume a social crème de la crème within the local community of families, families Greek in language and culture, although, in a place like ancient Ai-Khanoum, not necessarily in ethnic heritage.

The ancient name of this place is uncertain. Whoever the European settlers were who arrived here perhaps a generation after Alexander's death, around 300 BC, they did so on the coat-tails of his greatest imperial legacy, Macedonian military supremacy. Seleucus obtained this portion of Alexander's empire; one of his captains may have been the mysterious founder whose Greek name we know from that same inscription, 'Cineas'.

The French found dwelling houses that were not Greek but oriental in plan. They found temples which do not look Greek either. So there can be no doubt that the Greek settlers and their descendants lived here alongside Asian people.

Many of the ten thousand or so Macedonians discharged by Alexander in Mesopotamia in 324 BC had taken up with Asian women on campaign and had children by them. So it can safely be assumed that mixed marriage with local people, following the example of Alexander himself, was common from the start of this new wave of ancient Greek migration.

The pioneers from the Aegean world who settled in these new cities under the protection of Alexander or his Macedonian successors were tempted with plots of farmland in return for an expectation or requirement of military service. Fourth-century BC thinkers like Aristotle were probably not the only Greeks who imagined the perfect Greek-style state as a place where the hard work on the citizen farm, as in Sparta, was done by foreign serfs:

> Those who till the soil should best of all, if the ideal is to be stated, be slaves, not of the same ethnic group or spirited in character (for thus they would be both serviceable for their work and safe to abstain from revolt), but as second best they should be barbarian dependents of a similar nature.

Lack of evidence makes it hard to say whether conditions were this Helot-like in practice on the Greek settler farms of Asia and the Nile valley. But often, perhaps routinely, the farmhands must indeed have been local peasants, like their modern counterparts, the Qualang Pashtuns who tend the arable valleys of modern Afghanistan, or Egypt's fellahin.

So the settlers were, in one sense, economic migrants. They included army veterans, among them thousands of Greeks who fought for pay as mercenaries. Many were exiles from their home cities, where they had been on the losing side in Greek civil strife. For all these people, Alexander's conquests opened up new opportunities overseas, where the king could offer new farms to replace the confiscated homesteads of their old lives.

Founding a city and naming it after yourself was a regal tradition which went back to Philip. His 'City of Philip' (Philippopolis) survives as modern Plovdiv in Bulgaria.

Seleucus and his successors in particular were active as city-founders. The names of these new towns were memorials to the royal lineage long after their founders were dead. Antakya in south-easternmost Turkey still hints at its original name 'Antiocheia', Antioch, after Antiochus, the son and heir of the first Seleucus.

Apart from the self-advertisement derived from giving the royal name to a new city, there was the military aspect, as seen with Alexander. The male citizens were liable to call-up. The kings were also interested in maximizing the tax which they could cream off their lands. They seem to have viewed their kingdoms essentially as a profit-generating estate, to be run as efficiently as possible by an overall manager in the mould of a factor for a great estate in more recent times.

One can imagine tough characters entrusted with great responsibility in return for huge personal rewards. Finds of Egyptian papyri have revealed the figure of Apollonius, who served the grandson of the first Ptolemy as his *dioiketes*, a title derived from the Ancient Greek verb 'to manage a house'. In effect he was Ptolemy III's 'finance minister'. His writ extended well beyond Egypt to what in the third century BC was a very significant Ptolemaic empire overseas, including Cyprus and possessions in what is now southern Turkey and as far away as the north coast of the Aegean Sea.

Under this Apollonius in Egypt proper there were regional managers whose orders required them to take whatever practical steps were needed to ensure that all the arable land in the Nile valley was fully cultivated, such as delivering sufficient water for irrigation, listening to farmers' complaints and so on. In return King Ptolemy gave Apollonius, who presumably came from a Greek migrant background, a huge estate of over 10 square miles in the rich agricultural basin of the modern Fayum, south-west of Cairo.

Seleucus and his successors may have applied the same way of thinking – a kind of household economics of which Mrs Thatcher might have approved – to the business of founding cities. As well as in the frontier lands of Afghanistan, they seem to have planted these Greek-style new towns in rich but under-urbanized regions such as Syria and Mesopotamia, where barter rather than payment by coin had been the norm in Persian times.

The new urban markets were meant to promote a cash economy by introducing silver coins from the royal mint in exchanges with surrounding peasants. The cities recycled the coin to pay royal taxes. The Seleucid kings

1. The Greek goddess of grain, Demeter, despatches a demi-god in a winged chariot to teach agriculture to humankind. This scene features on an Athenian vase now in the Louvre, from around 470 BC.

2. Emperor Hadrian (AD 117–138) defends civilization from the barbarians. This modern plaster cast in Rome is taken from a marble statue from Crete, now in the Istanbul Archaeological Museum.

3. A young male with Minoan-style locks leaps over a bull. This fragment of a wall painting was uncovered in the excavation of an ancient Egyptian palace at modern Tell el-Dab'a. Here, the colours have been digitally restored by Clairy Palyvou. The painting is thought to date from roughly 1473–1458 BC.

4. One of the earliest texts in the new script which the ancient Greeks adapted from the Phoenicians. Scratched onto the shoulder of a wine jug from Athens, late 700s BC, it reads: 'He who of all the dancers now performs most daintily...'

5. Two armies of Greek heavy infantrymen about to collide as they march into battle to the sound of pipes. This scene is from a pottery jug made in Corinth about 640 BC, showing what at the time was a new style of group fighting in tight formation.

6. The remains of the paved haulage across the Isthmus which the Corinthians built around 600 BC to facilitate, and profit from, east–west trade.

7. An unfinished Greek-style temple (late 400s BC) commissioned by the city of Segesta, or Egesta, a pre-Greek community in Sicily which went on to adopt (and adapt) cultural traits from neighbouring Greek settlers.

8. The so-called Tomb of the Leopards at Tarquinii: an Etruscan tomb-chamber of about 480 BC showing men and women sharing couches as they recline at a banquet.

9. In the depiction on his tomb, Xerxes I, bearded and carrying a bow, stands on a platform-like throne supported by two rows of figures representing different groups of imperial subjects.

10. A modern lifesize replica of an ancient Athenian war galley with three banks of oarsmen per side (a trireme). Trialled at sea in the 1980s, the *Olympias* belongs to the Hellenic Navy and is now in a dry dock in Piraeus, Greece.

11. The so-called Ear of Dionysius, the most spectacular of the ancient quarries of Syracuse. The Syracusans kept Athenian prisoners of war in cruel conditions in one of these quarries after the failure of an Athenian expedition to Sicily in 413 BC.

12. A depiction of two actors holding their performance masks on an Athenian vase of about 400 BC. The club and the lion's head show that the left-hand figure took the role of Heracles.

13. A rare butt of cast bronze, all that survives from a spear made in the late 300s BC. The Ancient Greek inscription, MAK, identifies it as probably Mac(edonian) and perhaps state issue.

14. A stone water spout in the form of the type of mask worn by ancient comic actors, from Ai-Khanoum, an ancient Greek settlement in Afghanistan, early 100s BC.

15. Athena fights in a battle between the Greek gods and a primitive race of super-strong monsters, the Giants. This is probably an allegory of the threat to Greek civilization posed by invading Celts in the 200s BC. This depiction is from a monumental altar at Pergamum of 197–158 BC, now in Berlin.

16. The Tomb of the Scipios. Shown here are the sarcophagus of Scipio Barbatus, consul in 298 BC, with its two inscriptions, and the plaque with the epitaph of Paulla Cornelia, who was buried behind.

17. A rare scene of fighting between Roman troops with flat oval shields and Macedonians with round shields, under one of which slumps a dead infantryman (bottom right). This features on a monument celebrating a decisive Roman victory over the last Macedonian king in 168 BC and is now in Delphi Museum.

18. A marble statue of Livia Drusilla, the influential wife of Augustus and an exemplar of old-fashioned Roman morals. Here she is enfolded in the demure uniform of the Roman matron: a cloak which could be used as a partial veil, an undergarment reaching to the ground and a loose overgarment with sleeves for added modesty.

19. The largest fragment of an ingenious Greek-made mechanical calculator, the so-called Antikythera mechanism, which sank around 60 BC in a vessel laden with Greek artworks probably destined for the Roman luxury market.

20. The theatre at the Lycian city of Patara (south-west Turkey) which a local benefactress, Vilia Procla, repaired and provided with awnings around AD 147.

21. A posthumous head of Pompey the Great (died 48 BC) now in the Ny Carlsberg Glyptotek, Copenhagen. It was probably commissioned for the family tomb in Rome by his aristocratic descendants, who included Lucius Calpurnius Piso Frugi Licinianus, a claimant to the throne killed in AD 69.

22. A god with water flowing from his outstretched arms rescues a parched Roman army fighting Germanic invaders by miraculously sending rain, probably in AD 172. This scene features on the Column of Marcus Aurelius, Rome (about AD 185).

23. The ruins of the Roman amphitheatre at Lyon, where Christians were punished by exposure to wild animals in AD 177.

24. Constantine, the first Christian emperor, gazes heavenwards. This is part of a colossal statue now in the Capitoline Museum, Rome.

25. The sparkling mosaic dome of the fifth-century AD Christian church in Ravenna, Italy, now known as the Mausoleum of Galla Placidia (died 450).

26. Louis XIV's finance minister Nicolas Fouquet had himself painted as Hercules on a ceiling in his château of Vaux-le-Vicomte, France, late 1650s.

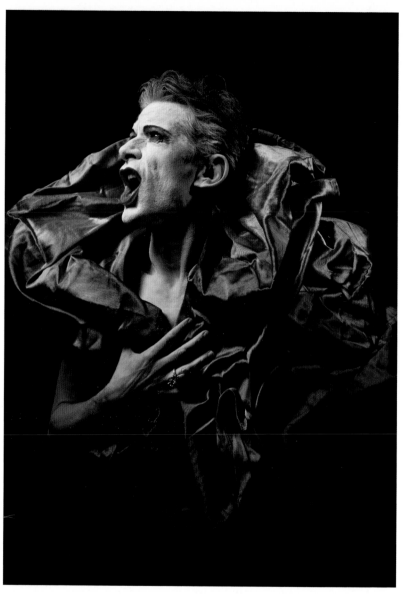

27. François Testory performing *Medea (Written in Rage)* at The Place, London, October 2017.

then had silver to pay for their outgoings in the more monetized Mediterranean – above all the wages of their troops. They regularly used armies, among other military operations, to contest with their Ptolemy cousins down in Egypt the disputed border region of what is now the Beqaa valley, modern Lebanon's chief agricultural district, famed in some circles today for Château Musar, Lebanon's top wine estate.

Apollonius was what now might be called a technocrat, a member of a technically skilled elite. As well as ordinary soldiers, this was the other type of migrant from Greek lands whom the Ptolemies and Seleucids sought to attract. These Greeks had the education and know-how to manage an economy, as well as to supervise production of strategic necessities, especially the paraphernalia of war. To help entice such Greeks to emigrate, in turn these early kings sought to present a cultured face to the old Aegean world. As rivals, as it were, for the same hands, each royal lineage sought to create the most brilliant royal capital.

Alexander founded only one city in the eastern Mediterranean, Alexandria in Egypt. This is now a rather dilapidated place of faded glories since Egypt's General Nasser 'encouraged' its Greek population to leave after 1952. Those Greeks were the remnants of a Greek presence in the city stretching back to the first settlers under Alexander, whose statue still adorned the forlorn premises of the old Greek school when I visited in 1995. The second and third Ptolemies deliberately promoted what was then still a young city as a capital of culture, of the Greek – meaning more or less the Athenian – kind.

Like that of Roman London, Alexandria's ancient past is buried beneath centuries of continuous occupation. There is little now to see apart from underground cemeteries. I remember in one of these tombs being struck by a Greek wall painting of an olive tree, its fruit a staple of Greek life which the incomers must have yearned to cultivate in their new home. In choosing the site, Alexander may have mainly had in mind the potential for a major Mediterranean harbour, one linked by natural waterways to the Egyptian interior. He would have had imports and exports in mind, and the duties that he could levy on these goods.

For the ancient city's lost architectural splendours we rely now mainly on Greek writings. A Greek geographical writer from the Black Sea region who lived in Alexandria just after the death of the last Ptolemaic ruler in 30 BC has this to say:

And the city contains most beautiful public precincts and also the royal palaces, which constitute one-fourth or even one-third of the whole circuit of the city; for just as each of the kings, from love of splendour, was wont to add some adornment to the public monuments, so also he would invest himself at his own expense with a residence, in addition to those already built.

The early Ptolemies also invested heavily in intellectual capital. Ptolemy I, Alexander's friend, established what is best described as a state-funded institute for advanced studies: 'The Museum is also a part of the royal palaces; it has a public walk, a portico with seats, and a large house, in which is the common mess-hall of the men of learning who share the Museum.'

To complement this institution of the 'Museum' the Ptolemies started to amass a library which aspired to contain the best of Greek writings up to that time. In the mid-200s BC one of Alexandria's Greek men of learning, Callimachus, produced what must have been one of the first-ever works of its kind, a catalogue of this library.

In 120 books, this was a pioneering exercise in what nowadays is called bibliography, the systematic description of books, arranged by subject matter. The overall heading gives in effect the mission statement of the library: 'Tables of Those Who Were Outstanding in Every Phase of Culture and Their Writings'. An academic myself, I cannot resist quoting this tetchy fault-finding by a Greek scholar two centuries later:

Seeing at once that neither Callimachus nor the grammarians of Pergamum [a rival library] had written accurately about him [Dinarchus, an Athenian orator and speechwriter], moreover that they had done no research on him and had missed the mark in reference to his most outstanding works.

With such facilities, the Alexandrian scholars produced groundbreaking research, with outcomes still with us today. They produced the first standard editions of Homer. The scholars compared different written versions of the two poems, evaluated the divergences, and produced corrected editions. Copied and recopied over the centuries, these form the basis for today's canonical texts of the original Homeric Greek.

There was also a dark side to the inquiries of the Alexandrian intelligentsia, to judge from this claim by a Roman doctor:

Herophilus and Erasistratus did this [anatomical study of human bodies] in by far the best way when they cut open live criminals they received out of prison from the kings and, while breath still remained in these bodies, they inspected those parts which nature had previously kept enclosed.

These two Greeks worked under royal patronage at Alexandria as doctors and medical researchers. Apologists for the ancient Greeks have naturally disliked this unwelcome evidence for the inhumane practice of human vivisection. If true, as is generally accepted nowadays, the criminals handed over by the Ptolemies to their scientists would certainly have been non-Greek and most probably native Egyptians, whom at least some of the Graeco-Macedonian settler class tended to see, and treat, as inferiors.

The existence of such colonial attitudes is suggested in a Greek letter preserved on a papyrus from Egypt. In it an indigenous employee in royal service complains of maltreatment:

They have treated me with contempt because I am a barbarian. I therefore request you, if you please, to order them to let me have what is owed to me and in future to pay me regularly, so that I do not die of hunger because I do not speak (or act) like a Greek.

Of course this might be a false charge of racism by a vexatious complainant and a single document, revelatory though this one is, hardly does justice to a complicated story of social and cultural interaction between settlers and settled, which modern experts are still trying to piece together. As in Asia there were mixed marriages, enough of them for a Roman writer of the later first century BC to record a claim that 'the Macedonians who hold Alexandria in Egypt . . . have degenerated into . . . Egyptians'. Clearly, this is not an unprejudiced opinion.

In 2001 the British Museum put on temporary display a colossal granite statue found in the shallow seas off modern Alexandria. It shows a second-century BC ruler of the Ptolemaic lineage in the traditional pose and costume of a pharaoh, complete with a headdress of the kind worn by Tutankhamun in the famous gold mask from his tomb.

So, in time, cultural interaction between the royal court and Egyptian culture hybridized the Ptolemaic royal image, once purely Greek. Presumably some contemporary viewers might have seen this statue as a Ptolemaic homage to the ancient civilization of Egypt. Archaeologists think that it stood in front of the lighthouse at the entrance to Alexandria's port: in full view of everyone coming or going by sea.

That complaint of maltreatment dates about a decade before the end of the long reign of the second Ptolemy (282–246 BC), the son who succeeded Alexander's childhood friend, Ptolemy I, in a successful transmission of regal power from the founder to his progeny. A striking feature of the son's rule was his queen. Five centuries later, for one Greek writer, she had still not shaken off her aura of scandal: 'Ptolemy was in love with his sister Arsinoe, and married her, flat contrary to the traditions of Macedonia, but agreeably to those of his Egyptian subjects.'

This marriage turned out to be the first of a series of full-sibling marriages among the Ptolemies. Greek writers thought that the Ptolemies were copying the Egyptian pharaohs of old. Ptolemy and Arsinoe consummated their incestuous marriage; their son succeeded his father as king. The Ptolemies like all ruling lineages gave prominence to royal women, in the last analysis because the transmission of hereditary power depended on the female womb. Since a sister's children were potential heirs, Ptolemy had kept his inheritance united by marrying Arsinoe. This, rather than the supposed practices of Egypt's former rulers, may be the real reason for the incestuous matches of the Ptolemies.

Arsinoe is a significant historical figure in her own right. Another text in the treasure trove of ancient documents on stone that is the Epigraphical Museum in Athens makes an extraordinary reference to her political influence over her brother-husband. It records a motion passed by the Athenian citizen assembly in 266 BC. This mentions that Ptolemy in the treatment of mainland Greece 'followed the policies of his ancestors and of his sister'.

What lay behind this reference is not really understood, but it makes history as the first open acknowledgement in a public document of the power of a Macedonian princess to influence state policy. In Shakespeare's play *Antony and Cleopatra*, Charmian describes her royal mistress's suicide in 30 BC as a deed 'well done and fitting for a princess descended of so many royal kings'. She might have added 'and royal queens'. These included Arsinoe and, very probably, the mother of this Cleopatra, the famous queen who was the last of the Ptolemaic lineage to rule in Egypt.

The royal palaces of Alexandria sank beneath the sea in the early Middle Ages, along with other ancient traces of Ptolemaic Alexandria's glories. To get an impression of the dazzling effects that Hellenistic rulers sought to create when they adorned their capitals, today's most rewarding archaeological site is in north-western Turkey.

Here a late-coming ruling family of Greek-speaking generalissimos took advantage of Seleucid difficulties in the mid-200s BC to establish themselves as independent rulers. They based themselves on a spectacular natural feature – a rearing massif of andesite rock which very obviously makes a natural fortress to anyone who sets eyes on it. Pergamum was the ancient name of this place.

The ancients called this nouveau lineage the Attalidae, after Attalus I, who ruled from 241 to 197 BC. For security the rulers established their palace quarter on the summit of the massif. This contained not just royal buildings, but sacred precincts, a library and a group of well-built granaries. Today's visitor walking through the debris of huge man-made terraces and the monuments that stood on them can sense the scale of this ancient undertaking, and enjoy the commanding views which made the pristine architecture visible from far and wide.

The museums in Berlin where many finds by the German excavators are housed hint at the stylish luxury of the royal court here. From one of the palaces, now reduced to stubs of walls, comes a fragment from a floor surface made of cubes of coloured stone. A skilled artist has handled them like paint to produce a brightly coloured image of a screeching bird from a species nowadays as familiar to Londoners, thanks to escaped pets, as it was once to Alexander's troops as they marched through Central Asia. In all the brilliance of its green, blue and red plumage, here we have a mosaic of an Asian parakeet.

Another archaeological find, of an altogether different order, has been hailed as 'one of the finest works in the history of world art'. On site you can still visit its huge footprint of 380 square feet or so. With permission from the then Ottoman sultan, the German archaeologists crated up the marble remnants for partial reassembly in a Berlin museum. Here visitors see something extravagant, fantastic even: a majestic flight of steps mounting a podium, round the outside of which runs a sculptured frieze over 7 feet high writhing with men and women in combat.

The latest theory is that this dramatic structure was meant to represent the heavenly palace of the king of the gods, Zeus. As you mounted the steps, flanked on both sides by the mêlée, the fighting would have seemed to continue to heaven's very portals. This battle was a mythical near-catastrophe, the assault on Zeus and his fellow Olympians by a primitive race of super-strong monsters, the Giants. In the end Zeus the almighty, here a magnificent figure who floors his assailants, prevails.

For the Pergamene people of the time, the meaning of the allegory was probably not in doubt. The bestial assailants stood for a strange people from the north who threatened the Aegean Greeks for a century or so. An ancient account of their attack on a town in central Greece in 279 BC conveys the terror inspired by this new foe: 'every male they put to the sword, and there were butchered old men equally with children at their mothers' breast. The more plump of these ... babes the Gauls killed, drinking their blood and eating their flesh ..'

Greek and Roman writers called the highly mobile peoples in central Europe by various names. A year after the descent on mainland Greece, a large group of these Gauls or Celts managed to cross the Dardanelles into Asia Minor. Much later, contained in what is now the region around Ankara and abandoning their marauding lifestyle, their descendants became the Galatians of the New Testament.

In earlier days, Attalus I and his son and successor, Eumenes II, had earned the gratitude of the settled populations of ancient Turkey's western seaboard by meeting, and defeating, these Gauls in battle. In fact it was his share of these victories which gave Attalus I the confidence to assume the Greek title of king, with its implied parity of status with the pre-existing kings of Macedonian stock. Eumenes II (ruled 197–158 BC) commissioned the great monument, which functioned as a giant open-air altar. Viewers could draw their own conclusions about who among the sculptured combatants stood for the Pergamene king.

Some scholars think that the Pergamene kings sought to pose as protectors from 'barbarians', not just of their region, but of a more generalized 'Greek identity'. Either the father or the son set up an offering of statues of defeated Gauls on the Athenian Acropolis. This is sometimes read as an attempt by an Attalid king to make the analogy between Attalid victories against the Celts and the famous Greek successes against the Persians. The Acropolis already displayed various mementoes of these Persian Wars, such as the supposed chair from which an incredulous Xerxes had watched the destruction of his fleet at Salamis.

It seems unlikely that either the Attalids or the older royal lineages, any more than Alexander himself, tried to spread the Greek way of life for its own sake in their domains. Be that as it may, in this Hellenistic world, dominated politically and culturally by Greek-speaking royal courts, an Egyptian or Asiatic who wanted to get on in life could see for himself the direction of cultural travel.

Learning to speak Greek was the key starting point of any attempt to claim a Greek identity. Some ethnic Greeks were now coming to think that the essence of Greekness was a Greek education. To pass as culturally Greek meant mastering the language. In turn the language itself slowly evolved in a way that eased its spread among an increasingly diverse population. A standard Greek, simpler to use in real life, now started to overtake the old dialects.

The pace of change was slow and uneven. To judge from their inscriptions, the Spartans held on to some of their Doric brogue as late as the first century BC. In the next century, the educated Greek-speakers of Near Eastern origin who composed the Christian Gospels couched them in the so-called 'common language'.

As well as a Hellenistic East, there was a Hellenistic West. In 2015 I found myself on an archaeological site in northern Sicily paying close attention to an information panel explaining the mysterious design on an ancient mosaic floor in front of me. It turned out that the criss-crossing curves framing a much smaller sphere at the centre are a unique ancient depiction of a Greek astronomical instrument.

The armillary sphere was a three-dimensional model of the heavens. As here, it had a ball at its centre standing for the earth, encased by a framework of bronze rings representing the main motions of the heavenly bodies around it (as we now know but the Greeks did not, these in fact rotate around the sun).

The Greek astronomers who invented the prototype lived and worked in Alexandria in the third and second centuries BC. Nothing could show more directly the fascination of the post-Alexander Greek world with scientific gadgets, or the advances of Greek astronomers of the time, or the learned culture that the Hellenistic Sicilians shared in common with the kingdom of the Ptolemies. As ever, these two regions were netted together by ancient mariners plying the coast whenever they could, the open sea if needs must.

The ancient house where I came across this mosaic was built in the Greek manner – rooms arranged round all four sides of a square courtyard framed by colonnades of Ionic columns. Running the length of one of these colonnades beneath the floor, archaeologists found an elongated, bath-shaped, cistern. This was a Phoenician, not a Greek, type of water-tank.

Twelve or so miles east of Palermo, this ancient community – called Soluntum – had begun on another site as a settlement of the Phoenicians. At the date of this culturally hybrid house – the second century BC – the way of life here, like the population, had long fused non-Greek and Greek, as happened in Ai-Khanoum.

By then the last great flowering of ancient Sicily had already been and gone. In the previous century, a Greek royal court flourished on the island, one to rival those of the east in riches and cultural patronage. Hieron II of Syracuse (about 271 to 216 BC) was the latest of Greek Sicily's many strongmen. His kingship was typically Hellenistic in its military origins. A successful general, he used the prestige of his victory over a rampaging band of Italian mercenaries to have himself declared king by a grateful population.

In Syracuse itself, Hieron's memory is perhaps most tangible in the Greek theatre. This magnet for today's tourists already existed in Hieron's time, but the king enlarged the seating capacity – what you see today is thought to be his work. On the back of the horizontal gangway halfway up the auditorium, a series of inscriptions in large Greek letters preserves the royal names which he gave to the different wedges of the upper level of seats. Still clearly legible is the labelling for the wedge 'of Queen Philistis'. She was a Syracusan noblewoman who brought Hieron the support of the city's old Greek families.

Major public works of this sort presuppose a well-supplied treasury. Some 75 miles away, on the western edge of Hieron's former domain, is the archaeological site of ancient Morgantina, met with already. Here the American excavators have identified two granaries erected in Hieron's time. The better preserved is a massive structure over 300 feet long, built of sturdy masonry and with buttresses as if to withstand the pressure of grain piled against the walls.

Archaeologists suspect that Hieron built these granaries to stockpile local grain levied as a tax in kind from his subjects here. They base these suspicions on the allusions in much later Roman writings to something called the Law of Hieron. This lost document seems to have laid down Hieron's rules for collecting taxes levied on agriculture. Hieron demanded a tenth of the harvest. At the threshing floor, piled with the harvested sheaves, tax collector and farmer reached, according to one scholar's perhaps rather rosy picture, a 'gentleman's agreement' over how much the government could take.

Hieron seems systematically to have overhauled agriculture in his eastern half of the island. In doing so he had the same hard-nosed aim as the Ptolemies: to maximize the revenues from the chief source of royal taxation, the land. Eventually stored grain from Morgantina and other regional depots would have found its way to the king's central granary on the offshore island of Ortygia, heart of ancient Syracuse. From here Hieron could dispose of it overseas, by sale or gift.

In Syracuse a particular challenge for modern tour guides is to make sense of the ancient defences, among the most complicated and most expensive of any Greek city. Their most impressive feature today is a massive fort, built to reinforce the protection of a main gate in the ancient wall circuit. Here visitors can spot what once were state-of-the-art design features like the tower-like masonry emplacements for a battery of stone-lobbing catapults. They can wander what ancient military manuals call 'secure passages', underground galleries in other words, allowing defenders to move troops around unseen by besiegers – a stratagem in use in the early twenty-first century among the Islamist defenders of Mosul and Raqqa. None of this had yet been built when the Athenians laid siege to Syracuse in 413 BC. Experts nowadays tend to see the fort – Euryalus was its name – as a work of the third century BC. Hieron among others contributed to these defences. Ancient writers record his installation of a dense array of artillery on the city walls, capable of an extraordinary volume of fire. As at other royal courts of the time, Hieron protected Greek scientific research. He had one of his men of learning, a Syracusan mathematician called Archimedes, make him 'engines accommodated to all the purposes, offensive and defensive, of a siege'.

An ancient Greek record of octogenarians includes Hieron, said to have died aged ninety-two. Early in his career this wily survivor had made an alliance with his immediate neighbours, the Carthaginians. They had long ago made good their defeat at Himera in 480 BC, and now controlled all of western Sicily. But Hieron, as a writer of the second century AD put it, almost at once abandoned Carthage because he found himself 'stronger, and firmer, and more reliable friends'.

Hieron's grain diplomacy tracks this new and enduring friendship. In 250 BC he sent grain to a Roman army besieging a Carthaginian stronghold in western Sicily. Thirteen years later, he visited Rome in person, bringing free grain for the citizens. In 216 BC, he sent another large consignment to Rome, and so on. The Roman alliance served Hieron and Syracuse well. 'He passed most of his life free from war and as if he was holding a festival,' as one Greek writer put it.

Within years of his death, Syracuse's fortunes abruptly changed. To find out why, it is time to return to the affairs of the Romans. By now, Greekness had long ceased to be a monopoly of ethnic Greeks. It had become a marker of a type of cultural civilization attractive to non-Greeks as well. As it turned out, in historical terms the Romans would be by far the most significant of the non-Greek peoples who succumbed to the allure of Greek cultural achievements.

PART II

THE ROMANS

CHAPTER 13

'SENATUS POPULUSQUE ROMANUS'

A ny society comprises a union, sometimes broadly consensual, some-times far less so, of many different groups. A Hellenistic-period tomb in Rome, reopened in 2011 after restoration works, illuminates the values of one of the most powerful of these groups in Roman society during ancient Rome's republican age. This lasted from the expulsion of the kings to the so-called 'fall' of the republic in 30 BC.

The tomb is an underground complex of corridors cut into the natural tufa of a hill on ancient Rome's main street of tombs, the via Appia. Niches in the corridors once contained an accumulation over a period of two centuries or so of at least eight sarcophagi of dead members of a single lineage. At the entrance the visitor now sees a modern replica of the earliest of these sarcophagi (the original is in a museum). The deceased's epitaph was inscribed on the lid: '[Lucius Corneli]us Scipio, son of Gnaeus.' On one of the long sides a descendant some three generations later (around 200 BC) added a fulsome poem of praise for his ancestor:

> Lucius Cornelius Scipio Barbatus, Gnaeus' begotten son, a brave man and wise, whose fine form matched his manly virtue surpassing well, was aedile, consul and censor among you; he took Taurasia and Cisauna, in fact Samnium; he overcame all Lucana and brought hostages therefrom.

The form of the Roman names is revealing. An Athenian citizen had just the one name. In formal naming contexts, this was coupled with his father's: 'Pericles, son of Xanthippus'. The official style of a Roman citizen included not just his own personal name ('Lucius') and that of his father ('Gnaeus'), but also a clan name ('Cornelius'), and sometimes a hereditary surname ('Scipio'). This system of naming must have helped Roman males to think of themselves as successive generations of a particular male line. Aristocrats could reinforce this sense of family identity by using the same burial ground over many generations, as the Cornelii Scipiones did.

Lucius's epitaph addressed an imaginary readership of fellow Romans. These passers-by were meant to stop, read and value the quality of the deceased as announced here. This Scipio's incarnation of a certain kind of masculine ethos of civic service is spelt out by some key Roman words.

Scipio was a fine specimen physically, he was 'brave' and possessed 'manly virtue' (*virtus*). He had served the state in three public offices, including those of consul and censor, which were particularly esteemed and fought over. Above all, his later family emphasized his services as a successful general, naming places in central Italy that he was supposed to have captured or subjected on behalf of the state.

The picture that emerges clearly enough from the remains of this family mausoleum is one of a society in which an aristocratic outlook counted for much. From generation to generation, families of men bearing the same hereditary name aspired to hold the highest magistracies of state, to command armies and to win wars. The males of these families were raised in a moral code familiar in other societies dominated by a warrior aristocracy. This emphasized reputation, glory and masculine excellence, all made manifest in public service. As in the epitaphs of the Scipios, republican Rome's aristocrats demanded public recognition of these virtues where they had brought benefits to the state.

The last family member to be buried in the tomb was a woman, thought to have died around 130–120 BC. Her epitaph reads as follows: 'Paulla Cornelia, daughter of Gnaeus, wife of Hispallus.' This Paulla Cornelia was a Roman aristocrat about whom nothing more is known. Her family chose to define her posthumously in traditional terms for ancient women of free birth, as one man's daughter and another's wife. This effacing style of commemoration, even for a Roman noblewoman, reflects deeply entrenched attitudes in ancient Rome.

Later Romans celebrated another female of the family of about this time, also a Cornelia, who died around 100 BC. In widowhood, this other Cornelia raised two aristocratic sons, who both achieved a brief prominence in Roman politics. A later writer claimed that she intervened successfully behind the scenes to dissuade the younger, Gaius, to abandon a planned attack on a political enemy.

In the heated style of Roman politics of the time, another enemy attacked this same son through his mother. We don't know what he said, but we have the son's supposed rejoinder: 'Have you brought forth children as she has done? And yet all Rome knows that she has refrained from the company of men longer than you have?'

The trading of sexual insults between competing aristocrats was quite typical of political discourse at republican Rome – as earlier it had been in Classical Athens. Here the jibe hinged, not just on the homosexual reputation of its target, but also on the 'virtues' of Cornelia. Not only could she vaunt wifely fertility – it is recorded that she had borne twelve children – but also she chose to remain true to her late husband's memory by not remarrying. Her family relationships with the politically prominent gave her chances to influence public life on rare occasions. Probably it was her austere embodiment of Roman matronhood that gave her the moral authority to do so, even in the eyes of her own son.

What did these Romans look like? A newish museum in Rome, the Centrale Montemartini, uses a disused power plant to display ancient sculpture amidst the pipes and dials of the machine age. One of these statues is as jarring as the setting: a balding middle-aged man holding two heads, also of balding, middle-aged men. In fact these hand-held heads depict sculptured busts. The statue references an old custom among the Roman aristocracy of displaying realistic 'masks' of ancestors in the more public part of their houses. Roman writers record how old families coupled these displays with painted family trees, the names highlighted with garlands.

Possibly the 'masks' were based on casts taken from the subject, in the style of the original Madame Tussaud. At any rate, the custom seems to have fed into what republican Romans of the governing class expected from the sculptors of their portraits.

With perseverance a visitor to the website of the Museo di Antichità in Turin in northern Italy can bring up an image of its ancient portrait of a middle-aged Julius Caesar. By modern standards the wrinkled forehead, sagging cheeks and receding hairline combine with the stern expression into something unpleasing. In profile, moreover, the top of the head is shown to be anomalously shaped: it has a congenital dip, a condition nowadays called clinocephaly. There are many other examples of what was a definite taste among Rome's republican nobility for seemingly true-to-life likenesses that relished presenting a harsh and pitilessly authentic face to the world.

Like their counterparts in other periods and places of history, the aristocracy of the Roman republic was a mixed bag when looked at more closely. The Scipios and the Caesars belonged to a core of supposedly ancient lineages, the *patricii*, or patricians, who traced their ancestry to the time of the kings and, in some cases, to individual kings. The much later Roman writers of the early history of their city record traditions of social conflict between these privileged patricians and the politically excluded mass of the citizenry, the plebeians or 'plebs'.

In their struggle for political equality, the extreme tactic hit upon by the arms-bearing plebs was to decamp en masse from the city:

> ... they withdrew to the Sacred Mount, which is situated across the River Anio, three miles from the City ... There, without any leader, they fortified their camp with stockade and trench, and continued quietly, taking nothing but what they required for their subsistence, for several days, neither receiving provocation nor giving any.

The plebs being the backbone of the early Roman army, these 'secessions', as the Romans called them, were something akin to going on strike – an obviously powerful weapon in the rivalry between the two groups. This first secession, dated to 494 BC, wrung from the patricians the right of the plebeians to have two magistrates of their own. The persons of these two annually elected 'tribunes of the people' were to be inviolable in any conflict between the plebs and the consuls.

Ancient Romans believed that popular pressure at around this time also brought about a major change in the safeguarding of the rights of the plebs. Their ancestors in the fifth century BC lived together according to long-established customs which had acquired the character of unofficial laws. Supposedly the plebs successfully agitated for these laws to be written down and displayed in public for all to see – something said to have happened around 450 BC. According to the Roman historian Livy, writing late in the first century BC, it was the stated claim of the ten magistrates charged with this task that they had 'equalized the rights of all, both the highest and the lowest'. This might have been a rose-tinted view of later times.

The original inscription, on twelve bronze tablets, is lost, and so is the original language. Modern scholars piece together much of the content from later writings of the Romans which cite, or refer to, the provisions:

> If he has broken a bone of a free man, 300, if of a slave, 150 [asses, Roman coins] are to be the penalty.

> He is not to send to pasture on fruit on another's land.

> Women are not to mutilate their cheeks or hold a wake for the purposes of holding a funeral.

As this random sample suggests, these are the archaic rules and regulations of a rustic society. Even if much became obsolete over time, the Romans held great symbolic store by what they came to call the Twelve Tables. Livy could claim that 'even now they are the fountain-head of all public and private law'.

Over two centuries or so, the plebeians struggled successfully to win other concessions, including the right to intermarry with patricians and (367 BC) a legal requirement that at least one of the annual consuls should be a plebeian – since the fall of the kings, the consuls had been the two chief annual magistrates at Rome. As a result, the recruitment of families of rich plebeians started to change the governing class.

By the second century BC there was nothing unusual in the marriage of the patrician Cornelia to a grandee of plebeian ancestry (called Tiberius Sempronius Gracchus). Both came from families in which members had reached the ultimate political prize of holding a consulship. It was this distinction that came to matter most. By the first century BC Romans called descendants of consuls *nobiles*.

Helped by its birth rate, one particularly fecund noble family achieved six consulships in two decades (123–102 BC). A Roman playwright of the time who poked fun on stage at leading Romans, rather in the manner of Aristophanes, was said to have included this family among his targets. He insinuated that actual merit played little part in its success, which was down to the procreative power of their loins:

> Naevius long ago composed the following witty and rude verse at the expense of the Metelli. 'By fate the Metelli are consuls at Rome.' Then Metellus the consul responded angrily to him with a verse ... 'The Metelli will do a bad turn to Naevius the poet'.

This vignette conjures up a conflicting image of free speech in republican Rome: on the one hand, the ordinary man whose satirical pen deflates the mighty in a way that sounds modern, on the other the haughty magistrate threatening violent reprisals for a personal slight, like a grand seigneur in pre-Revolutionary France.

In the second century BC a well-informed Greek outsider produced a description of republican Rome's political system which tries to resolve this seeming conundrum. This system was so finely balanced, he wrote, 'that no one could say for certain, not even a native Roman, whether the system as a whole was an aristocracy or a democracy or a monarchy'.

Polybius, the Greek historian in question (he died around 118 BC), provides an account of the system as he understood it to have been in the years shortly before his birth (around 200 BC). The two consuls of the year, he believed, were the king-like element: while in Rome they were 'masters of everything', and as commanders-in-chief of the legions in wartime they had power of life and death over all who were under their orders.

On the other hand, he says, when the consuls were off campaigning (more often than not the case), the Roman constitution seemed to resemble an aristocracy. This took the form of the Senate. This deliberative body of men of property, sitting annually at first, then for life (from the late 300s BC), included many ex-magistrates. It ran the state finances, acted as a court of law for all serious crimes, and received and replied to embassies from foreign states. Modern historians emphasize how senators seem to have monopolized civil, military, judicial and religious posts, not infrequently holding posts in all these categories – so there was no separation of powers as is taken for granted as desirable in western democracies.

Then again, Polybius states, the 'people' played an important part. He meant the mass of Roman citizens summoned formally by a magistrate to a public meeting. In legal cases involving the death penalty they had the final say. They deliberated on peace and war. They also – crucially – elected the executive, the annual magistrates. The haughty Metellus depended on the public vote. Even so, since Roman women, even exalted ladies like Cornelia, were by definition excluded from the vote, this was never a democracy in the modern sense.

Polybius spared his Greek readers an account of the Byzantine intricacies of these popular assemblies, as I shall spare mine. The two key points to grasp are, first, that there were different types of assembly for different types of business. Second, Roman society tended to think of itself in terms of groups rather than humans in isolation. Citizens rarely voted as individuals at these assemblies but usually in bodies, based on either property class or citizen tribe. Each of these groups voted by majority, one after the other, until an overall majority was reached. The way this system of block votes worked in practice meant that certain sections of the vote were favoured over others – the better-off over the poorer, the 'home counties' over the inner city.

On the other hand, Roman elections were lively affairs in which the citizen groupings exercised choice in a manner best described as, if not necessarily democratic, then at least involving ordinary citizens. This at any rate is the impression given in a short piece of Latin writing that claims to be one man's advice on electioneering to a brother standing for a consulship in 63 BC. Wherever he obtained his knowledge, its author seems to have found out a great deal about electoral politics at Rome in the mid-first century BC.

What it makes clear is that rival candidates had to work hard indeed to win votes. Some of their techniques are familiar from elections of more recent times in England, before universal suffrage and modern communications media. A candidate used a network of agents to help drum up support. The importance of the personal touch could not be overstated. The candidate should make himself as accessible as he could: everyone whose vote he needed should have had the chance to meet him. With ordinary people at the hustings, he should remember names and be charming – the ancient equivalent of kissing babies.

Reputation was everything. In this sort of society what passed for public opinion depended heavily on word of mouth. Naturally the candidate himself should speak out against his rivals. In doing everything possible to cultivate his own reputation, he should be mindful of even what the servants might say about him, since 'in general every rumour which becomes the common gossip of the forum originates from sources within one's own home'. This is an interesting passage for what it implies about the empowerment even of slaves, who served as domestics in the great households of Rome.

A candidate naturally had his own money and should be willing to spend it on his campaign. If, as in eighteenth-century England, he used his own pocket to feast potential voters, he should not disdain from showing up in person on these occasions. He should try to deter rivals from trying to corrupt voters with bribes by leaving them in no doubt that he was watching them carefully, and would not hesitate to bring charges of bribery.

There is much more in this vein, along with special advice for the addressee as a 'new man'. Romans used this expression to mean a man who was the first member of his family to become consul. Ancient lists of names of the two annual consuls leave in no doubt that the Roman electorate favoured political lineages. The irrational appeal of a familiar name is a feature of world politics today, western democracies included. In Roman society, where behind-the-scenes patronage was rife and great families were surrounded by deferential dependants whose votes they could count on, this dynastic tendency was far more pronounced.

That 'new men' did from time to time capture a consulship shows that the Roman aristocracy was not a closed caste. The 'new man' about whom the best information survives today is Marcus Tullius Cicero, who was murdered in 43 BC at the age of sixty-three. Cicero successfully stood for the consulship in 64 BC. He is the ostensible recipient of the electioneering treatise just discussed. Much is made there of the personal merits which should recommend him to the voters, above all his skill as a public speaker, tried and tested as an advocate in the Roman courts.

There was another story, a deeper one, explaining Cicero's pursuit of a career in Roman politics. It reveals something fundamental about the (relatively) inclusive nature of Roman society. Cicero's family did not come from Rome. They lived 87 miles south-east, in a hill-top settlement called Arpinum, now the town of Arpino. By heritage the inhabitants of Arpinum were not Roman. They descended from a neighbouring Italic people in this part of central Italy called the Volsci. Yet Cicero was born a Roman citizen.

True to their self-image as a people of mixed origins, from early on the Romans had shown a willingness to share some of their citizen rights with non-Roman neighbours within the Italian peninsula. They may have acted in this way chiefly to improve their military security by creating new oases of (they hoped) loyalty to Rome. They expected concrete services in return, above all, fighting in the Roman army. As these new citizens were not allowed to vote in the citizen assemblies at Rome, it must be wondered how they felt about the dubious honour of being awarded the obligations but not the rights of Roman citizenship.

Still, the Roman people kept the possibility of a status upgrade in their gift. This is what happened to Arpinum. Over a century after the Romans had first made the town's menfolk second-class citizens, in 188 BC they promoted them to full citizens. The Roman historian Livy describes this promotion, using the Latin term *municipium* (singular) to describe this and other townships of second-class citizens:

> Respecting the residents in the 'municipia' of Formiae, Fundi and Arpinum, Gaius Valerius Tappo, tribune of the people, proposed that the right to vote – for previously the citizenship without the right to vote had belonged to them – should be conferred upon them . . . The bill was passed with the provision that the people of Formiae and Fundi should vote in the tribe called *Aemilia* and the people of Arpinum in the *Cornelia* . . .

Much later, in AD 48, no less a person than the Roman emperor was said to have boasted of the superiority of the Roman treatment of outsiders to that of the great powers of Classical Greece:

> What was the ruin of Sparta and Athens, but this, that mighty as they were in war, they spurned from them as men of alien birth those whom they had conquered? Our founder Romulus, on the other hand, was so wise that he fought as enemies and then hailed as fellow-citizens several nations on the very same day.

A Roman historian of the years around AD 100 put these words into the mouth of the emperor Claudius. Although a specialist today would not give the emperor highest marks for his presentation of the 'facts', the speech does nail a lasting truth about Roman social attitudes. In the glory days of Athens and Sparta, to be a citizen of either Greek state was to belong to a closed caste which jealously guarded its privileges. The Romans on the other hand early on developed ways of incorporating outsiders into their political system.

Within Roman society there were outsiders of a different kind. This was a class of people whom free Romans did not consider fully human beings, but could think of as 'speaking tools'. Notwithstanding, the Romans shared their citizenship with them, too.

On display in the British Museum is a Roman gravestone, an upright slab just under 2 feet high, wider than it is tall. It depicts a married couple who clasp hands fondly. The husband is wrapped up in the voluminous piece of fabric that the Romans called the toga, the dress of a Roman citizen. Latin epitaphs for the deceased flank the scene – one for him, one for her. His reads:

> [Lucius] Aurelius Hermia, freedman of Lucius, butcher on the Viminal Hill. She who through fate preceded me [in death], chaste of body and gifted with a loving heart, was my only wife. She lived faithful to a faithful husband, with equal devotion. She abandoned her duties through no selfishness. Aurelia, freedwoman of Lucius.

Found in Rome, this monument dates to around 80 BC, when Cicero was turning twenty. Here we have a very different class of person, however. The husband was an ex-slave who had married another ex-slave, both freed by the same master. He had made a success of his butcher's business and his heirs could afford this tombstone.

It was not that the Romans treated their slaves less brutally than other ancient societies. Years ago I remember the wife of a colleague at a Canadian university telling me that she had a part in the 1960 film *Spartacus*, Hollywood's retelling of a revolt of Roman slaves in 73 BC.

At the end of the film, a woman holding her baby wants to show it to the father, who is Spartacus, the leader of the revolt. To find him she walks through a double file of men crucified on crosses that stretches out of sight, until she stops before one of them – Spartacus, just about alive. 'I was that baby,' my colleague's wife surprised me by saying.

The film takes a liberty with the facts, in that Spartacus fell in the final battle. Otherwise, the scene of the mass crucifixion is faithful to the ancient writings:

Since there were still a very large number of fugitives from the battle in the mountains, Crassus proceeded against them. They formed themselves into four groups and kept up their resistance until there were only 6,000 survivors, who were taken prisoner and crucified all the way along the road from Rome to Capua.

If the ancient information is correct, this was an extraordinarily laborious, as well as savage, punishment: six thousand crosses lining an ancient highway for a distance of some 118 miles. Its steely-eyed aim, to deter at all costs, hardly needs pointing out.

Yet there was a side to the routine Roman treatment of slaves that was unexpectedly humane, for all that it was also self-serving. To discourage work-shyness, owners allowed their slaves to save up assets and buy their freedom. Hermia perhaps started working as a butcher for his master. After accumulating his stash, he not only bought his own freedom, but maybe that of his future wife too.

If owners chose, there were ways of formalizing the slave's liberation in the eyes of the law. If a male, this gave the freed slave some citizen rights, and more for his freeborn sons, including the vote. Hermia's toga showed off his understandable pride in his status while alive. In this way, a large proportion of Roman citizens must have ended up descending from people who were once slaves.

By contrast, Cicero was an example of Roman social mobility at the vertiginous top of the social ladder. He had his personal talents, true, but he also inherited advantages. He was not just a Roman citizen by birth. As he said himself when it suited him, he was the son of a Roman 'knight'. This term, *eques* in Latin, needs some explaining.

Just as people whom the monarch 'knights' in the United Kingdom's archaic system of public honours do not literally go on to fight as mounted soldiers, neither any more did the Roman knights of Cicero's day. Instead they had evolved into a hereditary social grouping, with honorific distinctions. As a young knight, Cicero would have been entitled to wear a distinctive gold ring and to edge his Roman citizen's toga with a narrow purple stripe.

Because they were not members of the Senate, knights did not hold public office. Still, as a group they were influential stakeholders in the governance of the republic. This was especially true of those among them who made money as holders of lucrative state contracts. From 67 BC, the knights sat in their own reserved rows in the theatre. Here they are found expressing political opinions, for instance by standing and applauding politicians they liked.

What the knights all had in common, apart from being ostensibly apolitical, was wealth – at a minimum, if in land, roughly the equivalent of the estate of a country squire. As today, how the money was made, and how long ago, could be a source of snobbish anxieties. Under Augustus a Roman knight who was also a poet, Ovid, prided himself on coming from old money, 'not made yesterday from the workings of luck'.

He mentions parvenu knights of his times 'reared on blood', meaning on the profits of military contracts in Rome's recent civil wars, of which more in a later chapter. In a community like Arpinum, a centre of the wool industry in more modern times, Cicero's forebears were presumably part of the squirearchy.

The well-informed visitor to modern Rome who wishes to see ancient remains from the republican era is likely to end up gazing at a weathered rotunda near the banks of the Tiber which looks, somehow, disproportionate. This is because the marble colonnade of white marble columns has lost its ancient superstructure of curved blocks and the original roof above. Even so, this is a remarkable survival.

Archaeologists date it on style and materials to the later 100s BC – one of the oldest standing buildings from the ancient city. It was clearly once a temple. Roman deities who received round shrines included Hercules. This divine strong man is a definite candidate for the original recipient of the rotunda, because it stood in a part of the ancient city where deals were done, namely, the cattle market. Roman cattle merchants respected the power of Hercules to protect them and their stock from bad things because averting evil was the specialism of Heracles. This was a Greek god whose worship the Romans had been quick to take over – but not before Latinizing his name.

If we go back to the Greek Polybius, that intelligent and well-informed observer of Roman ways, he has some interesting comments on Roman religion in what survives today of the panoramic history that he wrote of Rome's rise to greatness in his lifetime (the second century BC):

> For I conceive that what in other nations is looked upon as a reproach, I
> mean a scrupulous fear of the gods, is the very thing which keeps the

Roman commonwealth together. To such an extraordinary height is this carried among them, both in private and public business, that nothing could exceed it.

He gives as an example the probity of Roman magistrates among whom financial corruption was extremely rare. This, he thought, was because they took their oaths of office, sworn by the gods, so seriously. The religious mindset of the Romans of republican times also emerges in an area for which the ancient evidence happens to be quite good, that of portents, or 'prodigies' as the Romans called them. Here is an entertaining ancient list of them for the year 203 BC:

And new religious fears were aroused in men's minds by portents reported from a number of places. On the Capitol ravens were believed not only to have torn away gilding with their beaks but even to have eaten it. At Antium mice gnawed a golden wreath. The whole region around Capua was covered by an immense number of locusts, while there was no agreement as to whence they had come. At Reate a colt with five feet was foaled. At Anagnia there were at first shooting-stars at intervals and then a great meteor blazed out. At Frusino a halo encircled the sun with its slender circumference, and then the ring itself had a greater circle bright as the sun circumscribed about it. At Arpinum in an open meadow the earth settled into a huge depression. One of the consuls on sacrificing his first victim found the lobe of the liver lacking. These prodigies were expiated by full-grown victims; the gods to whom sacrifices should be offered were announced by the college of the pontiffs.

The reader will spot that at least some of this list is amenable to rational explanation – the people of Arpinum seem to have reported a sinkhole, for instance. The Romans, faced with what to them was bizarre and inexplicable, saw signs of divine anger. It was the job of the state's representatives to carry out the delicate task of interpreting the signs. They then decided the correct measures to be taken, if any, in order to keep the gods on side ('the peace of the gods,' as Romans said).

This meant as here, deciding what kind of animal sacrifice was needed (full-grown animals in this case, not, say, calves) and which divinities needed propitiation. For expert advice the senators – the responsible body – turned to fellow members of the governing stratum serving as 'pontiffs,' from a Latin word for a priest. If need be the senators summoned the Etruscan soothsayers, hereditary specialists in this area.

Returning to Polybius, he explained this god-fearing morality as coming about not through deep personal conviction but because the Roman authorities recognized the force of religion as the glue of social cohesion:

> In my opinion their object is to use it [religious awe] as a check upon the common people. If it were possible to form a state wholly of philosophers, such a custom would perhaps be unnecessary. But seeing that every multitude is fickle, and full of lawless desires, unreasoning anger, and violent passion, the only resource is to keep them in check by mysterious terrors and scenic effects of this sort.

This was the sophisticated view of an educated Greek who thought that the philosophical training of the mind to think and act in the right way was beyond the reach of the masses, for whom the cult of the gods must suffice. It was the condescending view of a well-to-do Greek landowner contemplating 'the multitude'. The interesting question here is whether the religious mindset of the governing class of the Roman republic really was, as Polybius seems to have believed, sceptical (as he was) about divine influence on human affairs, but prepared to manipulate popular beliefs for political ends.

It was certainly the case that state priests whose job it was to interpret the signs could interrupt public business such as citizen assemblies on the basis of the omens, extraordinary though this may seem today. As just seen with the consuls in 203 BC, magistrates themselves had religious duties.

In 59 BC one of the consuls opposed his colleague's attempt to put a particular bill before the citizen assembly. He then retired home, where he spent the rest of his term exercising his consular right to observe the heavens for omens, an activity that would normally have caused public business to be suspended for the duration. Obviously enough, this manipulation of ritual was politically motivated.

If it were not for the religious dimension, this would seem like a filibuster, comparable to the British members of parliament who drone on for hours in the chamber, in the hope that the parliamentary day will run out of time before a vote can be taken. It is probably unwise to infer personal religious attitudes from the behaviour of the consul, a certain Bibulus, any more than personal levels of respect for the mother of parliaments from the behaviour of Westminster filibusters.

The history of the Roman Livy, writing late in the first century BC, is the main source for the annual lists of ancient portents which the republican senators were required to ponder, including the list of 203 BC just cited. Modern classicists have combed what is left of this major source for the history of the republic for signs of its author's personal religiosity.

Since Livy the historian was also a creative writer, his treatment of religious material cannot be supposed to be a straightforward reporting of the facts at his disposal. That said, recent scholars who have looked into this question tend to recognize in the author's presentation of prodigies the conflicting signs of someone who was both a believer and a sceptic.

The American philosopher William James (died 1910) seems to sum up the problem, which arguably has to do with the fundamental nature of human 'belief':

> The whole distinction of real and unreal, the whole psychology of belief, disbelief, and doubt, is thus grounded on mental facts – first, that we are liable to think differently of the same; and second, that when we have done so, we can choose which way of thinking to adhere to and which to disregard.

After this quality of mysteriousness to Roman, perhaps all, religion, there remains one quintessentially Roman activity yet to be explored since it was the key to their imperial success and all that flowed from it in terms of changing the course of world history. It is time now to go to war, Roman-style.

CHAPTER 14

BOOTS ON THE GROUND
BUILDING THE ROMAN EMPIRE

It is fair to say that army recruitment is rarely the subject matter of permanent public art in modern life. In the militarized society of republican Rome, things were different. This is precisely what is shown on a stone panel carved in the later 100s BC for some open-air monument in the ancient city, now lost.

Two young men in civilian clothing stand before two seated officials, one of whom writes down the personal details as he hears them in the latest of a mounting pile of ledgers. An infantryman armed with shield and sword stands watching. The scene is a military census, and the details being recorded will be used to assign these men their places in the Roman army.

The iron reality behind this marble scene of bureaucrats at work could once be viewed in the collections of Predjama castle in the highlands of south-west Slovenia. In the 1880s or thereabouts the princely owner started acquiring Roman weapons found on a nearby archaeological site, an ancient settlement of the indigenous people. Now in museums, the assortment of lethal devices includes barbed arrowheads, bolts from catapults, the heavy blades of the throwing spears favoured by Roman legionaries, and so-called incendiary spears. These have an opening in the head, like a bracket, for holding fireballs. This hoard of used weapons, unique for its date, ended up being buried during Roman wars against the population of the south-east Alps of the late third or early second century BC.

The Roman army of the second century BC, which wielded weapons like these, was carefully described by that same Greek historian, Polybius, a contemporary. His description is a marvel of detailed information and must reflect his friendship with well-informed Romans of high rank. It also conveys what he thought his Greek readers would want to know – how it was that the Roman military machine had become so seemingly unstoppable.

His description of Roman military discipline would surely have taken Greeks aback. There were military courts. In the event of a condemnation, the presiding officer

> takes a cudgel and merely touches the condemned man; whereupon all the soldiers fall upon him with cudgels and stones. Generally speaking men thus punished are killed on the spot; but if by any chance, after running the gauntlet, they manage to escape from the camp, they have no hope of ultimately surviving even so. They may not return to their own country, nor would any one venture to receive such a one into his house. Therefore those who have once fallen into this misfortune are utterly and finally ruined.

The crimes resulting in a death sentence included cowardice, theft, lying and 'misusing one's body' as the Ancient Greek puts it. That is, a fully adult trooper taking the passive role in sex with another male, whereby he compromised his soldierly virtue. Probably this was thought bad for morale.

As a result of this culture of harsh discipline, wrote Polybius,

> it sometimes happens that men confront certain death at their stations, because, from their fear of the punishment awaiting them at home, they refuse to quit their post: while others, who have lost shield or spear or any other arm on the field, throw themselves upon the foe, in hopes of recovering what they have lost, or of escaping by death from certain disgrace and the insults of their relations.

The professional-sounding army that Polybius describes had come a long way from the clan-based warrior bands that seem to have done much of the fighting in the early days of petty conflicts between archaic Rome and her neighbours. The fog that surrounds early Roman history makes the young republic's successive wars in Italy, which won her effective control of the whole peninsula south of the River Po by 275 BC, hard to reconstruct in the detail, even if the outline story is clear enough.

There was a series of sometimes overlapping struggles with Italic neighbours, Sabines, Volsci and Etruscans, proceeding to the Samnites of central Italy, the mixed Italian and Greek population of the Bay of Naples and its hinterland, and the Italic peoples and Greek cities of southern Italy, with the occasional invader thrown in – a band of Gauls who attacked Rome in 390 BC, and a Hellenistic king, Pyrrhus, who disembarked from his kingdom in north-west Greece in 280 BC to help a Greek ally, ancient Taras (Taranto), fight a non-Greek foe.

The Romans were not alone in history in liking to claim that they fought their wars for reasons that were 'just' and 'pious', to use their own language. They believed that from earliest times their ancestors had performed a religious rite when opening hostilities. A specialist priest in these matters called a *fetialis* would physically enter enemy territory to demand redress for an alleged wrong. If this was not forthcoming, 'It was customary for the fetial to carry to the bounds of the other nation a cornet-wood spear, iron-pointed or hardened in the fire.' After uttering a formula 'in the presence of no fewer than three grown men', the priest 'would hurl his spear into their territory'. The Romans took the observation of religious ritual seriously, whatever the real rights and wrongs in a quarrel with an enemy. So the custom of spear-throwing, even if the priest in so doing implied that blame lay with the enemy, does not in itself mean that the early Romans went to war only for defensive reasons.

The Romans of the early and middle republic seem to have been always fighting wars. Historians are still unsure whether they were mainly defending themselves from outside aggressors or whether (on the contrary) they were more warlike than even the standards of the time; and then, if so, whether they had long-term strategies of domination, first in Italy, then further afield.

So many actors over so many generations constituting the 'rise of Rome' warn against sweeping statements about Roman aims. It may be safest to assume a tangled knot of the defensive and offensive, of economic advantage and obligations to allies, along with a growing imperiousness as success followed success.

As seen in Chapter 6, the Romans had little to go on for earliest times when they started to write down their own history around 200 BC. The first account from a Roman pen available to us today was written even later, in the twenties BC and thereabouts. The writer – Livy – was a towering cultural figure in his time. A century or so after his death, a Roman letter-writer included this story in a missive to a friend:

> Have you never read of the citizen of Gades [Cadiz in Spain] so moved by the reputation and fame of Titus Livius that he came from the edge of the world to set eyes on him, and as soon as he had done so, went home?

It is impossible to imagine a historian today receiving such a tribute. Livy, as he is better known today, wrote patriotic history for a Roman readership ready for a version of the Roman past that would illustrate the peculiar virtues that had made the Romans great. He was certainly not averse to the truth, but he belonged to a society more tolerant than ours of embellishment, or even invention, of the facts, especially if, as here, the end product was a poetic vision of the past roughly consonant with what Romans thought they already knew, and in keeping with how they understood the Roman 'character'.

An example of Livy's approach is the account of a humiliating defeat suffered by the army of the consuls at the hands of the Samnites. The victors then inflicted the ultimate shame on the Roman soldiers of forcing them to stoop down to pass beneath an arrangement of three spears, which imitated the yoke attached to the necks of a pair of pulling oxen:

> First the consuls, little better than half-naked, were sent under the yoke, then their subordinates were humbled, each in the order of his rank; and then, one after another, the several legions. The enemy under arms stood on either side, reviling them and mocking them; many they actually threatened with the sword, and some, whose resentment of the outrage showing too plainly in their faces gave their conquerors offence, they wounded or slew outright.

In Livy's account, the Samnites have acted treacherously, but he admits that the Roman generalship was poor. Nature conspired against the Romans too, as he conveys in a confident description of the lie of the land in which the Samnites ambushed them, the so-called Caudine Forks – a feature that has proved challenging to locate today armed with just this armchair history. Livy provides additional padding – no fewer than five speeches which he gives to various protagonists, Roman and Samnite. He serves up the whole episode as a lesson to the Roman reader, but also dovetails his unpalatable tale with a dramatic, almost theatrical, tit-for-tat by the Romans six years later (the battle of Luceria):

> There is scarce any other Roman victory more glorious for its sudden reversal of fortune, especially if it is true, as I find in certain annals, that Pontius the son of Herennius, the Samnite general-in-chief, was sent with the rest under the yoke, to expiate the humiliation of the consuls.

The Romans expanded their sphere of influence not just by war but also by alliances and the use of treaties. Their diplomatic activity over the centuries can even be quantified. In AD 80 a fire at Rome destroyed no fewer than three thousand ancient records of 'the acts of the people, relative to alliances, treaties and privileges granted to any person'. A Greek writer of the later first century BC gives what is probably the authentic gist of a very early example of one of these treaties, between the Romans and their fellow Latins, drawn up in 493 BC:

> Let there be peace between the Romans and all the Latin cities as long as the heavens and the earth shall remain where they are. Let them neither make war upon another themselves nor bring in foreign enemies nor grant a safe passage to those who shall make war upon either. Let them assist one another, when warred upon, with all their forces, and let each have an equal share of the spoils and booty taken in their common wars.

This revealing agreement suggests how the Romans very early on involved their allies in their warring, expecting them to share the military effort and risks, but also the economic rewards. It hints at the scope for Romans to use the mutual aid agreement to embroil themselves in other people's wars, as well as to offer protection. It looks forward to a future when Rome's network of allies in Italy would give her a much greater pool of manpower to draw on than that provided by the population of one city-state, which is what republican Rome was.

The Romans also gave us the word 'colony'. They first started to gain control over large amounts of conquered territory from Italian neighbours in the fourth century BC. About 100 miles east of Rome, high up in central Italy, are the extensive remains of one of these colonies, a place called Alba Fucens. Today this is a scenic spot beneath the peaks of the Abruzzo range. You can see the rectangular layout which guided the future development of the settlement, and fortification walls of many-sided stone blocks which go back to the epoch of the colony's foundation in 303 BC.

A later Roman, Cicero, describes these old colonies in Italy as 'suitable places to guard against the suspicion of danger', so serving as 'a bulwark of empire'. Alba Fucens does seem to fit this bill. It occupied a fortified position on a hill, and at some point the Romans extended one of their existing military roads out here. Archaeologists have also detected traces of the work of Roman surveyors in the surrounding countryside. Using simple instruments they overlaid a grid of roads, paths and lines on the properties of the previous, now dispossessed inhabitants. This they then subdivided into rectangular plots for the new settlers. Livy writes of six thousand families sent here, a mix of Romans and their Latin kinsmen. Colonies could satisfy land hunger as well as strategic needs.

A recently renovated museum in north-west Greece, at Yannina, houses artefacts evoking kings related to Alexander the Great who ruled this part of the southern Balkans in the fourth and third centuries BC. One of them, called Pyrrhus, ruling from 319 to 272 BC, was the 'king' who had his Greek name and title punched into a shield of the Macedonian type, its remains displayed here. This shield must have been one of those that this Pyrrhus is said to have captured in 274 BC after a great victory over the next-door Macedonians, and taken home to offer to Zeus, in the sanctuary where archaeologists made this find.

The warring king had ambitions to build up power and territory like his contemporaries, the Macedonian Successors of Alexander. Six years earlier this warmongering spirit caused him to answer an appeal from a Greek city on the instep of Italy, the old Spartan settlement of Taras, Roman Tarentum, a regional power now feeling threatened by the Romans, whose tentacles reached this far south after their decisive victory over central Italian enemies in 295 BC.

While the Tarentine envoys made their speech, the king is said to have been thinking of the fall of Troy, 'and hoping that he might repeat that victory: the descendant of Achilles fighting against a Trojan colony'. The lineage of Pyrrhus did indeed claim descent from the Homeric hero. He seems to have voiced this morale-boosting line in his dealings with his Greek allies in southern Italy. In turn they must have been familiar with the Greek legends of Trojan refugees finding new homes in the Italian peninsula. As seen in an earlier chapter, among these were the legendary ancestors of the Romans.

Pyrrhus initially underestimated the Romans. The long-standing condescension of Greeks to 'barbarians' was a factor here. When he first encountered the orderliness of a Roman military encampment, the king supposedly commented, 'These may be barbarians, but there is nothing barbarous about their discipline.' In the campaigning that followed, there were successes on both sides. What daunted Pyrrhus was the constant stream of fresh troops with which the Romans and their allies seemed effortlessly to replenish their losses. Probably it was chiefly this that in the end prompted him to curtail his western adventure, and sail back across the Adriatic.

Eleven years later (264 BC), the Romans began what Polybius called 'the longest, most continuous, and most severely contested war known to us in history'. In a small archaeological collection in the Sicilian town of Castelvetrano I have seen for myself some of the exciting finds of war materiel from this conflict which divers and fishing nets have brought up since 2004 from the seas around the Aegates islands, today the Egadi group, off Sicily's north-west coast.

These finds comprise a group of well-preserved 'beaks', as the Romans called the bronze rams attached to the prows of their war galleys. Some still have the nails for attaching them to the ships' timbers. This helps to disprove one modern theory that a Roman ram detached on impact, like a bee-sting. Ten of the rams have Latin inscriptions naming the Roman magistrates whose job it must have been to 'sign off' the work of the contractors.

Unexpectedly, the names of these junior magistrates were actually cast with the ram itself, not merely engraved afterwards. This looks like an honorific gesture – as if there was personal kudos to be got from supervising these naval contracts successfully. Two magistrates had decoration added, a relief figure of a winged female who holds a crown. She is the goddess Victoria, and the reason for her invocation on these deadly weapons needs no comment.

Polybius describes the battle that the Roman fleet won off the Egadi islands in 242 BC. It was their third attempt to win by sea a war that had dragged on for twenty-two years. The Romans doggedly clung to the strategy of turning themselves into a naval power. With an empty treasury, they now appealed in desperation to the rich to make a patriotic sacrifice and pay for a third fleet from private funds. As for the consul in command, he was determined that this last chance would not be lost to poor seamanship:

> He practised and drilled his crews every day in the manoeuvres which they would be called upon to perform; and by his attention to discipline generally brought his sailors in a very short time to the condition of trained athletes for the contest before them.

The Romans needed sea-power because they were now at war with Carthage, the queen of the central and western Mediterranean. The history of Polybius, a first-rate informant, sympathetic to Rome but also, being Greek, somewhat more detached, covers this war. He gave his view as to how this clash came about between two states with a long history of treaty-relationships going right back, as we saw in an earlier chapter, to the years before 500 BC. The Romans, wrote Polybius,

> saw that the Carthaginians had not only reduced Libya to subjection, but a great part of Spain besides, and that they were also in possession of all the islands in the Sardinian and Tyrrhenian Seas. They were therefore in great apprehension lest, if they also became masters of Sicily, they would be most troublesome and dangerous neighbours, hemming them in on all sides and threatening every part of Italy.

This is defensive imperialism in modern jargon. Polybius believed that these considerations persuaded the Romans to support an immoral cause: they answered an appeal for help from a force of undesirables causing mayhem in eastern Sicily. The activities of these rogue mercenaries were an obstacle to Carthaginian plans – as the Romans saw them – to rule the whole island. Propping up the mercenaries suited the Roman interest, even if some Romans had misgivings. Western realpolitik suggests modern parallels.

The great Roman victory off the Egadi islands in 242 BC brought to an end this so-called First Punic War. Carthage now sued for peace. Rome required her to evacuate Sicily and gave her twenty years to pay a hefty, but not crippling, indemnity in silver. Just four years after the battle, the Romans seized the island of Sardinia, a Carthaginian domain.

They justified this 'theft', as Polybius calls it, with claims that Carthage was going to use the island to launch attacks on Italy. Polybius believed that this unfair act, kicking Carthage while already down, rankled enough with the Carthaginians to be the underlying cause of their attack on Italy twenty years later (218 BC). A Carthaginian general of great talent, Hannibal, launched this premeditated undertaking from Carthage's Spanish power base, boldly leading his army on a summer march across the Alps.

The Roman tradition presents Hannibal as a formidable adversary. 'To reckless courage in incurring dangers he united the greatest judgment when in the midst of them,' wrote Livy. Like Mrs Thatcher and Mr Trump, he made do without much sleep. It perhaps comes as no surprise that Livy also gives him flaws: 'His cruelty was inhuman, his perfidy worse than Punic; he had no regard for truth, and none for sanctity, no fear of the gods, no reverence for an oath, no religious scruple.'

This second war almost brought Rome to her knees. Roman fortunes reached their nadir in 216 BC near an ancient town called Cannae, in what is now the Puglia region of south-east Italy. Here Hannibal's generalship allowed him to annihilate a Roman army of eight legions led by the consuls of the year. On modern estimates the Roman dead ran into the many tens of thousands, including one of the consuls.

If the war was protracted, one reason was that Hannibal had no siege train and did not attack cities. Instead he aimed to break up the Roman network of alliances. He made a point of releasing Rome's allied soldiers, but failed in his aim of securing wholesale defections. As with Pyrrhus, Rome's larger manpower pool allowed the city, despite huge losses, to man fresh armies and to fight back. At one point the Romans were desperate enough to send teenagers and picked slaves into the field. By 209 they were able to attack Carthaginian positions in Spain. When a fearful Carthage, unable or unwilling to reinforce Hannibal, finally recalled him, the Romans followed him across to Africa. Here, in 202 BC, a Publius Cornelius Scipio won a decisive victory which forced Carthage to make peace.

Polybius was born in the Peloponnese at around this time. He grew up in a Greek world in which the Roman victory over Hannibal and its aftermath – more shortly of this – made nervous talk about Roman intentions a commonplace. There are echoes of these second-century BC Greek debates in his histories. He records his disagreement with fellow Greeks who thought that Rome's seemingly relentless rise was fortuitous and unplanned. His considered view was that the Romans were making a 'bold stroke for universal supremacy and dominion'. They had a Plan, in other words.

Historians debate Roman imperialism to this day. If Greeks at the time could argue either way, modern experts are unlikely to do better. We too can follow some of the controlling behaviour of the Romans which came to the attention of Greeks after the defeat of Hannibal. This released Rome to declare war on Carthage's Macedonian ally, Philip V, an aggressive expansionist in the usual mould of a Hellenistic king.

Among other signs of an imperialistic outlook Greeks, with the rest of the Mediterranean, had seen the Romans turn their overseas gains of territory from Carthage into provinces. First there was the Carthaginian half of Sicily, then Sardinia, then the Greek half of Sicily after a change of allegiance following King Hieron's death. This brought over a Roman army (211 BC), which all the ingenuity of Archimedes failed to prevent from capturing Syracuse, the Greek capital. Then, in 197 BC, the Romans started sending a pair of governors to Spain. Along with these governors came Roman demands for tribute.

For all that recent successes now made the Romans insist on recognition of their superiority, Greeks also saw that they were not invariably grasping for territory. They witnessed this in their own case, after the Romans defeated Philip V on a battlefield in central Greece. This defeat (197 BC) prompted Polybius to try to explain to his Greek readers how it was that a Roman force of infantry legions could beat Macedonian foot soldiers fighting in the same style as the invincible Alexander's men. These last lined up tightly so as to present the enemy with a bristling porcupine of long pikes of the distinctively Macedonian type.

Polybius thought that the Roman legionary had the edge because he was far more flexible. He fought in a more open order giving him space to deploy his shield and his different arms, either in the small units favoured by the Romans, 'or even by himself'. Given that Roman legions would go on to defeat more Macedonian-style armies in the future, this is that relatively rare thing in ancient accounts of warfare, a persuasive analysis.

In the ensuing peace talks the victorious general, whose name was Titus Quinctius Flamininus, showed a Roman capacity for diplomatic adroitness, as well as a knowledge of Greek history. Under Greek pressure to finish off the Macedonian monarchy for good, he pointed out that it was in the Greek interest to preserve it, because Macedonian arms shielded southern Greece from northern barbarians. Evidently the Romans were in no hurry to assume this burden themselves, or to remove a thorn in the Greek side.

Flamininus also declared in Rome's name that the Greek cities were to be free from Philip's garrisons. Plutarch describes jubilant celebrations breaking out in Greece:

> When [the Greeks] were tired of shouting about [Flamininus's] tent, and night was already come, then, with greetings and embraces for any friends and fellow citizens whom they saw, they betook themselves to banqueting and carousing with one another.

In practice Greece remained under the 'protection' of the Romans. They substituted their own for Macedonian garrisons in three strategic strongholds. The stated reason, or pretext, was the need to protect Greek freedom from the rumoured ambitions of another, and no less ambitious, Hellenistic king.

This was Antiochus III, of the Seleucid lineage. He and his army had recently been operating far from his kingdom's core lands in Syria and Mesopotamia. He aimed to recover territories in Asia Minor and Europe which his ancestors had lost to rival monarchs. Flamininus withdrew his army, but left Greece's door open.

Antiochus did cross the Dardanelles. The Romans sent back the legions. They defeated the king and his Macedonian-style army in two battles. Rome required him to evacuate all his recent conquests west of a snaking mountain range that starts in what is now central Turkey. This was a serious blow for what had once been the largest of the empires formed by Macedonian generals on Alexander's dismembered super-state.

Greeks in the space of a generation had to adjust to a new political landscape. The dominant power was non-Greek and did things differently. In the slower rhythms of life in ancient times, Greeks remained hazy about Roman customs in war. A Latin inscription on bronze, found in Spain, is a unique record of the Roman concept of unconditional surrender:

> The people of the Seaenoci put themselves and all their worldly goods in the good faith of Lucius Caesius the son of Gaius, the conquering general

. . . he ordered that they hand over the arms, hostages, deserters, captives, stallions and mares that they had taken. They handed these over. Then Lucius Caesius the son of Gaius the conquering general ordered that they should be free and restored to them the fields, and buildings, and all other things that had been theirs on the day before they handed themselves over.

The date, 104 BC, is given by mention of the consuls of the year. This Roman idea of 'good faith' left the capitulated enemy completely, and for all time, in the power of the Romans. It was new to the Greeks. In 191 BC, during the Roman war against King Antiochus, another Greek state hostile to the Romans entered peace talks with the Romans. The emissary of the general abruptly cut off the Aetolian representatives in mid-flow. Polybius describes what happened next:

The Aetolians, after some further observations about the actual situation, decided to refer the whole matter to Glabrio (the general), committing themselves 'to the faith' of the Romans, not knowing the exact meaning of the phrase, but deceived by the word 'faith' as if they would thus obtain more complete pardon. But with the Romans to commit oneself to the faith of a victor is equivalent to surrendering with no guarantees given to the surrendering party.

When the Romans finally made a treaty with these same Aetolians in 189 BC, they spelt out their insistence on their superiority in a bald statement of Aetolian dependence that must have surprised the Greeks, used to more temperate language in their own diplomatic traditions. The Latin word *maiestas* literally means 'greater-ness': 'The people of the Aetolians shall in good faith uphold the empire and majesty of the people of Rome.'

After Scipio defeated Hannibal at the battle of Zama, the grateful Romans bestowed on him an honorific byname, 'Africanus'. A slew of these names taken by victorious generals from the site of their victories charts some of the chief theatres of Roman warfare in the course of the second century BC: Asiagenes, Macedonicus, Achaicus, Balearicus, Delmaticus, and so on.

The Roman appetite for these victory names was a function of the same contest for military glory among Roman aristocrats, as the vaunting epitaphs of those male Scipios. Looking back, a Roman writer in the first century BC described the extraordinary zeal for fighting once typical of this stratum: 'There was intense competition among them for glory: each one of them hastened to strike down an enemy, to climb a rampart, and to be seen doing such a deed.'

The historian Livy even blamed these rivalries for what he saw as fake history in the displays of ancestral masks in Rome's aristocratic houses:

> The records have been vitiated, I think, by funeral eulogies and by lying inscriptions under portraits, every family endeavouring mendaciously to appropriate victories and magistracies to itself – a practice which has certainly wrought confusion in the achievements of individuals and in the public memorials of events.

How far this militarism of the great families fanned Roman warfare against other states for much of the second century BC is a modern debate. When consuls pushed for a declaration of war, and then received a command, one might feel entitled to make the connection. Livy wrote that Flamininus's victory in Greece 'commended' him to the Roman voters when they went on to elect him to the career-pinnacle of a consulship.

So did the fact that he had 'triumphed'. A Roman aristocrat in the second century BC could aspire to no higher expression of public esteem than the rare award by the Senate of a triumph. This centred on a public procession through the streets of Rome. Ancient writers indicate that there were criteria for an award. Among provisions at one time or another, we are told, a minimum number of enemy dead in a single battle (five thousand is the figure preserved) might be stipulated, and for the general to have left the theatre of war at peace. This meant that he could bring back his men, who were actors in the pageant almost as much as the general in his chariot.

In his details of Flamininus's triumph, Plutarch focuses on another Roman crowd pleaser, the display of booty:

> The amount of money exhibited was large. Tuditanus [a Roman histo-rian] records that there were carried in the procession three thousand seven hundred and thirteen pounds of gold bullion, forty-three thousand two hundred and seventy pounds of silver, and fourteen thousand five hundred and fourteen gold coins bearing Philip's effigy.

As this display suggests, the Romans saw the booty from a successful campaign as a communal good. Plundering was always part of the Roman ethos of war. The victorious general was allowed great latitude in distributing the more valuable booty. He could make additional cash payments to the men, an action understandably popular with the plebs, and hand over bullion to the treasury. He could also draw on the spoils to promote himself in the public esteem.

We hear of generals honouring battlefield vows by using booty to fund public games, or build temples. In the second century BC they started bringing back plundered artworks from the Greek world to advertise their victories. In 1952 archaeologists found an inscribed base for a lost statue in the ruins of Luna, a Roman colony on the Ligurian coast: 'I, Manius Acilius son of Gaius, consul, took [this statue] from Scarpheia.'

This was Manius Acilius Glabrio who campaigned in Greece. In 191 BC he had sacked a Greek town called Scarpheia, a stronghold of Antiochus. His men must have loaded this statue onto a ship bound for Rome. Probably they purloined it from one of the town's public shrines, favourite places for Greeks to set up offerings of sculpture. In its new life the statue was a trophy of victory. For aristocrats like Glabrio, booty was another weapon in their quest for personal glory.

In the archaeological museum at Delphi visitors rarely linger over a display of blocks carrying a sculptured frieze of men fighting. The theme is, after all, common enough in Greek art. The shields of the combatants hint at something unusual. Some wield a circular shield of Macedonian type, others the much larger oval shields, designed to protect the whole body, of the Roman legionary.

A Roman general had used this frieze to decorate an eye-catching pillar some 33 feet high, on top of which he placed his own statue. The frieze illustrated his victory over the Macedonian king Perseus, Philip's son, in 168 BC. For pilgrims to Delphi, one of Greece's holiest places, this monument was an unavoidable memorial to the final fall of the Macedonian monarchy.

Twenty-two years later, a Roman army invaded southern Greece in order to punish the disobedience of a Peloponnesian federation of cities, by now the only real military power left on the Greek mainland. The victorious army then razed to the ground the Greek city of Corinth. In the same year, another Roman army meted out the same treatment to the city of Carthage. Despite its being a shadow of its former self, the Romans mistakenly, but perhaps understandably, saw the African city as an existential threat.

As usual, Greeks were divided in their views of Roman behaviour. They included critics who thought that the Romans had been corrupted by power, just like (they said) the Athenians and Spartans before them. Their final war with Carthage, they said, was not fought in the honourable way of the Romans of old. They had employed 'stratagem and deceit', more like a Hellenistic king.

Polybius himself felt that the overseas wars of the Romans had started to change their character for the worse, whereas in the past they had 'retained their own habits and principles uncontaminated'. In the present time, he thought, it was no longer unthinkable that a Roman general would accept a bribe. Even so, Polybius himself, though an ex-hostage of the Romans, retained his Roman loyalties. He strongly disapproved of the Greek politicians who triggered the Roman invasion of Greece in 147 BC. After the Roman victory, he placed his local knowledge at the disposal of Roman officials settling Greek affairs. This would be the pattern for Roman rule over subject peoples: working with those who welcomed them.

Greeks at this time now referred openly to the Roman mastery of 'land and sea'. It is time to look at a by-product of this transformation – mounting tensions at home.

CHAPTER 15

HAIL CAESAR!
THE ADVENT OF THE AUTOCRATS

It is hard to forget a visit to the bare mass of limestone that is the Aegean island of Delos, either the brilliant blue sky, or (often) the wind and choppy seas beneath it.

When you step ashore, the island presents as a landscape of ancient ruins. Inscriptions abound, the island marble preserving their clarity. Visitors may well spot that letters are sometimes in the Latin alphabet, from which our own derives. Lying around is this Latin text, chiselled on a base for a lost portrait statue: 'The Italians and Greeks who do business on Delos [honour] L[ucius] Munatius Plancus son of Gaius . . .' Even before a Roman military presence appeared in the Greek Aegean, but especially after, businessmen followed. From the later second century BC a true diaspora of Italians fanned out round the shores of an increasingly Roman Mediterranean. The 'Greeks' here may well have hailed from the old settlements overseas in southern Italy. These invading money-men had fingers in all sorts of enterprises, from viticulture to the art market. To ease their dealings, they took good care to oil relations with important Romans, like the senator Plancus.

The Romans had made Delos a free port (166 BC). This privilege meant that cargoes were not taxed on ships arriving or leaving. Well placed in the centre of the Cyclades for shipping from all directions, Delos now developed into a Hong Kong, an entrepôt between east and west.

Despite all that Aegean light, Delos had a dark side. The archaeologists who work here are not sure where the merchandise was displayed and handled, and the deals struck, in one particular trade described by a Greek writer around the birth of Christ. Unusually for an ancient, he condemned it as 'villainy': 'Delos, which could both admit and send away ten thousand slaves on the same day . . . The cause of this was the fact that the Romans, having become rich after the destruction of Carthage and Corinth, used many slaves.'

Pirates of the eastern Mediterranean were important suppliers of this market, bringing their victims to an emporium with a reputation for always providing a buyer. That many of these slaves did end up in Italy is known from an eyewitness. In the 130s BC a young Roman nobleman travelling through Etruria was struck by what he saw. Where he expected to find free peasants doing the tilling and shepherding, instead he saw 'barbarian' slaves.

Addressing the citizens from the speaker's platform in Rome, Tiberius Sempronius Gracchus, the nobleman in question, later explained why this concerned him: 'The men who fight and die for Italy . . . though they are styled masters of the world, they have not a single clod of earth that is their own.' Ancient writers were much interested in this Gracchus, because they saw his proposed remedy for this problem in the Roman farming economy as the harbinger of a protracted age of civil unrest at Rome.

By way of explanation, the writers told a story of small farmers being edged off the land by rich landowners who brought in slave labour to work their increasingly large estates. This was land conquered by the Romans from Italian enemies like the Samnites. It was the source of the small farms in Italy that the Roman state made available to colonists and others. With these dispossessed smallholders no longer able to meet the property requirement for military service, nor to raise families, the levy – the traditional way of recruiting a Roman army – was becoming less dependable. The writers suggest that this was the real worry for Gracchus, son and grandson of renowned generals.

Today's historians are doing their job when they question whether Gracchus's reading of Rome's social ills was right. Creaky facts and figures about ancient Roman population size furnish fodder for lively discussion among experts, as does the inconclusive evidence from archaeologists for the existence of rural poor, or for slave quarters in farms.

What is certain is that the people egged Gracchus on. As seen, the voting procedures of the Roman public assemblies were weighed in favour of men of property and their concerns. For poor Romans, let alone Italians, protest took other forms – in this instance, one recalling the 'Democracy Wall' of the so-called Beijing Spring in the late 1970s. The Roman people, we are told, 'posted writings on porticoes, house-walls and monuments, calling upon him [Gracchus] to recover for the poor the public land'.

Using elected office, Gracchus disregarded constitutional niceties in order to bypass the opposition. Amid riotous scenes he pushed through a law, which did indeed institute a process of land reform. Contrary to custom, he then tried to get himself re-elected right away to the same office, which would protect him from his enemies' attempts to prosecute him for activity hostile to the state.

Just how divisive his politics were for his fellow aristocrats, landowners themselves, was revealed by what happened next. His own first cousin led a mob of like-minded senators and their retainers onto Rome's streets in search of Gracchus. He ended up being massacred in his civilian clothes by blows from sticks and stones, along with more than three hundred others. By going against the political values of the senatorial mainstream, Gracchus had undermined a long-standing consensus among republican Rome's ruling stratum. As the Greek writer Plutarch wrote around AD 100, 'This is said to have been the first sedition at Rome, since the abolition of royal power, to end in bloodshed and the death of citizens.'

This Gracchus had an admiring brother, Gaius, nine years his junior, fired up with the same reformer's zeal. Ten year later, in 123 BC, Gaius had himself elected to the same office of tribune of the people as a power base for continuing his brother's agenda. Unlike his brother, Gaius was a formidable orator, well aware that speech-making was a form of theatre. He was the first Roman, we are told, to use that stock ploy of the lively university lecturer – moving about on the speaker's platform, radiating energy and vigour. Later generations of Romans remembered sound bites from his speeches, including, 'That which is necessary for keeping alive is not luxury ...'. This may have been his defence of a new concept which disturbed conservative aristocrats. He set up a monthly dole of grain to adult citizens living in Rome at a subsidised price. Scorned by traditionalists, the move was popular with the landless city proletariat for obvious reasons; they were the most vulnerable to price hikes prompted by a crisis in supply.

Gaius was a serious politician who delivered on his commitments:

> He busied himself most earnestly with the construction of roads, laying
> stress upon utility, as well as upon that which conduced to grace and
> beauty. For his roads were carried straight through the country without
> deviation, and had pavements of quarried stone, and substructures of
> tight-rammed masses of sand. Depressions were filled up, all inter-
> secting torrents or ravines were bridged over, and both sides of the roads
> were of equal and corresponding height, so that the work had every-
> where an even and beautiful appearance.

This investment in Italy's infrastructure supported the programme of land
redistribution to impoverished farmers which his brother had begun and
Gaius continued. The Roman businessmen who bid for the road-building
contracts also benefited. They belonged to the oligarchically inclined, but
ostensibly non-political, stratum of the knights.

Gracchus also turned to this stratum when he sought to rein in senatorial
magistrates who abused their power by laying avaricious hands on the property of Roman subjects. This was an increasing problem as Rome's domination of the Mediterranean advanced, mainly because ancient societies did not
view what we call corruption with anything like the same disapproval. The
fair-minded Gracchus had other ideas. Gracchus now transferred from the
senators to the knights the duty of serving as jurors in the court that heard
provincial petitioners seeking redress for extortion by Roman magistrates.

Intentionally or not, this last reform handed the knights a potent weapon
in conflicts with senatorial magistrates arising from the execution of public
contracts. Gracchus himself fuelled this danger when he took the momentous step of giving knights the chance to bid for lucrative contracts to collect
taxes from provincials. Rome at this time was still essentially a city-state
with a rudimentary officialdom at best. Outsourcing saved the republic
from having to set up its own bureaucracy for tax-collecting. Inadvertently
or not, Gracchus had lit a fuse. In a matter of years, not decades, the knights
emerged as a new force in Roman politics, sometimes allies, sometimes
opponents of the conservative senators.

Gaius Gracchus is such an interesting figure because he really might
have been acting on principle rather than from partisan politics (that is,
acting merely to spite his brother's murderers). Whatever the case, his laws,

like his brother's, divided the aristocrats into opposing camps. When a hostile consul started to have them annulled, Gaius gathered armed supporters. Licensed by an emergency decree of the Senate, the consul announced that he would pay in gold the weight of Gaius's head. The story went that a friend of the consul brought it on the tip of a spear – but not before he had scooped out the brain and replaced it with molten lead.

The Gracchi brothers were not alone in letting political cats out of the bag. A generation after Tiberius Gracchus, one of the consuls of 107 BC tried another approach to Roman worries about army recruitment. Rather than relying on the annual levy of propertied conscripts, Gaius Marius enlisted volunteers from the poorest citizens. The ruling stratum traditionally saw the poor as unqualified for army service. To its way of thinking, men of property made the best defenders of the state, just as their politics were more 'reliable'.

The poor Romans who now enlisted seem to have included many of the dispossessed country-dwellers, descendants of earlier peasant soldiers, whose plight the Gracchi had tried to remedy. For these people, this chance to volunteer for a military livelihood in an era of seemingly never-ending Roman expansion offered a solution to their economic distress. The Roman army now moved definitively towards becoming a force of professional soldiers fighting for material reward. In due course, after a long service, these men would look to their general for the final gift of a secure retirement.

The Italian town of Palestrina, an hour's bus ride east of Rome, is located on a mountain spur and commands a sensational westward view of the country surrounding Rome. This is ancient Praeneste, a city of the Latini people. It sits on top of an ancient sanctuary, one so massive that the imprint of its ruins remains a striking feature of the modern town.

The unknown ancient architect obviously laid out this theatrical confection of seven levels of man-made terraces, ramps and colonnades to impress from afar. To anyone who has visited the Hellenistic shrine of Asclepius on the Greek island of Kos, likewise terraced into a hillside with monumental staircases and vast open courts, the visual effect is similar – as if the former were aware of the latter. In fact this is not unlikely. In the later second century BC, when this sanctuary of the goddess Fortuna was laid out, the distinctive names of leading families at Praeneste also turn up in the Greek world, among the Italian businessmen known from the inscriptions of Delos.

The cultural swerve eastwards of this Latin town in the second century BC is on show too in Palestrina's archaeological museum. The star exhibit is a mosaic pavement of superb workmanship. It depicts an exotic scene from Egypt, the teeming life of the River Nile, set in the time of the later Ptolemies. Evidently the top families of Praeneste had grown rich as Italian middlemen linking up Mediterranean commerce to the new spending power of the Romans. When they spent their wealth on civic monuments back home, they looked to Hellenistic Greek styles to express a proud local identity no longer rooted in the traditions of central Italy alone.

This independent spirit among the towns of central Italy took an explosive turn in 91 BC:

> One hundred and twenty years ago, in the consulship of Lucius Caesar and Publius Rutilius, all Italy took up arms against the Romans . . . The fortune of the Italians was as cruel as their cause was just; for they were seeking citizenship in the state whose power they were defending by their arms; every year and in every war they were furnishing a double number of men, both of cavalry and of infantry, and yet were not admitted to the rights of citizens in the state which, through their efforts, had reached so high a position that it could look down upon men of the same race and blood as foreigners and aliens. This war carried off more than three hundred thousand of the youth of Italy.

These are the words of a later Roman history-writer, a descendant of a prominent Italian who remained conspicuously loyal to Rome in this struggle. As for the rebels, they set up their own mint and used the designs on coins to express their feelings about Rome. On a typical specimen in the British Museum, a powerful Italian bull tramples a helpless Roman wolf, its snout raised in a howl of pain.

This ancient figure for the casualties of the war may not be precise, but it preserves a later memory of massive conflict. The previously reluctant Romans belatedly defused the struggle by passing two laws in 90 and 89 BC which finally opened Roman citizenship to the Italians. Even if parts of the insurgency aspired to complete independence from Rome, one Italian stratum interested less in trampling the wolf than in running with it was represented precisely by the ancestor of this history-writer: 'The Romans abundantly repaid his loyal zeal by a special grant of the citizenship to himself, and by making his sons praetors at a time when the number elected was still confined to six.'

If the upper classes of the Italian towns had been willing to go to war, it was because plenty of them chafed to play an active part in Roman political life as senators and magistrates, like these two praetors. As for the Romans, perhaps it is not so hard to understand why apprehension had got the better of them, despite their self-image as a society open to deserving newcomers. There is no exact figure for the number of eligible Italians, but it could have run into the hundreds of thousands.

Roman aristocrats worried about all these new citizens interfering with their long-standing manipulation of the popular vote. To quote the rhetoric of an early twenty-first-century British prime minister on the subject of migrants, a more primal fear of being 'swamped' was also there, to judge from the Roman politician who warned about the dangers of Romans losing their seats to new citizens at the games.

A professional soldiery motivated by rewards now gave a new twist to the traditional contest for military glory among the generals of the governing class. On campaign in Africa, the same Gaius Marius had claimed the credit for the surrender of an enemy leader captured by a junior officer at great personal risk. Marius went on to be one of Rome's most successful generals. Years later, the junior officer, Lucius Cornelius Sulla, now a famed general himself, had just helped to put down the revolt of the Italian allies, winning himself a consulship (88 BC). The Senate awarded the consul a major military command against a new enemy in the east.

Then Sulla's old rival Marius, despite advancing years, manoeuvred successfully to have it transferred to himself. The army awaiting its commander south of Rome was the same force that Sulla had lately led against the Italian rebels. He had already won their goodwill by promising them rewards. Reaching the camp first, he now had no difficulty persuading these six legions to march on Rome. His men fought their way into the city using indiscriminate violence. In their proximity, the senators sentenced Marius and his allies to death.

Sulla now disembarked with his army to confront yet another ambitious king in the Hellenistic mould. Mithradates was the scion of a royal lineage of Persian extraction based in modern-day northern Turkey. He aimed to enlarge his domain by appealing to Greeks and non-Greeks alike as their would-be leader in armed resistance to the mounting dominance of Rome. Sulla's fight-back began in Greece.

In 1990 a group of American archaeologists made an unexpected discovery on a hilltop overlooking the plain of Chaeronea, where Philip had defeated the Greeks in 338 BC. In a pile of rubble they found an ancient block with this Greek inscription: 'Homoloïchos and Anaxidamos the heroes.' The Greek writer Plutarch, a local man, records these same two heroes as fellow citizens of Chaeronea who in 86 BC led Greek allies of Rome up the hill to dislodge a contingent of men from the forces of Mithradates. This done, Sulla and his men went on to win a resounding victory on the plain below. Plutarch records the victory trophy which Sulla erected on the hill, inscribed with exactly this inscription 'in Greek letters'. In studied contrast to his rival Marius, Sulla was at pains to recognize and reward his military helpers.

After ejecting the forces of Mithradates from Greece, Sulla made peace with him. He then returned to Italy, where his political enemies controlled Rome. Sulla avoided disbanding his army, making him in effect an invader. Once again he marched on the capital, where he obtained from the senators, who included many of his supporters, the ancient post of dictator, a kind of emergency leadership used in the past for military crises.

Sulla was in favour of returning stability by shoring up the fragile dominance of conservative aristocrats like the noble clan into which he had married, the Metelli. These 'best men', as they called themselves, in effect were now counter-revolutionaries of varying shades. They wanted back the traditional system of city-state politics that had guaranteed the dominance of their class in the past.

Sulla sought to give them what they wanted by a reign of terror. Anticipating the political purges of more modern times, he had a list published of outlawed citizens, hundreds of whom became fair game for death-squads. While this was happening, he passed reactionary legislation targeting loopholes in the old constitution. The Gracchi had passed their reforms by using their powers as tribunes of the people. Sulla now sought to make the office unattractive to populist aristocrats by severely curtailing its powers.

Sulla did not forget his men. Wandering through the ruined streets of Pompeii the visitor soon notices the ancient graffiti. The author of one of them even joked about the habit: 'I'm amazed, O wall, that you have not fallen in ruins, you who support the tediousness of so many writers.' Their language is Latin. This is not such an obvious point as you might think. The original inhabitants of Pompeii were Italian allies of Rome who spoke and wrote their own Italic dialect, so-called Oscan. In 80 BC the ruthless Sulla punished the Pompeiians for their part in the allied rebellion by settling maybe two or three thousand of his army veterans here, with a plot of land for each in the fertile territory – a case of robbing Peter to pay Paul. The old inhabitants were downgraded in status and the new upper class of Latin-speaking Roman citizen-colonists made theirs the town's official language. An ancient writer says that Sulla was faced with veterans from as many as twenty legions to settle on Italian farmland – approaching 100,000 men, if true. The sheer scale of the disruption to existing patterns of landholding in many parts of Italy can only be imagined.

After Sulla, Romans continued to live through troubled times. Roman wars outside Italy, and the political need to identify competent generals to win them, meant that Sulla's methods remained available to members of the governing class with ambitions beyond the scope of the traditional politics which – paradoxically – Sulla had worked to restore. Only eight years after his death, the consuls themselves (70 BC) passed legislation restoring the full powers of the tribunes of the people. These powers, as the Gracchi had first shown, were a potent weapon for politicians who sought to appeal to the people over the heads of the conservative aristocrats.

One of these consuls, Gnaeus Pompeius, better known as Pompey, already a successful general, went on to obtain commands and win wars in the seventies and sixties which conferred on him exceptional personal prestige, or *auctoritas* ('authority') in Roman parlance. One of these commands tackled the unfinished business of Mithradates, still at large. Pompey forced the king to take refuge on the other side of the Black Sea, in the Crimea. Pompey then marched his devoted army into Syria, where he deposed the last Seleucid king and turned the remnant of this once great empire into a Roman province, Syria. People in this part of the Mediterranean world were put in mind of an earlier conqueror from the west, as was Pompey himself.

In Copenhagen's superbly housed collection of antiquities, the Ny Carlsberg Glyptotek, you can contemplate what must be one of the most peculiar products of Roman portraiture. By today's standards this fine marble head of a jowly male in early middle age with thin lips and furrowed brow does not demand admiration for its subject's good looks. The enviably full head of hair is another matter, not least the artfully rendered quiff of lustrous locks.

The subject is Pompey, of whom his ancient biographer, Plutarch, wrote:

> His hair was inclined to lift itself slightly from his forehead, and this,
> with a graceful contour of face about the eyes, produced a resemblance,
> more talked about than actually apparent, to the portrait statues of King
> Alexander. Wherefore, since many also applied the name to him in his
> earlier years, Pompey did not decline it.

Pompey liked the comparison. He was certainly a warlord, in the sense that
his military successes had given him an individual autonomy within a weak
state. But he did not want the kingly position to which warlords in history
sometimes aspire. A rival warlord, however, had different ideas.

Gaius Julius Caesar, the elder of the two men, came from the hard-up
lesser branch of an old patrician family. Like Pompey when it suited him, he
used populist methods to obtain personal advancement. To this end, the
two men for a while were political allies, sealing the deal by intermarriage,
like a pair of Hellenistic kings. Conservative aristocrats sought to obstruct
this alliance. The religious scrupulosity of Marcus Calpurnius Bibulus,
Caesar's colleague in the consulship of 59 BC, comes in here.

Using a tribune of the people to push through the legislation, Caesar
now got what he wanted, the opportunity for military glory in the west on
a scale to match Pompey's in the east.

> All Gaul is divided into three parts, one of which the Belgae inhabit, the
> Aquitani another, those who in their own language are called Celts, in
> ours Gauls, the third. All these differ from each other in language,
> customs and laws.

These are the opening words of one of the set books when I sat the pre-
university Latin exam at school in England. Exam setters like the plain style
of the Latin, which pitches the difficulty at about the right level. The author
is Caesar. Using the third person to depersonalize his writing, he gave here
his version of his achievements during this Gallic command.

They involved nothing less than extending the Roman conquest of what
is now France from the strip of Mediterranean coastland already acquired
as far north as the English Channel. In the east Caesar subdued territory up
to the west bank of the River Rhine in what is now western Germany. Not

that he saw the Channel as a definitive barrier to Roman arms either. He also made two seaborne expeditions against the southern 'Britanni'. These took him into what is now Hertfordshire.

Caesar used his writings to showcase his generalship and veil the self-promoting militarism that drove his conquests as accidental imperialism – the enemy were the aggressors. As for the scale of the mayhem, another ancient writer offers seeming facts and figures:

> For although it was not full ten years that he waged war in Gaul, he took by storm more than eight hundred cities, subdued three hundred nations, and fought pitched battles at different times with three million men, of whom he slew one million in hand to hand fighting and took as many more prisoners.

Military 'success' on this scale had political repercussions back in Rome. For one thing it pushed an eclipsed Pompey into the arms of the conservative aristocrats. Alarmed about Caesar's power and intentions, these men now threatened him with politically motivated prosecution for misconduct in office. Caesar's response was to follow Sulla's precedent and invade Italy with his victorious legions.

The ensuing war took civil strife at Rome to new levels, with theatres of conflict in North Africa and Greece. Pompey now fought for both his own political life and that of the republican system that Sulla had sought to prop up a generation earlier. After following Pompey's army into Greece, Caesar won a decisive victory at Pharsalus (48 BC). Pompey was killed in flight.

When Caesar finally returned to Rome after the mopping-up operation, he assumed, like Sulla, the office of dictator. Caesar's dictatorial style was far more challenging to conservative aristocrats. He acquired his own priest, a political crony called Marcus Antonius, whose duty was to supervise public worship of the dictator as a god-like being. Caesar then showed his determination to cling on to sole power by having his dictatorship extended 'for perpetuity'. Scenting the emergence of a tyrant, a young aristocrat called Marcus Junius Brutus and his fellow conspirators, intent on restoring what they called liberty, caught Caesar unawares in the senate house and stabbed him to death (44 BC).

Looking in my old guide book to Egypt I came across the form from Le Lotus Boat inviting comments on my cruise on one of their vessels from

Luxor downstream to Dendera, back in the days when the ancient sites along the Nile seemed safe enough to visit. I never filled it in, but would have given high marks to the entertaining and well-informed guide who showed us a wall in the ancient temple at Dendera carved with purely Egyptian images of the then ruler of Egypt making offerings to the gods – the famous Cleopatra.

This Ptolemaic queen projected a double identity in the long-standing tradition of her royal house. Alongside the image of a pious pharaoh which she carefully cultivated for her Egyptian subjects, Cleopatra was portrayed on coins meant for circulation in the world beyond Egypt in the Greek style, her hair tied back, wearing the cloth band signifying a Macedonian-style monarch in the tradition of Alexander the Great. Whether from the incompetence of the dye-cutters or because she had features – as some people do – which are hard for artists to capture, she looks unrecognizable from one coin issue to the next.

Cleopatra, a young Roman client-ruler of some importance, not for her power but for her treasury, had been on a visit to Rome when Caesar was murdered. Slipping away by ship, she left behind a capital in uproar. Those who saw themselves as the political heirs of the dead dictator swore revenge on his killers. For one of them, this was seized on as a filial duty: Caesar, with no legitimate son to succeed him, had adopted this would-be chastiser, Octavian, his sister's grandson, as his heir. This precociously astute nineteen-year-old was now able to raise a private army because Caesar's veteran soldiers transferred their loyalty to the avenging son.

An ancient biography of the son defined his political ascent in these terms:

> The civil wars which he waged were five, called by the names of Mutina, Philippi, Perusia, Sicily, and Actium; the first and last of these were against Marcus Antonius, the second against Brutus and Cassius, the third against Lucius Antonius, brother of the triumvir, and the fourth against Sextus Pompeius, son of Gnaeus.

After Caesar's death there was no return to senatorial business as usual, whatever his assassins might have hoped, but instead a complete break-down of the old order. Octavian found himself in immediate rivalry and conflict with the consul Marcus Antonius, Mark Antony as he is better known. The two men then allied in order to pursue Caesar's assassins, whom they brought to battle and roundly defeated at Philippi in what is now northern Greece (42 BC).

Together with Caesar's official deputy at the time of his death, Octavian and Antony now filled the political vacuum by having themselves legally constituted, along with a third strongman called Lepidus, as a three-man junta of so-called 'triumvirs'. Two and a half centuries later, a Roman historian had this to say about the new horrors that followed:

> Those murders by proscription which Sulla had once indulged in were once more resorted to and the whole city was filled with corpses. Many were killed in their houses, many even in the streets and here and there in the forums and around the temples; the heads of the victims were once more set up on the speaker's platform and their bodies either allowed to lie where they were, to be devoured by dogs and birds, or else cast into the river.

Among the victims of this new purge was Cicero, a believer to the end in the old way of politics, and a fiery critic of Antony. Next the triumvirs carved up the empire between them. Antony took the east, which is how he formed what at first was a purely political relationship with the Ptolemaic queen, or rather her treasury. Aided by Cleopatra's adroitness and personal charms, this developed into a Romano-Egyptian co-rulership based on Alexandria. While she dreamt of reviving the old Ptolemaic greatness in the east, Antony signed over Roman provinces to the queen and tried but failed to win military glory against a hostile empire based in Mesopotamia, the Parthians.

Back home, Antony's eastern politics handed Octavian in Italy a propaganda coup. Painting his behaviour as un-Roman, Octavian garnered enough support in Italy to declare war on the Ptolemaic queen. As the powerful 'Egyptian woman', she provided plenty of misogynistic ammunition for Antony's Roman enemies. In 31 BC Octavian's fleet decisively defeated Antony and Cleopatra's off the promontory of Actium in northwest Greece. Returning to Alexandria, her Roman lover, followed by the queen, committed suicide. Octavian added Egypt to Rome's empire, before returning home.

It could not have been foreseen, but Octavian, a delicate young man, lived for another forty-five years. Chance was therefore one of the historical factors allowing him after his victory to convert Rome from a broken republican system to what was a de facto monarchy. He did this step by step over a long lifetime. How much he made up as he went along, how much he planned from the outset: these are interesting questions and hard to answer.

More than entrenching himself in a position of supreme power unparalleled in Roman history, he died in his bed and succeeded in passing on his unofficial supremacy to a kinsman, Tiberius. Tiberius did the same on his death. This approach to the problem of how to arrange the transmission of power in an autocracy meant that Octavian had managed to found, in effect, a lineage of rulers. He was one of those individual leaders in history whom luck and personal qualities allowed to fashion a system of power not only new but also lasting. And if it lasted, this must have been because in many ways it went with the grain of the times. Key groups in Roman society were ready for hereditary monarchy.

For us, a stroke of luck is that Octavian composed a document in middle age which gives his own version of his political career and achievements. To say that this kind of contemporary testament from a ruler is rare in Roman history is an understatement. In of all places Ankara, modern Turkey's capital, which sits on top of what was the Roman town of Ancyra, a ruined wall preserves line after line of a long Latin inscription. After the heading, this is how it begins: 'At the age of nineteen on my own responsibility and at my own expense I raised an army, with which I successfully championed the liberty of the republic when it was oppressed by the dominance of a faction.'

Couched in plain and factual-sounding language, the very first sentence shows that the author is embarking on a self-serving, albeit broadly truthful, version of events. The threatening 'faction' was his enemy Antony. In opposing him Octavian claims to be acting to save the republican system. His position throughout the document is to present himself as the servant of the republic rather than a warlord with an appetite for one-man rule.

He also suggests where much of his political support lay. 'All Italy', meaning essentially the descendants of the new citizens of the 80s BC, had supported him against Antony and Cleopatra. He details how he provided for the retirement of his troops and his generous gifts in the established tradition of 'bread and circuses' to the proletarian citizens living in Rome – now a world city of over four million, as the author himself records here.

As he states of one of these staged hunts to the death of wild animals imported from Africa, 'about 3,500 beasts were destroyed'. He could afford to take these popular liberalities to unprecedented heights thanks to a huge personal fortune swollen by Egyptian booty.

It is unlikely that these groups cared much if anything about the 'liberty' of the republic. For those members of the old aristocracy that did, he claims to have 'restored' the republic, and studiedly refuses the office of 'dictator', his adoptive father's undoing. In a nostalgic appeal to the traditional values that Romans associated with their ancestors, he also claims to be leading the way in a 'back to basics' campaign: 'By new laws passed on my proposal I brought back into use many exemplary practices of our ancestors which were disappearing in our time, and in many ways I myself transmitted exemplary practices to posterity for their imitation.'

In projecting this moral conservatism Octavian (a name he dropped) drew a veil over his own rickety youth (more on this later). He also found a support in his second wife, an aristocrat of old-fashioned virtue. Madrid's archaeological museum displays a marble statue of a seated Livia Drusilla in the traditional dress of the upper-class Roman wife. Without entirely disguising her biological sex, it has the effect of enveloping her in voluminous fabric from veiled head to feet that peep from beneath floor-length drapes. After the shocking violence and unpredictability of the civil wars, it is almost as if Octavian and Livia sought to embody this much more recent definition of civilization:

> The essence of civilization, as we know, is dullness. In an ultimate analysis, it is only an elaborate invention, or series of inventions for abolishing the fierce passions, the unchastened enjoyments, the awakening dangers, the desperate conflicts, to say all in one word, the excitements of a barbarous age.

This same Victorian writer also wrote of the 'magic' of monarchy, that element of mystery hedging the ruler onto which 'daylight' should not be let. In Octavian's case, the turn towards magic came from the aura of sanctity which he colluded with the Romans themselves in drawing to himself. This began with his acceptance of a title not arrogated but bestowed, as he carefully records, 'by decree of the senate'. 'Augustus' was a Latin adjective connoting someone with a touch of 'holiness'. In the more forthright Greek world, the Athenians were not alone when they now appointed one of their citizens as 'priest of the God Augustus'.

In his moral crusade, Augustus also chose to make a stand on the question – morally vexed for many Romans – about their interaction with the civilization of the Greeks, their neighbours and now their subjects. This process of interaction was pivotal in ensuring that Greek civilization not only survived but flourished under the ensuing centuries of Roman rule. Indeed, Greek civilization made its mark on the cultural life of the Romans on a scale not remotely matched by any of the other cultures of Rome's multi-cultural empire, to the extent that imperial Rome can be thought of as an amalgam of the two cultures. The next chapter examines more fully the emergence of this 'Graeco-Roman' civilization.

CHAPTER 16

'FIERCE ROME, CAPTIVE'?
THE LURE OF GREECE

Around 60 BC an ancient freighter foundered in the treacherous waters off the south-eastern tip of mainland Greece. Two millennia later, fishermen happened upon remnants of its cargo still strewn on the seabed. Divers to the wreck site brought up ancient objects barely recognizable after their long immersion underwater. Only after restorers had done their painstaking work did the nature of the cargo become clearer. This was a treasure-ship of Greek luxury artefacts.

Divers found many marble statues. They include a fine figure of a boy in a wrestling position. One side of him is a delicate, almost translucent white. Walk round to his other side, and he is grotesquely deformed by centuries of attack from stone-eating organisms. Sculpturally the pièce de resistance is a luminous bronze of a young man, larger than life-size. The style is three centuries older than the date of the shipwreck. When it was loaded on board, this figure was already a prized antique.

Artworks ancient and modern were not the only cargo. Computer geeks as well as archaeologists have become enthusiastic about the find of a hand-sized lump of corroded bronze with a cogwheel embedded in it. Using twenty-first-century scanning tools, researchers have shown that inside the lump is a mass of interlocking gears. These once controlled dials and pointers on the two faces of an instrument housed in a wooden box.

This contraption would have faintly resembled an upright mantle clock. Despite modern media hype, it was not a 'computer', more a mechanical calculator. When the ancient operator turned its handle, dials and pointers on each face did a job not unlike the printed tables in a modern almanac. They gave out astronomical data along with information about the calendar, such as the day of the year, future eclipses and the position of heavenly bodies in the sky.

Whoever he was, the maker of this ingenious instrument would have needed great skill and precision to fashion the parts and fit them together. Equally unidentifiable is the Greek mastermind who designed the prototype – a scientific astronomer who could also invent machines. We have already encountered the most famous inventor of this type in Hellenistic Greek times, Archimedes, from the rich city of Syracuse.

One of his most renowned devices was an astronomical instrument in the form of a celestial sphere with moving parts. When the Romans captured Syracuse in 211 BC, the general in charge supposedly selected for himself this one object from all the available booty. At the time that our ship sank off the island of Antikythera, the other mechanism, this sphere, remained a precious heirloom of the general's descendants, the noble family of the Claudii Marcelli. They kept it in their town house in Rome, where they would show it to curious visitors.

The fate of Archimedes' sphere gives a strong hint as to the destination of our wrecked ship. Before the vessel foundered, the Antikythera mechanism was almost certainly bound for Rome.

The wreck site offers a watery window into a vast process of cultural transfer. It says much about what the Romans liked about Greek civilization: its arts, but also its scientific know-how, since both these instruments just mentioned modelled the scientific findings of Greek astronomers. By this date, the Greeks knew a great deal about the astronomical observations of the ancient Babylonians. For the first time in the history of classical civilization, we can follow how such a vast and prolonged process of cultural transfer worked in the detail.

As an imperial race the Romans could, and did, help themselves to the cultural goods of the conquered Greeks. Another archaeological site, this time in Italy itself, suggests what could happen to a cargo like this if it reached the safety of an Italian quayside. This site confirms that the rich and powerful at the topmost level of the Roman republic held a privileged position in the Roman acquisition and consumption of Greek culture.

In the years around 40 BC an unknown Roman plutocrat built a palatial villa halfway up the slopes of Mount Vesuvius just outside the town of

Herculaneum, in what was then a chic resort area for the Roman super-rich. During the long hot Italian summer, successive owners could enjoy sea views along a vast terraced frontage overlooking the bright blue of the Bay of Naples. They could take their ease in a grand walled garden shaded by colonnades and cooled by a miniature canal. They could enjoy a superb collection of Greek statues dotted about the property, their quality a match for those from the Antikythera wreck. They could order a slave to read to them from one of the Greek scrolls in the villa's library.

The eighteenth-century excavators of the site came across hundreds of charred lumps, which at first they mistook for charcoal or wood. They turned out to be two thousand or so papyrus scrolls, preserved by a flow of superheated gas, steam and mud which poured over Herculaneum during the eruption of Mount Vesuvius in AD 79. More so than the sculpture and the architecture, this is the true treasure of the so-called Villa of the Papyri today: the only ancient library to have survived from classical antiquity.

The library includes what are thought to be the personal books of a Greek philosopher called Philodemus, who hailed from an ancient city in what is now Jordan. He migrated to Rome in the early first century BC in the hope of finding a rich Roman patron (which he did). It is a mystery exactly how his books ended up in the villa. At any rate, one of its Roman owners was clearly an enthusiastic collector of books on Greek philosophy.

The best way of finding out more about how Romans from this elevated social stratum responded to Greek learning in the second and first centuries BC is to take a further look at the Roman statesman Cicero. His huge legacy of writings – over nine hundred letters alone survive – allows us to reconstruct his education into all things Greek in detail.

As a young knight in his twenties, he left Rome to study in the most prestigious centres of learning of the day. These were in the Greek world to the east. Cicero learnt Greek philosophy and the Greek arts of public speaking at the feet of masters in these subjects in Athens and on the island of Rhodes. Cicero would have had to learn the language. He not only spoke Greek fluently but he also could read the learned writings of the Greeks. This was a challenging task in the first century BC, by which time, as seen earlier, written Greek was increasingly remote from the living tongue.

Preening public figure he may have been, but Cicero possessed a formidable mind. He had an intellectual's passion for Greek higher learning. He immersed himself in Greek studies – far more so than the run of rich

Roman villa owners. As a refuge from the increasing stress and dangers of Roman politics in his lifetime, he started to channel his Greek studies into learned treatises. He was a gifted writer of Latin. He used this talent to try to popularize the difficult subject of Greek philosophy for Romans of his class. The aim was not to compete in intellectual originality with the Greek masters, but to pick out the more useful and relevant bits for practical Romans. Whether this amounted to homage or appropriation is a moot point.

Cicero captures a very Roman attitude to the cultural superiority of the Greeks. He saw a patriotic challenge in proving that Latin was up to the task of rendering the subtle ideas of Greek men of learning, despite its smaller vocabulary. He claimed that his mother tongue – at least sometimes – was actually superior. The argument – again this was typically Roman – ran on moral grounds. For instance, he pointed to the Latin word for a common meal, *convivium*. This placed the emphasis on sociability (hence our word 'convivial'), whereas the Greek equivalent, *symposion*, meant something more lowering – a drinking party.

In today's age of increasing free-for-all in the matter of language, with an average of a thousand words added yearly to the *Oxford English Dictionary*, the idea that words intrinsically reveal a society's morality may seem old-fashioned. In this respect Rome revealed herself as intensely moral, a characteristic that we run up against time and again, despite, or because of, ancient Rome's modern-day reputation for stupendous excess.

In Cicero's education, Moses went to the mountain. The reverse was also true in this complicated picture of what was not just cultural transfer but cultural exchange. The Greek philosopher Philodemus, he of the Herculaneum library, came in person to Rome to find buyers for his expertise. Philodemus was a follower of the Greek master philosopher Epicurus. Epicurean teachings in favour of pleasure proved tempting for a young nobleman called Lucius Calpurnius Piso Caesoninus. Later the father-in-law of Julius Caesar, this Piso is the preferred candidate of some scholars for the unknown proprietor of the Villa of the Papyri.

Young Piso and Philodemus became inseparable. Once the philosopher penned a Greek poem (it survives) which invites his Roman friend to his 'humble abode' to share a gourmet dinner of 'sow's udders and wine from Chios'. Philodemus sounds rather like a pet don serving up philosophy-lite to a high-living patron. The poem also highlights the bilingual cosiness by this date – around 70 BC – of Roman grandees and the Greek intellectuals who flocked to the capital in search of their patronage.

The Roman assimilation of Greek civilization was not just appropriation. It also provided opportunities for Greeks themselves to sell their cultural capital to their new masters. In the second and first centuries BC, not only Greek artefacts and ideas, but also Greeks themselves, were on the move to Rome. By the time of the birth of Jesus, Rome had become the new capital of Greek culture, succeeding Alexandria.

It is hard to overestimate just how much eloquence defined Roman society. Under the republic, as we saw, the capacity to speak well was essential above all for members of the Roman political class, whether a Gracchus or a Cicero. They routinely delivered speeches before large audiences of fellow citizens at trials, at popular meetings, and in the Senate.

As seen earlier, the ancient Greeks were the first society to believe that public speaking was teachable. Style, performance, subject matter, the state of mind of the audience and how to appeal to it: clever minds analysed these things, broke them down, produced manuals, gave classes. Romans started to think about how to apply this Greek expertise to public speaking in their own language. In the second century BC professional teachers of the Greek art of public speaking ('rhetoric') began to set up shop in Rome.

For Roman men, much was at stake here. 'There is no index of character so sure as the voice.' Modern research supports this dictum of Benjamin Disraeli: consciously or not, listeners today judge speech for trustworthiness, competence, masculinity and so on. Long before, the Romans developed their own approach to speech personality.

An orator embarking on the grave business of persuasion in the civic arena should be a 'good man' in the Roman moral sense. This ideal had the considerable weight behind it of a stern Roman statesman called Cato the Elder (died 149 BC). His phrase, 'the good man skilled in speaking', resonated with Romans for centuries to come. How the Roman orator spoke showed both his 'goodness' and so – since the two were inextricably linked in Roman thinking – his 'manliness'.

An outstanding speaker himself, Cicero took up his pen on behalf of Roman oratory as well. In his high-minded Roman way he wanted to promote the moral dimension to public utterance in Latin. He believed that a good speaker needed to be something of a philosopher too, since philosophy – in the absence of religious teachings on morality – offered Romans, like Greeks, the best self-help to becoming a better person.

Cicero became embroiled in a debate at Rome about the best Greek models of speaking technique. The Greek civilization of Asia Minor – modern Turkey – dominated Greek oratory in the second and for much of the first century BC. As seen, Rome's most dangerous enemy in the first century BC, king Mithradates, also held court in Asia Minor, where he found anti-Roman allies among the Greek-speaking citizenry of the cities on the west coast. It was no coincidence that by the mid-first century BC, in the bear pit of Roman politics, orating in an 'Asian' style had become a stick with which to attack an opponent. The great Cicero himself was not immune from this charge.

In reaction, a group of well-bred young Romans took to calling themselves Attics or 'men of Attica', as the countryside surrounding Athens is still known. Seeking to distance themselves from the 'Asian' technique, these oratorical enthusiasts claimed to be modelling their speech on the speakers of ancient Athens. Critics dismissed the rhetoric of the 'Asians' as flowery; Cicero found the manner of the 'Attics' rather dry. With no voice recordings, it is well nigh impossible to judge the essence of these contrasting styles. As today, their impact on listeners must have depended on cultural attitudes as well as on technique.

One thing is clear. In the end, Romans favoured the idea that the best public speaking should be modelled on the ancient Athenians. At the close of the first century AD, the oratory professor who tutored the young men of the emperor Domitian's family opined that 'to speak [Latin] in the Attic way is to speak in the best way'.

Romans harboured negative stereotypes about contemporary Greeks considered en masse: they talked too much, they were unwarlike, they were pederasts, they were wedded to luxury; they were not real men. Such stereotyping of subject peoples is not uncommon in the relations of dominance and submission at the heart of many empires.

Romans found it easier to admire long-dead Greeks, especially the high-achieving citizens of ancient Athens and Sparta. These were states, after all, which, like Rome, were not just Europe-based but had won glory on the battlefield (the Persian Wars) and imposed their rule on others (the Athenian and Spartan empires). Many Romans could relate to this Greek achievement of 'glory in war and command over others', as Cicero once put it.

Roman public speakers particularly revered the oratory of Demosthenes (died 322 BC). As seen, he was the Athenian statesman who made speech after speech urging his countrymen to resist Philip of Macedon. More than fifty Roman-period portraits of Demosthenes attest to his popularity with Romans. The Metropolitan Museum of Art describes its own example as showing the great man in a 'characteristically harsh, unhappy yet determined expression'. This portrait perhaps captures something of the 'mood music' of upper-class Romans when they gave speeches in what they thought was the 'Attic' manner.

Contradictory attitudes among Romans towards Greek culture made leanings in that direction something of a guilty pleasure among republican Rome's upper class. Romans from the great families preferred to indulge this pleasure privately. Away from prying eyes in a suburban villa, surrounded by Greek-speaking attendants and Greek luxuries, they might even energize their 'inner Greek' by throwing on a Greek-style mantle. For public appearances in the capital, however, they took care to envelop themselves in the national costume of the Roman male, the voluminous toga.

The traditional elite – the senators in Rome – enjoyed the lion's share of all this imported Greek culture in the last two centuries BC. As so often with expensive luxuries, in time the nouveaux riches lower down the Roman social pyramid started to want these symbols of wealth and status too. One of Cicero's surviving courtroom speeches depicts an ex-slave of the dictator Sulla (died 78 BC) living in a house crammed with costly Greek goods, including some of the renowned bronzes originating from the lately destroyed Greek city of Corinth.

Rome's upwardly mobile had a particular penchant for these bronze totems of conspicuous consumption, prized for the distinctive pale hue of their metal alloy. A miniature donkey of Corinthian bronze, with panniers holding olives, graced the table of the most famous Roman parvenu of them all, the Gatsby-like ex-slave Trimalchio, one of the colourful characters in the Roman novel usually known as the *Satyricon*, authored in the mid-first century AD.

The urban poor of republican Rome may only have seen such Greek collectibles from afar, when they craned their necks at the parade of booty in the triumph of a Roman general back from the east, such as that of Flamininus. The Greek civilization of southern Italy and the eastern Mediterranean also seeped into their lives in other types of Roman show.

Broadly speaking, the Romans learnt how to write and stage plays from the Greeks. The first Roman playwright to make a Latin adaptation of a Greek play lived in the third century BC. For the next century or so Romans flocked to watch popular comedies based on Greek originals which Roman magistrates commissioned for performance on festival days. The texts of some twenty-six of these plays survive. They are Greek-style situation comedies full of songs – so musicals, really. Or panto even, if they really did deploy – as one scholar suggests – the painfully obvious joke which gets the audience laughing, or rather groaning.

In the surviving plays the humorous plots can seem harmless and even familiar to a modern ear, until, that is, they become desperately inappropriate. So (in one play) a youth disguises himself as a eunuch in order to befriend a girl he adores from afar ... then rapes her. This particular twist cannot be blamed on the Roman adaptor. The ancients assigned the invention of comic 'rapes of maidens' to a playwright of two centuries earlier – a Greek.

Roman theatregoers sat and watched these crowd-pleasers, as well as tragedies based on Greek myths, from temporary wooden stands. The presiding magistrate would have these specially erected; afterwards, he would have them taken down. In the heyday of the comic playwrights (second century BC), the aristocrats whose fierce rivalries drove public building in Rome did not provide their city with what at that date was standard civic kit in even a middling Greek town: a fine stone theatre.

In the mid-century workmen did actually start to build a stone theatre in the city of Rome. An influential nobleman – a member of the Scipio family – then stood up in the Senate and denounced Greek-style theatre-going as immoral, and therefore un-Roman. He carried the day: the masons ended up having to demolish their own handiwork. Roman attitudes to Greek cultural sophistication never entirely lost this ambivalent edge.

In the second century BC the urban centre of the expanding Roman Empire did not yet look the part. Over in the southern Balkans the anti-Roman courtiers of Philip V of Macedon, who died in 179 BC, sneered that the city of Rome lacked fine buildings. On Rome's doorstep, the cities of her Italian allies could look far more impressive, as with lofty Praeneste, modern Palestrina.

Rome would have to wait a long time for anything like this. The rivalries among the senators discouraged cooperation around *grands projets*.

Individual nobles were keen to gain credit with gods and voters for public buildings in a Hellenistic Greek style, like the marble rotunda in the cattle market encountered in an earlier chapter. However, such fine buildings were put up piecemeal. There was no master plan, as there was in the planned cities of the Greek world.

Ordinary Romans watched their urban space become more Greek in other ways. A generation after Philip V's death, Romans could inspect at their leisure what had once been the most famous artwork in Macedonia – now displayed in Rome. Around 146 BC, the Roman general whose job it was to mop up after Rome's toppling of Philip's dynasty had hauled off as booty a group of at least twenty-five bronze figures set up by the great Alexander himself in the Macedonian 'national' sanctuary. Back in the capital, the general built two new temples and put the statues on permanent public view there.

As an earlier chapter noted, in the last two centuries BC many victorious generals decorated the city of Rome in this way. Did contemplation of these objects teach the Roman plebs to appreciate Greek art? It is easier to believe that sight of them promoted 'national' pride. As for the overpowered, there is the poignant tale of Greek visitors in the early first century BC who recognized some of their stolen statues on show in the Roman Forum. They promptly burst into tears.

After the civil wars and his capture of autocratic power, the victorious Octavian, soon to be Augustus, took on a huge task of 'national' restoration. In this exceptional political atmosphere, Augustus and his political helpers turned to what the twentieth century would call 'hidden persuaders' on a scale unprecedented in Roman politics.

This technique may sound, and indeed was, rather modern. Techniques of manipulation formed the core of the rhetoric lessons that upper-class Romans learnt as young men. Like other ancient societies, Romans also understood, somehow, the power of symbols: otherwise, why all those phallic plaques and amulets protecting Roman homes and persons?

As the Romans themselves observed, an absolute monarch makes his decisions in secret. We can only guess why Augustus commissioned a crowd of fifty statues of mythical Greek women to stand in his new shrine of Apollo on Rome's Palatine Hill. In the legend a Greek king called Danaus married his fifty daughters to the fifty sons of his mortal enemy with instructions to the brides to kill their husbands on the wedding night.

The Palatine group included the king, his sword drawn, instigating the slaughter.

Augustus decorated his lavish new forum in Rome with another host of marble women. These so-called Caryatids represented all the wives of a Greek town called Caryae. So the story went, they were forced to endure perpetual punishment for the treachery of their husbands, who sided with the enemy when the Persians invaded Greece in the far-off days of the Persian Wars.

These spectacular public displays of miscreant wives on the gleaming new buildings of Augustan Rome seem to express the mood of moral re-armament which Augustus and Livia tried to promote by example, despite the origins of their own union – the young Octavian had forced a pregnant Livia to divorce and then marry him. Determined – notwithstanding – to return Roman society to supposedly traditional Roman values, an older Augustus passed harsh laws against Roman wives who committed adultery, almost as if he was trying to pin at least some of the blame for Rome's recent ills on 'misbehaving' women.

This conservative aspect of the politics of Augustus was divisive – we hear of resistance to this legislation. But it is unlikely that the pragmatic Augustus took these steps unless he thought that there was also public support for them. What is striking is how a Roman leader and his advisers opted unreflectively for the cultural idiom of Greece when offering citizens – as it seems – marble parables of bad wives.

In his political testament, the so-called *Res gestae*, Augustus made much of the wide-ranging makeover that he gave the city of Rome:

> In my sixth consulship [28 BC] I restored eighty-two temples of the gods in the city on the authority of the senate, neglecting none that required restoration at that time.

> I built the temple of Mars the Avenger and the Forum Augustum on private ground from the proceeds of booty. I built the theatre adjacent to the temple of Apollo on ground in large part bought from private owners, and provided that it should be called after Marcus Marcellus, my son-in-law.

What must have been a vast building programme involved both the repair of existing buildings and the construction of new ones. The urban agenda of Augustus dwarfed the comparable programmes of earlier states that we have already come across: Pergamum notably, or, before that, Athens.

Augustus turned Rome into a far more Greek-looking city. Rome now caught up with and far surpassed Italian neighbours such as Praeneste. To do so he relied heavily on architects and artists who were either Italian adaptors of Greek ideas or actual Greeks. The sculptor of the female figures for his new forum was probably an Athenian.

On the surface, this dependence on Greek talent does indeed look like the 'capture' of Rome by her Greek subjects. A Roman poet of the time, Horace, sang lines to this effect which probably made some in his Roman audience wince on their Greek-style couches. On the other hand, in a way that a visiting Greek might have found disconcerting, the total effect of this new Rome was un-Greek. The visual messages projected concerns that were distinctly Roman.

The ruins of Rome still convey some idea of the grandeur of these new buildings – what is left in situ of the Forum Augustum still impresses. Some scholars would say that the greatest monument nowadays to the Rome-centred civilization that Augustus seems consciously to have aimed to restore and magnify is not a building, but a poem:

Arms and the man I sing, who first made way,
predestined exile, from the Trojan shore
to Italy, the blest Lavinian strand.
Smitten of storms he was on land and sea
by violence of Heaven, to satisfy
stern Juno's sleepless wrath; and much in war
he suffered, seeking at the last to found
the city, and bring o'er his fathers' gods
to safe abode in Latium; whence arose
the Latin race, old Alba's reverend lords,
and from her hills wide-walled, imperial Rome.
O Muse, the causes tell! What sacrilege,
or vengeful sorrow, moved the heavenly Queen
to thrust on dangers dark and endless toil
a man whose largest honour in men's eyes
was serving Heaven? Can gods such anger feel?

The United Kingdom retains a poet who is asked to write about important public occasions. Still, it can safely be said that by and large Western societies do not have the cultural habit of reading or listening to extremely long poems in a lofty idiom freshly commissioned to celebrate nationhood. So the importance for the ancient Romans of the Augustan poet Virgil's twelve-book epic about the hero Aeneas, the Trojan refugee who crossed the sea to settle in Italy and found the Roman race, is harder for us to grasp. Latin literature had produced nothing like it before, nor would it do so again. For the Romans, Virgil's poem the *Aeneid* quickly became a classic.

In these opening lines, the 'heavenly Queen' is the goddess Juno. She tries to thwart Aeneas, son of a rival, the goddess Venus, by causing a storm to blow his vessel off course and into the arms of Queen Dido of Carthage – a failed attempt, it will transpire, to distract him from his destiny, since Juno's husband, Jupiter, king of the gods, is willing him on.

From the very beginning Virgil shows how consciously he modelled his epic poem on Homer's Greek poems, the *Iliad* and the *Odyssey*. It was not just in the subject matter – a hero who wanders the seas after the fall of Troy. It was also in the clear echoes of the structure of the poem and, in Virgil's Latin, of Homer's Greek. My great-great-grandfather's copy of Pope's translation of the *Odyssey* begins:

> The man, for wisdom's various arts renown'd,
> Long exercis'd in woes, oh Muse! resound.
> Who, when his arms had wrought the destin'd fall
> Of sacred Troy, and raz'd her heaven-built wall,
> Wand'ring from clime to clime, observant stray'd,
> Their manners noted, and their states survey'd.
> On stormy seas unnumber'd toils he bore [etc.]

Without much effort the reader can see the similarities – 'the man', the Muse, the fall of Troy, the suffering wanderer, the stormy seas. Educated Romans will have 'got it' at once. Virgil was in his fifties when he composed this poem. By means of minute comparison between this and Greek poetry, scholars now know that he must have been totally immersed not just in Homer but in a whole raft of lesser Greek poets writing in the epic genre, off all of whom he endlessly 'riffs'.

Poetry like this is subtle and elusive. Interpreting the poet's own attitude to his work is not easy. It seems unlikely that Roman audiences took the Latin *Aeneid*'s emulation of the Greek Homer as deferential appreciation of Greece's cultural gifts. Not least since Virgil's patron was Augustus, the first man in the state, it is easier to imagine their competitive enjoyment of a Roman poem which seemed to measure up to, if not outclass, its Greek model.

The political shadow of Augustus shows too. In building consensus around his unique position, Augustus deployed his own family traditions, which Virgil dutifully wove into his national epic. The poet presents Augustus as predestined to rule Rome by virtue of being a descendant of the Trojan Aeneas and so of Venus herself. Augustus could parade this ancestry thanks to his adoption by Julius Caesar, whose ancient family claimed to spring from a grandson of Aeneas named Iulus. In Virgil's hands, it is Jupiter himself who foresees the rule of this younger 'Iulus':

Of Trojan stock illustriously sprung,
Io, Caesar comes! whose power the ocean bounds,
whose fame, the skies. He shall receive the name
Iulus nobly bore, great Julius, he.

As Augustus notched up a third and then a fourth decade of sole rule, for many Romans memories of the civil wars were receding into the background – but not for the ageing emperor. Another Roman poet in a different mould, Ovid, composer of risqué lines making light of adultery, found himself bundled off to the provincial purgatory of Tomis – modern Constantsa in Romania. That was in AD 8, six years before the old autocrat died.

Over the next century and a quarter, the attitudes of Romans to the Greek civilization on their doorstep continued to be troubled. There were influential Romans who felt that Romans would no longer be 'Roman' enough unless they reminded themselves of the differences – minor in more and more ways though these were in fact – between being a Roman and being a Greek.

When Augustus died in AD 14, his political bequest to Rome was a shaky succession of four interrelated emperors, about as secure on their thrones as the Romanov tsars. Nero, a great-great-grandson of Augustus, was the last. Every now and then historians try to rehabilitate him from the lurid tales of the ancient writers, spun after Nero's murder when it was safe to attack him. The sheer awfulness of his alleged crimes – including matricide, fratricide and uxoricide – makes this a testing task.

Without this bloodshed, there is a certain resemblance between Nero and Ludwig II, the Bavarian king and patron of Wagner who died mysteriously in 1886. Both were young eccentrics who pursued artistic obsessions in ways that put them on a collision course with the establishment. Both also won the affection of ordinary people and kept it after untimely deaths.

Nero considered himself not just a patron of the arts but also a performing artist in his own right. He loved to appear on the theatre stage where the Roman plebs received him rapturously. In the eyes of the upper class, this budding stage career was undignified for a man who was emperor and head of state. Despite his apparently weak and husky voice, the field in which Nero competed was that of a Greek-style singer, accompanying himself on the lyre.

He was also an enthusiastic actor. This Roman emperor would appear before adoring audiences in the capital in the full fig of a Greek-style tragic actor. For male roles, Nero had one actor's mask with his own features. For the female parts that he performed, he had another, modelled on the face of his wife, Poppaea Sabina – she whose eventual death while pregnant, it was said, was caused by a kick from her imperial spouse.

To provide a public platform for these musical and thespian activities, Nero founded a Greek-style cultural and athletic festival, a permanent one, to be celebrated on a five-yearly cycle like the Olympiads in ancient Greece. This was the first of its kind in Rome, and a landmark in the halting Roman embrace of Greek culture.

When he was not yet thirty, Nero took his passion a step further. He sailed across the Adriatic Sea to compete in the true Olympics. Called back by the rebellion of a senior general, he was so anxious to protect his voice, the story goes, that he neglected to give rallying speeches to either the senators or – more thoughtlessly – his imperial guard. Cornered by his enemies, he committed suicide. Nero's opponents then abolished his short-lived 'Neronian Games'.

As emperor, Nero had drastically misjudged. Yet he was one of many Romans who relished watching Greek cultural shows. To stand today in one of Rome's liveliest and most elegant plazas, the Piazza Navona, is to catch faint echoes of the continuing culture wars of the Romans after Nero's death. The elongated U-shape of this mid-seventeenth-century public space preserves the footprint of an ancient athletic stadium, the ruins of which survived into Renaissance times.

The emperor Domitian, who died in AD 96, was the donor of this popular amenity. With a seating capacity estimated at fifteen to twenty thousand, it was the first permanent stadium for Greek-style athletics in the capital. Domitian's grandiose athletic track was a crowd-pleasing response to popular taste. Unlike Nero, however, at performances Domitian remained firmly in his spectator's seat.

The reign of the emperor Hadrian (AD 117–138) is often seen as marking the high tide of the flow of Greek culture into ancient Italy. Hadrian had come to the throne as a middle-aged man. As with Nero, there was a personal dimension to Hadrian's enthusiasm for Greek culture. He commissioned an unknown sculptor to create the lost original behind one of the most famous Greek faces from antiquity, a handsome, downcast youth with tousled hair and a hint of a pout, celebrated in over a hundred surviving statues. This was Antinous, Hadrian's Greek boy, who drowned during an imperial cruise on the Nile in AD 130.

Hadrian's promotion of everything Greek took other forms. In particular, he devised for provincial Greece the ancient equivalent of the USA's Marshall Plan for post-Second World War Europe – roads, bridges, public buildings, land reclamation, even a Rome-style annual dole of grain for his favourites, the Athenians. All this Hadrian poured into a run-down and strategically worthless corner of his empire. Today's visitor who wanders through the Plaka area of central Athens, the old Turkish town in effect, finds the domes of an Ottoman bathhouse side by side with a monumental ruin faced with a row of columns in a marble veined with thick waves of green and white. This was part of a vast and luxurious cultural centre, including a library, that Hadrian gave to the Athenians.

Back in the capital, senatorial wags had long ago had the 'size' of Hadrian. He was a 'Greekling'. This insult amounted almost to a charge of un-Roman behaviour. He stoked this prejudice when he mourned 'like a woman'. That was how one Roman historian described his grief when his beloved Antinous drowned in the Nile.

Hadrian's gifts to Greece suggest one way of answering the question posed by the next chapter: 'What did the Romans do for their empire?' In the next two chapters I shall say more about the Roman peace that Hadrian imperator was so keen to defend, as well as the mounting tally of threats to it during the second century AD.

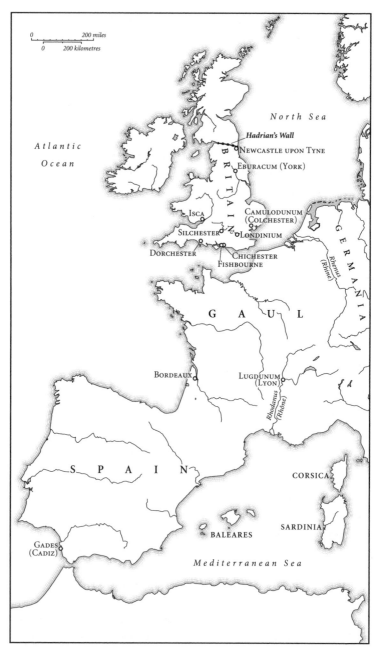

Scale bar:
0 — 200 miles
0 — 200 kilometres

Atlantic Ocean

North Sea

Hadrian's Wall
Newcastle upon Tyne
Eburacum (York)

BRITAIN

Isca
Camulodunum (Colchester)
Silchester
Londinium
Dorchester
Chichester
Fishbourne

GERMANIA

Rhenus (Rhine)

GAUL

Bordeaux
Lugdunum (Lyon)

Rhodanus (Rhône)

SPAIN

CORSICA

BALEARES

SARDINIA

Gades (Cadiz)

Mediterranean Sea

5. The West.

CHAPTER 17

WHAT DID THE ROMANS DO FOR THEIR EMPIRE?

If this question replaced 'their empire' with 'us', a mischievous answer would be that the Romans gave us endless entertainment, thanks to the alleged antics of those emperors from the death of Augustus onwards deemed black sheep by the Romans, or rather by the highest echelons of Roman society, the imperial-period quasi-service aristocracy of senators and knights.

Augustus cut the Senate down to size – six hundred – and discreetly furthered its slow transformation into a body of men drawn from the suitably rich and well born among the Roman citizens not just of Italy but also the provinces. He also nurtured a dwindling core of families from the old republican nobility. Their continuing service to the state as magistrates helped maintain the façade of constitutional business-as-usual. Augustus saw this as necessary for the consensus he sought to build around the new political reality. For the same reason he had opted for a low-key term to describe his unofficial position at the top – *princeps* or 'leading citizen'.

In 1884 construction workers in Rome stumbled on an underground tomb, since destroyed. Poorly documented at the time, the purported finds of inscriptions, marble portrait busts and sarcophagi identified the owners of what might in reality have been a group of tombs as one of these ramified houses of the old nobility.

That fine head of Pompey the Great with the Alexander-like quiff now in Copenhagen is said to have been found here. A posthumous creation, the sculpture celebrated one of the intermarriages that knitted together descendants of Pompey with two other lineages, the Licinii Crassi and the Calpurnii Pisones. Art historians identify another bust said to be from here, this time of a young woman, as a daughter of the emperor Claudius whom her imperial parents married into this same clan.

The historical interest of another find is even greater: a stone altar, now displayed in the patched-up ruin of a Roman bathhouse serving as the Roman National Museum. In effect an epitaph, the heirs of the man whom it commemorates had this funerary altar dedicated in finely carved Latin letters to 'The Shades of L[ucius] Calpurnius Piso Frugi Licinianus'.

'Piso was the son of Marcus Crassus and Scribonia, thus being noble on both sides; his look and manner were of the ancient school, and he had justly been called stern . . .' This is how a Roman historian a generation or so later admiringly described the qualities recommending this Piso to an old man who had declared himself emperor in AD 68. This was at the start of a year of political chaos after Nero's style of rule triggered a revolt among army commanders. Galba, as the new emperor was called, wanted to adopt a son and political heir. He started a practice which the serendipity of human fertility made the norm for much of the second century AD: a child-less emperor adopted a meritorious fellow Roman from the senatorial elite as his 'Caesar'.

The epitaph for Piso gives no hint of the fate awaiting both him and his new father. Aged thirty-one at the time, he had been Caesar for just four days when the soldiers of a rival to Galba killed them both. They stuck the two heads on poles 'side by side with the eagle of the legion'. This episode showed clearly enough that the professional army bequeathed by the republic was now the real 'king-maker' in the imperial system devised by Augustus.

The senator Tacitus, the historian in question, wrote historical works in the years around 100. With a biting irony he gave his version of the reigns of the four emperors who succeeded Augustus, and also of this so-called Year of the Four Emperors following the suicide of Nero, the last descendant of Augustus to rule.

A mournful theme of Tacitus inspired the title of my favourite chapter in a book that was required reading for my Ancient History exam at pre-university level in England: 'The Doom of the Nobiles'. Savouring the names of the old families with a Proustian relish, Tacitus tracked what he depicts as their ceaseless persecution by the successors of Augustus who saw them in some ways as equals – emperors intermarried with them after all – and therefore feared them as rivals. The eligibility of Piso in AD 68, fatal for Piso though it turned out to be, shows that these early emperors were right – up to a point.

The imperial elites might contemplate an alternative emperor-in-waiting who seemed to incarnate the 'old school' as Piso did. Unfortunately for him, troopers were unimpressed with historic names. Modestly paid professionals, they wanted incentives in cash, as we have seen before. On this point Galba had shown himself to be mean, even towards the crack bodyguard of the emperor, the praetorians. They ended up conniving in his murder. Tacitus gave Piso an obituary, adding him to Piso's close family's tally of violent deaths: 'His brother Magnus had been put to death by Claudius, his brother Crassus by Nero.'

The suspicion in which emperors held the top layers of Roman society, senators and the most prominent knights, was mutual. On the one hand, each needed the other to fulfil the possibilities of their allotted roles in Roman society. The emperor was now the fount of patronage. He also depended on officials recruited from both senators and knights in the running of the state. On the other hand, the inequality of the power relationship turned senators – whose best hope for retaining or improving their status lay in flattery – into courtiers. The emperor in turn might action his suspicions by murderous crackdowns, as happened to Piso's brothers. Or he might use his stupendous purchasing power in effect to buy loyalty, of the already rich and powerful too, not just of troops. Apart from disobedience with all its risks, the elite of senators and knights had little defence against an emperor who erred too far in repressing their class.

One option was to die philosophically. The emperor Nero suspected his tutor, Seneca, a rich senator, of complicity in a plot against him and decided to have him summarily killed. Seneca, like many upper-class Romans of his time, was an adherent of a philosophical doctrine which the ancients called the Stoa, after the *stoa*, or roofed colonnade, in central Athens where its Cypriot Greek founder used to teach in the years after 313 BC.

At the real risk of doing an injustice here to a complicated set of tenets, the Stoics believed that humans alone among animals were endowed with reason, that the exercise of reason in the right way conferred mental well-being derived from living virtuously, and that emotions, triggered by things which were not valuable to this way of thinking, were bad – even grief for the loss of one's child.

Nero sent troops who surrounded Seneca's house. A centurion went inside, where Seneca was dining in company, including his wife. Refused a request to write his will before dying, he told tearful friends that his greatest bequest to them would be their memory of the moral pattern of his life, and rebuked them for forgetting the preparation of so many years of philosophical study against 'evils to come'. Seneca and his impressive wife there and then entered a suicide pact, opening their veins with daggers.

Taking too long to die and retaining an extraordinary presence of mind, Seneca then recalled the death of Socrates and tried for an assisted death:

> Seneca . . . begged Statius Annæus, whom he had long esteemed for his faithful friendship and medical skill, to produce a poison with which he had some time before provided himself, the same drug which extinguished the life of those who were condemned by a public sentence of the people of Athens. It was brought to him and he drank it in vain, chilled as he was throughout his limbs, and his frame closed against the efficacy of the poison . . . He was then carried into a bath, with the steam of which he was suffocated.

For survivors, there was always the pen. This offered the educated elite a weapon once an emperor deemed 'bad' by these strata was safely dead. Most writers of contemporary or recent history in imperial times were either senators – like Tacitus – or knights. One modern school of thought wonders if some of the outlandish stories of imperial excess – the consulship which the third emperor, Caligula, was said to have conferred on his horse, for instance – might not have been, as we now say, fake news. As seen with Alexander, ancient monarchs, living as well as dead, were vulnerable to this kind of libellous treatment.

Piso's widow lived on for thirty or so years, a pillar of respectability. The society gossip of a Roman letter-writer of the time recounts this great lady's vulnerability as she died. A conman inveigled his way to her bedside. Claiming astrological expertise, he predicted her recovery, went away, and returned to announce that a soothsayer on inspecting a sacrificial liver had agreed with him. Suffering and credulous, she called to alter her will in his favour, but then died anyway. Shorn of Roman detail, this story of legacy hunting is not so different from the testamentary dramas of today's rich and infirm.

Verania came from a different background from her husband. There is no record of the blue-blooded Piso deigning to hold public office before Galba singled him out. In terms of social background, his father-in-law, Quintus Veranius, was more typical of the Senate under the emperors. He earned his consulship in AD 49 through dutiful service. His career included appointments to two provinces at opposite ends of the empire – opposites too in history, culture and climate.

In recent years Turkey's longest beach has been regularly hailed as 'unspoilt'. On long walks across the sands of Patara on the south-west coast I like many have seen the evidence for why this beach has protected status – tyre-like tracks left by the flippers of the logger-head turtles who haul themselves ashore here to lay their eggs. Beyond the sand dunes edging the beach lies another sight, the impressive ruins of a Roman provincial city.

These ruins tick boxes in any list of the standard amenities of a Roman town of the first two centuries or so AD. There is a large theatre for open-air shows; a paved high street flanked by colonnades sheltering shops, the portal of one of them protected by a carving of an erect phallus; the mighty portal of a temple; Turkish-style public baths; a roofed council house; a handsome triple arch spanning an approach road; and stretches of an ancient pipeline once bringing fresh water under pressure to city fountains.

The summer visitor willing to brave the heat can tramp pathways to two rarer types of Roman monument. When I visited one in 2011, it was completely deserted. Dug out of the dunes, this stub of what was once a tall cylindrical tower encasing a spiral staircase is nothing less than a lighthouse erected in the name of the emperor Nero, as the remains of an inscription in big bronze letters tells us.

The other monument is reached by following the edge of what now looks like a swampy lake, in fact an ancient harbour, now landlocked. This large and well-preserved building, divided into compartments, declares its ancient purpose 'on the tin', or rather in a Latin inscription on the façade.

This states that the emperor Hadrian had built a granary here (AD 129). Experts debate whether Hadrian meant this as a benefit to the provincials. Perhaps he intended imported grain to be stockpiled here, or to encourage commerce by providing storage space for local merchants to rent. Lighthouse and granary bear witness to the seaborne trade that supported

Roman city life, and specifically to ancient Patara's importance as a port, before windblown sands eventually blocked up the harbour mouth.

The Turkish archaeologists who work here have not yet put all their finds on display. In 1993 a mysterious act of arson set fire to the undergrowth that still covers much of this sprawling expanse of ruins. The fire exposed by chance a mediaeval wall built from inscribed blocks taken from the dismantling of a pillar-like monument of Roman date.

This find has caused a stir among specialists: there is nothing quite like the subject matter of the inscription. Picked out in red, the letters on the pillar recorded a quintessential feature of Roman imperial rule – road-building, in this case 'throughout all Lycia', as the Romans, following the Greeks, called this part of their empire. The inscription then records regional roads and their distances, as if there had been a concerted programme to measure existing roads, and to construct at least some new ones.

The monument also sheds light on how the Romans came to impose direct rule on the region. Almost certainly, it once supported a statue of the emperor Claudius (reigned AD 41–54). On the main face the Lycians, or those who now spoke for them, enthusiastically describe themselves as 'Rome-loving and Caesar-loving faithful allies'. They thank the Roman emperor as the 'saviour of the [Lycian] nation'.

This was because he had rescued the Lycians from an outbreak of 'faction, lawlessness and brigandage'. In this crisis the emperor's agents had stepped in to transfer control of the league of Lycian cities away from the 'rash majority' to 'councillors drawn from among the best people'. It is not hard to see the imperial interest in the region's roads at this juncture as a reflection of security concerns. Roman roads above all were military and strategic.

One thing that the Romans did not do for the empire was to support democracy. The verbiage of this monument masked what seems to have been a popular movement with anti-Roman undertones. This challenged the usual political dominance of the region's pro-Roman upper stratum. To sort out the mess, Claudius sent in Quintus Veranius in AD 43. Quintus's solution was to form a new council of local oligarchs. This was to run the Lycian federation in place of an assembly with a broader social base that was now discredited in Roman eyes. Quintus oversaw this enforced stability by remaining for four years as Lycia's first Roman governor.

The names are known of many men and women from the class of people whom Veranius put back in local control. One Greek inscription that visitors to Patara can easily see still occupies its original place on the wall of the theatre, where it was framed for greater publicity in a panel recessed into the stone. After a loyal dedication to the emperor of the day (AD 147), a certain Vilia Procla, 'citizeness of Patara', proclaims a generous gift to her fellow citizens. She completed expensive repairs to the earthquake-struck theatre begun by her late father.

These two rich donors claimed a Roman as well as a Lycian identity. They literally had dual citizenship, Roman as well as Pataran. Both of them also bore names that were Roman, not local. They admired Roman ways of doing things. The inscription translates into Greek letters the Latin word for one of their embellishments – Roman-style 'vela'. How welcome these often brightly dyed coverings could be in the Mediterranean heat is suggested by a story about the alleged cruelty of an early Roman emperor, Caligula (reigned AD 37–41). Sometimes during gladiator shows in the capital he supposedly had the awnings retracted while the sun was hottest 'and gave orders that no one be allowed to leave'.

Modern visitors to Roman city-sites through much of the Mediterranean can see traces of a similar way of life from Spain to Syria. Socially, local government mirrored the plutocracy of the empire's service elite. Well-off town councillors meeting a property qualification ran local services, including the collection of Roman taxes. A skeleton staff of higher officials sent from Rome, sometimes but by no means invariably backed up by troops, kept a collusive eye on them.

Rich men and women in the provinces engaged in an ancient version of Victorian 'philanthrocapitalism' in towns like Patara, where poverty and plenty must have rubbed shoulders. Augustus and his successors had rebuilt Rome as an architectural showcase reflecting the majesty (that word 'greater-ness' again) of Roman power. Local benefactors like Vilia Procla hoped to curry favour with Roman patrons, not to mention the distant emperor, by promoting a scaled-down version of the same urban vision.

The values motivating her might also have included true feelings of patriotism towards her 'dearest fatherland', as she calls not Rome but Patara in her inscription. But putting money into immortalizing her name in marble did not make Procla a Florence Nightingale. Charity in the Christian sense lay in the future, even if the inhabitants of Patara enjoyed shows in the local theatre and other amenities, including the dubious benefits of the public baths.

In 2014 I heard an illuminating lecture by a Finnish expert in public health with a sideline in ancient sanitation. His essential point was that neither Greeks nor Romans had a concept of waterborne disease. So dysentery, typhus and diarrhoea must have been major killers. He noted that Roman cities often placed public toilets near or in the bathhouses and private facilities next to the kitchen.

Patara's impressive Roman baths with their Turkish-style suites of rooms would have been unhealthy unless the authorities maintained a constant throughput of clean water. With no understanding of these health risks, they had other priorities when they built the aqueduct fetching water from 12 miles away. This would have been a status symbol for the town as much as anything. In sum, we should not be too rose-tinted about Roman sanitation. It is not clear that it contributed to higher standards of living in the cities of the empire.

After Lycia, Quintus Veranius died serving the next emperor in a very different province:

> Veranius, after having ravaged the Silures in some trifling raids, was prevented by death from extending the war. While he lived, he had a great name for manly independence, though, in his will's final words, he betrayed a flatterer's weakness; for, after heaping adulation on Nero, he added that he should have conquered the province for him, had he lived for the next two years.

Tacitus had a sharp eye for the necessary vice of flattery. It was part of the performance which men of his class felt obliged to put on to convince the emperor of their loyalty. As for this last posting of Veranius, the Silures were Britons inhabiting what is now the county of Monmouthshire in south Wales. For today's second homeowners from London this is an under-three-hour commute by motorway. Local shops stock the same luxuries as those of the capital. It is hard to put ourselves in the place of the Romans. Before they conquered it, Britannia was so remote as to be almost a land of legend.

But conquer it they did. In AD 43 Claudius, a mere step-grandson, not a direct descendant, of Augustus, decided to continue where Julius Caesar had left off in order to burnish his credentials as emperor. After his death, his successors persevered with the fighting. A Roman emperor campaigned in Scotland as late as AD 208. By then the Romans had largely contented themselves with the annexation of most of what is now England and Wales.

I recently visited the archaeological site in south Wales which the Romans called 'Isca of the Silures'. In recent times the staff here have offered a range of children's events linked to the Roman finds. A 'Summer of Stories' features the Roman fortress and baths. Children can paint a Roman actor's mask, or use stickers to make their own Roman gladiator, an activity referencing the most imposing monument here, an earthwork amphitheatre.

These children's activities do indeed convey something about the Roman way of life of the legion stationed here from around AD 74. Isca was a Roman army camp guarded by a strong wall of stone. The rural landscape hereabouts, part of the borderlands between what is now England and Wales, suggests the fertile – and taxable – terrain which the Romans were mainly interested in holding in their island possession.

The Romans would have seen a real difference between Britons and Lycians. We have seen how the latter, an indigenous Anatolian people, were early adopters, and adaptors, of Greek culture. Four centuries later, Romans could lump them together with their Aegean neighbours as 'Greeks'. Local benefactor Vilia Procla did not need reminding of the benefits of the Roman way of life. So much of this, as we have seen, was anyway Greek-inspired.

The Romans like the Greeks saw lands where this pan-Mediterranean lifestyle held little or no sway in a less favourable light. One of the more interesting archaeological finds of recent years is a wafer-thin writing tablet of wood from a Roman rubbish heap on Hadrian's Wall (of which more later). On it a Roman of the military persuasion had penned a Latin letter to a comrade in the years around AD 90: 'The Britons are unprotected by armour. There are very many cavalry. The cavalry do not use swords nor do the Brittunculi mount in order to throw javelins.' In Latin 'Brittunculi' is an offensive diminutive. Modern translations include 'nasty' or 'wretched little Brits'. Here we have what nowadays would be labelled casual racism. Like most Greeks, many Roman minds arranged the world into a hierarchy of ethnicities. Indigenous peoples whose way of life differed markedly from their own, where chiefs, tribes and buildings of wood replaced the familiar world of Mediterranean-style cities, many Romans viewed with less respect.

Tacitus for one thought that high-level encouragement to promote Roman civilization took place in conquered territories of this type. The passage is worth quoting in full:

> To accustom to rest and repose through the charms of luxury a population scattered and barbarous and therefore inclined to war, Agricola gave private encouragement and public aid to the building of temples, courts of justice and dwelling-houses, praising the energetic, and reproving the indolent. Thus an honourable rivalry took the place of compulsion. He likewise provided a liberal education for the sons of the chiefs, and showed such a preference for the natural powers of the Britons over the industry of the Gauls that they who lately disdained the tongue of Rome now coveted its eloquence. Hence, too, a liking sprang up for our style of dress, and the 'toga' became fashionable. Step by step they were led to things which dispose to vice, the lounge, the bath, the elegant banquet. All this in their ignorance, they called civilization, when it was but a part of their servitude.

Here by the way is a wonderful example of why Tacitus remains so readable today. Tacitus was an imperial insider. This Agricola, governor of Britain from AD 77 to 84, was Tacitus's own father-in-law, whom he respected and admired; he himself was a senator and proconsul. This did not prevent him from offering a cynical critique of methods of imperial pacification employed by people like himself. His critique is tinged, it will be noted, with condescension towards the Britons. He portrays their chiefly families as blinkered colluders with the occupying power.

Generally speaking, it is the leaders of a dominated society who are best placed, by their wealth and position, to mobilize resistance movements. Like Alexander with the Persian nobles, the Romans therefore favoured a collaborationist system of governing their provinces. All things being equal, they preserved and worked with traditional local hierarchies. They hoped that the prominent people with the most to lose would make their peace with the new 'facts' and set an example of peaceable co-existence with the newcomers.

In the portico of the Council Chamber in the town of Chichester in southern England the notice 'No cycles' aims to protect the object displayed on the wall just above it. This mutilated slab of Dorset marble has had a colourful afterlife. Found nearby in 1723, it was quickly purloined by the local duke to adorn his estate.

Having the taste for the antique of the men and women of his class and time, he built a folly which he called the Temple of Neptune and Minerva for the express purpose of displaying the slab. In 1907 the then duke returned the slab to Chichester after demolishing the folly, supposedly because King Edward VII complained that it blocked the view from his bedroom window when he came to stay.

The slab's collectability comes from the fine lettering of its ancient Latin inscription, its great historical interest from the content:

> To Neptune and Minerva, for the welfare of the Divine House by the authority of Tiberius Claudius Togidubnus, great king of Britain, the guild of smiths and those therein gave this temple from their own resources, Pudens, son of Pudentinus, presenting the site.

With its mention of mainstream Roman deities, the loyal wishing well of the imperial family, the artisans organized into a guild, the civic philanthropy of private donors, and the purely Roman names of this 'Pudens son of Pudentinus', here we have an inscription which on the face of it could come from any town – Chichester was once Roman Noviomagus – in the western, more Latin-using, parts of the Roman Empire.

The name and title of the authorizing grandee are another matter. Personal names beginning 'Togi-' are quite common in ancient Celtic. As the title leaves in no doubt, this is a friendly British chief transformed into a Roman client ruler of these parts. To judge from his additional names, Claudius in person had negotiated with him, sealing the political deal with a gift of the Roman citizenship to Togidubnus individually, in or around AD 43.

This Togidubnus also refashioned his cultural identity, along the lines that Tacitus's father-in-law envisaged for leading British families. In the 1960s archaeologists dug up the remains of a luxurious Roman-style country house not far from the waters of Chichester harbour. Built in the AD 70s, the complex is so unexpected and so exceptional – over a hundred rooms, many Italian-style mosaic floors, formal gardens with water features and so on – that its original owner had to be someone of unusual eminence in the area. Togidubnus is the obvious candidate.

The Romans were used to encountering societies where inequality was the norm, like their own. A shared acknowledgement of high social status could bridge the cultural gap between a Veranius and a Togidubnus – especially if common pleasures were there to promote personal affinity. An unusual find from the villa site – called Fishbourne – suggests the possibilities.

This is a small piece of onyx, originally set into a ring to be worn on someone's finger. Engraved into the stone is a horse and a palm frond – the symbol of victory in the Greek and Roman world. Given the date, the AD 60s, the excavators could not resist speculating: 'It wouldn't be unreasonable to suggest that it belonged to the putative owner of the Palace, King Togidubnus. Perhaps future excavations should look for a racecourse!' As for the Romans, a person only has to see a *Ben Hur* film to know something of their fanatical love of the horsey spectacle of chariot racing.

In earlier times I used to help set questions on Roman Britain for the pre-university exam in British secondary education. A favourite was on the lines of 'How widespread was the use of Latin in Roman Britain?' The underlying aim was to get candidates thinking about the cultural impact of the Roman occupation on the indigenous population. The Chichester inscription shows the early appearance of Latin as the public language of a British tribal centre, as Noviomagus was.

Another tribal centre outside Reading, in the Thames valley, has produced Latin graffiti left by the town's artisans in the clay of roof tiles and building bricks. One brick, broken, is incised with the Latin word *puellam*, 'girl'. As a book on Roman Britain published in a politer age puts it, it is 'part of an amatory sentence otherwise lost'. It is interesting to find literacy among the town's brickmakers, not to mention a knowledge of Latin, absorbed perhaps from the concentration of Latin-speakers in this centre of local administration, as Roman Silchester was.

A smattering of Latin hardly proves that the lower orders of society in Roman Britain felt shared interests with the occupying power to the same degree as a rich and powerful Briton like Togidubnus. Some archaeologists talk about the 'creative' blending of cultures in the hands of natives who – possibly – were far from bending over backwards to adopt Roman ways.

So with diet: domestic rubbish from Romano-British sites produces evidence for an ancient fusion cuisine – meals of native mutton accompanied by the so-called ketchup of the Roman world, a mass-produced fish sauce. Still, archaeologists realize that inferring a political outlook from a food recipe is not straightforward.

Under the emperors the officials sent out to govern provinces were by and large no longer as oppressive as in the bad old days of the republic. Caesar had mostly abolished the system of tax-farming, in which governors often colluded. When they were not fighting wars, governors spent much of their time presiding as judges in periodic courts held around the towns of their province. Around AD 100 a Greek writer nicely caught the bustle of the annual governor's assizes in a town in the province of Asia (western Turkey): 'The courts ... bring together an innumerable multitude of people – litigants, judges, orators, governors, attendants, slaves, pimps, muleteers, shopkeepers, prostitutes, and craftsmen.' This was a system of justice which looks impressive on paper, but which in practice, as in other pre-industrial empires, was easier to access for the better off, who had the time and means to make the – often long – journey to the governor's court, not to mention pay the legal costs of preparing for an appearance before his tribunal.

Even in assize towns (the minority in a province), most people probably relied on the extensive powers of local magistrates where petty disputes and crimes were concerned. These two jurisdictions operated different legal systems, local law on the one hand, Roman on the other. It is easy to imagine the chaotic co-existence of overlapping or even conflicting legal rights. The Romans were less concerned about this than they were in monopolizing the right to impose the death penalty – the power of the governor that the Romans grimly termed the 'right of the sword'.

A modern judge describing his day is likely sooner rather than later to mention the paperwork – the papers for the day's cases, the writing of judgements and so on. Egyptologists and amateurs rifling the waste paper, or rather papyrus, of Roman Egypt have opened a vivid window onto the workings of the courts in this corner of the empire with their finds of thousands of ancient legal documents.

The mature system is illustrated by this extract dating from AD 245. It formed part of a petition by an Egyptian woman to the governor of Egypt, sitting in Alexandria as he had done since Octavian's conquest in 30 BC:

> To Valerius Firmus, prefect of Egypt, from Aurelia Arsinoe. I ask, my lord, that you grant me as guardian in accordance with the Julian and

Titian Law and decree of the Senate Aurelius Herminus. [Year] 2, 26th [day of the Egyptian month] Pachon. Sheet 94, Roll 1.

The sheet number identifies the place of the document in the governor's archive. Here legal papers were arranged in numbered 'sheets', each sheet made up of a series of 'rolls', the end of one glued to the start of another. So here is a hint of what once must have been a governor's dusty archive in Alexandria, filling up with shelves of legal papyri.

The petitioner shows familiarity with the specifics of Roman law – she cites the legislation that gave Egypt's Roman governor the competence to appoint guardians. Roman law traditionally saw women as legally impaired by their lack of good sense, so the unmarried Arsinoe needed a male guardian to run her affairs now that her father was dead. Ruled by the Romans for over 250 years, Egyptians like Arsinoe had become increasingly familiar with how to operate the Roman legal system.

She needed to be, because she was a Roman citizen. So were all Egyptians by AD 245. Three decades previously a Roman emperor had decided that all free men and women in the empire were to enjoy this status (the so-called Antonine Constitution). The long-term effect was to promote a shared Roman identity throughout the empire.

In other ways too Arsinoe lived in a Roman world undergoing rapid change. At the date of her petition the ruling emperor, despite his Greek name (Philip), was a Roman of Arabian heritage from what is now southern Syria. At exactly this time of growing unity in diversity that Philip's accession seems neatly to symbolize, however, the cohesion of the empire began to be tested by mass migration.

A growing levelling of Roman and non-Roman, as well as concerns for the empire's security, had older roots. To think more about these matters, I return now to the reign of the emperor Hadrian (AD 117–138).

CHAPTER 18

'BARBARIANS' AT THE GATE

At the time of writing an outlay of around £480 or US$600 buys a nice silver coin of the emperor Hadrian, presenting him in the role of peacemaker. Minted at Rome, this was an issue showing on one side a bust of Hadrian depicted as a wreathed ruler, and on the other a draped woman whom the Latin legend identifies as 'PAX', Peace. She holds a horn-shaped container overflowing with natural produce. This ancient symbol of abundance and prosperity was called a cornucopia, meaning 'horn of plenty'.

The symbolism here is not subtle. By his feats of arms the emperor as commander-in-chief keeps the empire safe from enemies. The resulting state of peace brings prosperity for the empire's inhabitants. Although this is a positive image of peace as something more than the absence of war, the coin also emphasizes the martial success of the emperor that alone made peace possible.

Military victory was the demonstration of Rome's supremacy from which all else flowed – the empire of peace and the orderly life which it permitted, as well as imperial displays of clemency for the conquered, humiliation for impertinent people daring to challenge Roman power, and so on.

Tacitus wrote that Augustus 'won over everyone with the sweetness of repose'. He meant provincials as well as the Romans of Rome and Italy. Had he been more interested in the provinces, Tacitus might have expanded on the sheer extraordinariness of the lengthy peace which much of the Mediterranean had enjoyed for nigh on four generations by his day. Surely this was the greatest boon of the ancient Romans to their subjects.

Peace did not just promote greater prosperity. It also spread a psychological sense of the world as a more stable place to a degree that must have been unprecedented in antiquity. The great outpouring of inscriptions on durable stone and of monumental architecture in town after town of the Roman Empire during the first two centuries AD had something to do with this sense of a securer future into which the pax Romana had lulled many people.

The Romans inherited a them-and-us division of the world from the Greeks. Outside the empire were the so-called barbarians, savage and insolent until humbled by Roman arms. In 122 the emperor Hadrian visited Britain. Here he did something that the Romans had never done before.

When I taught a course on Hadrian at Newcastle University I used to take the class into the archaeological museum on the campus. It includes a collection of artefacts from the line of Hadrian's Wall, which runs less than a mile away. Here I showed them a not especially impressive block of Roman masonry with this Latin inscription: '[Work] of Emperor Caesar Trajan Hadrian Augustus. Legion II Augusta [built it] under Aulus Platorius Nepos, propraetorian legate.' The wording underlines that this was a project dear to the heart of Hadrian – a personal commission. Squads of legionaries working in sections built a continuous wall – not terribly well, the archaeologists say – in what is now northern England running from one side of the island to the other. It was no light undertaking: the wall covered a length of 74 miles. While half of it was built of turf, the other half was stonework mostly 8 feet thick and perhaps 12 feet high.

Hadrian's Wall was the talk of this corner of the Roman Empire. Visitors wanted a souvenir. In the British Museum you can see a modern replica (the original is in private hands) of a remarkable bronze bowl. Around the outside runs an enamel-work frieze showing a battlemented wall and above it Latin letters spelling out the Roman names of forts on Hadrian's Wall. The original once belonged to the owner of a Roman villa some 300 miles away in south-west England.

Specialists hotly debate Hadrian's purpose in commissioning this wall, whether it was a defensive fortification to protect the province from northern 'barbarians', or more like a customs barrier, controlling the movement of people and goods, or mainly a massive show of Roman resources and will, meant to cow the enemy. Or even a training task for a frontier soldiery in need of discipline.

As well as being any or all of these things, I myself believe that Hadrian wanted news of his wall to filter back into the imperial heartlands to reassure provincials that the Roman emperor was primed to protect them against barbarians. A generation later a rich Greek landowner in Asia Minor seems to have got wind of the British wall when he praised the benefits of the Roman Empire in a public speech:

> An encamped army like a rampart encloses the civilised world in a ring ... [The walls] have not been built with asphalt and baked brick nor do they stand there gleaming with stucco. Oh, but these ordinary works too exist at their individual places – yes, in very great number, and, as Homer says of the palace wall, 'fitted close and accurately with stones, and boundless in size and gleaming more brilliantly than bronze'.

The quotation from the great Homer is apt in a eulogy by a Greek magnate for the Roman frontier armies and barriers defending his way of life. The metaphor of gleaming metal is interesting too: it would suit Hadrian's Wall if this was originally whitewashed, as some specialists think.

There are signs that some provincials under Hadrian were jittery about the Roman delivery of the empire's main promise to conquered subjects – security. When he succeeded Trajan in AD 117, the middle-aged Hadrian, a seasoned Roman general, had to take immediate measures to restore 'pax'.

These included an unheard-of thing – Hadrian evacuated the conquests of his predecessor on the eastern front. Here the Romans had as a troublesome neighbour on the east bank of the River Euphrates another warlike people, the Parthians, whose kings ruled a ramshackle empire stretching to Pakistan. To some onlookers this evacuation must have seemed like an admission that Rome had met its match.

Hadrian's regime sought to offer reassurance. As seen in the prologue, Hadrian was the subject of a statue type popular in parts of the eastern Mediterranean. It shows him as a victorious general resting a foot on a prone captive, whose 'barbarian' trousers and a bow and arrows identify the figure as one of the Parthians. Notoriously Parthia's mounted archers could turn and release 'Parthian shots' to their rear in mid-gallop – a redoubtable feat of horsemanship before the mediaeval invention of the saddle.

The regime probably approved of the lost prototype of the statue and made clear that it was its pleasure if eastern provincials took the initiative and created their own versions. Some in Hadrian's circle might have hoped to reinforce an attitude of provincial confidence in the traditional claim of the Romans to an unbeatable supremacy. There were also 'enemies' within:

> They would eat the flesh of their victims, make belts for themselves of their entrails, anoint themselves with their blood and wear their skins for clothing; many they sawed in two, from the head downwards; others they gave to wild beasts, and still others they forced to fight as gladiators. In all 220,000 persons perished. In Egypt too, they perpetrated many similar outrages, and in Cyprus . . .

This description belongs to a Roman historian's account of a violent uprising by Diaspora Jews living in what is now Libya, then a Roman province. To Greeks and Romans these atrocities marked the rebels as barbarians, outside the pale of civilization.

The truth of this Roman account cannot now be established. But it is clear that this Jewish revolt two years before Hadrian's accession was serious. There might have been a concerted plan among different Diaspora communities in Libya, Egypt and Cyprus. Some scholars think that the rebels had an ultimate aim, to wrest Jerusalem, the traditional centre of Jewish cult, from Roman control.

No other subject people still resisted Roman rule so long after conquest. The Jews inside the Roman Empire shared a uniquely strong identity. This was based on ethnicity, language and customs, and memories of a glorious history of independence under their own kings – David, Solomon and the rest. These markers of Jewish identity were all bound up with their distinctive religion, based on holy writings familiar to all Jews.

In an earlier revolt in the Roman province of Judaea itself, the Romans burnt down the Jewish Temple. In an annual day of fast, Jews to this day remember the destruction of AD 70, a half-century before Hadrian's accession. To say that this Roman action would have appalled ancient Jews, wherever they lived, must be an understatement.

Hadrian did not just keep a weather eye on the Jews. It is hard to resist the conclusion that this intelligent but complex man provoked the Jewish revolt that broke out in AD 132. Traditionally Roman in so many ways, Hadrian was also said to be an amateur sculptor and architect. His admiration for Greek civilization extended to its cultural practice of pederasty. When he visited Egypt in AD 130, his travelling companion was Antinous, a comely youth of Greek heritage.

A Roman history of Hadrian's reign compiled over two centuries later claimed that the Jews began this new war 'because they were forbidden to practise circumcision'. Greeks saw circumcision as unsightly. Did the 'Graecizing' Hadrian share this aesthetic prejudice, as one scholar has suggested?

In addition, amid the rubble of Jerusalem he decided – provocatively as it transpired – to found a colony of Roman soldiers. A coin from the colonial mint, up and running almost at once, commemorates Hadrian in person marking with plough and oxen the limits of the farmland in a traditional Roman rite. He meant Aelia Capitolina – as he now renamed the place after himself (Aelius Hadrianus) and Jupiter (Capitolinus) – to be a Roman bridgehead in potentially hostile terrain.

The ensuing revolt developed into full-blown war. The rebels had a leader and claimed to be an independent state. Hadrian had to take command himself. When it finally came, Roman retribution was terrible. According to an ancient Jewish tradition this is what happened southwest of Jerusalem at ancient Bethar, where the rebels made their last stand:

> Hadrian the blasphemer had a great vineyard of eighteen square miles, as much as the distance from Tiberias to Sepphoris. He surrounded it with a fence made from those slain at Bethar as high as a man with outstretched arms.

Again, it seems superfluous to judge with modern hindsight this iron-fisted episode of ancient imperialism. At much the same time as he was fighting this war, Hadrian himself seems to have authorized what experts call the 'province' coinage. This torrent of coin types issued at Rome in all the denominations of the official mint has a unity of theme and originality of subject matter that only the summit of power could have orchestrated.

These coins are important because they show that Hadrian's imperial thinking was running along new lines.

On one side the different types all show the same head of Hadrian. On the other they celebrate different regions of the empire – twenty-five all told – and Hadrian's visits and gifts to them. A typical example shows Hadrian dressed in his toga raising a kneeling woman, along with a Latin legend: 'For the restorer of Gaul.'

What this coinage celebrated was the regional diversity of the empire and the equal care of the ruler for its constituent parts. This was a more benevolent image of Roman rule than the provincials were used to receiving from the centre of power. It was an official attitude tending to gloss over the traditional distinction Romans made between citizens and non-citizens: all were the concerns of the caring emperor. It was this idea of the Roman state as one huge unit which a later emperor took further in AD 212 by giving the citizenship to pretty much everyone of free status in the empire.

Hadrian's concerns about the perimeter defences of the empire led him to undo an engineering feat of his predecessor. A century later even what was left, twenty stone arches 'placed in a river so deep, in water so full of eddies, and on a bottom so muddy', impressed Roman visitors. This great river was the Danube.

Walking its length in more recent times, the travel writer Patrick Leigh Fermor relayed the local stories told him of the fishy invaders sometimes swimming upstream as far west as Vienna and even beyond. These included giant sturgeon-like creatures, their true home 'the Black Sea and the Caspian and the Sea of Azov'. Trajan and Hadrian were concerned about invasive use of the river, not from the east, but from the north.

The Romans tended not to see their empire as the British saw theirs – a mass of territory colouring much of the known world in British pink. True to their militaristic ethos, the Romans thought more in terms of what they called their 'imperium', their power to order other people around, mainly thanks to their victories and conquests.

Still, in time they did come to crystallize a sense of this imperium as a geographical space with limits. To their north, they conceived the Danube and the Rhine as two great rivers at the southern and western edges respectively of a vast area largely beyond their empire, and to a large extent their ken. They called it 'Germania'.

Around AD 100, this region was the subject of what one twentieth-century ancient historian called 'among the one hundred most dangerous books ever written'. What attracted German nationalists of more recent times to this work, Nazis included, was the way in which its Roman author – Tacitus again – presented the Germanic peoples as independent and, after their fashion, moral, as well as being truly Germanic. Supposedly they had always lived where they did.

This was not unstinting admiration, it must quickly be added. Tacitus did full justice to the Roman stereotype of the Germanic 'barbarian' who had once annihilated a Roman army led by a kinsman of Augustus himself:

> The Harii, besides being superior in strength to the tribes just enumerated, savage as they are, make the most of their natural ferocity by the help of art and opportunity. Their shields are black, their bodies dyed. They choose dark nights for battle, and, by the dread and gloomy aspect of their death-like host, strike terror into the foe, who can never confront their strange and almost infernal appearance.

By Hadrian's time there was already a history of migrating Germanic tribes seeking Roman lands on which they could settle. In their heyday, the Romans had a history of refusing these requests, probably from wariness about sharing land with unconquered and independent people from outside their empire. When they did do so, they presented the action as a form of subjection. So a Roman general boasted how, governing what is now Serbia in the AD 60s, he 'transplanted – and forced to pay tribute – more than 100,000 Transdanubians with their wives and children, chiefs and kings'.

A generation after Hadrian, his successors had to confront a major crisis on the Danube. In the mid-160s an alliance of tribes from the other side crossed the river and plundered Roman territory to the south. The situation worsened before it improved, with the enemy reaching as far south as Aquileia, an Italian city at the head of the Adriatic Sea that now found itself under siege. In the capital there was such 'terror' that the emperor Marcus Aurelius summoned non-Roman priests from all over the empire to do their best.

In 1890–91 a French archaeologist recovered twenty-four pieces of a marble inscription broken up as building material for a mediaeval wall some 50 miles north-west of Athens. The Ancient Greek text records 'the names of the young soldiers who left voluntarily on campaign for the very great and very divine Emperor Caesar M[arcus] Aurelius Antoninus Augustus'. There follows a list of the eighty local men together with their doctor – a large corps of able-bodied youth from what was only a country town, a place called Thespiae. Although called volunteers, these were in fact conscripts levied by the Romans as part of the massive recruitment for an imperial fight-back on the Danube.

As well as levies in peaceful provinces like Greece, we hear of gladiators, brigands and slaves being pressed into service. The emperor Marcus Aurelius helped fund this emergency army by selling off the family silver, or rather, the luxuries of the imperial court – 'besides clothes and goblets and gold cups he even sold gold statues, together with paintings by great artists'.

In Rome an ancient column still stands in its original place, less famous than its older sibling, Trajan's Column. The so-called Column of Marcus Aurelius is decorated with a narrative spiral that celebrates victory in the ensuing war, and what Romans must have hoped was a permanent restoration of the security of the northern limits.

One peculiar scene is of greater historical interest than a first sighting suggests. It shows a long-haired, bearded divinity of enormous size from whose head and outstretched arms wavy lines flow onto the battle scene below – envisaged rather predictably by the sculptor as an orderly grouping of Roman troops and a pile of Germanic bodies. What is depicted is a moment – famous at the time – in the emperor's northern wars, when a Roman army snatched an unexpected victory over a Germanic one.

Hemmed in by the enemy in the heat of the summer and cut off from drinking water, the parched Roman troops were starting to fail, 'when suddenly many clouds gathered and a mighty rain, not without divine interposition, burst upon them'. A child at the time, the Roman historian Cassius Dio also recorded the tale that an Egyptian magician in the emperor's entourage had employed his arts to alter the weather. On the column, what is pouring off the colossal winged figure is the victory-bringing rainwater.

Other people had strong convictions about where divine responsibility alone could lie for what was understood by contemporaries as a miracle: 'The Germanic drought was removed by the rains obtained through the prayers of the Christians who chanced to be fighting under him [the emperor].' Also a child at the time, this writer – called Tertullian – grew up to be a prolific author of Christian tracts.

What is striking is the indeterminate identity of the divinity on the column. It was as if the sculptor deliberately sought to portray not a recognizable Roman god such as Jupiter helping the Romans in their peril, as you might expect, but an undefined deity, one whom viewers of different religious persuasions could identify according to taste. In the late second century AD, the tectonic plates of ancient religion were shifting, and official Roman art here seems to take account of it. The next chapter will say more about the rising sect of the Christians.

When I was a PhD student I spent many weeks in southern Greece studying the remnants of ancient Sparta. A nineteenth-century creation, today's town of Sparti partly overlies its more famous forebear. A wander round the back streets takes you past building sites where work is held up by the discovery of ancient remains. These are likely to be Roman. Dusty plastic coverings may well protect mosaic floors, or hypocausts, the underfloor heating system of Roman baths. In their copper age, the descendants of the famous Spartans of old survived as a prosperous town of the Roman Empire.

In these later times the Spartans were as fond of carving inscriptions as any other Greek provincial city. On the northern outskirts of the town you can walk through olive groves to the ancient theatre – in the monumental form you see today, with seating of local marble, a Roman creation of the time of Augustus. Here you can stand in front of a masonry wall covered with inscribed records of proud town councillors.

At Sparta as elsewhere, fluctuations in this 'epigraphic habit', as experts call the ancient world's enthusiasm for writing on stone, can be a barometer of the larger mood of the times.

The Romans themselves held that their empire enjoyed its golden age under the rule of a series of five 'good' emperors. On the death of Marcus Aurelius, an emperor was succeeded for the first time since the reign of Titus, who died in AD 81, by his own flesh and blood. Of this moment the Roman senator and historian Cassius Dio wrote, 'Our history now descends from a kingdom of gold to one of iron and rust.' This was Dio's perspective half a century later, after living through turbulent times, including the reign of the vicious son of Marcus Aurelius, Commodus, and then a civil war ending with the advent of a new imperial lineage of mixed North African, Syrian, and perhaps Italian, heritage.

Judging from what has survived, Sparta's town councillors were at their most lively in flaunting their parish-pump politics on stone during the first sixty years of the second century AD. Under Marcus Aurelius, whose reign, despite his 'goodness', was a time of insecurity for the Roman Empire, as we just saw, Sparta's epigraphic appetite fell off. It was as if sombre events in the wider world had punctured their parochial enthusiasms.

If so, the Spartan mood might have lifted under the new emperor. In my studies I re-examined two inscribed blocks found in the 1960s during the building of modern Sparti's vegetable market. They belonged to what was once an imposing monument, a base perhaps 25 feet long, supporting a lost row of statues. This must have been the commission of all time for their local sculptor.

The life-size images showed a new imperial family. There was the emperor Septimius Severus, who ruled from AD 193 to 211 and came from a family based in Roman Africa, his Syrian wife Julia Domna, their two sons and their daughter-in-law. The empress's title shows how close relations were between this new imperial family and the army. She is styled 'Mother of the Camp'.

In AD 235 the murder of a teenage emperor and his mother brought the Severan lineage to a violent end. In this youth's name his generals had waged war to protect the empire both in the east and the north. The deed was done while the emperor – Alexander Severus was his name – was with his troops on the west bank of the Rhine preparing for war with Germanic tribes. A senior army officer, the instigator of the murders, had already been hailed by Roman troops as emperor. He inaugurated a new breed of Roman ruler, as this snobbish assessment by a contemporary writer conveys:

... by his birth and normal behaviour he was a barbarian. Possessing the bloodthirsty temperament derived from his ancestors and his country, he devoted himself to strengthening his rule by cruel actions. He was afraid that the senate and his subjects would despise him, forgetting his present good fortune and fixing their attention on the humble circumstances of his birth. There was a scandalous story widely circulated that he was supposed to have been a shepherd in the Thracian mountains until he offered himself for service in the small, local army because of his physical size and strength. It was the hand of chance that had brought him to rule the Roman empire.

Here are the ingredients for the following half-century of Roman history. External enemies on more than one front put the defences of the empire under increasing threat. A mounting atmosphere of military crisis favoured the careers of talented soldiers no matter what their background, and could take them to the very top, as here. Lacking legitimacy among the traditional stakeholders of the imperial system, notably the senatorial aristocracy and the Roman plebs, men swept by the military tide into the highest office relied on the fickle loyalty of the soldiers.

Here is the end of this Thracian ex-shepherd (if he really was), just three years later (AD 238), at the hands of his own soldiers:

> With great daring the men went to Maximinus' tent about mid-day, and tore down his portrait from the standards with the assistance of the bodyguards. When Maximinus and his son came out of their tent to try and negotiate, the soldiers killed them both without listening. Their bodies were thrown out for anyone to desecrate and trample on, before being left to be torn to pieces by dogs and birds.

The Spartan town councillors felt less optimistic now. Under mounting financial pressure from the state, they also went in for cost cutting. Whereas once they honoured a dignitary with a full-length statue of bronze or marble on a stone base, now, when they bothered at all, they tended to make do with a squared shaft of stone with a carved head on top. By the later 240s, the local masons who used to cut inscriptions were more or less out of work.

After the mid-third century, the Athenians too become a dramatic gauge of a changing world. Rule by Roman emperors had been good for Athens as for Sparta. The descendants of Themistocles, Pericles and the like, as members of the aristocratic lineages of Roman Athens styled themselves, had seen their city outgrow its former walls. There were many new amenities, not all of them gifts of emperor Hadrian.

In the middle of the AD 200s this sense of relative well-being late in the life of ancient Athens evaporated when the Roman emperors no longer seemed able to deliver protection. Visitors to the Acropolis begin their visit by passing through an ancient gateway flanked by two towers. They may notice that the ill-fitting blocks look as if the ancient builders reused them. Closer scrutiny shows that they did so with some art. They flanked the portal (for instance) with a decorative band of grey marble that contrasts with the surrounding white.

In a way, the building of this defensive work in the later third century AD was a case of the Athenians closing the stable door after the horse had bolted. In recent years Austrian scholars using digital technology have performed the heroic feat of reading the earlier Greek writing on a manuscript in a Vienna library which eleventh-century scribes had recycled for a fresh text. Underneath the scholars discovered a fragment of an ancient account of barbarian invasions of Greece early in the AD 260s.

We learn that the invaders moved southwards through Greece intending to plunder the rich sanctuaries of Athens and elsewhere. With no Roman troops in sight, the Greeks elected their own generals and prepared to block the invaders at the historic pass of Thermopylae. One of the generals harangued this Greek home guard with stirring talk: 'Your ancestors, fighting in this place in former times, did not let Greece down and deprive it of its free state, for they fought bravely in the Persian wars . . .' This time the invaders turned back before reaching Athens. What happened a few years later, in AD 267/8, we already know from ancient writings: the luck and pluck of the Athenians failed them.

The Heruli, a migrant people originating in Scandinavia, captured the city despite stout resistance from the locals. Modern excavations show that the ancient civic centre, the agora, full of historic and famous buildings, now reached the end of its long life. Devastated by the Heruli, it was left as a quarry of ruins. Reusing whatever they could, the Athenians now fortified a shrunken core of their city, including new defences for the Acropolis. This was the diminished urban pattern of the future in many parts of the empire.

In the following two decades or so a continuing combination of military crisis and political instability threatened to break up the empire. On the south-eastern edges of the Roman province of Syria an ancient oasis city flourished under imperial rule thanks to its location on caravan routes servicing the trade in luxuries between the Roman Empire and the east. This was a place of mixed population, culture and language, where Greek-speakers lived alongside speakers of a Semitic tongue, Aramaic. As Pope Francis reminded Israel's prime minister in 2014, this would have been the everyday language of Jesus.

Great architecture sprang up at Palmyra, as did great ambitions among the leading families. They sensed an opportunity as Roman authority over the region faltered and the Roman subjects in these parts cried out for protection from the Sasanian Persians, a menacing new power with origins in what is now Iran.

Out of this environment emerged Zenobia, widow of a Palmyrene prince with an Arabian name. She took Roman imperial titles, briefly turned Palmyra into an eastern Athens by attracting Greek intellectuals to her court, and invaded neighbouring Roman provinces, capturing Alexandria in 270.

Later Roman writers claimed that she compared herself to Cleopatra. Certainly she must have been formidable. She seems to have aroused the same fears in Rome, fuelled by orientalism and misogyny, as the 'Egyptian woman' of three centuries earlier. Finally a Roman soldier-emperor marched out to suppress her.

Franks, Sarmatians by the thousand, once and once again we've slain.
    Now we seek a thousand Persians.

Supposedly Roman soldiers sang this song after an officer of humble origins led them to victory against the Franks, Rome's name for a grouping of Germanic peoples who had invaded Roman Gaul. As a garrison commander on the Danube, Aurelian, as he was called, also killed in one day forty-eight Sarmatians – these were a nomadic people on the move under pressure from Germanic tribes. Other stories, possibly tall, accrued to this Aurelian. He was a stern disciplinarian in the harshest Roman tradition. The soldiers feared him. Hailed as emperor by his troops, he quickly moved against Zenobia.

Defeating and capturing her, he returned again to extinguish a final flame of Palmyrene rebelliousness. A Roman tradition claimed that on this occasion Aurelian stopped the slaughter, asking, 'To whom, at this rate, shall we leave the land or the city?' In a curious foretaste of today's concerns, he was also said to have given orders to use Zenobia's treasure to restore Palmyra's war-damaged monuments.

In the chaos of the times, there were chances too on the other side of the empire for would-be rulers of Roman-style breakaway states. In 2010 British media carried the story of the chance discovery in a Somerset field of a buried hoard of 52,000 Romano-British coins. First reports claimed that nearly eight hundred of these were minted under the authority of one Carausius.

The thin written sources of the Romans about this man describe him as another soldier risen from the ranks. Roman tradition records his orders 'to clear the sea, which the Franks and Saxons infested' – the English Channel in other words. Supposedly to avoid the death penalty for misappropriating the booty from this campaign, Carausius seized Britannia, assumed Roman imperial titles as Zenobia had done, and for seven years ruled a breakaway domain until an underling murdered him (AD 293).

What is interesting about Carausius – of whom little in truth can be known – is precisely his coins. Uniquely in Roman coinage, Carausius quoted the Roman 'national' poet. An example found in 2005, by a chap with a metal detector on land in Hertfordshire, depicts a rough-and-ready-looking Carausius with his usurped titles 'Imp[erator]' and 'Aug[ustus]'. On the other side a woman, Britannia probably, and a Roman soldier clasp hands. The Latin legend reads 'EXPECTATE VENI'.

In effect a speech bubble for the female figure, this means 'O longed for one, come!' It took a good knowledge of Virgil's long poem, the *Aeneid*, for a modern expert to recognize this legend's seemingly deliberate echo of a question which Aeneas in Book 2 puts to a fellow Trojan in a dream: 'From what shores do you come ['venis'], longed-for ['expectate'] Hector?'

This is all very interesting. It shows that Carausius wanted to project himself as a man of (Roman) culture. If you contemplate who might be reassured by this display of refinement, and important enough to be targeted in this way, one constituency that springs to mind are the civilian owners of the rich villa-estates of Roman Britain – themselves, perhaps, a more cultivated class than we suspected.

One other issue of coins by this rogue emperor merits a pause. It shows him trying to insinuate for contemporaries who handled them his legitimate place in the new arrangements of imperial power emerging on the Continent at the end of the third century AD. One side shows not one but three bearded emperors in overlapping profile. The Latin legend reads 'Carausius and his brothers'. Carausius here cheekily proposes himself as a colleague, equal indeed, of soldier co-emperors who were restoring stability to the Continental empire.

The faux team spirit of this coin is reminiscent of a famous sight in Venice. Visitors stop to take photographs of a curious group of sculptured figures built into the outside of the Doge's Palace. Clearly ancient, they catch the eye because they are carved in the purple stone known as porphyry.

Roman emperors – as depicted here – favoured this material for their portraits because in real life they wore purple clothes as a sign of their rank.

Art historians used to shudder at the style of these figures as evidence for the decline of classical art. Four mature men, similar looking and identically dressed in military garb, stand together in pairs, each twosome clasped in fraternal embrace. All stare intensely at the viewer. Nowadays experts see here the sculptor's success in conveying a political ideal of group solidarity and martial hardiness.

As to who they are, identification cannot be entirely certain, but this foursome seems to represent a new political system inaugurated in AD 293 – a team of emperors: two senior ones, shown earlier with Carausius, and now joined here by two junior ones. They wanted to present the Roman public with an image of harmonious industry as each one in his theatre helped to put the empire back to rights. The first to obtain the imperial power was the initiator of these arrangements. His name was Diocletian, an important reformer, as we shall see in a later chapter.

Under Diocletian's college of four (the so-called Tetrarchy), the Roman state once more persecuted the sect of the Christians. It is time to think more about the religions of the early Roman Empire, since one of them turned out to have the power to transform the empire into a monotheistic state, with longer-term consequences still with us today.

CHAPTER 19

THE 'JESUS MOVEMENT'

For twelve or so years in my former university I worked next door to the professor of Latin. John and I were often in and out of each other's offices. I marvelled that his made mine look positively tidy. When he came into mine, it was usually because his fine brain was whirring and he needed someone to talk at. In his fifties and early sixties, John was increasingly consumed by his researches into the New Testament.

Among specialists, the origins and early days of Christianity, no less than those of Islam, are fiercely controversial. John's researches in this area were no exception. I remember going to hear him give a paper in the School of Divinity of a university neighbour. A senior Anglican prelate sporting clerical purple beneath his grey suit had his eyes raised heavenward for much of the talk, as if silently praying for strength to hear John out.

The early Jesus movement, as John sometimes called it, crystallized around a charismatic healer figure of Jewish ethnicity who never left his native Judaea – a Roman province – during his short life. His public stance as a religious expert brought him to the attention of the Roman authorities. They saw him as politically dangerous and sentenced him to death, probably because Pontius Pilate, the governor, did not want to be seen as soft on possible sedition.

Within two generations of Jesus' crucifixion around AD 30, Greek writings offering accounts of his life and afterlife, as well as the teaching activity of his first followers in cities of the Roman world, were in circulation. Five of these survive today as books of the New Testament – the four Gospels and the Acts of the Apostles. What fascinated John was how the Greek-speakers who read or listened to readings of these first Christian writings might have 'heard' the Greek.

He was convinced that these writings were not just addressing an ideal audience of Greek-reading Jews, including Jewish followers of the new movement. Their authors also, he thought, wrote in a particular way so as to snag the interest of educated Greek-speaking people in the non-Jewish world. These would-be readers were used to, and appreciative of, the allusive tricks typical of Greek literature of the higher sort.

Such literary tricks included punning on people's names. John pointed out that the name 'Iesous' is a Greek rendering of a Hebrew name translatable as 'Yaweh saves'. He charted how often in the Gospels 'Iesous' is coupled with the Greek verb meaning 'to cure' or 'heal' (*iasthai*). Greek readers would have 'heard' this pun in sentence after sentence, like subliminal advertising. What the pun helped to paint, John thought, was a vivid picture of Jesus as a healer, or rather, the Healer, a figure far outstripping the pagan competition.

Among scholars, John's views are not quite mainstream. Competition there certainly was, however. As the title of a book on the subject put it, the Roman Empire was 'a world full of gods'. All over the empire, towns funded and organized the worship of their local pantheons. In Ephesus in western Turkey the evangelizing Paul of Tarsus had a memorable brush with a silversmith who feared for his livelihood. He made images of his city's world-renowned divinity, Artemis, and here was Paul impudently teaching that man-made gods were, well, just that.

Today you can walk the well-preserved thoroughfares of Roman Ephesus, one of the great cities of the empire. Paved marble streets and plazas take you past impressive public buildings. The pièce de résistance, a marvel of modern restoration, is a public library, fronted by a gorgeous façade of marble columns and sculptures personifying the donor's 'Wisdom', 'Knowledge', 'Intelligence' and so on.

The walls of another public amenity, the theatre, spectacular for its size, once hosted a long Greek inscription – 568 lines, no less. This was a heroic act of letter-cutting by ancient masons perched on ladders or scaffolding, since the letters were placed well above human height. It was as if what mattered was the general impression on the ancient passer-by of the great mass of lettering picked out in red.

The curious stranger in this harbour entrepôt asking a local person what it all meant might have learnt the following – that the text recorded a rich donor's gift to his fellow Ephesians of gold and silver religious images that were to be carried in a great annual procession through the city.

The Greek lists the images. The lion's share (ten) were to depict Artemis, the city-goddess par excellence. The remainder included statuettes of 'our lord Emperor' – Trajan in this case, who ruled from 98 to 117 – and his empress; the 'deified' Augustus; other Greek divinities; personifications – the 'revered Senate' and Roman People, along with various civic bodies; and the city's founders. This blend of pagan piety, imperial loyalism and civic patriotism is a reasonable snapshot of how many inhabitants of the empire experienced this 'world full of gods' when they joined in the crowded calendars of religious celebrations laid on by their local authorities.

The religious prominence of Roman emperors deserves more thought. Not just in Ephesus, but everywhere throughout the empire, there were temples, statues, priests, altars, sacrifices and processions all given over to venerating the Roman emperor as if he were a god. Scholars trace the origins of Roman ruler worship back to the Greeks.

As seen, among Greeks this way of thinking and acting had rapidly spiked when they found themselves ruled by the phenomenon that was Alexander. After his death Greeks venerated his successors, the Hellenistic kings. When Rome conquered the east, they worshipped the new power as Roma, a goddess, not to mention individual Romans, usually generals, like Flamininus, 'liberator' of Greece. When Octavian became Augustus, they took to worshipping him and his wife; and on it went.

Here is how a Japanese believer in 1912 wrote about the divinity of the late Emperor Meiji for the benefit of scoffing Westerners:

All soldiers and sailors were ready to die for their Mikado, and the generals and admirals, too, commanded those soldiers and sailors with their own devotion towards the Mikado ... If the Mohammedans concentrate[d] their souls by the faith in Mohammed, and if the Christians concentrated their souls by the faith in Christ, the result should be all the same. I often meet so-called philosophers who are laughing at the superstitions of the religious people or the Mikado-worshipping of Japanese. However right and accurate may be their reasoning, I must say their philosophies are only too shallow. They ought to proceed one step further and think what influence has the concentration of the whole nation's souls! The concentration of our hearts and souls is itself our own God who reigns over us.

Roman subjects of the pre-Christian emperors have left behind no statements which can match this heady mixture of religious and nationalist fervour. In their case, how much was encouragement from above, how much spontaneous initiative by the local authorities? What were the private views of the urbane men and women who served as imperial priests and priestesses all over the empire, people more often than not from much the same cultured background as Polybius in the second century BC, with his startling capacity for treating religious rites as the 'opium of the masses'? Whether we can know if even the huddled masses 'believed' in the divinity of (say) Trajan in the same way that they 'believed' in the other powers to whom they addressed prayers for miraculous help with their lives; how much one can generalize, ever, about what, even nowadays, individuals over a lifetime think, as opposed to say or do, about God – all this and more is part of a modern debate that we cannot go into here.

What we can say is that for some in the Roman Empire the worship of the emperor was another form of flattery; and that for some his local temple symbolized Roman rule, and not always in a good way – when the British queen Boudicca led a revolt, the rebels targeted 'the temple raised to the deified Claudius' in what is now Colchester: this 'continually met the view, like the citadel of an eternal tyranny'.

For many, perhaps the majority, used to taking divinity for granted, the monuments and rites of emperor worship in their town provided entertainment – there were shows of gladiators, wild beast hunts and much more, as well as festive distributions, sacrificial dinners and so on. It may also have given them reassurance of the reality and 'god-like' powers of a distant ruler whom few would ever see in person.

Today many people do not hold with religion being the basis of statehood. As we have seen time and again, this was not true of the ancient states encountered in this book. At Rome, the emperor, as well as being godlike himself, was pontifex maximus, head of Roman religion. He was responsible for maintaining good relations between the Roman gods and the Roman people. Among other things he monitored the state priests of Rome. This was a deadly serious business.

In the AD 80s emperor Domitian felt obliged to mete out the traditional punishment of burial alive when one of the six Vestal Virgins in Rome itself – they tended the sacred fire symbolizing the continuity of the state – was charged with sexual impurity. To the very end she protested – performed, rather – her chastity:

> Whether she was innocent or not, she certainly appeared to be so. Nay, even when she was being let down into the dreadful pit and her dress caught as she was being lowered, she turned and readjusted it, and when the executioner offered her his hand she declined it and drew back, as though she put away from her with horror the idea of having her chaste and pure body defiled by his loathsome touch.

Beyond the state religion and the more or less official cults of the provinces, there existed a sea of unofficial and largely unregulated religious expression.

In the early nineteenth century a slightly mysterious figure who called himself Jean d'Anastasi, perhaps Armenian, washed up in the Ottoman client state of Egypt. Here he befriended the pasha and started to buy ancient Greek papyri offered to him by dealers in Egyptian antiquities. Eventually he sent his collection for auction. It ended up divided between various top museums in Europe. Here is an extract from one of his papyri:

> Take a sprig of laurel and write the two names on its leaves, the one: '[AKRAKANARBA] KRAKANARBA RAKANARBA AKANARBA KANARBA ANARBA NARBA ARBA RBA BA A'; the other: 'SANTALALA ANTALALA NTALALA TALALA ALALA LALA ALA LA A.' Take another sprig with twelve leaves on it, and inscribe on it the following heart-shaped name, while you begin with a sacred utterance [etc.].

Readers of J. K. Rowling might be forgiven for feeling themselves back at wizardry school. The ancient user of this hocus pocus (the spell and accompanying instructions continue on the papyrus for many lines) would have felt himself in terrain both strange and familiar – a land of ancient Egyptian wisdom, yes, but mixed in with major Greek divinities: this spell goes on to invoke Apollo and Zeus among others.

This is not the same sector of humanity's religious experience as the one explored by the twenty-first-century American psychologist Jonathan Haidt in his researches on the link between exposure to moral elevation or beauty and the religious impulse. Earlier we came across fear of ghosts among the Greek settlers of Selinus in Sicily back in the fifth century BC. In the early Roman Empire beliefs and activities nowadays distinguished from conventional religion as the 'supernatural' or 'paranormal' were a more seamless part of the religious spectrum. The Roman world teemed with freelance soothsayers, magicians, sorcerers, astrologers, dream interpreters, fortune-tellers and the rest of it.

The attitude of the state to these activities in the main was one of tolerance. Emperors, indeed, might have such people at their court. As we saw in the last chapter, some said that the miraculous rain saving the Roman army under Marcus Aurelius was brought about by a member of the imperial entourage. This Egyptian magician, called Arnouphis, supposedly invoked the god of the air, Mercury, and thus attracted the rain.

So it is a surprise in some ways to find a Roman emperor persecuting the Jesus movement just over a generation after its founder's crucifixion. At least, that is what the ancients came to believe. In AD 64 a fire devastated the city of Rome. Rather like the Great Fire of London in 1666, it broke out in shops, raged for days and left parts of the city a smoking ruin.

Another similarity was the scapegoating. In 1681 the aldermen of the City of London added an inscription on Christopher Wren's column commemorating the fire, blaming it on 'Ye treachery and malice of ye popish factio'. In imperial Rome, the finger pointing was directed – so we are told – at 'Christiani'.

To get rid of the rumour [of arson], Nero found and provided the defendants, and he afflicted with the most refined punishments those persons whom, hated for their shameful acts, the common people were accustomed to call Chrestiani ... a very large number were convicted, less on the charge of having set the fire than because of their hatred of humankind ... Covered with the hides of wild animals they perished by being torn to pieces by dogs or, fixed to stakes [or, crosses] they were set afire in the darkening evening as a form of night spectacle.

But can we believe the Roman historian who alone recounts this tale of Neronian villainy? Tacitus wrote his history of the first Roman emperors some two generations after these events. Like Thucydides he was an ancient historical writer of high quality, well worth reading in his own right for anyone who wants to experience how good the history-writing of the ancient Romans can get.

It may be that Tacitus inadvertently set down what in fact was an embroidered version of events circulating in his day. Leaving Christians aside, Nero perhaps did seek to appease the populace by finding 'culprits'. By using them as human torches, he then sanctioned a Roman-style penalty. This would have mimicked, not the Crucifixion, as often thought, but the crime of arson: burning alive.

If 'Christians' got into the story later, this could be because in the early second century the new sect was starting to seep into the Roman consciousness. This was as a result of developments not in Rome, but rather where they might be expected, the Greek-speaking provinces of the Roman east. Here early proselytizers for the Jesus movement – the Apostles – are well documented, as we saw in the case of Ephesus.

On 24 August AD 79, Mount Vesuvius in the Bay of Naples erupted. One of the observers was a Roman polymath whose daily routine, his nephew tells us, included an afternoon's sunbathe – an early record of heliotherapy. The uncle's fascination with the unfolding eruption proved fatal. He died from the dense fumes before he could reach safety.

Later (around AD 110) the nephew, known to us as Pliny the Younger, a Roman consul, was sent to govern one of Rome's Black Sea provinces in what is now northern Turkey. Here he found himself at a loss when local people denounced some of their fellows to him as 'Christians'. His interrogations of the accused produced information offering the earliest 'official' view of the movement that survives. He was told about praying to Christ, about pledging under oath to abide by moral precepts such as not committing adultery or telling lies, and about common meals.

The movement had acquired some purchase in the towns, where there were Christians in sufficient numbers to cause a perceptible decline in the sale of sacrificial meat in the markets. Christians abhorred animal sacrifice and refused to take part in it in any shape or form. This marked them out as different in an age where sacrifice was a more or less universal religious practice for inhabitants of the Roman Empire, no matter what their local cultural heritage.

Pliny thought that there were rural Christians too. He had carried out a basic test by asking the accused to 'offer worship with wine and incense' before a portable statue of the emperor, which he had had brought in to the courtroom specially. Observing the status-based gradations of legal privilege in Roman society of this time, he had executed those provincials who were not Roman citizens and who refused to recant.

In his uncertainty as to whether, and how, these people merited punishment, he went on to write to the emperor for further instructions. The letter survives, as does the emperor Trajan's reply, which is worth quoting in full for its enormous historical interest.

It is not possible to lay down any general rule for all such cases. Do not go out of your way to look for them. If indeed they should be brought before you, and the crime is proved, they must be punished; with the restriction, however, that where the party denies he is a Christian, and shall make it evident that he is not, by invoking our gods, let him (notwithstanding any former suspicion) be pardoned upon his repentance. Anonymous informations ought not to be received in any sort of prosecution. It is introducing a very dangerous precedent, and is quite foreign to the spirit of our age.

One only has to think of examples of religious intolerance in more recent times to recognize that this was a relatively 'mild' position on the part of the imperial state. Despite being general overseer of the state religion, the emperor does not seem to harbour 'theological' objections to people becoming Christian.

On the other hand, the early emperors were periodically prone to autocratic crackdowns on the activities and influence of individuals who behaved as freelance authorities offering 'soapbox' wisdom in public places, whether religious or philosophical. As well as the gamut of magicians and other religious quacks, experts such as priests of foreign gods, along with their followers, could from time to time be targeted in this way by the Roman authorities. Wandering preachers of the newfangled Jesus movement and the circles around them could be seen as undesirables for similar reasons.

This perception was exacerbated by imperial suspiciousness of club-like gatherings of all kinds as potentially subversive. The communal character of their religious observations could have made early Christian groups permanently insecure. Pliny records that in his particular province in what is now north-west Turkey, Trajan had completely banned private associations. This had deterred Christians from holding their pre-sunrise prayer meetings.

Another problem touching the political was the refusal of Christian converts to recognize the divinity of the existing gods. When the emperor was himself a god, in Roman eyes this refusal became tinged with politics. It might seem to imply hostility to the Roman Empire.

It also risked alienating Christians from their own cities and villages. Here, people's identification with the local pantheon by taking part in religious festivals and the like was a vital part of the building of community. So the early Christians could be unpopular in the wider society. This might help to explain in turn why people saw them as 'other' and sometimes denounced them to the authorities.

In modern Lyon today's roads and buildings beset what is left of the amphitheatre of the ancient Roman colony here, called Lugdunum. At the start of the fourth century AD the author of the first-ever history of the Christians set down an account of what he thought had happened here back in AD 177. His story is the earliest record of Christianity in Roman Gaul.

For reasons unknown, the account went, one or more mobs set on local people perceived to be Christians. They dragged them before the chief magistrate, who locked them up to await the Roman governor's arrival. When they were brought before his tribunal, the governor tested the accused in much the same way as Pliny had. Those who did not recant were sent to the arena to be killed by wild animals, a Roman punishment usually reserved for criminals seen as lower class. Our writer – his name was Eusebius – describes the deaths in gruesome detail.

Ten or so years before these events, another Greek writer – a pagan – had ridiculed Christian belief in a life eternal, 'in consequence of which they despise death'. As a Christian himself, Eusebius spelt out the torments of the amphitheatre because they testified to the sufferers' sense of themselves as Christians – their willingness to die for their faith exemplified what a Christian person really was.

He would also have known that these heroic 'martyrs' would have expected rewards in the Christian afterlife. So the Christian tradition had its reasons for showcasing these persecutions. That need not make the core of this story untrue, or of others like it. Religious persecution still exists today, as do martyrs who die believing in heavenly rewards.

In AD 249 a new emperor called Decius issued an edict requiring all inhabitants of the empire to sacrifice to the gods. Some of the evidence for what happened next comes from an archaeological site in Egypt's Nile valley where excavators between 1904 and 1906 found masses of papyri dumped as ancient rubbish.

> To the commissioners of sacrifices at Oxyrhynchus from Aurelius Gaion, son of Ammonius and Taeus. It has always been my habit to make sacrifices and libations and pay reverence to the gods in accordance with the orders of the divine [i.e. imperial] decree, and now I have in your presence sacrificed and made libations and tasted the offerings with my wife, my sons and my daughter, acting through me and I request you to certify my statement.

Written in Greek, this certificate shows that the emperor's order required individuals, not just in Egypt but all over the empire it seems, to obtain an official document proving that they had performed a sacrifice before local officials, tasted the meat, and testifying that they had always revered the gods in this way.

These certificates – there are others from Roman Egypt as well as this one from ancient Oxyrhynchus – lift the lid on the empire-wide bureaucracy that must have swung into action to implement this imperial order. Decius's edict was an extraordinary extension of the religious reach of the ancient state. The usually easy-going attitudes of the Roman authorities meant that organized religion was essentially a local matter – the province of the priests and priestesses of the cities and villages of the empire. No emperor had ever before ordered an empire-wide religious observation in which all individuals were required to take part – and obtain an official piece of writing to prove it.

Many Christians who did not deny their faith suffered for it. Of a Christian sage called Origen, who escaped death at this time but only just, a later historian wrote of 'how many things he endured for the word of Christ, bonds and bodily tortures and torments under the iron collar and in the dungeon.' So there is no denying the horror to which the imperial order exposed staunch Christians. Even so, nothing in the certificate of Aurelius

Gaion above suggests that he and his family had been singled out to provide religious proofs because they were suspected of being Christians. So scholars no longer think that Decius had solely Christianity in his sights, even if he must have been aware – and disapproving – of the 'nonconformity' of this numerous sect.

By demanding that all inhabitants of the empire observed the practice at the heart of traditional Roman religion, Decius gave a religious dimension to the new type of 'universal' Roman identity grown up in recent years. This went back at least to AD 212, when an earlier emperor gave Roman citizenship to almost all inhabitants of the empire, no matter their ethnicity and first language. To be a Roman was also, Decius was now saying, to perform animal sacrifice to the gods.

The last chapter introduced Diocletian, yet another tough soldier-emperor. As part of the fight-back against Rome's enemies, this conservative-minded ruler tried, like Decius before him, to reset the traditional bonds between the Romans and their gods by stamping out religious 'deviancy'. Christians must now have been perceived to exist in sufficient threatening numbers for the emperor to launch the following all-out assault in AD 303:

> In the nineteenth year of the reign of Diocletian ... an imperial letter was everywhere promulgated, ordering the razing of the churches to the ground and the burning of the holy writings, and proclaiming that those who held high office would lose their civil rights, while those in households, if they persisted in their profession of Christianity, would be deprived of their liberty.

Intended as an existential assault on the sect, this so-called Great Persecution naturally added to the early Christians' already-swollen narrative of heroic martyrs. The rubbish once more of Roman Egypt reveals the ducking and weaving of ordinary Egyptian Christians – the spiritual ancestors of contemporary Egypt's beleaguered Copts – as they sought to dodge the blunt instrument of the emperor's decree.

One papyrus concerns the sworn testimony of a church reader in an Egyptian village. This Ammonius would have been an important figure for the largely illiterate churchgoers, to whom he recited Holy Scripture. In an official affidavit he testified that his church – which the authorities had destroyed – possessed 'neither gold nor silver nor money nor clothes nor cattle nor slaves [!] nor building-sites nor possessions, neither from gifts or bequests'.

The list suggests what the authorities might expect to find when they visited even an Egyptian village church at this date. That they discovered nothing of the sort here might mean that the church in question was a poor one. It could also point to concealment of at least some of the more valuable movable property by Ammonius – church plate for instance – or even to collusive officials turning a blind eye.

Despite being the church reader, Ammonius got someone else to write his sworn signature on his behalf, claiming 'not to know letters'. An illiterate reader is not beyond the bounds of possibility – Ammonius might have recited from memory.

Perhaps, though, his alleged illiteracy was a Christian's ruse to get him out of having to swear, as required, on the Good Fortune of the emperors. So between the lines of this document, there are hints of small-scale resistance to the almighty Roman emperor. How widespread this sort of thing might have been depends on the unknowable answer to the question of Christian numbers by this time.

As seen, Diocletian instituted a college of four emperors, two senior (the Augusti) and two junior (the Caesars), to share the challenges of ruling the Roman Empire. In 305, probably in his early sixties, Diocletian did something unprecedented in the annals of imperial rule: he abdicated. In poor health, he retired to a fortified palace he had prepared for himself at what is now Split in Croatia – the modern town is built into its ruins – and died in his bed there some seven years later.

Without his dominating presence, the new system of power sharing descended into civil war. This was triggered by the death of one of a new pair of Augusti in 306. His army promptly proclaimed as his successor this emperor's son, an army officer in his thirties. Six years later, in 312, this Constantine, as he is best known today, was on campaign with his army when he experienced a supernatural event.

A most marvellous sign appeared to him from heaven, the account of which it might have been hard to believe had it been related by any other person. But since the victorious emperor himself long afterwards declared it to the writer of this history, when he was honoured with his acquaintance and society, and confirmed his statement by an oath, who could hesitate to accredit the relation, especially since the testimony of after-time has established the truth? He said that about noon, when the day was already beginning to decline, he saw with his own eyes the trophy of a cross of light in the heavens, above the sun, and bearing the inscription, Conquer by this. At this sight he was struck with amazement, and his whole army also, which followed him on this expedition, and witnessed the miracle.

This supposed vision raises the same issues for historians as all claims of past miracles. Recently I visited the pilgrimage church of Our Lady of Tears in modern Syracuse. This gleaming tent of stone and marble is built around a cheap plaster image of the Madonna, now encased above the main altar.

In 1953, so the story goes, this image hung in the bedroom of a young Syracusan couple, of whom the wife suffered from partial blindness. One morning she woke up cured, and the first thing she saw was the image of the Madonna, weeping tears. The image went on weeping for a while, as witnesses affirmed. Experts analysed a sample of the tears and declared it consistent with human secretions. The next year Pope Pius XII publicly acknowledged the reality of the event.

In 1995 an Italian chemist sought to debunk Syracuse's weeping Madonna by making a similar image of his own. He argued that water absorbed by the plaster would appear as droplets if scratches were made in the impermeable glazing around the eyes. Two years earlier, in 1993, a respected German scholar had argued that Constantine's vision was the result of a natural phenomenon, a solar halo, although this would not explain the heavenly letters.

Already met with, it was the churchman Eusebius who authored this account of the emperor's vision. He was a member of the entourage of Constantine, who now began to recruit Christians to advise him. Eusebius shores up the truth of his report by being the first to admit that it was hard to believe. He then gives as his unimpeachable source the emperor himself, who, moreover, had confirmed his recollections under oath. Constantine's regime evidently realized how important it was for Romans to believe in a miracle which showed that his rise to power was God's work.

Contemporaries were not sure exactly what had happened. Before Eusebius, another Christian writer had already penned his alternative version. According to this, Constantine had invaded Italy to wage war on a rival. Marching south along the main Roman road to Rome from the north, he prepared for battle outside the ancient city's newly rebuilt walls not far from the old bridge carrying the road across the River Tiber, the Milvian Bridge. In his sleep he was told to have the shields of his soldiers marked with 'God's heavenly sign'. Having done so, he went on to win a great victory against the odds.

Constantine certainly came to believe that he owed his success to the Christian God. In some sense he became himself a Christian believer, with historic consequences. He extended official support to Christians for the first time, reversing the recent persecutions. After a second victory over a rival in 324, which left him sole emperor, he also inaugurated church building at state expense.

A work known as the 'Book of the Pontiffs', dating from the early sixth century AD, states that it was Constantine who commissioned the first church of Saint Peter in Rome. The site chosen was an area outside the city walls where Christians of the time gathered around a monument believed to mark the burial place of the apostle Peter.

Here architects adapted a tried and tested form of Roman public building. This was a large rectangular hall supported by internal columns known as a basilica, suited to gatherings of large numbers, as a Christian service required. The same source records that Constantine and his mother, Helena, who also turned Christian, donated the church's gold cross, inscribed with their names.

Helena is a historically shadowy figure. The writer Evelyn Waugh brought her to life in his historical novel of that name. He made her a Briton and based her no-nonsense character on his friend Penelope, the wife of the poet John Betjeman. In his retelling, the aged empress goes on pilgrimage to Jerusalem and is told in a dream where to dig for the True Cross. She sets labourers to work in the torchlight. Eventually they reappear, 'bearing a baulk of timber'.

Nowadays historians think that Helena's discovery of the True Cross was a legend that grew up later in the fourth century AD. The kernel of truth was her visit in about 327 to the Christian sites of what at the time was still Aelia Capitolina. This was the name that the emperor Hadrian gave to Jerusalem when he founded his colony of legionary veterans there. After being shown what passed for the holy sites, she reported back to her son, who commissioned another church in the basilica form, that of the Holy Sepulchre, which survives, much altered, today.

The religious trajectory of the Roman Empire had changed course. At the same time, reforms in the age of Diocletian and Constantine gave a radically new mood to imperial governance, as the next chapter explores.

CHAPTER 20

UNITED WE STAND
THE FINAL CENTURY

In my early twenties I was sent off to Greece by the estimable supervisor of my PhD, under orders to see for myself the terrain of the region I was studying. So it was that one day I found myself eating a midday snack while examining the ancient fragments built into a pretty mediaeval church in a remote part of southern Greece.

These turned out to be of major historical interest. Framing the door were reused slabs from a large inscription. This was once on display in the market of a Roman provincial town in these parts, a small place called Geronthrae. I could make out bits of the Ancient Greek. For instance, there were lines listing three grades of linen headband, each followed by a different price per woven piece.

In fact this was nothing less than a Roman emperor's attempt to fix maximum prices for a range of well over a thousand goods and services in the empire, from lentils to lions. Parts of the same imperial edict have been found on other sites too – so it was meant to have a wide application, even if experts aren't certain whether the whole empire was targeted.

The emperor was Diocletian, acting in nominal concert with the other three members of the team of four rulers that he had created in AD 293. Passed eight years later, this edict belonged to a body of imperial reforms aimed at stabilizing the empire after the military crises of the last sixty years. As seen in an earlier chapter, these had badly affected economic life. A series of (usually) short-lived emperors had struggled to fund their ceaseless campaigning by raising taxes and also by skimping on precious metal when minting new coins. This in turn caused people to hoard the older, better-quality issues and even to prefer barter to cash payment.

A near-contemporary writer thought that the runaway prices that the edict tried to control were the result of Diocletian's own policies – in particular, further hikes in taxes to pay both for the army and for the new capital cities required by the fact that there were now four emperors ruling different parts of the empire. The same writer – a Christian, hostile to Diocletian's memory and so not necessarily trustworthy – claims that the edict was a flop and had to be repealed.

In a political manoeuvre not without modern parallels, the imperial team on the other hand put the blame for economic hardship on the greed of businessmen. They were especially concerned about the suffering caused to one section of society in particular:

> Who therefore can be ignorant that an audacity that plots against the good of society is presenting itself with a spirit of profiteering, wherever the general welfare requires our armies to be directed, not only in villages and towns, but along every highway? . . . that sometimes by the outlay upon a single article the soldier is robbed both of his bounty and of his pay, and that the entire contributions of the whole world for maintaining the armies accrue to the detestable gains of plunderers, so that our soldiers seem to yield the entire fruit of their military career, and the labours of their entire term of service, to these profiteers in everything . . . ?

The military recovery of the Roman Empire at the end of the third century AD made one thing clear – the Roman war machine was still proving its superiority centuries after Roman ancestors had turned the Mediterranean into *mare nostrum*, or 'our sea'. Self-evidently, the welfare of the army was an affair of state at the highest level. A verbal exchange which happens to have come down to us during a visit by the emperor Constantine to some of his veterans shows the close relationship between emperor and soldiers at this time:

> The assembled veterans cried out, 'Constantine Augustus! To what purpose have we been made veterans if we have no special privilege?'

Constantine Augustus said, 'I should more and more increase rather than diminish the happiness of my fellow veterans.'

On the south bank of the River Danube lies modern Serbia's second city, Novi Sad, overlooked by the site of a Roman fort helping to guard this part of the empire's border area. In the local museum here you can see an impressive Roman helmet from this period. Made of iron coated with gilded silver and studded with glass and gems, it is a parade version of what archaeologists call a 'ridge helmet'.

The military fight-back at this time triggered a large-scale reorganization of the army. Among the innovations was new equipment including this type of helmet, so-called from the central ridge joining the two half-bowls that form the head piece. In its basic form it was well suited to mass production. There was also restructuring of the army:

> Constantine did something else which gave the barbarians unhindered access to the Roman empire. By the forethought of Diocletian, the frontiers of the empire everywhere were covered, as I have stated, with cities, garrisons and fortifications which housed the whole army. Consequently it was impossible for the barbarians to cross the frontier . . . Constantine destroyed this security by removing most of the troops from the frontiers and stationing them in cities which did not need assistance.

Here too there is more than a whiff of religious bias. This extract comes from a Roman history by another writer whose pagan sympathies prejudiced him against a Christian emperor. Change in the army establishment under Diocletian and Constantine there certainly was, however. A distinction now emerged between field armies, elite troops stationed inside the empire and commanded by the emperor in person, and garrison troops stationed in border regions like Hadrian's Wall. These mobile striking forces were meant to speed up the military response to any breach in the empire's security.

The Romans may have adapted the so-called ridge helmet from the armour of an eastern neighbour. The 'Arch of Khosrau', or *Tāq i Kisrā* in Arabic, is an ancient ruin some 15 miles south of Baghdad. An online photograph dated 2009 shows American army officers and Iraqi officials standing in front of it while they discuss post-war renovations.

Muslim writers used to admire this gravity-defying archway of fired brick as a wonder of the world. It once ornamented the palace of the great power that arose on Rome's eastern border early in the third century AD. Persian in origin, the kings of the Sasanid line were as aggressive as the Romans. It was partly to counter their threat that Constantine seems to have taken the other fateful decision for which his name is still remembered.

In old Istanbul you can catch the tram to Çemberlitaş Square, where pigeons peck around the base of an ancient column. Its lower part sheathed in a stone buttress of Ottoman date, its upper part blackened by fire and reinforced with iron hoops in the 1970s, this battered monument suggests glorious origins only in the stone from which its drums are quarried: porphyry, the hard purple stone from Egypt which the Caesars favoured as a symbol of their rank.

This is almost the only visible memory today of the founder of Constantinople. Originally the column supported a golden statue of Constantine and stood in the forum of his new Roman capital, created here in 324 by rebuilding an old Greek settlement, Byzantium. By this time, Constantine had emerged as sole ruler of a unified empire after years of struggle with rivals. Diocletian's collegiate system of four emperors was dead.

Apart from chasing his own glory, as the name of the new city makes clear enough, the emperor was now thinking strategically. Military roads on both sides of the Bosporus linked Constantinople to vulnerable Roman borders to the north (the Danube) and the east (the Sasanians). This was to be both a base and bulwark of imperial power. Spear in hand, Constantine himself paced the line of the wall which he hoped would protect his new foundation on its one vulnerable side, the landward approach from the west.

Constantine also had novel ideas about his image. In one of Rome's treasure houses of ancient art, the Palazzo dei Conservatori, lined up in an inner courtyard, is a row of supersized body parts. Carved in marble, they include a hand, an elbow and an eye-catching head of an adult male, about eight times life-size, exuding calm command.

This colossal statue of Constantine – for it is he – shows him clean-shaven, the first emperor to revive this look after a long series of soldier-emperors portrayed as hard men with stubbly beards and cropped hair. Perhaps he wanted to remind people of the founding father of the Roman

Empire, the beardless Augustus, also depicted, like Constantine here, with hair combed forward and ever youthful – or of Alexander, the original beardless wunderkind. But the eyes tell a different story, and a new one. They are enormous, as if all-seeing, and they gaze upwards, like a ruler whose absolute power is sourced from a higher realm.

Constantine's recipe for stabilizing the state included the familiar one of handing power to his family. A son succeeded him as emperor, called Constantius (reigned 337–361). An ancient description shows Constantius apparently trying to embody his father's image of all-powerfulness in real life.

In 356, aged thirty-nine, he appeared in the streets of Rome alone in a golden chariot, surrounded by troops in parade armour. The emperor himself, this writer says, was 'shining with all kinds of precious stones which seemed to spread a flickering light all around'. Commenting on an exhibition in 2009 at Versailles of the similarly bejewelled costumes of the old French court, the fashion designer Karl Lagerfeld observed: 'Dazzling the people was the best way to keep them at a distance. This type of costume created virtually insurmountable barriers.' In the case of Constantius, the real *coup de théâtre* was his extraordinary comportment on this occasion. As with some heads of state today, the effect could have been comical, if it weren't so frightening:

> For though he was a man of short stature, yet he bowed down when entering through the city's high gates, looking straight ahead, as if he had his neck in a vice; he turned his eyes neither to right nor left, as if he were a graven image of a man; nor did he sway when jolted by the wheel of his chariot, nor was he ever seen to spit or wipe or rub his face or nose, or to move his hands about.

The ducking beneath gates is particularly striking – as if the vertically challenged Constantius even so saw himself as superhumanly tall by virtue of his godly office. This new image of the fourth-century Roman emperor included a spiky crown, something carefully avoided by earlier emperors as smacking too openly of one-man rule and therefore likely to upset traditional Roman values.

The military instability of the third century had prompted radical solutions. What had emerged under Diocletian and Constantine was a new kind of Roman Empire. This reformed state needed to be much stronger and more centralized to do what had become the much more demanding job of keeping Romans safe. To this end, the old provinces had been divided up into a hundred or so smaller units to enable a greatly enlarged bureaucracy – between 30,000 and 35,000 personnel on one estimate – to extract more tax from provincials.

These personnel mainly came from the social stratum beneath the old senatorial aristocracy, namely, the knights. More numerous than the more exclusive senators, and more adaptable to the managerial ethos increasingly called for in running the state, knights now more or less replaced senators as a specialized professional class of imperial administrators.

This bigger tax pot in turn funded the larger defence budget that the empire now needed. To legitimize these expanded powers of the state, the image of the figure at the pinnacle of the system needed reinvention. He was now conceived as an autocrat whose authority was limitless, universal and divine.

As seen, Constantine's conversion had introduced into the heart of the Roman state something entirely new – an exclusive monotheism. Constantine held synods of bishops to try to get agreement on what all Christians believed about their faith. At the first of these, convened in 325 at Nicaea, modern Iznik in north-west Turkey, the council of prelates – over three hundred of them – agreed on a general statement of Christian tenets. This was the first version of what is now known as the Nicene Creed. His son and successor Constantius was also Christian.

This new visibility of Christians both at court and in society at large was not a neutral development for the other religions of Rome. In the second and third centuries AD pilgrims flocked to a mighty building on the west coast of Turkey. Inside, the god Apollo was believed to give oracles by communicating through his priestess. Today's visitor can still admire the fine ashlar passageways and the vast open courtyard of what was once a Greek temple so ambitious in scale that the builders were still at work when Constantine first came to power, half a millennium after the monument was begun.

A few years earlier, an undecided Diocletian had consulted Apollo's oracle here at Didyma about whether to proceed with persecuting Christians. A Christian writer describing this episode not long after writes that the oracle responded to the diviner sent by the emperor as 'one would expect of an enemy of God's religion'.

Ten years later, when the religious boot was on the other foot, there was an unprecedented turn of events – Christian reprisals. In 313 Christians instigated the arrest of a senior priest at Didyma, one of the men who turned the prophetess's meandering utterances into graceful Greek. He was among a number of prophetic personnel at this time who 'under cruel tortures before the Roman courts declared that the whole delusion was produced by human frauds, and confessed that it was all an artfully contrived imposture'.

This too is a Christian voice – that of Eusebius once more, a member of Constantine's circle. No doubt it suited him to see the persecutions as part of a conspiracy against Christians in which traditional oracles of the gods had connived. In fact the priestly establishment at Didyma – no matter what might be confessed under torture – could simply have been seeing the world in their traditional way when they gave Diocletian the god's reply.

When the norms of the community seemed to be threatened, the suspicions of the Roman authorities were aroused. From Constantine's time these 'norms' were Christian, now that the emperor had officially sanctioned Christianity and redirected imperial patronage towards Christian churches. In this revolutionary period for Christians, most people were probably not interested in stirring up disturbances on religious grounds. Still, a relatively small number of zealots can cause a lot of trouble for the many. A new guardedness can be detected among practitioners of the old religion as the fourth century got under way.

Dominating the Greek island of Patmos in the eastern Aegean is a Greek Orthodox monastery dating from the eleventh century. It is dedicated to the early Christian saint who supposedly authored the New Testament's Book of Revelation in a nearby cave around AD 90, John the Evangelist.

Among other sights, visitors to this monastery get to see a well laid-out museum. Amid the chrysobulls and firmans of imperial patrons, the mediaeval manuscripts and all the liturgical paraphernalia, somewhat incongruously a corner of the display is devoted to finds from the island's pre-Christian past. Here there is one inscription which far surpasses the neighbouring fragments in historical interest.

Attached to the museum wall, a more or less intact slab preserves a sixteen-line poem in Ancient Greek. The inscription is hard to date, but the style of the lettering could be as late as the early fourth century AD. An unknown poet was commissioned to celebrate the good works of a woman called Vera in the service of the goddess Artemis, who had a shrine on the island.

As the inscription recounts, she was the daughter of a successful doctor, born on the island but brought up on the nearby mainland of Asia Minor. She returned to Patmos to serve the goddess as her priestess. As the poet graphically describes, the first duty of her office was 'to sacrifice by the altar the foetus of goats slaughtered in the proper way and just twitching, to the Patmian goddess'. The poet doesn't say as much, but this Vera presumably wielded the sacrificial knife herself. This was a traditional role for priestly personnel in the old cults. The odd thing about the inscription is that it puts so much emphasis on this perfectly normal act of Greek and Roman religion in the first place.

Some scholars wonder if Vera's action was stressed in this way because, at the date of the poem, blood sacrifice was no longer quite so routine as it used to be. Vera and her co-religionists might have travelled to sleepy Patmos because they were frightened of performing blood sacrifice in the mainland towns of Asia Minor. Under Constantius, for instance, ancient writings record attacks by Christian zealots on pagan temples in the eastern half of the empire, sometimes in collusion with Roman officials.

It is usually a good sign of the subject's historical liveliness when a Roman ruler attracts the novelist. The American writer Gore Vidal tackled the emperor Julian (ruled 361–363) in a historical novel published in 1964. One of its reviewers described the genre of historical fiction as 'not history but imaginative re-creation; a kind of dream-edifice'. It could be said of Julian himself that he was hard at work on a similar project: 'a kind of dream-edifice'.

Constantine's nephew, Julian was another member of the family 'of short stature'. He ruled for a mere sixteen months before being killed in battle with the Persians in 363, aged thirty-two – around the same age as Alexander the Great when he too died in Mesopotamia. In another respect there was more a touch of Hadrian about Julian. Carefully educated, he admired Classical Greece's legacy, including the Spartans and, especially, the Athenians.

Julian was an idealistic young ruler who set about shaking up the status quo. A contemporary writer, an admirer, describes how he attacked soft living, cutting down luxury among the eunuchs at court and restoring the discipline of the army in the best traditions of old-fashioned Roman morality. Unexpectedly, he also turned out to want to interfere in religion, on the side of the gods. A secret pagan in a Christian family, he 'came out' when on the throne.

Not least because he inherited power through the fluke of birth, experts are not sure how popular his plans for Roman religion were – or indeed, quite what they were. He passed decrees, we are told, which 'ordered the temples to be opened, victims brought to the altars, and the worship of the gods restored'. This fight-back chimes with a definite impression from the ancient sources that by this date Christian encroachment on the old religion was worsening.

Julian was told, for instance, that Christians had been bringing the relics of their holy people near, or right into, the oracles of the gods in an apparent bid to silence them by putting the divinity off his stride. At Didyma he responded by having churches near Apollo's temple in which relics were being placed for this purpose burnt to the ground.

What we call religious intolerance was on both sides. Even the admiring Roman historian Ammianus Marcellinus thought that Julian, his contemporary, went too far when he barred Christians from teaching literature or public speaking. Here Julian's Machiavellian aim seems to have been to restrict Christian influence on future generations of young people from the elite classes of society.

Experts wonder if he had more ambitious plans to 'reform' paganism. This debate is bound up with the murky problems of his personal religious attitudes, about which we know quite a lot from his own writings, which survive. Suffice to say that in his day, for a sophisticated mind like Julian's, the old religion had come a long way since the 600s BC, when a devotee in central Greece had an inscription incised on a bronze figurine which he offered to Apollo: 'Mantiklos donated me as a tenth to the far shooter, the bearer of the Silver Bow. Do you, Phoebus [Apollo], give something pleasing in return.' This crude 'I give so that you may give' was a core creed of the old religion, channelled through offerings of all sorts, including countless generations of animal victims like Vera's kid and its mother. By Julian's time, for the educated few, more esoteric fare was on offer from 'those who wear the long cloak and look supercilious'.

Thus did a Christian writer of the fourth century AD offer a fairly typical ancient caricature of philosophers. Their shabby cloaks – *hommage* to the frayed and dirty garb of Socrates – were almost a professional uniform.

One ancient writer met the philosopher with whom the young Julian had studied. By then an old man, this Maximus still made a great impression, especially his speech:

> His voice . . . was such as one might have heard from Homer's Athene or Apollo. The very pupils of his eyes were, so to speak, winged; he had a long grey beard, and his glance revealed the agile impulses of his soul . . . In discussion with him no one ventured to contradict him, not even the most experienced and most eloquent, but they yielded to him in silence and acquiesced in what he said as though it came from the tripod of an oracle; such a charm sat on his lips.

In the manner of his times, this Maximus was a philosophical holy man. He was steeped in a mystical reworking of Plato's philosophy fashionable among pagan intellectuals at this time. He also staged the performance of wonders, as an ancient eyewitness recounts:

> He burned a grain of incense and recited to himself the whole of some hymn or other, and was so highly successful in his demonstration that the image of the goddess first began to smile, then even seemed to laugh aloud. We were all much disturbed by this sight, but he said: 'Let none of you be terrified by these things, for presently even the torches which the goddess holds in her hands shall kindle into flame.' And before he could finish speaking the torches burst into a blaze of light. Now for the moment we came away amazed by that theatrical miracle-worker.

Although the young Julian was absorbed by this style of higher wisdom, he was no religious lightweight. He knew his Christian scripture well enough to argue that the biblical God lacked the divine quality of goodness. Where his attempts as emperor to turn back the religious clock might have led is hard to say, not least because within six months of becoming Rome's autocrat he embarked on a long-contemplated war against the Sasanian power on Rome's eastern border.

Like too many earlier forays by Roman generals into the eastern borderlands, this one went badly wrong, and the commander-in-chief got himself killed. According to Ammianus, who was serving in Julian's army, a Persian ambush took the emperor by surprise. 'Forgetting' to don his armour, he entered the fray on foot, armed just with a shield, which failed to stop an enemy spear from lodging 'in the lower lobe of his liver'.

Julian died in his tent. The consequences of this setback for imperial security were far more serious than his short-lived tinkering with Roman religions. In order to evacuate the rest of the army safely, the Romans agreed to a shameful surrender to the Persian king of their five provinces on the east side of the River Tigris. Among the Roman fortresses handed over was the only one where the merchants of both empires could legally trade, a city called Nisibis – now Nusaybin, a Kurdish town on the Turkish border with Syria. The Romans never recaptured it.

Around this time a nomadic people north of the Black Sea began to make life untenable for their westerly neighbours, the Gothic milieu beyond the Danubian limits of the Roman Empire. Our Roman historian of these times, Ammianus, an urbane gentleman from the great Roman city of Antioch, modern Antakya down in south-east Turkey, painted these trouble-makers from the steppes in vivid colours for his readers.

Their clothing consisted of the skins of field mice sewn together. They lived, and could sleep, on horseback. They ate the raw flesh 'of any animal whatsoever', warming it up while astride by putting the cut of meat between their thighs and the backs of their horses. They cut the cheeks of boys at birth so that the scars would show through the beard after puberty. Inevitably, these people were 'monstrously ugly' and 'exceed every degree of savagery'. Enter the *Huni*, or Huns as we call them today, a Mongolian people prone to 'seizing and destroying everything in its path'.

Violent nudging by these Huns now destabilized the peoples in south-eastern Europe known to the Romans as *Gothi*, or Goths; 'Germans' in the linguistic sense – speakers of the earliest of the Germanic dialects known to us. Under their chiefs, Gothic refugees started to stream down to the Danube's north bank. They sent messages to the Roman emperor, prom-ising to lead a peaceful life and to fight for him if he would let them settle inside the empire in what is now Bulgaria.

From weakness more than strength, the emperor Valens acquiesced. A sad scene then unfolded:

> They were ferried over for some nights and days embarked by compa-nies in boats, on rafts, and in hollowed tree-trunks; and because the river is by far the most dangerous of all rivers and was then swollen by

frequent rains, some who, because of the great crowd, struggled against the force of the waves and tried to swim were drowned; and they were a good many.

The emperor gave orders that the refugees, numbering in the tens of thousands, be fed and given land to cultivate. However, the authorities bungled this instruction and the newcomers received appalling treatment. Two of the Roman generals in charge even profiteered by trading dogs as food in exchange for Gothic children as slaves. The refugees were driven to ravaging Roman lands. This in turn triggered the march of Valens himself at the head of an imperial army to 'the most frequently contested spot on the globe'.

The words are those of a distinguished military historian today, who points to fifteen battles or sieges in the vicinity of Edirne in European Turkey. Here 'avenues of movement' down three river valleys converge on one side of a great plain, on the other side of which stands Istanbul – Constantinople as was. Down one of these avenues had come the Goths, who perhaps set up their camp outside Edirne – the Adrianople of the Romans – at today's village of Muratçali. To protect their women and children, they drew up their wagons into a laager here.

On an August day in AD 378, the battle went well for the Goths. The emperor, who was no great shakes as a general, had ignored advice to wait for reinforcements. The Goths set fire to the crops to irritate the enemy with smoke; then they attacked the Romans before they were even in battle formation. Two-thirds or more of the army fell, including, shockingly, the emperor.

In the ensuing emergency a new emperor, Theodosius I, took over the Gothic command. Despite four more years of war, he was unable to defeat the Goths properly. Instead the two sides signed a treaty in 382. As first promised by Valens, the Romans now gave the Goths land – somewhere in modern Bulgaria most probably – in return for military obligations.

The disaster of Adrianople meant that Roman manpower had not been enough to subjugate these Goths completely, to turn them into Roman subjects in the time-honoured way. Politically the Goths now formed an enclave of their own, under their own chiefs, keeping their own customs including in many cases, no doubt, the beards, the trousers, the animal-skin clothes and other accoutrements of a non-Roman appearance.

While this migration crisis played out on the plains of south-east Europe, the wheels of an ancient world still turned. In southern Greece, at this very time, two teenage brothers were binding their hands with leather thongs in training for the events of their lives. Painters of clay pots in Athens nine centuries earlier had first depicted the two combat sports in which these youths were to excel: the *pankration*, a combination of boxing and wrestling, and boxing proper.

We know about these youngsters thanks to a scrap of inscribed bronze found at Olympia in 1994. It shows that both became adolescent Olympic champions, one after the other. The true revelation from this find is the dating. Given in the Greek inscription as the 290th and the 291st of the ancient sequence of Olympiads, these victories fell in AD 381 and AD 385. The ancient Olympics were still going. A few years later, in AD 391, the same Theodosius I, another Christian emperor, decreed the following ban:

> No person at all, of any class or order whatsoever of men or of dignities, whether he occupies a position of power or has completed such honours, whether he is powerful by the lot of birth or is humble in lineage, legal status and fortune, shall sacrifice an innocent victim to senseless images in any place at all or in the city.

In the ancient world blood sacrifice had been the core of communal and private worship of the gods since the night of time. The new edict now made clear to the great and good throughout the empire that to worship the old pantheon was to back a loser. Theodosius did not target specific festivals, but the games at Olympia now ceased, as did the sacrifices on the many altars there, including the great ash cone of Zeus. The priestly personnel, long supplied by the families of local landowners, now melted away.

Just before this edict, the imperial entourage had witnessed an astonishing public demonstration of the new power of the Church. In 390 the same Theodosius, an emperor prone to anger, had let his troops loose on the civilian population of Thessalonice in what is now northern Greece. This was in reprisal for a popular uprising during which the locals had lynched a 'master of the soldiers', one of the most senior generals in the empire.

After the lawless slaughter, it was said, of seven thousand people, the pious emperor went to pray as usual, only to find that a reproachful bishop stopped him from entering church – excommunication in other words.

When the two powers, temporal and spiritual, eventually reached a deal, it included another foretaste of the Middle Ages – this extraordinary spectacle of imperial penitence:

> The Emperor, who was full of faith, now took courage to enter holy church where he prayed neither in a standing, nor in a kneeling posture, but throwing himself upon the ground. He tore his hair, struck his forehead, and shed torrents of tears, as he implored forgiveness of God.

The lynching of that general opens more windows onto a changing world. His name, Butheric, points to Germanic heritage. In the 400s AD a history-writing Roman lawyer claimed that the trigger for his death was his earlier imprisonment of a popular charioteer who had clapped eyes on the general's cupbearer and made a pass at him. When the charioteer's passionate fans among the Thessalonicans clamoured for his release ahead of the chariot games, the general's refusal sparked a riot.

Suffice to say that in an elite household such as the general's, the cupbearer would have been a youth, and a comely one at that, in the tradition of the mythical Ganymede, cupbearer of Zeus. Some modern writers have seen a culture clash here between the upright 'German' (the general) and the decadent 'Greek' (the charioteer). Alternatively, the general was simply jealous because he fancied the youngster himself.

What the figure of Butheric highlights more convincingly is the increased reliance of the Roman field armies on 'barbarian' recruits, and at the highest level. In the emperor Julian's day it was common for troops of this kind to fight for Rome only on condition that they weren't led to regions beyond the Alps. This was a humiliating stipulation coming from mere auxiliaries, one that the Roman imperial state must have been fairly desperate to accept.

There has been a modern debate for years about what historical trends underlay this use of foreign troops, although, to cut a long story short, we do not really know. As one historian has said of this period, 'who bore arms was a very serious matter, [and] the decision involved delicate and complex calculations'.

Did the state recruit 'barbarians' because there was a manpower shortage, for instance, or was the reverse true, that the imperial state wished to avoid recruitment of its own subjects because their able bodies were needed for the agricultural labours generating so much of the tax base? Were the emperor's poorer subjects less willing to fight, whether from long inurement to civilian life in the core provinces of the Mediterranean, or disenchantment with an increasingly authoritarian and controlling imperial state, or because Christianity had the side effect of focusing more minds on preparing for the hereafter?

Meanwhile, those uninvited guests, the Gothic settlers, were not happy, as events would now show.

CHAPTER 21

DIVIDED WE FALL
A TALE OF TWO EMPIRES

Modern Istanbul preserves another towering monument of the later Roman emperors, this time a pharaonic obelisk. Emperors had a decided taste for these tapering towers of Aswan granite intimating the grandeur and exoticism of ancient Egypt. Under Theodosius I, as under Augustus four hundred years before, transporting and re-erecting an Egyptian obelisk in a Roman setting was an impressive display of imperial power.

This particular obelisk sits on a stone base decorated with sculptured scenes along with a Latin inscription boasting that 'Everything cedes to Theodosius and his everlasting descendants'. On one side Theodosius I is shown in the imperial box in the hippodrome of Constantinople, displaying himself to his subjects and flanked by the 'everlasting descendants', meaning his two sons – boys at the time. This was AD 390.

Among the Roman ideas underpinning this vision of imperial rule was the pervasive notion of a threatening world of 'barbarians' outside the empire of civilization inhabited by the Romans. This old idea, with its roots in Greek thinking, had lost none of its force in the late fourth century AD, when the emperors of this time propounded it as zealously as their predecessors.

A gold coin of the same Theodosius shows the fully armed Roman emperor – 'Our Lord', as the Latin legend describes him – holding an image of the goddess Victory while he tramples a conquered barbarian. The message seems to be that the everlasting rule of the Roman emperor is the best defence against the un-Roman foes always pressing against the limits of empire.

The din of this rhetoric of Romans versus barbarians was increasingly at odds with the reality. As seen, the fourth-century AD Roman Empire happily recruited 'barbarians' into the army, settling them on Roman territory in greater numbers than ever before. Through the officer corps, a man like Butheric could rise to fame and fortune in the imperial state. He had become Roman in his way. In plain sight, the ethnic and demographic fabric of western Roman society was changing in the fourth century.

When Theodosius died in 395, he had already organized the succession so that his two sons succeeded as co-emperors, the elder (aged twelve) taking the eastern half, his brother, a year younger, the western. This division of the empire for practical purposes of ruling had happened before, with mixed results. This time such arrangements were about to be sorely tested by – in the supposed words of British prime minister Harold Macmillan – 'events, dear boy, events'.

Within twelve years, Germanic invaders were committing grave assaults on the European provinces of the empire. These assaults were so hard for the Roman military to fend off because consciousness of Roman imperial might had encouraged different Germanic groups to cooperate. Experts debate whether these groups already felt a common 'German' identity. They could certainly understand each other, even if mutual intelligibility must always have been easier between some early Germanic languages than others.

In 407 a large grouping of peoples known to the Romans as Vandals, Alans and Suevi crossed the River Rhine, throwing Roman Gaul into chaos. Screened by this disaster, a Roman general in Britain proclaimed himself emperor. Fear of Britain being next seems to have triggered this action, because the usurper now crossed the Channel with the British field army to challenge the invaders, driving them south.

Unfortunately, the minders of the western emperor, a weak man now in his twenties, already had a military crisis elsewhere on their hands – the Goths settled within the empire under Theodosius I in what is now Bulgaria were also on the move. It did not help either that the two imperial courts were squabbling, so that the east helping the west was not on the cards at this time.

Under the pressure of finding themselves unwelcome guests inside the Roman Empire, these Goths had meanwhile reformed themselves by uniting with other Germanic subgroups into a larger polity. A sixth-century Roman writer was the first to call these amalgamated people 'Visigoths'. Greater strength raised Visigothic hopes of challenging the fragile treaty agreed with Theodosius I. This caused discontent – the late emperor had used these military settlers as the ancient equivalent of cannon fodder in the front ranks of his battles.

The Visigothic leader's name was Alaric. He was 'Roman' as well as 'Gothic', having already served in the Roman army commanding his own people. Now he wanted something more honourable, a normal Roman generalship. A year after the Rhine frontier crumbled, Alaric led his men across the Alps.

At the start of the fifth century AD the city of Rome had a population in the hundreds of thousands. It was a treasure house of art and architecture and public and private wealth, the accumulation of centuries. At the city's social summit were the senators. Amid the ruins of the forum you can still visit their meeting house, well preserved thanks to an afterlife as a mediaeval church.

The emperors had long since stopped consulting these senators of Rome on weighty matters of state. So it was that in AD 410 a somewhat rusty corporation found itself having to manage a real crisis. The Visigothic army – perhaps as large as forty thousand men – was camped outside the city walls. When negotiations failed, the angry besiegers gained entry to the city.

History has overstated what happened next, modern scholars now think. Rereading the ancient writers, they find evidence for a limited destruction of buildings, a great deal of pillage and some rape. An influential churchman of the time and future saint, Augustine, offered his cold comfort to the Christian women among these victims: 'Some most flagrant and wicked desires are allowed free play by the secret judgment of God.'

The Visigothic sack did not mark a decisive turning point as such. Rome as a city seems to have recovered. Some of the rich got out, fleeing as refugees to the shores of Africa and Egypt. Others stayed put, such as the family of a leading senator of this time called Acilius (pronounced Akilius) Glabrio Sibidius. It would be nice to believe in the hoary pedigree which the first two names advertised – one stretching back, in theory, to a Roman general encountered much earlier in this book (Chapter 14), Manius Acilius

Glabrio, consul in 191 BC. Seventy years after the Visigothic sack of 410, the descendants of this Sibidius could still be found on the benches of the senate house in Rome.

After the attack, the western empire's commander-in-chief, an able general, recruited these same Visigoths in the fight against the invaders from across the Rhine, whom he drove – with this Germanic help – into Roman Spain. In 418, by mutual agreement, he then settled the Visigoths as military colonists in the Gallo-Roman province whose capital lies beneath today's Bordeaux.

Exactly how these settlers lived is a thorny question, but rather an important one. The answer would offer further clues to what the Visigoths wanted from the empire. Some could have been billeted with the provincials, who would have had to feed and clothe them and give them money. An ancient writer states for sure that some received land to farm. It is not clear whether this was appropriated from Roman estate holders, or took the form of uncultivated fields abandoned by their owners. The least that can be said is that the Visigoths sought a settled life inside the Roman Empire. Because they have left no archaeological traces, some experts suppose that they must have adopted a Roman lifestyle as well.

Meanwhile, vigorous Roman counter-attacks prompted the wandering Germanic groups from across the Rhine, who had left Gaul for the provinces of Roman Spain, to strengthen their organization. Their talented ruler now deemed it prudent to lead them to pastures new in Roman North Africa, crossing in 429 from what is now Cadiz into today's Morocco. One eastern Roman writer gives as eighty thousand the number of fighting Vandals, as the Romans called this grouping. Another has left a surprisingly respectful description of their ruler, whose name was Gaiseric:

> . . . [he] was a man of moderate height and lame in consequence of a fall from his horse. He was a man of deep thought and few words, holding luxury in disdain, furious in his anger, greedy for gain, shrewd in winning over the barbarians and skilled in sowing the seeds of dissension to arouse enmity.

Over a long and successful career Gaeseric and his followers defeated the Roman armies of North Africa and helped themselves to land and property, gradually bringing into being a lasting state centred on modern Tunisia. In

439 they conquered the leading Roman city of these parts, the great port of Carthage, long since re-founded as a Roman colony.

This gave them access to the sea. Using the short crossing to Sicily so crucial to the Phoenician Carthaginians of old, Gaeseric and his newly acquired ships could now intervene in Italy. In 455 he and his men followed Alaric's example and sacked Rome. This time they did a more thorough job, stripping the imperial palaces of their treasures and capturing three female members of the imperial family.

An eastern Roman writer of the sixth century presents the experience of civilians under the Vandal occupation in a harsh light:

> He [Gaeseric] robbed the rest of the Libyans [that is, the Roman Africans] of their estates, which were both numerous and excellent, and distributed them among the nations of the Vandals, and as a result these lands have been called 'shares of the Vandals' up until the present time. And it fell to the lot of those who had formerly possessed these lands to be in extreme poverty and to be at the same time free men; and they had the privilege of going away wherever they wished.

As this historian implies, there was now a reverse flow of Roman refugees out of Africa northwards to Sicily and Italy. Favouring Gaeseric's ambitions was a new threat to the European provinces. In the usual way, western Roman generals in recent years had been recruiting barbarians – now it was the Huns – in their attempt to reimpose central control on the northern frontier region. Here this combined force defeated another Germanic people, the Burgundi. In another familiar pattern, the formidable leader of the Huns, Attila, had received a Roman command and vast subsidies of cash disguised as military pay.

Not content, in 441 Attila led his battle-hardened Huns across the Danube, just as the two halves of the empire were managing to cooperate in mounting an invasion of Vandal Africa – a plan now hastily dropped. These Huns were no longer the wild men clad in mouse skin of fourth-century Roman nightmares. They now had a siege train and captured Roman fortresses. They even besieged Constantinople, where the mighty land walls proved, not for the last time, their near-impregnability.

There are various signs that Attila's men were chiefly driven by a lust for plunder. One contemporary writer notes how Attila would cynically send his friends to Constantinople as envoys, because they could expect the eastern Roman court to load them with gifts. This source was Priscus, an eastern Roman diplomat who left behind a remarkable eyewitness account of an embassy from Constantinople to Attila in 449.

Priscus and his fellow envoys crossed the Danube and were led through lands unknown to them to Attila's residence, somewhere near the modern border between Hungary and Serbia. He describes the great man: 'He was short, with a broad chest and large head; his beard sparse and flecked with grey, his nose flat and his complexion dark.'

As Priscus noted, despite the gold with which his wooden palace groaned, Attila drank simply from a wooden bowl. Among the Roman diplomats, the impression was that, like Alexander of Macedon centuries earlier, the Hunnic leader himself was thirsty not so much for plunder as for power and domination. There was talk of Sasanid Persia being in his sights. In fact, after being bought off by Constantinople with an agreement by the eastern Romans to pay an annual tribute, Attila turned his attentions to the western empire.

Here, however, he unexpectedly met his match. The western emperor of the time, an ineffectual grandson of Theodosius I, was ruled in turn by his commander-in-chief. This able soldier put together a Roman army including Visigoths from south-west France, who by now had evolved into a state within a state, with their own king. He then defeated Attila resoundingly in what is now the Champagne country of north-east France (451). Two years later, the Hunnic leader unexpectedly died of natural causes and his empire, like Alexander's, promptly fell apart.

Not only Africa, but other parts of the western empire, were now moving into a sub-Roman world. After the breach of the Rhine frontier region in 407, references in Roman writings show that the western emperor abandoned Roman Britain, leaving it without central officials or field troops. A mediaeval manuscript in the British Museum records what happened next. It preserves a Latin chronicle of events compiled in its original form in the mid-400s. The entry for the year 441 reads: 'The British provinces, which up to this time had suffered various disasters and misfortunes, were reduced to Saxon rule.'

These Saxons were a Germanic people, and their raids across the Channel had first caused trouble two centuries earlier. As for what it was like living in fifth-century Britain, archaeologists struggle to find signs of life at all in this period. As late as 450, maybe, the Romano-British people in and around Dorchester in south-east England were still making their distinctive brand of coarse pottery. And the experts now think that there were people still living in forts on Hadrian's Wall in the earlier 400s. Who they were is pure guesswork.

As for fifth-century Italy, it continued to develop a mediaeval feel. In the hill country of today's Basilicata region, inland from the Greek temples of Paestum on the coastal plain south of Naples, archaeologists excavated what was left of a substantial country house of this time. Called San Giovanni di Ruoti, the site produced fine mosaic floors, now in a nearby museum. However, the excavators were surprised to find un-Roman features as well.

The shape of the likely dining room was long and thin. This would have suited diners sitting at a rectangular table rather than lolling, as high-status Romans of this period did, on a shared semicircular couch with tables in front. And instead of removing their rubbish as house-trained Roman slaves should have, the occupants dumped it just outside the front door and even in empty rooms inside. The archaeologists think that the inhabitants were Germanic settlers. These newcomers wanted to live like Roman aristocrats, but only up to a point. They kept their own customs as well.

Faltering on the military front, the western Roman Empire could still project soft power. Years ago I visited a small fifth-century chapel in Ravenna, a day trip from Venice where I was staying. I can still remember the dazzling sight when I looked up to the dome – hundreds of gold stars twinkling in a night sky of deep blue, all revolving around a golden cross. Superb mosaics like this clad all the inside of the building. It was like stepping into Aladdin's cave.

The donor of this jewel was a princess, a daughter of Theodosius I. Some of her fairly short life – she was about forty when she died in 450 – she spent in Ravenna. In insecure times the western imperial court had transferred here, sheltering in the marshy delta of the River Po, with an escape route by sea to imperial kin in the east. It was not just her birth but also her personal qualities that made this Galla Placidia a politically influential figure – even if, as so often with the famous women of Greece and Rome, it was her relationships with powerful men that gave her the chance to shape events.

After the sack of Rome, she spent three years in the Visigothic camp as a hostage, before marrying Alaric's successor as Visigothic leader, by whom she had a son who died in infancy. A detailed description of the marriage, by the diplomat Priscus once more, gives no hint that she was a reluctant bride. Experts nowadays assume that she willingly consented, despite likely Roman prejudice against a match between an emperor's daughter and a barbarian associate of the detested Alaric. Following her husband's death she remarried, a Roman this time, and for twelve years served as regent for their son, who, as Valentinian III, succeeded as western emperor in 425.

After Attila's death, there were one or two short-lived western emperors who continued to lead Roman armies against barbarian foes in attempts to win back more of Gaul, or Africa. But circumstances by this time conspired against any successful fight-back. The loss of so many provinces, not least the riches of Roman Africa, meant that the western war chest funding military pay had shrunk drastically, along with the pool of recruits, as shown by the ingrained western custom by now of using barbarians to fight barbarians. The details are far from clear, but by the 470s the Roman army in the west had started to melt away.

Nor was the age of migrations – the trigger for the western empire's reverses – yet spent. It was not just that earlier invaders and their descendants, having become settlers, had started to consolidate themselves into states on formerly Roman soil. Others were still on the move. In particular, more Goths, the grouping known to Romans as the Ostrogoths, were massing south of the Danube.

This was the background to a further development, a western barbarian who deposes an emperor. This is what Odoacer, a commander in Roman service, did in 476:

Then he entered Ravenna, deposed Augustulus from his throne, but in pity for his tender years, granted him his life; and because of his beauty he also gave him an income of six thousand gold-pieces and sent him to Campania, to live there a free man with his relatives.

Odoacer's men hoped that he would settle them on Italian lands. However, instead of claiming the purple himself, Odoacer was content to be 'king of Italy'. In the next century there were eastern Roman writers who portrayed this moment as the 'fall' of the western empire. This was by way of justifying the sixth-century reconquest of 'barbarian' Italy by an eastern Roman emperor, of which more below.

In Italy at the time, the deposition of the youth Romulus, to give this 'little Augustus' his proper name, does not seem to have marked a great break with the past. It was a few years later, in the 480s, that the three great-grandsons of Acilius Glabrio Sibidius, that Roman of glorious lineage, held their run of consulships in Rome. Still, the line of western emperors had finally petered out. Another king of Italy followed Odoacer, this time a Romanized Ostrogoth.

The age of migrations put severe pressure on the eastern Romans too. However, geopolitics favoured them. The fourth-century Huns had pushed Germanic neighbours towards the Roman frontier regions along the Danube and Rhine rivers. Attila's Huns could approach Constantinople by land, but they never acquired the sea-power they would have needed to mount attacks from the Balkans on the rich Roman provinces of Asia Minor, Syria and Egypt. These assured the fiscal base of the emperors in Constantinople and provided the resource needed to resist the Sasanian Persians on the eastern flank.

One of these emperors, a towering figure in the sixth-century Mediterranean, was targeted for perhaps the most venomous character assassinations of a Roman ruler ever penned by a subject.

> This Emperor was insincere, crafty, hypocritical, dissembling his anger, double-dealing, clever, a perfect artist in acting out an opinion which he pretended to hold, and even able to produce tears, not from joy or sorrow, but contriving them for the occasion according to the need of the moment, always playing false.

This was opposition literature, dangerous to write in this case, since its subject was still on the throne. This was a secret work meant for private circulation among like-minded members of the Constantinopolitan elite, among whom this ruler had his critics, just as he did among ordinary people.

Interestingly, the author is clear from the start that he is taking joint aim at an imperial partnership – an empress as well as an emperor, and with no holds barred:

> And often even in the theatre, before the eyes of the whole people, she stripped off her clothing and moved about naked through their midst,

having only a girdle about her private parts and her groins, not, however, that she was ashamed to display these too to the populace, but because no person is permitted to enter there entirely naked, but must have at least a girdle about the groin. Clothed in this manner, she sprawled out and lay on her back on the ground. And some slaves, whose duty this was, sprinkled grains of barley over her private parts, and geese, which happened to have been provided for this very purpose, picked them off with their beaks, one by one, and ate them.

Erotic performance artists were hardly unknown in those days, any more than now. Women in history who achieve extremes of upward mobility have rarely been spared what now we would call sexist attacks. For the author, an eastern Roman male in the imperial service, the real shock value of this story lay in the contrast between humble origins and a lofty destiny. In her earlier career this empress had indeed been a low-status actress.

Once empress, she did not let her husband hog the limelight. Her independent activity in public life further fuelled the hostility of our author. Procopius – his name – also tried to distort the empress's championing (as we would say today) of good causes, such as her help for prostitutes. Probably drawing on personal knowledge of the milieu, she tackled this in a modern way as a by-product of poverty:

Theodora also concerned herself to devise punishments for sins against the body. Harlots, for instance, to the number of more than five hundred who plied their trade in the midst of the market-place at the rate of three obols – just enough to live on – she gathered together, and sending them over to the opposite mainland she confined them in the Convent of Repentance, as it is called, trying there to compel them to adopt a new manner of life. And some of them threw themselves down from a height at night and thus escaped the unwelcome transformation.

Despite this ancient besmirching of their reputations, Theodora's husband Justinian, a ruler of great vigour (527–565), was a reformer too, on the grand scale. A modern tribute to his achievement in a key area of ancient Roman life takes the form of 4,521 pages of type which now reside in the University of Wyoming. An American judge – he died in 1971 – laboured for years on this unpublished English translation, from the original 'lawyers' Latin', of a great collection of Roman laws commissioned by Justinian in the first years of his reign.

Purportedly in his own words, Justinian explained what prompted this endeavour, on which he employed a small army of professionals:

> Whereas, then, nothing in any sphere is found so worthy of study as the authority of law, which sets in good order affairs both divine and human and casts out all injustice, yet we have found the whole extent of our laws which has come down from the foundation of the city of Rome and the days of Romulus to be so confused that it extends to an inordinate length and is beyond the comprehension of any human nature.

Roman law had come a long way since the archaic Twelve Tables met with earlier. Justinian's huge operation aimed to purge what was now a mighty legal edifice of the contradictory laws arising from centuries of Roman legislation. The practical benefit was to speed up the business of Roman courts, as well as providing reliable textbooks for students in the eastern empire's two law-schools at this time. A book about the Roman legacy – which this is not – would highlight Justinian's work here, since his codification was the written source by which Roman law came to influence legal systems in mediaeval Europe and beyond.

Another enduring monument is now Ayasofya Müzesi, a museum in old Istanbul, in Justinian's day the 'Great Church' of a contemporary description, and a marvel thanks chiefly to its 'golden dome suspended from Heaven'. Justinian built on a scale reminiscent of emperor Hadrian, and not just because both were patrons of daring and innovative architecture, as here with Haghia Sophia. Both also built fortifications.

In my twenties, on my way to the dusty storerooms of the archaeological museum at Corinth to study ancient inscriptions for my PhD, I regularly passed a slab inscribed in Greek which was displayed on a wall in the museum courtyard: 'Light of Light, True God of True God, guard the emperor Justinian and his faithful servant Victorinus along with those who dwell in Greece living according to God.' Originally this stone was probably set into a defensive wall nearly 5 miles long running across the Isthmus of Corinth, lengths of which can still be seen. Through Victorinus, an official, Justinian carried out repairs to this wall. This was part of a much bigger programme of defensive military works. Greece is an example of a provincial territory which was relatively free from invasion under Justinian and flourished at this time.

The words with which the inscription opens are Christian theology, taken from the Nicene Creed. This statement of correct Christian doctrine first formulated by a council of bishops under Constantine was necessary because Christians, then as now, could not agree on what they believed. Justinian, an enthusiastically Christian emperor, wanted to promote religious uniformity by advertising, as here, where the regime stood in the theological debates of the time.

Under Christian influence he also intervened in sexual morality, as Augustus once had done for very different reasons. Justinian's law code reiterated a law of the first Roman emperor punishing with death citizens 'who dare to practise abominable lust with men'. In fact the imperial authorities had traditionally taken a laissez-faire attitude to same-sex relations among males. This now changed for good thanks to Justinian, who persecuted this activity in an unprecedented way: 'The emperor ordered that all those found guilty of pederasty be castrated. Many were found at the time, and they were castrated and died. From that time on, those who experienced sexual desire for other males lived in terror.'

Justinian's military posture was not just defensive. He went on the offensive on a massive scale – his generals 'recaptured' North Africa from the Vandals and Italy and Sicily from the Ostrogoths. Campaigning on this scale was in the best traditions of the imperial role as defined by centuries of Roman emperors. But Justinian's personal choices also drove his wars, especially in Africa, a risky venture which he probably launched despite the misgivings of influential advisors.

After Justinian's death in 565, the relentless movements of peoples reversed much of his military effort. In 568 a Germanic group, the Lombardi, migrated into Italy and rapidly established their own state in the centre and north. Over the next sixty years in Greece alone we hear of twelve barbarian raids, prelude to a much longer 'dark age' there. And in the lifetime of a monk born in Damascus a few years after Justinian's death, explosive forces would change Roman rule in the east for ever.

Years ago, when I first visited Topkapi Palace, seat of the Ottoman caliphs until the nineteenth century, I viewed the room now known as the Chamber of the Holy Relics. Here I saw a motley collection of objects supposedly linked to the Prophet Muhammad such as hair from his beard and one of his teeth, as well as his sword and his bow. If authentic, these last items presumably would be the 'arms' that an Islamic *hadith* or traditional saying states were among the Prophet's very few possessions when he died.

Authenticity apart, what struck me in my naïve way at the time was the contrast between this display of military memorabilia and Christ's purported relics, with their marked focus on passive suffering – nails and wood from the Cross, the Crown of Thorns and so on. I am far from qualified to write about the religious levers that put in motion the attacks by the first Muslims on the Roman Empire. However, the militarization of Islam was certainly close to being an original feature of the new religion.

After the Prophet's death in Medina (632), one of his close companions emerged as his religious successor and new Muslim leader. The Anglicized version of the Arabic term for this role is 'caliph'. The following year the first of the caliphs, Abū Bakr, had launched the determined campaigns by Muslim Arab soldiers that resulted in the capture of Jerusalem around 637.

This rapid overthrow of Roman rule happened first in a region strategically placed between Constantinople and the Sasanian Persians. These two old enemies had recently fought a draining war. At one time (622) this saw the Persian king overrun Palestine and Egypt and lay siege to Constantinople itself, before the Romans drove him back into Mesopotamia. So it was an exhausted Roman Empire in the east that the Muslims attacked. By 642 the first caliphs had gone on to conquer Egypt, and from there they started to conquer the lands 'reconquered' by Justinian from the Vandals.

The Arab armies could move rapidly. These were hardy Bedouin fighters who travelled light, dismounting from horses and camels for battle, including the archers. To follow the detail of the early Islamic conquests in the Mediterranean is not for this book. Suffice to say that within a generation the eastern Roman Empire had been shorn of some of its richest territories. What was left was now a regional power, rivalled in the Mediterranean by the burgeoning Muslim state.

I remember once passing the time in the company of the head of Classics of a well-known independent school in England. When I nosily asked to see what it was that he was scribbling on the back of an envelope, he showed me a short poem in Ancient Greek that he was halfway through composing – 'One of my ex-pupils asked if I'd mind penning something for him to read out at a business dinner.'

I laboured rather fruitlessly with Greek verse composition when I was a schoolboy. It is a rare skill indeed in the early twenty-first century. Back in the early 600s, eastern Romans with a good education were still trained in the knack of composing Greek verses in a classical manner. If Arabic sources can be trusted, it was one of these amateur poets, that same Damascus monk, now the elderly bishop of Jerusalem, who discussed terms when Abū Bakr's successor as caliph visited the newly conquered city of Jerusalem in person (637).

Sophronius, as the bishop was called, has left behind a three-line epigram in an ancient poetic form about a holy place in Jerusalem which he revered, the Rock, otherwise known as Golgotha:

Thrice-blessed rock, who didst receive the blood that issued from God,
The fiery children of Heaven guard thee around,
And Kings, inhabitants of the Earth, sing thy praise.

This book ends with the encounter between a caliph and a Christian Roman prelate who wrote Greek verses in a tradition stretching back to the elegists of Archaic Greece. It is as good a symbol as any of two worlds, both with long futures, now meeting each other for the first time.

EPILOGUE

When I was twenty-one I went on my first dig, at York Minster, where the need to underpin the mediaeval foundations had given archaeologists a chance to explore deeper layers. I was handed a pick, and was gouging away, when suddenly the voice of the long-suffering director, inspecting our trench from above, cried: 'Stop! That's a Saxon floor you're destroying!'

Perhaps I was not quite as blameworthy as might be supposed. The floors of Roman York had been made of opus signinum, small pieces of tile mixed with concrete to give a hard, smooth finish which even my pick could not have ignored. The inhabitants of Anglo-Saxon York made do with beaten earth. Archaeologists think that living standards, not just in Britain, but in other parts of the post-Roman west, saw a definite material decline.

Even so, there were glimmerings. In this impoverished world a few people still tried to read the writings of ancient Rome. A municipal library in a town in north-east France possesses the earliest example of an English dictionary. Made in the AD 700s, this rare manuscript lists difficult Latin words in one column, and next to them a Latin or Old English equivalent. By studying the Latin words carefully experts can work out the Latin works that the original compilers – probably British monks – were reading, or trying to: mainly, it turns out, the Christian learning of the sub-Roman Mediterranean world, but also the pagan pleasure of Virgil, the great poet of Augustan Rome.

The mediaeval world never ceased to connect with ancient Greece and Rome. The labours of its scribes and scholars, their copies and their translations, preserved at least a fraction of the fragile writings of the ancient Greeks and Romans for us. In the west this achievement owed much to the monastic communities of the post-Roman successor kingdoms. Far away to the east, in ninth-century Baghdad, an open-minded caliph called Ma'mūn gathered the best translators into Arabic to put the writings of Greek philosophy and science at the disposal of the world of Islam. This great transfer of knowledge also helped to save these writings, some known today only from the Arabic translations.

Among the Greek-speaking 'Romans' of mediaeval Constantinople, also known as Byzantium, classical Greek authors remained a staple of a higher education down to the fall of the city to the Ottoman Turks (1453). Preserved in this way, these ancient authors found their way to Renaissance Italy as manuscripts in the baggage of Byzantine refugees. Only by this means were giants of such stature as Homer, Aristophanes, Thucydides, Euripides and Plato preserved for today's world.

The Renaissance was a cultural movement led by the curiosity, the talent and the patronage of enlightened men (and women) in the republics and principalities of central and northern Italy. It was marked by a new sense of wonder at, and openness towards, the pagan civilizations of the ancient Romans and Greeks. Recently I stood under the painted ceilings of Vaux-le-Vicomte, a stately French château built in the 1650s. This experience brought home to me just how far-reaching the influence of this rediscovery of the ancient world was.

The original builder was an overambitious finance minister of the French crown. When he wanted to see himself and his services to the king glorified in the décor of his new house, he naturally turned to the only possible source of inspiration in that era. So in one ceiling we see the hero Hercules (but really Nicolas Fouquet, seigneur of Vaux) ascending by chariot to heaven, where his labours will earn him deification, while Glory crowns him and Renown blasts her trumpet before reciting his great deeds. On the front of his chariot can be read a Latin word, *ascendet*, hinting at the owner's boastful motto, 'Quo non ascendet?', or 'How far will he not climb?'

Other visitors, like me, may find it well-nigh impossible to grasp the cultural trends of those times producing this kind of image. In seventeenth-century Europe, educated people were obsessed – an advisedly strong word –

by the Greek and Roman myths: 'Intellectually, men of the seventeenth century lived in a mythological world. Their imagination was haunted by the divinities whom they saw everywhere in the residences and gardens of the time'.

How and why the flotsam and jetsam of classical civilization has inspired the societies of mediaeval and early modern times is a story for another time. Suffice to say here that, since the Renaissance, the rediscovery of the artistic legacy of Greece and Rome has served the needs of timeless grandeur well, as shown by a place like Vaux and by the exteriors and interiors of countless churches, palaces, stately homes and public buildings in Europe, North America and elsewhere.

What of today? I remember the piteous state of the plaster casts of famous classical sculpture at my old university, no longer used by lecturers in the art department and left out to be vandalized by boisterous students. Despite such changes in western taste arising from the swerve towards modernism at the start of the twentieth century, the image-making abilities of ancient artists and the classical harmonies of ancient architects still seem to please a wide public.

The coaches filling the car parks make clear the popularity of famous ancient wonders such as the dazzling mosaics in the great Roman villa near Piazza Armerina in Sicily. In a world of selfies and self-fashioning, ancient Greek and Roman bodies perfectly crafted in marble and bronze have a marked appeal, to judge from the admiring crowds gathered round, say, the naked Zeus of Artemisium in the National Archaeological Museum of Athens. As a bystander over the years pondering these popular responses on sites and in museums, I have come to wonder if a measure of the achievements of a great civilization is a quality of irresistibility.

For the benefit of theatregoers, today's writers, directors and performers continue to draw on the treasure house of ancient Greek and Roman literature. In 2017 I was present at the opening night of a thought-provoking one-man show in a London theatre. It explored the grim subject of what nowadays is called maternal filicide – when a mother kills her children, a crime all too well known in modern times.

For eighty minutes with no interval, the performer, a man dressed in an extravagant gown and unfeasible platform shoes, threw himself into the role of Medea. In Greek mythology Medea was a witch and, as we might now say, a wronged woman. In the fifth century BC the Athenian dramatist

Euripides wrote a tragedy named after her in which Medea – a man would also have played her in the original staging – avenges herself by slaughtering her two children by the husband who has abandoned her for a younger woman. What I saw was a contemporary reimagining ultimately inspired by the ancient story. The unsettling performance left me haunted by something I'd not really grasped before – the extreme explosiveness to which jealousy can drive a human being.

Reflecting on the ancient Greeks and Romans while writing this book, I have neither minimized nor dwelt unduly on the obviously disturbing features of those societies, although ancient slavery and ancient attitudes to women and to sexuality seem to me as good a starting point as any for putting changing human behaviour into a historical perspective. In general, it seems dubious to me to shun the pleasures bequeathed by the contemplation of a great civilization, just because this civilization was founded on human weaknesses as well as strengths.

There remain for sure the beauty and, yes, the humanity: the aesthetic fineness which allowed Greek and Roman artists to capture images and effects – the bright plumage of a mosaic bird, or the cool curve of a marble limb – which arrest us still; the human understanding of the ancient writers, their clear-eyed reckoning of what constitutes our short human lives. These are things which suspend despair about the shortcomings of human nature. They bring joy, and hope.

TIMELINE

The East

BC

c. 7000–3000 Neolithic Greece

c. 3200–2000 Cycladic culture

c. 2000 Oldest Mesopotamian version of the Epic of Gilgamesh

c. 2000–?1370 Minoan 'palaces' in Crete

c. 1575–1200 Mycenaean civilization in Greece

c. 1473–1458 Hatshepsut reigns in Egypt

c. 1550 Gold death mask 'of Agamemnon'

c. 1500 Warrior tomb in Pylos

c. 1300 Uluburun shipwreck

c. 1200 Hittite capital destroyed

1183 Ancient date for the 'fall of Troy'

c. 1050–700 Geometric pottery in Greece

c. 1000 Lefkandi burials

776–491 Greek 'Archaic' period

776 First Olympic games

c. 740 New Greek alphabet based on Phoenician script

The West

BC

c. 825–730 First Greek settlements in the west

814/3 Ancient date for the Phoenician foundation of Carthage (modern Tunisia)

753 Ancient date for the foundation of Rome

The East   ## The West

c. 720 'Nestor's Cup', Pithecusae (modern Ischia)

c. 700–500 Etruscan civilization flourishes in Italy

c. 700 Phoenicians found settlement at Motya in Sicily

664–610 Foundation of a Greek trading station, Naucratis, in Egypt

c. 650 Dreros inscribed law

c. 610–575 Sappho active

594/3 Solon's reforms at Athens

c. 570–*c.* 549 Reign of Phalaris, tyrant of Acragas

565 Thales predicts an eclipse of the sun

c. 560–510 Tyranny of Pisistratus and his sons at Athens

c. 560–546 Reign of Croesus, king of Lydia

c. 557–530 Cyrus the Great founds the Persian Empire

c. 510 Red figure pottery technique invented in Athens

509 Expulsion of the last king of Rome

508 Political reforms of Cleisthenes at Athens

499 Ionian Greeks revolt against Persian rule

c. 499–458 Aeschylus active

494 First secession of the Roman plebs

493 Treaty between Rome and the Latins

490–336 Greek 'Classical' period

490 Persian invasion of Greece; Battle of Marathon

480 Second Persian invasion of Greece; Battles of Thermopylae and Salamis

480 Battle of Himera, Sicilian Greeks defeat the Carthaginians

479 Battle of Plataea

479/8 Athens founds a Greek naval alliance against Persia

474 Battle of Cumae, victory of Hieron of Syracuse over an Etruscan fleet

c. 468–406 Sophocles active

c. 460–430 Herodotus active

c. 455–408 Euripides active

454 Athens moves treasury of the Greek naval alliance from Delos to Athens

c. 450 Publication of the Twelve Tables, Rome's first law code

The East

The West

447–432 Building of the Parthenon, Athens

431 Peloponnesian War begins; Funeral Oration of Pericles

c. 431–400 Thucydides active

c. 427–388 Aristophanes active

415 Athens captures and punishes the islanders of Melos

415–413 Athenian expedition to Sicily

404 Athens surrenders to Sparta

399 Trial and execution of Socrates

390 Gauls attack Rome

371 Battle of Leuctra, the Boeotians under Thebes defeat Sparta

360/359–336 Reign of Philip II, king of Macedon

347 Death of Plato

338 Battle of Chaeronea, Philip defeats the allied Greeks

336–323 Reign of Alexander of Macedon

335 Alexander destroys Thebes; Aristotle founds the Lyceum

334 Alexander invades the Persian Empire

333 Battle of Issus, Alexander defeats Darius III

331 Foundation of Alexandria; Battle of Gaugamela, Alexander defeats Darius III a second time

323–30 Greek 'Hellenistic' period

323 Alexander prepares to attack Arabia; death of Alexander at Babylon

323–c. 281 Alexander's generals divide up his empire

322 Death of Demosthenes

321 Battle of the Caudine Forks

c. 300 Foundation of Greek city at Ai-Khanoum (modern Afghanistan)

285–246 Callimachus active

280 King Pyrrhus invades southern Italy

279 Celts invade Greece

c. 271–216 Reign of Hieron II, king of Syracuse

264–241 First Punic War

241–197 Reign of Attalus I, king of Pergamum

241 Carthage's domain in Sicily becomes the first Roman province

218–201 Second Punic War

The East	The West
	216 Battle of Cannae, Hannibal annihilates a Roman army
	211 Roman capture of Syracuse; death of Archimedes
	202 Battle of Zama (modern Tunisia), Romans defeat Hannibal
197 Battle of Cynoscephalae, Greece, Roman victory over Philip V of Macedon	
192–188 Syrian War between Rome and the Seleucid Antiochus III	
after 184 Great Altar of Pergamum	
168 Battle of Pydna, Greece, Flamininus defeats Perseus of Macedon	
166 Rome makes Delos a free port	
	c. 150–100 Sanctuary of Fortuna, Praeneste
146 Roman destruction of Corinth; Greece in effect a Roman province	146 Roman destruction of Carthage
	133 Land reforms of Tiberius Gracchus
	123 Land reforms of Gaius Gracchus
c. 118 Death of Polybius, Greek historian of Rome's rise to world empire	
	107 Army reform of the consul Marius
	91–89 War between Rome and her Italian allies ('Social War')
	81 Dictatorship of Sulla
	73–71 Revolt of Spartacus
c. 70 onwards Greek philosopher Philodemus active in Rome	
69 Birth of Cleopatra, future Egyptian queen	
	63 Pompey's settlement of the east; the last Seleucid king deposed; Syria a Roman province; death of Mithradates, king of Pontus
c. 60 Antikythera shipwreck	
	58–51 Caesar's campaigns in Gaul
	55–54 Caesar's two invasions of Britain
	48 Battle of Pharsalus, Greece, Caesar defeats Pompey
	44 Caesar's on-off dictatorship made perpetual; murder of Caesar
	43 Antony, Octavian and Lepidus form ('Second') Triumvirate; murder of Cicero
	42 Battle of Philippi, Antony and Octavian defeat republicans

The East	The West
	31 Battle of Actium, Octavian defeats Antony and Cleopatra
30 Suicide of Cleopatra; Egypt a Roman province	30 Octavian sole ruler
	27 Octavian claims to have restored the republic; Senate bestows the title of Augustus
	19 Death of Virgil
AD	**AD**
	8 Ovid exiled to Tomis (modern Romania)
	14 Death of Augustus
c. 30 Traditional date for the death of Jesus, Jerusalem	
	37–41 Gaius ('Caligula') emperor
	41–54 Claudius emperor
43 Lycia (south-west Turkey) a Roman province	43 Claudius invades Britain
	54–68 Nero emperor
	64 Great Fire of Rome
	65 Suicide of Seneca
66–68 Nero's tour of Greece	
	68–69 Year of the Four Emperors
	79 Eruption of Mt Vesuvius, Pompeii and Herculaneum destroyed
	81–96 Domitian emperor
	98–117 Trajan emperor
	c. 100–120 Tacitus the historian active
c. 110 Pliny corresponds with Trajan about Christians	
115 Jewish revolt in North Africa and Cyprus	
	117–138 Reign of Hadrian; Hadrian's Wall built in Britain
132–135 Hadrian suppresses a revolt in Judaea; Jerusalem renamed Aelia Capitolina	
147 Vilia Procla repairs the theatre at Patara, Lycia	
	161–180 Marcus Aurelius emperor
	177 Trials of Christians in Lugdunum (Lyon)
	193–211 Septimius Severus emperor
	c. 202 Cassius Dio starts his Roman history
	212 'Antonine constitution' extends Roman citizenship to most inhabitants of the empire
	235–238 Maximinus reigns

The East

246 Sasanid lineage comes to power in Persia

267/8 Herulian Goths devastate Athens

270 Zenobia of Palmyra seizes Alexandria

324 Constantine re-founds Byzantium as Constantinople

325 Council of Nicaea; Nicene Creed

c. 327 Empress Helena visits Jerusalem

363 Julian killed fighting Sasanid Persia

378 Battle of Adrianople; Goths defeat and kill the emperor Valens

c. 393 Ammianus Marcellinus writes his history

527–565 Justinian emperor

632 Death of the Prophet Muhammad

637 Arab conquest of Jerusalem

The West

249 Edict of Decius requiring pagan sacrifices of all Romans

c. 270–275 Aurelian emperor

284–305 Diocletian emperor

293 Tetrarchy created; murder of Carausius, usurper based in Britain

301 Diocletian's Price Edict

306–337 Constantine I emperor

312 Battle of the Milvian Bridge

337–361 Constantius II emperor

379–395 Theodosius I emperor

395 Division of the empire between west and east

410 Visigoths sack Rome

429 Vandals cross into Roman Africa

450 Death of Galla Placidia

451 Roman victory over Attila (north-east France)

476 Odoacer deposes the last western emperor

NOTES

NB. I have limited myself in the main to citing sources for the book's direct quotations.

Prologue

'repeated human experiences': the formulation of the novelist Hilary Mantel in her fourth Reith Lecture broadcast on BBC Radio 4, 11 July 2017.

'Wonders are many': Sophocles, *Antigone*, line 332.

'On, you men of Greece!': Aeschylus, *Persians*, lines 402–5.

Freedom as a 'criterion of civilized modernity': David Kelly and Anthony Reid editors, *Asian Freedoms: the Idea of Freedom in East and Southeast Asia* (Cambridge, 1998), p. 11.

'For if it were proposed': Herodotus 3, 38, 1.

'the kinship of all Greeks': Herodotus 8, 144, 2.

'super-culture': Christopher Dawson, *The Dynamics of World History* (New York, 1956), p. 402.

'He immersed himself in the studies': Pseudo-Aurelius Victor, *Epitome de Caesaribus* 14, 2.

'What is more precarious': Maximus Confessor, *Letters* 14 (*PG* 91, 540A–541B).

1 The Dawn of Greek Civilization

'harsh, rustic': Aelius Aristides, *On Rome* 1, 31–38 (165–168D), trans. Charles Behr.

'Minos is the first': Thucydides 1, 4.

2 The Rise of the Hellenes

'the country now called Hellas': Thucydides 1, 1.

'No arts, no letters': Thomas Hobbes, *Leviathan*, chapter 13.

'killed' ritually (Lefkandi building): see now Angélique Labrude in Anastasia Dakouri-Hill and Michael J. Boyd, eds, *Staging Death* (Berlin, 2016), pp. 307–8.

'Achilles' wrath': Homer, *Iliad* 1, 1–8. Quoted from Alexander Pope, *The Iliad of Homer*, vol. 1 (London, 1801), p. 4, lines 1–8.

'Like leaves on trees': Homer, *Iliad* 6, 146–148. Quoted from Alexander Pope, *The Iliad of Homer*, vol. 1 (London, 1801), p. 177, lines 181–3.

'A well-prov'd casque': Homer, *Iliad* 10, 261–265. Quoted from Alexander Pope, *The Iliad of Homer*, vol. 1 (London, 1801), p. 296, lines 309–12.

'He who of all the dancers': Rosalind Thomas, *Literacy and Orality in Ancient Greece* (Cambridge, 1992), p. 58, citing Lilian Jeffery, *Local Scripts of Archaic Greece*, 2nd edn, revised Alan Johnston (Oxford, 1990), p. 76, no. 1.

'The swarming populace': Homer, *Iliad* 23, 257–260. Quoted from Alexander Pope, *The Iliad of Homer*, vol. 2 (London, 1801), pp. 324–5, lines 321–5.

'And from Hellen': Hesiod, *Catalogues of Women*, fragment 4.

3 New Things

'Menelaus' Helen': Hector Catling and Helena Cavanagh, *Kadmos* 15 (1976), pp. 145–57. The translation of the Greek is that of Robert Parker: www.academia.edu/22684765/The_Cult_of_Helen_and_Menelaos_in_the_Spartan_Menelaion (accessed 7 October 2016).

'May God be kind' (Dreros inscription): Russell Meiggs and David Lewis, *A Selection of Greek Historical Inscriptions to the End of the Fifth Century* BC (Oxford, 1969, revised edn 1988), no. 2.

'the warfare in which those spear-famed lords': Archilochus fragment 3.

'All wars were fought individually': Thucydides 1, 15.

'to attend the funeral of Amphidamas': Plutarch, *Moralia* 153f.

'I gave the common folk' and 'shaking off': Plutarch, *Solon* 18. 4 and 16. 3.

'heralds ran before them': Herodotus 1, 60.

'They [the Greeks] invented mathematics': Bertrand Russell, *History of Western Philosophy* (London, 1962), p. 25.

'Whence things have their origin': 'Anaximander (*c.* 620–546 B.C.E.)', by Dirk L. Couprie, *The Internet Encyclopedia of Philosophy*, ISSN 2161–0002, http://www.iep.utm.edu/ (accessed 8 October 2016).

'Thales, who was in the encampment': Herodotus 1, 75.

'Choræbus, the Athenian': Pliny, *Natural History* 1, 7, 56.

'Now is the floor clean': Xenophanes, fragment 1 (Diels), trans. John Burnet.

4 As Rich as Croesus

'You yourself wait': Hesiod, *Works and Days*, lines 630–640.

'Thus saith the Lord of hosts': Jeremiah 7, 21.

'The chief magistrates who are in office': *Inscriptiones Graecae* 12, 5, no. 647, lines 6–16.

'afterwards, when the victim was burnt': Porphyry, *On abstinence from animal food*, 4, 15, trans. Thomas Taylor.

'while fighting as an ally of the Babylonians': Alcaeus, fragment 350 (Lobel-Page).

'the day was suddenly turned to night': Herodotus 1, 74, 2.

'Like a lioness': Epic of Gilgamesh: *Gilgamesh* 8, 61–2.

'The lion thus': Homer, *Iliad* 18, 318–323. For the comparison with the Epic of Gilgamesh see Johannes Haubold, *Greece and Mesopotamia* (Cambridge, 2013), pp. 22–3.

'When King Psammetichus came': Russell Meiggs and David Lewis, *A Selection of Greek Historical Inscriptions to the End of the Fifth Century* BC (Oxford, 1969, revised edn 1988), no. 7.

'But you keep babbling' (new Sappho): Dirk Obbink, *Zeitschrift für Papyrologie und Epigraphik*, 189 (2014), pp. 32–49.

Charaxus and Rhodopis: Herodotus 2, 135.

'executed columns – fine works': Apollo-temple inscription in Gillian Shepherd in Nick Fisher and Hans van Wees, eds, *Aristocracy in Antiquity* (Swansea, 2015), pp. 367–70.

'The Lydians . . . were the first men': Herodotus 1, 94, 1.

'Walwet': Koray Konuk in William Metcalf, ed., *The Oxford Handbook of Greek and Roman Coinage* (Oxford, 2012), p. 47.

ΚΡΟΙΣΟΣ (Croesus) inscription, Ephesus: BM GR 1872.4–5.19, discussed in Brian Cook, *Greek Inscriptions* (London, 1987), pp. 17–18.

'after hearing at Lydian feasts': Pindar, fragment 125 (Snell).

'dainty ways learnt from the Lydians': Xenophanes, fragment 3 (Diels).

Statue from near Miletus: Berlin inventory 1664; noted in Erich Kistler's discussion of Lydian luxury in Linda Marie Gunther and Paolo Filigheddu, eds, *Tryphe und Kultritual im archaischen Kleinasien* (Wiesbaden, 2011), p. 60.

'Clearchus says that Polycrates': Clearchus of Soli, fragment 44 (Wehrli) cited by Athenaeus, *Deipnosophists* 12, 540f.

'Stay ten miles off Cape Malea': www.cruiserswiki.org/wiki/Elafonisos (accessed 25 January 2018).

'The one leads straight to Asia': Strabo 8, 6, 20.

5 Great Greeks

'Great Hellas': Strabo 6, 1, 2; Pliny, *Natural History* 3, 95 ('Magna Graecia').

'by earthquakes, and by eruptions of fire' (Pithecusae): Strabo 5, 4, 9.

'the delicious cup of Nestor': I follow the translation of this graffito in Rosalind Thomas, *Literacy and Orality in Ancient Greece* (Cambridge, 1992), p. 58.

'bare hillsides flaming yellow': Giuseppe Tomasi di Lampedusa, trans. Archibald Colquhoun, *The Leopard* (London, 1988), p. 55.

ΠΙΒΕ graffito, Morgantina: Carla Antonaccio and Tim Sgea in Laura Manicalco, ed., *Morgantina duemilaquindici: La ricerca archeologica sessant'anni dall'avvio degli scavi* (Palermo, 2015), pp. 59–67.

'When the men of Acragas': Polyaenus, *Stratagems* 5, 1, 3.

Sixty talents of gold: Selinus temple inscription in Russell Meiggs and David Lewis, *A Selection of Greek Historical Inscriptions to the End of the Fifth Century* BC (Oxford, 1969, revised edn 1988) no. 38, now on display in the reopened Palermo Archaeological Museum.

Ghosts at Selinus: Michael H. Jameson, David R. Jordan and Roy D. Kotansky, *A Lex Sacra from Selinous* (Durham, North Carolina, 1993), pp. 15 and 17 (translation). See Robert L. Fowler, *Early Greek Mythography* II. *Commentary* (Oxford, 2015), pp. 70–1 with n. 267.

A Carthaginian 'portion' of Archaic Sicily: Justin 18, 7.

'the part of Sicily which the Carthaginians control' (509 BC): Polybius 3, 22, 10.

'chief poet of comedy': Plato, *Theaetetus* 152e.

'in plan and size': Polybius 9, 27, 9.

'lord of Sicily' (Gelon): Herodotus 7, 157.

6 Meet the (Western) Neighbours

Roman translation of Mago's manual: Columella, *De re rustica* 1, 1, 12.

'Presently a man': G. Flaubert, *Salambô*, trans. May French Sheldon (London and New York, 1886), p. 354.

'so that each of the children': Diodorus Siculus 20, 14, 6.

Abraham: Genesis 22, 1–19.

On the debate about Carthaginian child sacrifice: Paolo Xella, Valentina Melchiorri and Peter van Dommelen, *Antiquity* 87 (2013), pp. 1199–207; Maria Giulia Amadasi Guzzo and José Ángel Zamora López, *Studi Epigrafici e Linguistici*, 29–30 (2012–13), pp. 159–92.

Carthage's political stability: Aristotle, *Politics* 2, 1272b.

'judgment and training': Cicero, *On the Republic* 1, fragment 1, trans. David Fott.

Punic amphorae: Babette Bechtold and Roald Docter in *Motya and the Phoenician Ceramic Repertoire* (Rome, 2010), pp. 85–116; Laura Portas and five others, *Journal of Biological Research* 88 (2015), pp. 166–9.

'The intervening country': Diodorus Siculus 20, 8, 3–4.

Supplies from Sardinia (480 BC): Diodorus Siculus 11, 20, 4.

'At the present day': Pseudo-Aristotle, 'On marvellous things heard' (traditionally known by its Latin title, 'De mirabilibus auscultationibus'), 100, trans. L. D. Dowdall, in J. Barnes, ed., *The Complete Works of Aristotle: The Revised Oxford Translation* (Princeton, NJ, 1984), vol. 2, p. 1282.

Sardinian survey results: Andrea Roppa and Peter van Dommelen, *Journal of Roman Archaeology* 25 (2012), pp. 49–68.

'In Etruria': Pseudo-Aristotle, 'On marvellous things heard' (as above), 93, trans. L. D. Dowdall, in J. Barnes, ed., *The Complete Works of Aristotle. The Revised Oxford Translation* (Princeton, NJ, 1984), vol. 2, p. 1284.

Sostratus inscription: *Supplementum Epigraphicum Graecum* 26 (1976), no. 1137.

'no one could compete': Herodotus 4, 152, 3.

'it is a law among the Etruscans': Theophrastus fragment 204 cited by Athenaeus, *Deipnosophists* 12, 517d-e (trans. C. B. Gulick).

'Before the Roman supremacy': Livy 5, 33, 7–8.

'Hieron [son] of Deinomenes and the Syracusans' (inscription on Hieron's helmet): Russell Meiggs and David Lewis, *A Selection of Greek Historical Inscriptions to the End of the Fifth Century BC* (Oxford, 1969, revised edn 1988), no. 29.

Date of battle: Diodorus Siculus 11, 51.

'Romulus and Remus lived': Dionysius of Halicarnassus, *Roman Antiquities* 1, 79, 11.

'obscure and lowly': Livy 1, 8, 5–6.

'dregs of Romulus': Cicero, *ad Atticum* 2, 1, 8.

'pleading the irresistible force of their passion': Livy 1, 9, 16.

'mothers of free men': Livy 1, 9, 14–15.

'filled with wonder': Livy 1, 1, 8.

Vulci vase: Munich, Antikensammlungen, 1546.

'no wrong [to the] Latins who are [Roman] subjects': Polybius 3, 22, 11.

7 'Lord of All Men'?

'Lord of all men': Aeschines, *Against Ctesiphon* 132, trans. C. D. Adams.

'Leader of the Greeks': Thucydides 1, 132, 2–3.

'Behold, I will stir up': Isaiah 13, 18.

'I am Darius, the Great King': Behistun inscription (DB): § 1–4, trans. Maria Brosius, *The Persian Empire from Cyrus II to Artaxerxes I* (London, 2000), p. 30.

Royal tombs, throne-platform inscriptions: Amélie Kuhrt, *The Persian Empire* (London, 2007), vol. 2, pp. 483–4.

'richest under the sun': Diodorus Siculus 17, 70, 2.

'an arena for meditation': Madawi al-Rasheed, *A History of Saudi Arabia*, 2nd edn (Cambridge, 2010), pp. 77–8.

'When they reached the place' (Asidates): Xenophon, *Anabasis* 7, 8, 9–16.

'the whole treasure': Strabo 15, 3, 9.

USA figures: http://minerals.usgs.gov/minerals/pubs/commodity/silver/mcs-2012-silve.pdf.

'the retail merchant': Herodotus 3, 89, 3.

'father of history': Cicero, *Laws* 1, 5.

'the more one studies him': J. L. Lazenby, *The Defence of Greece 490–479 BC* (Warminster, 1993), p. 15.

'The Persians saw [the Athenians]': Herodotus 6, 112, 2–3.

'Cynegirus son of Euphorion': Herodotus 6, 114, 1.

'I do not wish that a man': Naqš-i Rustam inscription (DNb) § 4, trans. Maria Brosius, *The Persian Empire from Cyrus II to Artaxerxes I* (London, 2000), p. 64. See Thomas Harrison in A. Fitzpatrick-McKinley, ed., *Assessing Biblical and Classical Sources for the Reconstruction of Persian Influence* (Wiesbaden, 2014), pp. 3–11.

'wood-built wall' oracle: Herodotus 7, 141, 3–4.

'Stranger, go tell': Herodotus 7, 228, 2.

'display some feat to the king': Herodotus 8, 89, 2.

'the Persians were akin to him': Herodotus 8, 136, 1.
'by courage and constant effort': Herodotus 9, 70, 2.
'that freedom of theirs': Herodotus 7, 147, 1.
'As it is, to say that the Athenians': Herodotus 7, 139, 5.

8 The Same but Different

'in a ghastly graveyard marble': Nancy Mitford cited in Charlotte Mosley, ed., *A Talent to Annoy* (London, 1996), p. 107.
Dining crockery: Ann Steiner, *Classical Antiquity*, 21 (2002), pp. 347–90; also an unpublished paper on the Tholos pottery which Professor Steiner generously made available to me.
'taking the people into his *hetaireia*': Herodotus 5, 66, 2.
'*nébuleuse*': Jean Duma, *Les Bourbon-Penthièvre (1678–1893)* (Paris, 1995), p. 14.
'Cimon, son of Miltiades': *Supplementum Epigraphicum Graecum* 46 (1996), no. 79.
'it was also used to remove': ?Aristotle, *Athenian Constitution* 22, 6.
'golden brooches shaped like cicadas': Thucydides 1, 6, 3–4.
'if anyone else': Plato, *Protagoras* 319b-d, trans. W. R. M. Lamb, adjusted.
Pericles' 'ability' and 'personal repute': Thucydides 2, 65, 8.
'works of Pericles': Plutarch, *Pericles* 13, 3.
'treat everyone equally': Thucydides 2, 37, 1.
'poverty'; 'excellence': Thucydides 2, 37, 1.
'Great is your glory': Thucydides 2, 45, 2.
'the name of the good woman': Plutarch, *Moralia* 242e.
'Like donkeys': Tyrtaeus, fragments 6–7 West.
'the most high-spirited': Thucydides 4, 80, 3.
Nocturnal bands: Plutarch, *Lycurgus* 28.
'governed at all times': Thucydides 4, 80, 3.
'about eight thousand men': Herodotus 7, 234, 2.
'not even a thousand': Aristotle, *Politics* 2, 1270a.
'For among the Spartans': Polybius 12, 6b, 8.
'from early childhood': Thucydides 2, 39.
'It has come about that some of the Spartans': Aristotle, *Politics* 2, 1270a.
'He (Lycurgus) made it a point of honour': Xenophon, *Spartan Constitution* 2, 9.
'most shameful': Xenophon, *Spartan Constitution* 2, 13.
'embraces and lying together': Cicero, *On the Republic* 4, 2a (trans. David Fott).
Masks: Jonah Lloyd Rosenberg, 'The Masks of Orthia: Form, Function and the Origins of Theatre', *Annual of the British School at Athens* 110 (2015), pp. 247–61.
'Don't you see?': Alcman, *Partheneion* lines 50–57, trans. Gregory Nagy: http://chs.harvard.edu/CHS/article/display/5294 (accessed 10 January 2017).

9 'Unprecedented Suffering'?

'Mecypernians': lines 10–16 of *Inscriptiones Graecae*, vol. 1, 3rd edn, no. 259; translation in Robin Osborne and P. J. Rhodes, eds, *Greek Historical Inscriptions 478–404 BC* (Oxford, 2017), p. 97.
'on the stage': Isocrates, *On the Peace* 82.
'And surely Greece is insulted': Plutarch, *Pericles* 12, 2.
Parthenon payments: see the commentary of Robin Osborne and P. J. Rhodes, eds, *Greek Historical Inscriptions 478–404 BC* (Oxford, 2017), p. 262.
'For his part, Pericles': Plutarch, *Pericles* 12, 3.
'And you have never considered': Thucydides 1, 70, 1–3.
Comparison with Troy: Simon Hornblower, *The Greek World 479–323 BC*, 4th edn (London, 2011), p. 156.
'I detest the Spartans': Aristophanes, *Acharnians* lines 509–12.

'You know as well as we do': Thucydides 5, 89.

'put to death all the grown men': Thucydides 5, 116, 3–4.

'the most important action': Thucydides 7, 87, 5.

'a longing for foreign sights': Thucydides 6, 24, 3. Compare www.quora.com/What-made-you-join-the-military (accessed 14 January 2017).

'exceedingly ambitious of a command': Thucydides 6, 15, 2.

'who seeks to be admired': Thucydides 6, 15, 3.

'enthusiasm of the majority': Thucydides 6, 24, 4.

'more than twenty thousand slaves': Xenophon, *Ways and Means* 4, 14.

'corrupted by flattery': Xenophon, *Spartan Constitution* 14, 2.

Cynisca: *Palatine Anthology* 13.16; *Sayings of Spartans, Agesilaus* 49 (*Apophthegmata Laconica* 212b).

'eat the full citizens': Xenophon, *Hellenika* 3, 3, 6.

'The impact of one single battle': Aristotle, *Politics* 2, 1270a.

10 Examined Lives and Golden Mouths

'many Athenians who reached home safely': Plutarch, *Nicias* 29.3 (Syracuse).

'left the theatre abruptly': Plutarch, *Pelopidas* 29.

'I grieve, I grieve': Vienna fragment: translation and musical arrangement in Eric Csapo and William J. Slater, *The Context of Ancient Drama* (Ann Arbor, MI, 2001), Plate 21A.

Naples vase: the museum website has photographs and a description in English: http://cir.campania.beniculturali.it/museoarcheologiconazionale/thematic-views/image-gallery/RA84/view (accessed 25 January 2018).

'That being agreed': Aristophanes, *Knights*, lines 1384–1386 (contrasted translations of Gilbert Murray (1956) and Kenneth Dover (1978)).

'We two have a master': Aristophanes, *Knights*, lines 40–49, trans. Jeffrey Henderson.

'train you, if you give them money': Aristophanes, *Clouds*, lines 98–9.

'For you yourselves saw': Plato, *Apology* 19c.

'For if I did not believe': Plato, *Phaedo* 63b-c.

'[pregnant] with things that it is fitting': Plato, *Symposium* 209a.1–2, ed. C. J. Rowe.

'For I imagine': Plato, *Symposium* 209c.1–5, ed. C. J. Rowe.

'correct kind of boy-loving': Plato, *Symposium* 211b.6, ed. C. J. Rowe.

'trying to get hold of truly beautiful things': Plato, *Symposium* 218c.6–219a.1, ed. C. J. Rowe.

'in the Academy': Diogenes Laertius, *Lives of Eminent Philosophers, Life of Plato* 3, 9, trans. Mark Joyal and others, *Greek and Roman Education: A Sourcebook* (London, 2009), p. 110, no. 5.15a.

'I saw a group of boys': Epicrates, fragment 10 Kassel-Austin, trans. Mark Joyal and others, *Greek and Roman Education: A Sourcebook* (London, 2009), p. 112, no. 5.17.

'disguising for some considerable time': Themistius, *Oration* 33, 295c-d, trans. Mark Joyal and others, *Greek and Roman Education: A Sourcebook* (London, 2009), pp. 111–12, no. 5.16b.

'he had a lisping voice': Diogenes Laertius, *Lives of Eminent Philosophers: Life of Aristotle* 5, 2.

'And generally, the molluscs': Aristotle, *Historia Animalium* 544a, 16–22.

'Things do not appear the same': Aristotle, *Rhetoric* 2, 1377b30–1378a2 and 1378a 20–2, trans. Terence Irwin and Gail Fine, *Aristotle: Selections* (Indianapolis, 1995), pp. 534–5.

Spear butt: Pat Foster, *Greek Arms and Armour* (Newcastle upon Tyne, 1982), p. 13. See John Ma, 'Chaironeia 338: Topographies of Commemoration', *Journal of Hellenic Studies*, 128 (2008), pp. 72–91.

11 'A Brilliant Flash of Lightning'

'Philip used to train': Polyaenus, *Stratagems* 4, 2, 10.

'he draws no distinction': Demosthenes, *Philippic* 3, 50.

Inscription about landed estates: Miltiades Hatzopoulos, *Une donation du roi Lysimaque* (Athens and Paris, 1988).

'[c]areless of what they had': Theopompus, *History of Philip*, fragment 225b cited by Athenaeus, *Deipnosophists* 6, 260d–261a.

Chaeronea: Polyaenus, *Stratagems* 2, 1, 9.

'he dispensed with his horse': Plutarch, *Artaxerxes* 24, trans. Timothy Duff.

'stormed, plundered': Plutarch, *Alexander* 11, 5.

'a brilliant flash of lightning': Appian, *Roman History* Preface 10.

'insatiable thirst for extending his possessions': Arrian 7, 19, 6, trans. Aubrey de Sélincourt.

'The wealth of their [i.e. the Arabs'] country': Arrian 7, 20, 2, trans. Aubrey de Sélincourt.

'observations from Babylon': Simplicius, Commentary on Aristotle's *De Caelo* 2, 12.

'myrrh was burnt': Ephippus fragment 5 = Athenaeus, *Deipnosophists* 12, 538a.

Alexander dresses as Artemis: Ephippus fragment 5 = Athenaeus, *Deipnosophists* 12, 537e-f. I first offered my reinterpretation of this alleged transvestism in an online journal (http://research.ncl.ac.uk/histos/HISTOS62012.html, accessed 25 January 2018): 'The pamphleteer Ephippus, King Alexander and the Persian royal hunt', *Histos*, 6 (2012), pp. 169–213.

'there is nothing left for the king than to become a god': Isocrates, *Letters* 3, 5.

12 Game of Thrones, or the World after Alexander

'When a child': Ai-Khanoum inscription: M. M. Austin, *The Hellenistic World*, 2nd edn (Cambridge, 2006), no. 192.

'Those who till the soil': Aristotle, *Politics* 7, 1330a, 25.

'And the city contains': Strabo 17, 1, 8.

'The Museum is also a part': Strabo 17, 1, 8.

'Seeing at once': Dionysius of Halicarnassus, *Dinarchus* 1, trans. Gladys Shoesmith.

'Herophilus and Erasistratus': Cornelius Celsus, *On medicine*, Proem 23–24, translated in James Longrigg, ed., *Greek Medicine: From the Heroic to the Hellenistic Age: A Source Book* (London, 1998), no. VII, 2.

'They have treated me with contempt': M. M. Austin, *The Hellenistic World*, 2nd edn (Cambridge, 2006), no. 245 (dated around 255 BC).

'the Macedonians who hold Alexandria in Egypt': Livy 38, 17, 10 (invented speech of a Roman general supposedly in 189 BC).

'Ptolemy was in love': Pausanias 1, 7, 1.

'and of his sister': M. M. Austin, *The Hellenistic World*, 2nd edn (Cambridge 2006), no. 61 (dated between 268 and 265 BC).

'well done and fitting': William Shakespeare, *Antony and Cleopatra*, Act 5, Scene 2, lines 320–321.

Pergamene altar: Andreas Scholl in Carlos Picón and Seán Hemingway, eds, *Pergamon and the Hellenistic Kingdoms of the Ancient World* (New Haven and London, 2016), pp. 44–53.

'every male they put to the sword': Pausanias 10, 22, 2.

'gentleman's agreement': R. T. Pritchard, 'Cicero and the Lex Hieronica,' *Historia* 19 (1970), p. 357.

'engines accommodated to all the purposes': Plutarch, *Lucullus* 14, 9.

'stronger and firmer': Pausanias 6, 12, 3–4.

'He passed most of his life': Plutarch, *Marcellus*, 14, 9.

13 'Senatus Populusque Romanus'

Inscriptions for the Scipios and Paulla Cornelia: *Inscriptiones Latinae Selectae* nos 1, 4 and 10.

'Have you brought forth children': Plutarch, *Caius Gracchus* 4, 6.

The head of the statue of the so-called Togato Barberini, although ancient, is a modern addition according to the museum website: http://www.centralemontemartini.org (accessed 23 January 2018: click on 'Collezioni', then on 'Tutte le Opere', then on 'Togato Barberini').

Caesar's portrait: see http://museoarcheologico.piemonte.beniculturali.it. (accessed 22 February 2017). Discussion in John Pollini, *From Republic to Empire: Rhetoric, Religion and Power in the Visual Culture of Ancient Rome* (Norman, OK, 2012), pp. 51–2.

'they withdrew to the Sacred Mount': Livy 2, 32, 2–4.

'equalized the rights of all': Livy, 3, 34, 3.

'If he has broken a bone' and other extracts from the Twelve Tables: M. H. Crawford, *Roman Statutes* II (London, 1996), pp. 607 (Tabula I, 14), 681–2 (Tabula VIII, 3), 707 (Tabula X, 4).

'even now they are the fountain-head': Livy 3, 34, 6.

'Naevius long ago': Pseudoasconius in T. Stangl, *Ciceronis Orationum Scholiastae* (Vienna and Leipzig, 1912), p. 215.

'no one could say for certain': Polybius 6, 11.

'masters of everything': Polybius 6, 12.

'in general every rumour': ?Quintus Cicero, *Commentariolum Petitionis*, trans. D. W. Taylor and J. Murrell as *A Short Guide to Electioneering* (London, 1974), p. 5 (17).

'Respecting the residents': Livy 38, 36, 7–9.

'What was the ruin of Sparta': Tacitus, *Annals* 11, 24.

Lucius Aurelius Hermia tombstone: British Museum 1867,0508.55, viewable online, with the curator's translation of the Latin: http://www.britishmuseum.org/research/collection_online/collection_object_details.aspx?objectId=465522&partId=1 (accessed 25 January 2018).

'Since there were still a very large number': Appian, *Civil War* 1, 120.

Cicero's 'knightly' status: *Pro Murena* 17.

'not made yesterday': Ovid, *Tristia* 4, poem 10, line 8.

'reared on blood': Ovid, *Amores* 3, 8, 10.

'For I conceive that what in other nations': Polybius 6, 56.

'And new religious fears': Livy 30, 2, 9–13.

'In my opinion their object is to use it': Polybius 6, 56.

'The whole distinction of real and unreal': William James, *The Principles of Psychology*, vol. 2 (New York, 1890), p. 290, cited by Henk Versnel, *Coping with the Gods: Wayward Readings in Greek Theology* (Leiden, 2011), p. 470.

14 Boots on the Ground

Grad hoard: Jana Horvat, 'The Hoard of Roman Republican Weapons from Grad near Šmihel', *Arheološki vestnik* 53 (2002), pp. 117–92.

'takes a cudgel': Polybius 6, 37.

'it sometimes happens that': Polybius 6, 37.

'It was customary for the fetial': Livy 1, 32, 13.

'would hurl his spear': Livy 1, 32, 14.

'Have you never read of the citizen': Pliny, *Letters* 2, 3, 8.

'First the consuls': Livy 9, 6, 1–2.

'There is scarce any other Roman victory': Livy 9, 15, 8.

'the acts of the people, relative to alliances': Suetonius, *Vespasian* 8, 5.

'Let there be peace': Dionysius of Halicarnassus, *Roman Antiquities* 6, 95.

'suitable places . . . bulwark of empire': Cicero, *De lege agraria* 2, 73.

'and hoping that he might repeat that victory': Pausanias 1, 12, 2.

'These may be barbarians': Plutarch, *Pyrrhus* 16, 5.

'the longest, most continuous': Polybius 1, 63.

Rams: see Francesca Olivero, 'Bronze rams of the Egadi battle,' *Skyllis* 109 (2012), pp. 117–24; Jonathan Prag, 'Bronze rostra from the Egadi islands off NW Sicily: the Latin inscriptions,' *Journal of Roman Archaeology* 27 (2014), pp. 33–59.

'He practised and drilled his crews': Polybius 1, 59.

'saw that the Carthaginians': Polybius 1, 10.

'theft': Polybius 3, 30, 4.

'To reckless courage . . . no religious scruple': Livy 21, 5–9.

'or even by himself': Polybius 18, 32.

'When [the Greeks] were tired of shouting': Plutarch, *Flamininus* 11.1.

Seaenoci inscription (Latin text): *L'Année Épigraphique* 624 (2006).

'The Aetolians, after some further observations': Polybius 20, 9 with Álvaro M. Moreno Leoni, *Histos* 8 (2014), pp. 146–79, reasserting the traditional interpretation.

'The people of the Aetolians': Livy 38, 11, 2.

'There was intense competition': Sallust, *Bellum Catilinum* 7.6.

'The records have been vitiated': Livy 8, 40, 4.

'commended': Livy 35, 10, 4.

'triumphed': Livy 35, 10, 5.

'The amount of money exhibited': Plutarch, *Flamininus* 14.

'I, Manius Acilius son of Gaius': for Glabrio's base see Dylan Bloy, 'Greek war booty at Luna and the afterlife of Manius Acilius Glabrio', *Memoirs of the American Academy in Rome* 43/44 (1998/9), pp. 49–61.

Delphi victory monument, on display in the archaeological museum at Delphi: see now Michael J. Taylor, *Hesperia* 85 (2016), pp. 559–76.

'stratagem and deceit': Polybius 37, 1.

'retained their own habits and principles uncontaminated': Polybius 18, 35.

15 Hail Caesar!

'The Italians and Greeks who do business on Delos': *Inscriptiones Latinae Selectae* nos. 8961a–b.

'Delos, which could both admit': Strabo 14, 5, 2.

'barbarian' slaves: Plutarch, *Tiberius Gracchus* 8, 7.

'The men who fight and die for Italy': Plutarch, *Tiberius Gracchus* 9, 5.

'posted writings on porticoes': Plutarch, *Tiberius Gracchus* 8, 7.

'This is said to have been the first sedition': Plutarch, *Tiberius Gracchus* 20, 1.

Tiberius Gracchus: Plutarch, *Tiberius Gracchus* 19–20, 1.

'That which is necessary for keeping alive': Aulus Gellius, *Attic Nights* 9, 14, 16–17.

'He busied himself most earnestly': Plutarch, *Gaius Gracchus* 7.

'One hundred and twenty years ago': Velleius Paterculus, *Roman History* 2, 15.

'The Romans abundantly repaid his loyal zeal': Velleius Paterculus, *Roman History* 2, 16.

Seats at the games: Gaius Julius Victor, *Ars rhetorica*, p. 402, lines 12–15 in C. Halm, ed., *Rhetores Latini Minores* (Leipzig, 1863), trans. Andrew Wallace-Hadrill, *Rome's Cultural Revolution* (Cambridge, 2008), p. 446.

'Homoloïchos and Anaxidamos': Plutarch, *Sulla* 19, 5. Jeremy McInerney and others, *American Journal of Archaeology*, 96 (1992), pp. 443–55.

'I'm amazed, O wall': *Corpus Inscriptionum Latinarum* 4, 1904 translated in Jennifer Baird and Claire Taylor, eds, *Ancient Graffiti in Context* (New York, 2011), p. 2.

'His hair was inclined to lift itself': Plutarch, *Pompey* 2.

'All Gaul is divided into three parts': Caesar, *Gallic War* 1, 1.

'For although it was not full ten years': Plutarch, *Caesar* 15, 3.

'The civil wars which he waged were five': Suetonius, *Divus Augustus* 9.

'Those murders by proscription': Cassius Dio, *Roman History* 47, 3.

'At the age of nineteen'; 'All Italy'; 'about 3,500 beasts'; 'By new laws passed on my proposal'; 'by decree of the senate': Peter M. Brunt and John M. Moore, *Res Gestae Divi Augusti*, 2nd edn (Oxford, 1967), sections 1, 1; 25, 2; 22, 3; 5; 34, 2.

'The essence of civilization': 'Empedocles on Etna', *Inquirer* (27 August 1853), pp. 548–9, an anonymous article attributed to Walter Bagehot by Robert H. Tener, *Biographical Society of the University of Virginia* 29 (1976), pp. 349–53.

16 'Fierce Rome, Captive'?

'convivium'/'symposion': remarks in Alan Wardman, *Rome's Debt to Greece* (London, 1976), p. 144.

'humble abode': *Palatine Anthology* 11, 44.

'There is no index of character': Benjamin Disraeli, *Tancred: Or, the New Crusade* (Leipzig, 1847), book II, chapter 1.

'the good man skilled in speaking': Quintilian, *Institutio Oratoria* 12, 1, 1.

'to speak [Latin] in the Attic way': Quintilian, *Institutio Oratoria* 12, 10, 26.

'glory in war': Cicero, *Pro Flacco* 64.

Demosthenes portrait in the Metropolitan Museum of Art, New York: www.metmuseum.org/collection/the-collection-online/search/257882 (accessed 25 January 2018).

Painfully obvious joke: Michael Fontaine, *Funny Words in Plautine Comedy* (Oxford, 2010), p. 41.

'In my sixth consulship': Augustus, *Res gestae* 20, 4.

'I built the temple of Mars': Augustus, *Res gestae* 21, 1.

'Arms and the man I sing': Virgil, *Aeneid* 1, lines 1–11.

'The man, for wisdom's various arts renown'd': Homer, *Odyssey* 1, lines 1–5 (lines 1–7 in the 1801 edition of Alexander Pope's translation).

'Of Trojan stock illustriously sprung': Virgil, *Aeneid* 1, lines 290–293.

'Greekling': Scriptores Historiae Augustae, *Hadrian* 1, 5.

'like a woman': Scriptores Historiae Augustae, *Hadrian* 14, 5.

17 What Did the Romans Do for Their Empire?

'The Shades of L[ucius] Calpurnius Piso': *Corpus Inscriptionum Latinarum* 6, 31723.

'Piso was the son of Marcus Crassus': Tacitus, *Histories* 1, 14.

'side by side with the eagle of the legion': Tacitus, *Histories* 1, 44.

'The Doom of the Nobiles': chapter 32 of Ronald Syme, *The Roman Revolution* (Oxford, 1939, reprinted from 1960 on), pp. 490–508.

'His brother Magnus': Tacitus, *Histories* 1, 48.

'Seneca . . . begged': Tacitus, *Annals* 15, 64.

Patara granary: Marie-Brigitte Carre in Javier Arce and Bertrand Goffaux, eds, *Horrea d'Hispanie et de la Méditerranée* (Madrid, 2011), pp. 28–30.

Patara pillar monument: Mustafa Adak and Sencer Şahin, *Stadiasmus Patarensis. Itinera Romana Provinciae Lyciae* (Istanbul, 2007). For an English summary see the presentation by Professor Nalan Eda Akyürek Şahin (with bibliography) on the website of Akdeniz University, Antalya, Turkey: http://adkam.akdeniz.edu.tr/sp-en-text (accessed 22 March 2017).

Patara theatre inscription: *Tituli Asia Minoris* 2, no. 420.

'and gave orders that no one be allowed to leave: Suetonius, *Caligula* 26, 5.

Sanitation: lecture by Heikki Vuorinen of Helsinki University at the Finnish Institute at Athens (20 March 2014).

'Veranius, after having ravaged': Tacitus, *Annals* 14, 29.

Isca website: Welsh Government Website, page for Caerleon Roman Fortress and Baths, http://cadw.gov.wales/daysout/Caerleon-roman-fortress-baths/?lang=en (accessed 21 March 2017).

'The Britons are unprotected by armour': A. K. Bowman and J. D. Thomas, *The Vindolanda Writing Tablets (Tabulae Vindolandenses II)* (London, 1994); *Vindolanda Tablets Online*, tablet 164: http://vindolanda.csad.ox.ac.uk/4DLink2/4DACTION/WebRequestQuery?searchTerm=164&searchType=number&searchField=TVII (accessed 22 March 2017).

'To accustom to rest and repose': Tacitus, *Agricola* 21.

'To Neptune and Minerva': the most up-to-date edition of the Chichester inscription is the website *Roman Inscriptions of Britain Online*, no. 91: https://romaninscriptionsofbritain.org/inscriptions/91 (accessed 22 March 2017).

Onyx ring: John Manley and David Rudkin, 'Fishbourne Roman Palace Final Interim 1995–9': https://sussexpast.co.uk/wp-content/uploads/2011/08/FBE–95–99.pdf (accessed 25 January 2018).

'puellam': Francis Haverfield, *The Romanization of Roman Britain*, 4th edn (Oxford 1923), p. 30 with Figure 2.

Diet: Gillian Hawkes, 'Beyond Romanization: The creolization of food. A framework for the study of faunal remains from Roman sites', *Papers from the Institute of Archaeology* 10 (1999), pp. 89–95.

'The courts . . . bring together': Dio Chrysostom, *Oration* 35, 15–17.

'To Valerius Firmus': James Keenan and others, eds, *Law and Legal Practice in Egypt from Alexander to the Arab Conquest* (Cambridge, 2014), no. 3, 3, 5.

18 'Barbarians' at the Gate

Augustus 'won over everyone with the sweetness of repose': Tacitus, *Annals* 1, 2, 1.

'[Work] of Emperor Caesar': *Roman Inscriptions of Britain Online*, no. 1638: https://romaninscriptionsofbritain.org/inscriptions/1638 (accessed 29 March 2017).

'An encamped army': Aelius Aristides, *Oration* 14 (Dindorf), 219–20.

'They would eat the flesh': Cassius Dio 68, 32.

'because they were forbidden to practise circumcision': Scriptores Historiae Augustae, *Hadrian* 14, 1–2.

'Hadrian the blasphemer': Jerusalem Talmud Taan 4, 8, folio 69a.

'placed in a river so deep': Cassius Dio 68, 13.

'the Black Sea and the Caspian': Patrick Leigh Fermor, *A Time of Gifts* (London, 2004), pp. 183–4.

'among the one hundred most dangerous books': Arnaldo Momigliano, *Studies in Historiography* (London, 1966), p. 112.

'The Harii': Tacitus, *Germania* 4.

'transplanted – and forced to pay tribute': Latin inscription in *Inscriptiones Latinae Selectae* no. 986.

'the names of the young soldiers': Greek inscription in Paul Roesch, *Les Inscriptions de Thespies*, Fascicule I (2007, revised 2009), no. 37: www.hisoma.mom.fr/sites/hisoma.mom.fr/files/img/production-scientifique/IT%20I%20%282009%29.pdf (accessed 25 January 2018).

'besides clothes and goblets': Scriptores Historiae Augustae, *Marcus* 21, 9.

'when suddenly many clouds gathered': Cassius Dio 71, 8.

'The Germanic drought was removed': Tertullian, *Apologeticus* 5. I follow the interpretation of the divinity on the Column of Marcus Aurelius argued by Ido Israelowich, 'The Rain Miracle of Marcus Aurelius: (Re-)Construction of Consensus', *Greece & Rome*, 55 (2008), pp. 83–102.

'Our history now descends from a kingdom of gold': Cassius Dio 72, 36, 4.

Spartan inscription: Antony Spawforth, 'A Severan Statue Group and an Olympic Festival at Sparta', *Annual of the British School at Athens* 81 (1986), pp. 313–32.

'by his birth and normal behaviour': Herodian 7, 1, 2.

'With great daring': Herodian 8, 5, 9.

'Your ancestors, fighting in this place': Vienna manuscript translated by Christopher Mallan and Caillan Davenport, 'Dexippus and the Gothic Invasions: Interpreting the New Vienna Fragment (*Codex Vindobonensis Hist. gr.* 73, ff. 192ᵛ–193ʳ)', *Journal of Roman Studies* 105 (2015), p. 206 (7).

'Franks, Sarmatians by the thousand': Scriptores Historiae Augustae, *Aurelian* 7, 2.

'To whom, at this rate': Scriptores Historiae Augustae, *Aurelian* 31, 5.

'to clear the sea, which the Franks': Carausius: Eutropius, *Breviarium* 9, 21.

'Expectate veni': this particular coin recorded by the Portable Antiquities Scheme (UK) as with the unique ID: BH-059652. Virgil, *Aeneid* 2, lines 282–3.

'Carausius and his brothers' (CARAVSIVS ET FRATRES SVI): see N. Shiel, 'Carausius et fratres sui', *British Numismatic Journal* 48 (1978), pp. 7–11.

19 The 'Jesus Movement'

John Moles, 'Jesus the Healer in the Early Gospels, the *Acts of the Apostles*, and Early Christianity', *Histos* 5 (2011), pp. 117–82.

List of gold and silver images: see Guy Rogers, *The Sacred Identity of Ephesos* (London, 1991), pp. 83–5, discussing the detailed information contained in the long Greek inscription published as *Die Inschriften von Ephesos* no. 27.

'All soldiers and sailors were ready to die': New Zealand's *The Northern Advocate* (Tuesday 24 September 1912), p. 2, citing a letter to the *Daily Mail* from the expatriate Japanese artist and author Yoshio Markino, who lived in Edwardian London: https://paperspast. natlib.govt.nz/newspapers/NA19120924.2.3 (accessed 25 January 2018).

'the temple raised to the deified Claudius': Tacitus, *Annals* 14, 31.

'Whether she was innocent or not': Pliny, *Letters* 4, 11, 8–9.

'Take a sprig of laurel': H. D. Betz, *The Greek Magical Papyri in Translation* (Chicago, IL, 1986), p. 14, citing *PGM* II, 65–8.

'Ye treachery and malice': John Timbs, *Curiosities of London: Exhibiting the Most Rare and Remarkable Objects in the Metropolis; With Nearly Sixty Years' Personal Recollections* (London, 1867), p. 571.

'To get rid of the rumour': Tacitus, *Annals* 15, 44. The translation is that of Brent D. Shaw, 'The Myth of the Neronian Persecution', *Journal of Roman Studies* 105 (2015), pp. 73–100, whose larger argument I follow.

'It is not possible to lay down any general rule': Pliny, *Letters* 10, 97.

Early Christians as freelance experts: Heidi Wendt, '*Ea superstitio*: Christian Martyrdom and the Religion of Freelance Experts', *Journal of Roman Studies*, 105 (2015), pp. 183–202.

Lyon 'martyrs': Eusebius, *Ecclesiastical History* 5, 1.

'in consequence of which they despise death': Lucian, *On the Death of Peregrinus* 13.

'To the commissioners of sacrifices at Oxyrhynchus': Alan Bowman, *Egypt after the Pharaohs, 332 BC – AD 642: From Alexander to the Arab Conquest* (London, 1986), p. 191, citing P. Oxy. 1464.

'how many things he endured': Origen: Eusebius, *Ecclesiastical History* 6, 39, 5.

'In the nineteenth year of the reign of Diocletian': Eusebius, *Ecclesiastical History* 8, 2, 4.

'neither gold nor silver nor money': P. Oxy. 33, 2673 with the discussion by Annemarie Luijendijk in *Journal of Early Christian Studies* 16 (2008), pp. 341–69.

'A most marvellous sign appeared to him': Eusebius 1, 28, 2.

'God's heavenly sign': Lactantius, *De morte persecutorum* 44, 5.

Saint Peter's: *Liber Pontificalis* (Book of the Pontiffs), trans. Raymond Davis (Liverpool, 1989), pp. 16–24.

'bearing a baulk of timber': Evelyn Waugh, *Helena* (Penguin, 1963), p. 154.

20 United We Stand

'Who therefore can be ignorant': Edict of Diocletian, trans. Roland G. Kent, *University of Pennsylvania Law Review* 69 (1920), p. 43.

'The assembled veterans cried out': *Theodosian Code* 7, 20, 2, trans. N. Lewis and M. Reinhold, *Roman Civilization: Sourcebook II: The Empire* (New York, 1966), p. 530.

'Constantine did something else': Zosimus 2, 34.

Arch of Khosrau: https://commons.wikimedia.org/wiki/File:Arch_of_Ctesiphon_assessment_ DVIDS221914.jpg (accessed 6 June 2017).

'shining with all kinds of precious stones': Ammianus Marcellinus 16, 10, 6.

'Dazzling the people': Karl Lagerfeld in *Fastes de Cour et cérémonies royales* (Paris, 2009), p. 13.

'For though he was a man of short stature': Ammianus Marcellinus 16, 10, 10, cited by Rowland Smith in A. Spawforth, ed., *The Court and Court Society in Ancient Monarchies* (Cambridge, 2007), p. 210.

'one would expect of an enemy of God's religion': Lactantius, *De morte persecutorum* 11.

'under cruel tortures': Eusebius, *Praeparatio Evangelica* 4, 2.

'to sacrifice by the altar the foetus': lines 4–5 of the Vera inscription, with new readings by Tibor Grüll: *Supplementum Epigraphicum Graecum* 39 (1989), no. 855. An English translation and commentary are available in that author's *Patmiaka* (Budapest, 1989). See also

George Deligiannakis in *The Dodecanese and the Eastern Aegean Islands in Late Antiquity, AD 300–700* (Oxford, 2016), pp. 318–20.

'not history but imaginative re-creation': Dudley Fitts's review of Gore Vidal, *Julian* (1964) in the *New York Times*, www.nytimes.com/books/98/03/01/home/vidal-julian.html (accessed 25 January 2018).

'ordered the temples to be opened': Ammianus Marcellinus 22, 5.

'Mantiklos donated me': John Boardman, *Greek Sculpture: The Archaic Period* (London, 1991), p. 30, no. 10.

'those who wear the long cloak': Eusebius, *Praeparatio Evangelica* 4, 2.

'His voice . . . was such as one might have heard': Eunapius, *Lives of the Sophists* 427.

'He burned a grain of incense': Eunapius, *Lives of the Sophists* 435.

'Forgetting': Ammianus Marcellinus 25, 3, 3.

'of any animal whatsoever'; 'monstrously ugly'; 'exceed every degree'; 'seizing and destroying everything': Ammianus Marcellinus 31, 2, 1–3.

'They were ferried over': Ammianus Marcellinus 31, 4, 5.

'the most frequently contested spot': John Keegan, *A History of Warfare* (London, 2004), p. 70.

Olympic victories of AD 381 and 385: *Supplementum Epigraphicum Graecum* 45 (1995), no. 412.

'No person at all, of any class': *Theodosian Code* 16, 10, 12.

'The Emperor, who was full of faith': Theodoret, *Ecclesiastical History* 5, 17–18, trans. William Stearns Davis, ed., *Readings in Ancient History: Illustrative Extracts from the Sources* (Boston, 1912–13), vol. 2: *Rome and the West*, pp. 298–300.

Butheric and the cupbearer: Sozomen, *Ecclesiastical History* 7, 25 with the discussion of Robert M. Frakes in Robert M. Frakes and others, eds, *The Rhetoric of Power in Late Antiquity* (New York, 2010), pp. 47–62.

Bearing arms a 'serious matter': Moses Finley in *Journal of Roman Studies* 48 (1958), p. 159.

21 Divided We Fall

'Everything cedes to Theodosius': Latin inscription on the Obelisk of Theodosius: *Inscriptiones Latinae Selectae* no. 821.

'Visigoths': Jordanes, *Getica* 5, 42.

'Some most flagrant and wicked desires': Augustine, *City of God* 1, 28.

Acilius Glabrio Sibidius and family: Alan Cameron, *Journal of Roman Studies* 102 (2012), pp. 148–50.

'[he] was a man of moderate height': Jordanes, *Getica* 168.

'He [Gaeseric] robbed the rest of the Libyans': Procopius, *History of the Wars* 3, 5.

'He was short, with a broad chest': R. Blockley, *The Fragmentary Classicising Historians of the Later Roman Empire*, vol. 2 (Liverpool, 1983), Priscus fragment 12.

'The British provinces': Gallic Chronicle of 452, *Chronica minora* 1, 660 (*c.* 126).

Dorchester pottery: James Gerrard in *Britannia*, 41 (2010), pp. 293–312.

Hadrian's Wall: Rob Collins, *Hadrian's Wall and the End of Empire* (New York and Abingdon, 2014), chapter 2.

'Then he entered Ravenna, deposed Augustulus': Anonymus Valesianus 8, 38.

'This Emperor was insincere': Procopius, *Secret History* 8, 24; 17, 5–6.

'And often even in the theatre': Procopius, *Secret History* 9, 20–21.

'Theodora also concerned herself': Procopius, *Secret History* 17, 5–6.

American translator: Timothy G. Kearsley, *Law Library Journal* 99 (2007), pp. 525–54.

'Whereas then, nothing in any sphere': Alan Watson, *The Digest of Justinian*, revised edn, vol. I (Philadelphia, PA, 1998), p. xxxiii.

'golden dome suspended': Procopius, *On Buildings* 1, 1, 46 (Great Church).

'Light of light': Timothy Gregory, *Isthmia*, vol. 5 (Princeton, NJ, 1993), pp. 12–13, no. 4.

'who dare to practise abominable lust': *Institutions* 4, 18, 4.

'The emperor ordered that all those found guilty': Malalas, *Chronographia* 18, 168 (PG 97: 644).

Sophronius and the caliph: see Phil Booth, *Crisis of Empire. Doctrine and Dissent at the End of Late Antiquity* (Berkeley and Los Angeles, CA, 2011), pp. 234–5.

'Thrice-blessed rock': Alan Cameron, *Classical Quarterly* 33 (1983), pp. 284–92 (translation and commentary).

Epilogue

Earliest English dictionary: for traces of Virgil in the so-called Épinal glossary see Michael Lapidge in Malcolm Godden and others, eds, *Anglo-Saxon England* (Cambridge, 2007), p. 44.

'Intellectually, men of the seventeenth century': Henri Lamonnier, *L'art français au temps de Louis XIV* (Paris, 1911), p. 226, cited by Jean Cordey, *Vaux-le-Vicomte* (Paris 1924), pp. 48–9.

Medea, Written in Rage, by Jean-René Lemoine, translated, adapted and directed by Neil Bartlett, starring the performer, dancer and vocalist François Testory, opened in London at The Place on 5 October 2017, which is when I saw it.

FURTHER READING

Many of the renditions into English from ancient writers, unless otherwise stated, are based on the Loeb Classical Library. This is an invaluable and ongoing series of ancient writers in translation, the English and the Greek or Latin set out side by side, which Harvard University Press has been publishing since 1912. It now available digitally as well: http://www.hup. harvard.edu/collection.php?cpk=1031.

The reader who wants to find out more about ancient Greek and Roman individuals, places and themes and so on mentioned in this book might find of use this reference work, which I helped to edit: Simon Hornblower, Esther Eidinow and Antony Spawforth, eds, *The Oxford Companion to Classical Civilization*, 2nd edn (Oxford, 2014). This illustrated volume is the slimmed-down child of a much more comprehensive parent: Simon Hornblower, Esther Eidinow and Antony Spawforth, eds, *The Oxford Classical Dictionary*, 4th edn (Oxford, 2012), which has well over six thousand entries aiming to cover all aspects of the ancient Greek and Roman world, with bibliographies. It can also be consulted for further information about individual ancient authors and editions and English translations of their writings.

In addition, the following is a short and (therefore) highly selective list of suggestions for further reading on particular topics:

Austin, M. M., and P. Vidal-Naquet, *Economic and Social History of Ancient Greece: An Introduction* (London, 1977)

Beard, M., J. North and S. Price, *Religions of Rome* (Cambridge, 1995)

Boardman, J., *Oxford History of Classical Art* (Oxford, 1993)

Briant, P., *Alexander the Great and His Empire: A Short Introduction* (Princeton, NJ, 2010)

Cornell, T., *The Beginnings of Rome* (Abingdon and New York, 1995)

Dickinson, O., *The Aegean from Bronze Age to Iron Age* (London and New York, 2006)

Garnsey, P., and R. Saller, *The Roman Empire, Economy, Society and Culture*, 2nd edn (Oakland, CA, 2015)

Goodman, M., *The Roman World 44 BC–AD 180*, 2nd edn (Abingdon and New York, 2011)

Heather, P., *The Fall of the Roman Empire: A New History of Rome and the Barbarians* (New York, 2006)

Hornblower, S., *The Greek World 479 BC–323 BC*, 4th edn (Abingdon and New York, 2011)

Howatson, M. C., *The Oxford Companion to Classical Literature*, 3rd edn (Oxford, 2011)

Lane Fox, R., *Pagans and Christians* (1986, reissued London, 2006)

Mattingly, D., *An Imperial Possession: Britain in the Roman Empire, 54 BC–AD 409* (London, 2006)

Ogden, D., *A Companion to Greek Religion* (Chichester, 2007)

Osborne, R., *Greece in the Making 1200–479 BC*, 2nd edn (Abingdon and New York, 2009)

Sabin, P., H. van Wees and M. Whitby, eds, *The Cambridge History of Greek and Roman Warfare* (Cambridge, 2007)

Talbert, R. J. A., *Barrington Atlas of the Greek and Roman World* (Princeton, NJ, 2000)

INDEX

300, film 106

Abraham 92
Abū Bakr, first caliph 328, 329
Abu Simbel 68
Academy *see* Athens
Achaemenids 107, 116
  Macedonian intermarriages 165, 172
  see also Artaxerxes II; Cambyses; Cyrus
    the Great; Darius I; Darius II; Darius
    III; Xerxes I
Achilles, Greek hero 32, 215
Acilius Glabrio, Manius, Roman consul
  (191 BC) 221, 223, 318–19
Acilius Glabrio Sibidius, Roman senator 318
  his great-grandsons 324
Acragas, modern Agrigento 81–3, 87
Acropolis *see* Athens
Actium, battle of (31 BC) 237
actors 151, 172
  Nero as 254
  see also drama
Acts of the Apostles 287
adoption 236, 258
Adam, and Eve 44
Adrianople, modern Edirne 312
adultery 250, 253
Aegates islands, modern Egadi islands
  216–17
Aelia Capitolina *see* Jerusalem
Aeneas of Troy 102–4, 251–3, 284
Aeneid see Virgil
Aeschylus, Athenian playwright 4, 87, 151–2

Aetolia, Aetolians 221
Afghanistan 6, 30, 162, 172, 180, 181, 182
Africa, North 89, 90, 94, 231, 280, 318, 319,
  320, 323, 327 *see also* Carthage;
  Cyrene; Gaeseric; Libya; Septimius
  Severus; Vandals
Agamemnon, mythical Greek king 28, 29,
  40, 152
Agamemnon, play by Aeschylus 151–2
Agesilaus II, Spartan king 146
Agricola, Roman governor of Britain
  (AD 77–84) 266
agriculture 18, 25
  Aristotle on 181
  Carthaginian manual on 90, 93
  Law of Hieron 191
  Sparta disrupts Athenian 140, 144
  see also animal husbandry; bull-leaping;
    farmers; landowners; olive; trade
Ai-Khanoum 6, 180–1, 190
Aidone, Sicilian town 80
Ajax 43
Alba Fucens 215
Alaric 318, 320, 322, 323
Alcibiades 143
Alexander III of Macedon ('the Great') 6,
  109, 162, 163–76, 177–81, 183, 184,
  186, 187, 236, 249, 260, 266, 305,
  308, 321
  deification and 174–6, 215, 220
  economy and 171, 183
  Greek civilisation and 189
  Persian customs and 172–6

Pompey and 234, 257
see also hairstyles
Alexander Severus, Roman emperor 280
Alexandria, Egypt 183–7, 189–90, 237, 269, 283
alliance, ally 114
  Hieron II and Rome 192
  Italians and Rome 214, 218, 230–1, 232
  Macedonians and Greeks 169
  Spartans and Peloponnesians 139, 147
  see also Athens, naval alliance
Al-Mina 61, 67, 68, 77
alphabet
  Etruscan 99
  Greek 5, 39, 77, 81, 99
  Phoenician 39, 99
Alps 314, 318
altars 288, 313
  Pergamum 187–8
Alyattes, Lydian king 71
Amazons 79
Amphidamas of Chalcis 49
Ammianus Marcellinus, historian 311
amphora
  Carthaginian 92–3
  see storage jar; trade
Anaximander, Greek philosopher 53, 54
Andros, island 21
ancestor worship 46
animal husbandry *see* cattle; sheep and goats
animals *see* bears; camels; hippopotamus; horses; lions; sacrifice, animal
Ankara, ancient Ancyra 238
Antigonids, Macedonian dynasty 179, 249
  see also Perseus; Philip V
Antigonus I, Macedonian king 179
Antikythera, Roman shipwreck 241–2
  mechanism 241–2
Antinous 255, 275
Antiocheia, Antioch, modern Antakya 182, 311
Antiochus I, Seleucid king 182
Antiochus III, Seleucid king 220–1, 223
Antonius, Marcus, Mark Antony 235–8
Antony and Cleopatra, Shakespeare play 186–7
Apollo 41, 70, 86, 102, 152, 249, 306, 309
Apollonius, Ptolemaic finance minister 182–3
Apology, Plato 156
Apries, Egyptian pharaoh 69
aqueducts *see* water supply
Aquileia 277
Arabia, Arabs
  Alexander III of Macedon and 171

ancient 10, 270, 283, 328
  modern 108
Arabic language 329, 331
Aramaic 282
'Archaic smile' 80
architects, Greek 52, 53, 70, 139
archery 173, 273–4, 328
Archimedes, Greek inventor 191, 242
archons, Athenian 122
aristocracy, aristocrats
  Athenian 120, 121, 122, 123, 125
  Greek 41, 43, 44, 47–9, 53, 65, 71, 86
  French 98
  Homeric 40
  Persian 109, 172, 175, 266
  Roman 196–200, 202, 221–3, 227–9, 231, 232, 235, 248
  see also dress; *nobiles*
Aristophanes, Athenian comic playwright 152–5, 199, 331
Aristotle 92, 158–60, 172
  barbarians and 181
  drama and 150
  Sparta and 129, 147
armies, Arab 328
armies, Macedonian 164–5, 219
armies, Roman 199, 210–12, 258, 302
  'king makers' 258, 280–1
  late Roman 303, 319, 323
  protectors of civilization 273
  see also armour; artillery; cavalry; discipline; infantry; militarism; military recruitment; Romans; shields; war; weaponry
armillary sphere 189
armour
  Greek 49
  late Roman 303, 314–15
  Macedonian 164–5
  Persian 117
  see also shields
Arpinum, modern Arpino 202–3, 206
Arsinoe, Egyptian petitioner 269–70
Arsinoe II, Ptolemaic queen 186–7
art market, Roman 225
Artaxerxes II, Persian king 167, 170
Artemis, Greek goddess 71, 173, 287, 308
Artemisium 332
Arthur, King 111
artillery, Greek 191
Asclepius, Greek healing god 229
Ascra, Boeotian village 61
Asia *see* Alexander III of Macedon; Attici; Babylon; barbarian; Mesopotamia; orientalism; Parthian Empire; Persia;

Pompeius; Sasanian Persians; Seleucid dynasty
Asidates, Persian landowner 109
Aspasia 125
assemblies
    Athenian 123–4, 143, 153, 186
    Homeric 40
    Lycian 262
    Roman 201, 208, 226–7
astrologers, astrology 260, 291
astronomical instruments 189–90
    see also Antikythera, mechanism
astronomy 67, 159, 172
Aswan 316
Athena, Athana, Greek goddess 8, 18, 51, 132, 134
Athens, Athenians 119–28, 164
    Academy 158
    Acropolis 1, 50–1, 115, 125, 134, 135, 136, 137, 144, 168, 188, 281
    agora 119, 282
    Apollo as ancestor 102
    cultural achievements 148–61
    cultural prestige 183
    democracy 119–24, 126–7, 139, 149, 152, 153, 155
    Hadrian and 255
    Heruli and 282
    Lysicrates Monument 123
    Macedon and 167
    naval alliance against Persia 134–9, 141, 144
    Parthenon 2–3, 8, 87, 119, 125, 138, 149, 164–5
    Persian Wars and 114–18
    Pnyx 123, 153
    Roman attitudes to 8, 9, 246–7
    Roman provincial town 281–2
    Stoa 259
    Theatre of Dionysus 137, 151, 155
    Tholos 119–20, 122
    women 127
    see also Attalus II, Stoa of; Attici; Demosthenes; Epigraphical Museum; Goulandris Museum; law courts; Athenian; National Archaeological Museum; Pericles; Piraeus; potters
athletes, athletic contests, Greek 43, 55, 313
    Alexander III of Macedon and 172
    Rome and 255
    see also Olympia
Attalidae, Attalids 187
Attalus I, Pergamene king 187
Attalus II, Stoa of 119

Attici, 'Attics', group of Roman orators 246, 247
Attila, Hunnic leader 320–1, 323, 324
auctoritas 233
audiences, rulers' 108–9, 173
Augustine, churchman 318
Augustulus see Romulus
Augustus, first Roman emperor 238–40, 249–51, 257, 259, 264, 316, 327
    title 239
    see also Livia Drusilla; Octavian; Virgil; worship of rulers
Aurelian, Roman emperor 283
Axiothea 158

Babylon, Babylonians 36, 57, 67, 105, 170, 171, 242
Bactria 170
Baghdad 67, 174, 303, 331
Balkh, Afghanistan 175
Baltimore, USA 171
barbarian, barbarians
    Aristotle and 181
    Germanic peoples as 277
    Greek ideas of 4–5, 168, 185, 216, 274
    Macedonians as 164
    modern ideas 57
    Pergamum and 188–9
    Roman ideas of 8–9, 272–4, 277, 316–17
    see also civilization; migrants, migration
barter 182
bathing, bath houses, Roman 261, 279
    sanitation and 264
bathrooms, Greek 166
beards 106, 305, 312, 324 see also hairstyles
bears 128
Beijing Spring 227
'belief' 209, 289
Ben Hur, film 268
benefaction, benefactors, benefactresses 263
Benghazi 89
Berlin 187
    Altes Museum 72, 97, 99
Bethar 275
Betjeman, John and Penelope 299
Bible 39, 65, 105–6 see also Acts of the Apostles; Gospels; New Testament
Bibulus see Calpurnius Bibulus, Marcus
bibliography, ancient 184
bilingualism 243–4
biography, ancient 236 see also Alexander III of Macedon; Caesar, Julius; Augustus
bisexuality 164

bishops *see* Augustine, churchman;
   Eusebius, Christian writer; Sophronius
Black Sea 75, 158, 183, 233, 276, 311
Boeotia, region of central Greece, Boeotians
   60, 147 *see also* Ascra; Chaeronea;
   Thebes, central Greece; Thespiae
Bon, Cape, Tunisia 85, 94
books and booksellers, ancient 110, 120,
   184, 243 *see also* libraries; papyrus
booty 89, 100, 109, 169, 318
   Alaric and 320–1
   Carausius and 284
   Roman 222–3, 239, 249
   see also empire; war
Bordeaux 319
Bosporus 304
botany, Greek 158
Boudicca 289
'bread and circuses' 238
bribery 146, 202, 224 *see also* corruption
Britain, Roman Britannia 234–5, 264–9,
   272, 283–4, 321–2, 330
Britanni 235
British Museum 23, 54, 55, 61, 64, 68, 71,
   100, 108, 125, 131, 139, 149, 185, 204,
   230, 272, 321
British School at Athens 35
'Brittunculi', insulting Roman diminutive
   265
bronze, bronze-making 21, 30
   Corinthian 247
   inscriptions 199, 220, 261, 309, 313
Bronze Age 22, 23, 28, 30, 32, 73
Brutus *see* Junius Brutus, Marcus
Bulgaria 106, 181, 312
bull-leaping 24
Burgundi, Germanic people 320
businessmen 229–30, 302
Butheric, Roman general 314
Byzantium 304, 331

Cadiz, ancient Gadir 64, 319
Caecilii Metelli, Roman noble family 200,
   232
Caere, modern Cerveteri 97
Caesar, Julius 234–7, 264, 269
   ancestry 253
   author 234
   portrait 197–8
Caesar, title 258
Caligula, the Roman emperor Gaius 260,
   263
caliph, caliphate, Muslim 10, 328, 329, 331
   see also Abū Bakr, caliph; Ma'mūn,
   caliph

Callimachus, Alexandrian scholar 184
Calpurnii Pisones, Roman noble family 258
Calpurnius Bibulus, Marcus, Roman consul
   (59 BC) 208–9, 234
Calpurnius Piso Caesoninus, Lucius,
   Caesar's father-in-law 244–5
Calpurnius Piso Frugi Licinianus, Lucius,
   imperial claimant 258–9, 261 *see also*
   Verania
Cambyses, Persian king 106
camels 328
Canaanites 64, 84
cannibalism, ancient allegations of 188, 274
Carausius, Roman imperial usurper 284,
   285
   coinage and 284
Caria, Carians 23, 135
Carthage, Carthaginians 85, 88, 90–5, 104,
   143, 320
   Aeneid and 252
   Hieron II and 191–2
   Roman colony 320
   Roman wars with 216–18, 223–4
   see also Punic Wars
Caryae 250
Caryatids 250
Cassius Dio, Roman historian 278, 279
Castelvetrano, Sicily 84, 216
castration, of homosexuals 327 *see also*
   eunuchs
Catania, Sicily 77
catapults 191
Cato the Elder, Roman statesman 245
cattle 24, 93 *see also* animals; Rome
   (ancient city), cattle market; sheep and
   goats
Caudine Forks 213–14
cauldrons 42, 43
cavalry
   British 265
   Macedonian 162, 169
   Persian 117
   Roman 230
   see also horse-breeding
Cecrops, mythical king of Athens 1, 2
centaur 36
Celtic 267
Celts 234 *see also* Gauls
censor, Roman magistracy 196
Ceos, modern Kea, Aegean island 65
Chaeronea 161, 232
   battle of (338 BC) 161–2, 164, 167
   battle of (81 BC) 232
Chalcis, Euboea, modern Chalkida 48–9
Champagne 321

chariots, chariot-racing, charioteers 146, 169, 173, 222, 268, 305, 314
Chicago 55
Chichester, Roman Noviomagus 266–7
children 115, 188
Delphi maxims and 180
enslavement 142
Plato's utopia and 157
sacrifice of 91–3
Spartan 130
see also Medea
China 165 *see also* Beijing Spring; Mao
Chios, Greek island 69
wine 244
Christ, relics of 299, 300, 328 *see also* crucifixion; Jesus
Christianity, Christians 174, 278, 279, 285, 286–300, 306, 308, 309, 310, 313–14, 315, 318, 326–7, 328, 329, 330
charity and 263
Gospels 189
persecution of 291–7, 299
see also paganism, late Roman
churches 309 *see also* Haghia Sophia; Constantine I; Galla Placidia; Helena; Justinian; Ravenna; Rome (ancient city), St Peter's basilica
Cicero, Marcus Tullius, Roman politician, orator, intellectual and writer 92, 102, 202, 205, 243–7
on Sparta 131
Cimon son of Miltiades 121
circumcision 275
cities
Alexander III and 170, 172
Etruscan 97
Hellenistic 180
Philip II and 181
Roman provincial 261–4, 279–80
Seleucids and 182
see also bathing, bath houses; drainage; fortifications; houses; sanitation; theatres
city-state, Greek (*polis*) 44, 47
Archaic Greek settlement overseas and 78
Aristotle and 181
civil strife and 181
local identity and 55
city-state, Rome as 214, 228
citizens, citizenship
Athenian 120–1, 126–7, 203–4
Roman 102, 202–3, 205, 227, 230–1, 263
Roman provincials and 263, 267, 270, 276, 293, 296

Spartan 147, 203–4
civil strife 227–39
civil wars, Roman 235, 236–7, 258 *see also* proscriptions
civilization 75, 162
Alexander and Greek 172, 189
Greek ideas about 1–7
Greek prehistory and 15–31
modern ideas about 15, 24, 137, 148, 239, 331–2, 332–3
Roman ideas about 7–10, 240, 251, 265–6, 316–17
Rome and Greek 240, 241–55
see also barbarian; cities; Mycenae
Classical, classical, definition 148
Claudii Marcelli, Roman noble family 242
Claudius, Roman emperor 203–4, 258, 262, 264, 267, 289
Claudius Togidubnus, Tiberius, great king of Britain 267–8
Cleisthenes 120–1
Cleon, Athenian politician 153–4
Cleopatra VII, last Ptolemaic ruler 186–7, 236–8, 283
client rulers, Roman *see* Boudicca; Cleopatra VII; Claudius Togidubnus
coinage, coins
Carausius and 283–4
Cleopatra and 236
Greek 54
Hadrian and 275–6
Italian rebels and 230
Lydian invention 70–1
urbanisation and 182
Colchester 289
colonial attitudes, Greek 185
colonies, colonists, Roman 213–14, 226, 233, 275, 319
colonisation 23
Hellenistic 181
'libidinous' 80
Macedonian 172
see also Greeks, ancient
comedy, Greek 87
Athenian 140, 150, 152–5
Roman adaptations 248
see also drama; music
Commodus, Roman emperor 279
competition, competitiveness 55 *see also* athletes
computer *see* Antikythera, mechanism
Constantine I, Roman emperor 297–300, 302–4, 306, 307, 308
Constantinople, modern Istanbul 10, 105, 304, 312, 316–17, 320, 321, 324, 326,

327, 331 *see also* Haghia Sophia; hippodrome; Topkapi Palace
Constantius II, Roman emperor 305, 308
constitution, Roman republican *see* Romans
consulate, consuls, Roman 103, 196, 98, 199, 200, 213, 202
  Caligula and 260
  religious duties 208
convivium, Roman drinking party 244
Copenhagen, Ny Carlsberg Glyptotek 160, 233
copper 21, 30, 31, 96
Copts 296
Coressia 65
Corinth, Corinthians 49, 55, 73–4, 77, 78, 86, 139
  archaeological museum 326
  Roman destruction 223, 247
Cornelia, mother of the Gracchi 197, 199
Cornelia, Paulla 196
Cornelii Scipiones, Roman patrician family 196, 222, 248
Cornelius Scipio Africanus, Publius, Roman consul (205 BC) 218
Cornelius Scipio Barbatus, Lucius, Roman consul (298 BC) 195–6
Cornelius Sulla, Lucius, Roman dictator (81 BC) 231–3
corruption 207, 228 *see also* bribery
Corsica 95, 100
courts, courtiers, 164, 189, 190, 259, 278, 283, 308
  late Roman 305, 321
  see also audience, rulers'; dress; eunuchs; flattery; palaces
courtesans *see* Aspasia; Rhodopis
Crassus *see* Licinius Crassus, Marcus
Crete 23
Crimea 233
Croesus, Lydian king 71
Cronus, Greek god 58, 91
cross-dressing 174
crucifixion 204–5, 292 *see also* Jesus
Cumae 100
Cyclades, 18, 22, 141
Cycladic figurines 22–3
Cynegirus son of Euphorion 112
Cynisca, Spartan princess 146
Cyprus 30, 36, 61, 66, 68, 182, 274
Cyrene 89
Cyrus the Great, Persian king 106, 107, 109, 113

Damascus 327, 329

Danaus, mythical king 249–50
Danube, River 276, 278, 283–4, 303, 304, 311, 323, 324
Dardanelles 114, 116, 117, 167, 169, 188, 220
Darius I, Persian king 106, 107, 110, 116
Darius II, Persian king 145
Darius III, Persian king 169–70, 172
Decius, Roman emperor 295, 296
deification *see* Alexander III of Macedon; worship of rulers
Delian League *see* Athens
Delos 135, 229
  slave market 225–6
Delphi 70, 87, 88, 89, 105, 114, 135
  inscribed maxims 180
  Romans and 223
  see also oracles
Delphic Charioteer 86
Demeter, Greek goddess 18, 19
democracies, western 124, 154, 200, 202
democracy
  Greek *see* assemblies; Athens, Athenians; law courts, Athenian; lottery; merit, meritocracy
  Roman 200–2
Demosthenes 160–1, 166, 247
Dendera, Egypt 235–6
diaspora
  Jewish 274
  Italian 225
  Persian 109
dialectic 155 *see* Socrates
dictator *see* Romans
Dido, Carthaginian queen 252
Didyma 306–7, 309
Diocletian, Roman emperor 285, 296, 297, 300, 304, 306
  edict on prices 301–2
dining
  Alexander III of Macedon and 173
  Athenian democracy and 122–3
  Etruscan 98
  Germanic 322
  Greek 59
  Near Eastern influence 77
  Roman 244, 247
  see also symposium; *convivium*
Diodorus Siculus, Greek historian 91, 93
dioiketes, Ptolemaic finance minister 182
Dionysus, Greek god 18, 150, 151
  Athenian festival of 137, 150
diplomacy, diplomats 94, 164, 166, 219, 221, 321
  grain diplomacy 192

see also alliance, ally; treaty
disease *see* epidemic; sanitation
discipline, military
    Greek 130, 166
    Macedonian 165–6
    Roman 211, 216, 273, 283, 308
    Spartan 130, 147, 166
divination
    Etruscan 99
    Greek 117
    Roman 207–9, 291
Domitian, Roman emperor 246, 255
Dorian, Dorian Greeks, Doric 33, 44, 46,
        89, 141, 143, 189
Dorchester 322
drainage 24 *see* bathrooms; sanitation
drama
    Alexander III of Macedon and 172
    Greek 87, 123, 150–4
    origins 132, 150
    Roman 248
    women in the audience 153
    see also actors; Aeschylus; Aristophanes;
        comedy; Epicharmus; Euripides; mask,
        theatrical; Medea; Sophocles;
        Stesichorus; theatres; tragedy
Dreros, Crete 47–8, 53
dress
    Alexander III of Macedon and 172–4
    Aristotle and 159
    Athenian democracy and 122, 123
    effeminacy and 173
    Goths 312
    Huns 311
    late Roman emperors 305
    Livia and 239
    Lydian influence on Greek 73–4
    philosophers and 309
    Romans and Greek 247
    see also cross-dressing; toga
drought 31, 78, 378
dynastic principle, dynasty 107, 177, 202,
        238

earthquakes 24, 77, 140, 263
Ecbatana 170
economics, household 182
economy
    farming 94
    Hellenistic royal 182–3
    and Linear B 29
    see also agriculture; empire;
        farmers; imperialism; landowners;
        metallurgy; mines, mining; piracy;
        slavery; trade

education
    Greek 189
    Roman 243–5, 329, 331
    see also gymnasium; orators;
        philosophers; rhetoric
Edward VII 267
Egesta *see* Segesta
Egypt, Egyptians 39, 43, 57, 68, 235, 235–7
    Alexander III of Macedon and 168, 169
    Christianity and 295–7
    Greek colonial attitudes and 185
    Greek temple building and 70
    Minoans and 25
    Persians and 167, 169
    pharaohs 186
    Ptolemies and 179, 182–7, 189
    Roman province 237, 269–70, 274, 304,
        316, 318, 324, 328
    see also Alexandria; Apries; Aswan;
        Cleopatra VII; Dendera; obelisk;
        Oxyrhynchus; Psammetichus; Thebes,
        Egypt
Elba, ancient Aethalia 96
electioneering, elections *see* lottery;
        Romans
Elgin Marbles 149
Elizabeth II 146
Elpinice 121
emperors, Roman, ideology and role 259,
        272, 285, 288–90, 305–6, 316–17 *see
        also* Augustus; courts; monarchy;
        princeps; Tetrarchy; worship of rulers
empire, empires 23, 24, 71, 85, 95, 100, 106
    Alexander's approach to 174
    Athenian 137, 246
    Macedonian 167, 169
    Ptolemaic 182
    Spartan 145–7, 246
    Roman 210–24, 257–70
see also Alexander III of Macedon; Athens,
        naval alliance; Carthage; imperialism;
        land hunger; Lydia; Macedon; Persia;
        Rome; tribute
engineers, engineering, Greek 51, 67
England 265, 266, 272
English Channel 234–5, 284, 321
Ephesus 55, 71, 287–8, 292
Ephippus, Greek writer 174
Epicharmus, Sicilian Greek poet 87
Epicurus, Greek philosopher 244
Epidaurus 150
epidemic, Athenian 140–1
Epigraphical Museum, Athens 134, 186
eques, equestrian, *equites see* Romans,
        knights

Erasistratus, Greek scholar and medical researcher 185
Eretria 41, 48–9
erōs, Greek sexual love 157
estates, landed
  Hellenistic kingdoms as 182
  Macedonian 166–7, 170
  Persian 109
  Roman 206, 284, 319, 320
  Spartan 128
Etna, Mt 80
Etruria, ancient Italy 96, 226
Etruria, Staffordshire, England 95
Etruscan language 99
Etruscans, ancient 95–100
  kings of Rome 103
Etruscomania 95
Euboea, Greek island, Euboean 40, 48, 61, 68, 77 *see also* Lefkandi
Eumenes II, Pergamene king 188
eunuchs 308 *see also* castration
Euphrates, River 171, 273
Euripides, Athenian playwright 87, 149–50, 331, 332–3
Europe 246 *see* Asia
Eurotas, River 130
Eurymedon, River 136
Eusebius, Christian writer 294, 298–9, 307
Evans, Sir Arthur 23, 24, 25, 26, 27
Eve, and Adam 44
exchange
  Minoan 25
  see also trade
exiles, Greek 181
extispicy 99, 260 *see also* divination

fake news 173
farmers, farming, farmland, farm produce 117, 128
  Archaic Greece 46, 50, 60–1
  Athenian 140
  Bronze Age Greece 22
  Carthage 92–3
  Hellenistic 181
  Macedonian 165, 166–7
  Megara Hyblaea 78
  Neolithic Greece 19–20
  Roman 226
  see also agriculture; estates
Fayum 182
feasting, feasts
  Etruscan 98
  Lydian 71
  Macedonian 164, 173
  Minoan 27

sacrificial, Greek 43, 65
  see also symposium
fertility, female 23, 79, 197
fetialis 212
film 106 *see also* Ben Hur; *Spartacus*, film; *300*
fish 92
Fishbourne, Roman villa 267–8
Flamininus *see* Quinctius Flamininus, Titus
flattery 176, 259, 264
Flaubert, Gustave 90–1
fortifications 179–80, 191, 282, 320
  Justinian and 326–7
  see also Hadrian's Wall
France 75, 92, 234, 321, 330 *see also* Gaul, Gauls
Franchthi Cave 18
Franks 283, 284
freedmen, freedwomen, Roman 204, 247
freedom 4, 118, 220 *see also* liberty
friendship 159
frontiers 273, 276 *see also* Hadrian's Wall

Gaeseric, Vandal leader 319, 320
Galba, Roman emperor 258
Galilee, Lake 31
Galla Placidia 322–3
Galla Placidia, 'mausoleum of' 322
galleys
  Greek 115, 136
  Persian 113
  Roman 216
  see also triremes
Game of Thrones, TV series 177–8
Ganymede 314
gardens 93
Gaugamela, battle of (331 BC) 169–70
Gaul, Gauls 188, 234–5, 266, 276, 294, 319
Gela 81, 86
Gelon, Sicilian tyrant 86–9, 93
genealogies 44, 165
  Roman 197, 253
geographers, geography, Greek 170, 183
Germania, Roman definition 276
Germani, ancient peoples known as 277, 278, 280, 283
  appearance 277
  Tacitus's book about 277
  see also Burgundi; Butheric; Lombardi; San Giovanni di Ruoti; Saxons; Visigoths
Germanic dialects 311
Germany 234
Geronthrae 302
Getty Museum, California 19, 39, 84

ghosts, Greek belief in 84, 291
Gibbon, Edward, historian 10
Gilgamesh, Epic of 67–8
Glabrio *see* Acilius Glabrio, Manius
gladiators 274, 278
Golan Heights 10
gold 28, 36, 117, 123, 164, 229, 278
    coins 70
Golgotha 329
Gospels 287
Gothi, Goths 311–12, 315, 318, 323 *see also*
    Ostrogoths; Visigoths
Goulandris Museum, Athens 22
Gracchus, Sempronius *see* Sempronius
    Gracchus, Gaius; Sempronius
    Gracchus, Tiberias, brother of Gaius;
    Sempronius Gracchus, Tiberias,
    Roman consul
graffiti 68, 121, 122, 232–3 *see also*
    inscriptions
grain 93, 94, 145, 190–1
    doles, Roman 227, 238, 255
granaries 190, 261
'Graecia', 'Graeci' *see* Greeks
'Graeco-Roman', definition 240
Great North Museum, Newcastle upon
    Tyne 161
Greece, Roman
    conquest 224
    'dark age' 327
    Justinian and 326
    see also Athens; Hadrian; Heruli; Sparta
Greek, Ancient, language 28, 33–4, 168,
    243, 328
    'common language' (*koine*) 189
    see also inscriptions; literature; papyrus
'Greekling', Roman insult 255
Greekness, definition 6, 192
Greeks, ancient 28
    origin of name 33
    identity 43–4, 189
    overseas settlements 75–89 *see also*
        Naucratis
    Rome, resistance to 231
    see also civilization
gymnasium
    aristocracy and 123
    Athenian 158, 159
gymnastic exercises 98 *see also* sport

Hadrian, Roman emperor 8–9, 261, 269,
    308, 326
    Greek culture and 255, 275, 281
    Jews and 275
    military concerns and 272–6

provinces and 275–6
Hadrian's Wall 265, 272–3, 303, 322
Haghia Sophia, Istanbul 326
hairstyles 234, 236
Halicarnassus, modern Bodrum 4, 135
Hannibal 218–19
haruspices 99 *see also* divination
Hatshepsut, Egyptian pharaoh 25, 26
Hattusa, Hittite capital 30–1
Helen 'of Troy' 45–6
Helena, Roman empress 299–300
Helicon, Mt 60–1
Hellas, Hellen, Hellenes 33, 44, 87, 89 *see*
    also Greek; Greeks
'Hellas, Great' *see* Magna Graecia
Hellenistic, definition 179
Helots, Spartan 128–9, 140, 147
hēmerotēs see civilization, Greek ideas
    about
Hera, Greek goddess 52
Heracles 33, 75, 102, 151, 165
Herculaneum 242–3
Hercules 206, 331
Herodotus, 4–5, 6, 67, 69, 70–1, 88–9, 121,
    129
    Persian Wars and 112–18
    truthfulness 110–11
Herophilus, Greek medical researcher 185
Hertfordshire, England 235
Heruli, migrating people 282
Hesiod, Greek poet 44, 60
hieroglyphs, Egyptian 25, 30, 69
Hieron I, Sicilian tyrant 100
Hieron II, Sicilian king 190–2, 219
Himera 88
    battle 88, 93, 192
hippodrome *see* Constantinople; horses
hippopotamus 24
history-writing, ancient 110
    Alexander III of Macedon and 168–9,
        173–6
    Greek 110
    Roman 103, 212–14, 230, 260
    see also Ammianus Marcellinus; Cassius
        Dio; Diodorus Siculus; fake news;
        Herodotus; Livy; Polybius; Tacitus;
        Thucydides; Xenophon
Hittite Empire 30
Hobbes, Thomas 34–5
Hollywood 106 *see also* film
Homer 36–40, 45, 49, 140, 159, 215, 273,
    331
    Alexander III of Macedon and 172
    Alexandria and 184
    Iliad 29, 37, 38, 40, 42, 77, 102, 252

Mesopotamia and 67
Odyssey 37, 252
Virgil and 252
homoerotic graffiti 122
homosexuality
  Athenian comedy and 152–3
  Justinian penalises 327
  Macedonian 164
  late Roman 314
  Plato and 157
  Romans and 211, 275
  Spartan 131
  see also bisexuality; males; symposium
honey 80
Horace, Roman poet 251
horses, horse-breeding 78, 82, 93, 163, 167,
    268, 274, 328 *see also* Caligula; cavalry
houses
  Greek 166
  Roman 197, 242
  Soluntum 290
human-centred culture, humanity, Greek
  57
Hungary 321
Huni, Huns 311, 320, 324
hunt, hunters, hunting 163, 164
  Alexander III of Macedon and 173–4
  staged, Roman 238
hunter-gatherers 18
Hyblon, Sicilian ruler 80
hybridity, cultural 81, 190, 268 *see also*
  Ai-Khanoum

Iliad see Homer
imperial cult, Roman *see* worship of rulers
imperialism, imperialists 24
  Macedonian 169, 174
  Roman 212, 217, 218–19, 224, 242, 274
  see also civilization; colonisation; empire;
    peace; tax
'imperium', Roman idea of 276
Inca emperor 173
incense 171, 173
incest 121, 177
  Ptolemaic 186
India, ancient 170
Indus, River 171
infantry
  Greek 49, 117, 136
  Roman 230
  see also armies
inscriptions
  Ai-Khanoum 180
  Athenian 134–5, 139, 144, 186
  'epigraphic habit' 279–80

Etruscan 99
Greek 47, 70, 71, 84, 86, 100, 105, 117,
  131, 146, 166, 167, 189, 190, 232,
  279–81, 287–8, 301, 307–8, 309, 313,
  326–7
Latin 195–6, 199, 216, 220–1, 223, 258,
  261, 267, 268, 272, 316–17
Persian 106, 113
Phoenician 91
see also Epigraphical Museum; graffiti;
  Res gestae
Ionia, Ionian Greeks 34, 44, 52, 71, 108,
  113, 145
Ionian Revolt 113
Iraq 169
Iran 106, 114, 167, 171, 283
  shah 108
iron, ironworking 31, 96
  roasting spits 70
Iron Age 92, 100, 101
irrigation 182
Isca 265
Islam 286, 328, 331 *see also* caliph;
  Muhammad, prophet; Muslim;
  Topkapi Palace
Israel 21, 30, 282
Issus, battle of (333 BC) 169
Istanbul *see* Haghia Sophia;
  Constantinople; obelisk; Topkapi
  Palace
Isthmus of Corinth 72, 116, 117, 127, 326
Italians, revolt against Rome (91 BC) 230–1
Italic peoples *see* Latini, Latins; Oscan
  dialect; Sabini, Sabines; Samnites;
  Volsci
Italy 74, 75, 89, 103, 226
  Justinian's reconquest 323, 327
  support for Octavian 238
ivory 24, 36

James, William, philosopher 209
Japan, 11, 288–9
Jerusalem 274–5, 299–300, 328–9
Jesus 282, 286–7 *see also* Christ;
  Christianity
Jews, ancient 274–5
John the Evangelist *see* Patmos
jokes, Roman 248
Jordan 243
Judaea, Roman province 286 *see also*
  Hadrian; Jerusalem; Jews
Julia Domna, Roman empress 280
Julian, Roman emperor 308–11, 314
Julius *see* Caesar, Julius
Junius Brutus, Marcus, conspirator 235

Jupiter 253, 275, 279
Justinian, Roman emperor 324–7

Kalamata 128
kalos inscriptions *see* homoerotic graffiti
Kashmir 172
kings, kingship
    Greek ideas about 176
    Hellenistic 179, 188, 190, 219, 224, 232
    Macedonian 116, 164, 179
    Pergamene 188
    Persian 106–10, 113, 137, 170
    Roman 103, 234
    Spartan 146
    see also courts; monarchy; worship of
        rulers
Knossos, Crete 23–8
Knights, comedy by Aristophanes 153
Kommos, Crete 64
Kos, ancient Cos 229
Kopanaki 128

Lagerfeld, Karl 305
Lampedusa, Giuseppe di, Sicilian writer 77
land hunger 78, 167, 215
land reform, Roman 226–7, 233
land tenure
    Macedonian 166
    Roman 226–7
    Vandal 320
landowners, landownership 109, 120, 123
    Macedonian 166–7
    Spartan 130
    see also agriculture; estates; farmers
language *see* Greek, Ancient, language;
        Latin language
Latin language 90, 93, 94, 99, 232, 244, 330
    spread of 268
    see also inscriptions; literature
Latini, Latins 100, 104, 229
Lavrion, ancient Laurium 144
law courts, Athenian 126, 139, 152
    trial of Socrates 155–6
law courts, Roman 202, 228
Law of Hieron 191
law, Roman
    Justinian's codification 325–6
    provinces and 269–70
    schools 326
    Twelve Tables 198–9, 327
laws, Greek 47, 159
    Spartan 130
    see also Lycurgus
lead 96, 229
Lebanon 30, 64, 169, 183

Lefkandi, archaeological site on Euboea
        35–6, 38, 40, 41
Leigh Fermor, Patrick, writer 276
Lelantine plain, Euboea 49
Leonidas, Spartan king 115, 118
Lesbos, modern Lesvos, 67, 69, 71
    Aristotle and 159–60
letters, letter-writing 243, 260, 265, 293
liberty, Roman ideal of 235 *see also*
        freedom
libraries
    Alexandria 184
    Athens 255
    Ephesus 287
    Herculaneum 243
    Pergamum 184
    see also bibliography; books and
        booksellers; papyrus
Libya, modern state 75, 89, 274
Licinii Crassi, Roman noble family 258
Licinius Crassus, Marcus, Roman consul 70
        BC 205
lighthouses, ancient 186, 261
Linear A, Minoan script 25–6, 27
Linear B, Mycenaean script 27–8, 29, 33,
        39, 42, 66
lions 2, 64, 67–8, 173, 301 *see also* hunt
literature, ancient *see* biography; drama;
        history-writing; letters; novel; poems;
        Procopius; puns
Livia Drusilla, second wife of Augustus
        239, 250
Livy, Roman historian 102, 103, 199, 209,
        212–14, 218, 222
    personal religiosity 209
Lombardi, 327
London, Great Fire of 291
lottery 120, 126
Luceria, battle of (315/314 BC) 214
Ludwig II, king of Bavaria 254
Luxor 235 *see also* Thebes
Lycia, region and Roman province 262 *see
        also* Nereid Monument; Patara; Vilia
        Procla
Lycurgus, Spartan lawgiver 131
Lydia, Lydians
    coinage and 70–1
    'customs' 71–2
Lyon, ancient Lugdunum 294–5

Macedon, Macedonians 116, 148, 161–2,
        163–76, 186
    Antigonids and 179
    Asian women and 181
    Rome and 219–20, 249

see also Alexander III of Macedon; Philip II; Ptolemies; Seleucid dynasty
Madonna, weeping, Syracuse 298
Madrid 239
magic, magicians 278, 290–1, 293
Magna Graecia 75
maiestas 221, 263
majlis, audience 108
Malea, Cape, Peloponnese 73
males, manliness, masculinity 20, 30, 42, 58
    Roman 196, 255
    see also beards; nudity; war; women
Ma'mūn, caliph 331
manpower, Roman 214, 218 *see also* population
Mao, Chairman 176
Marathon 112
    battle (490 BC) 112–13, 117, 121
marathon race 113
marble 119, 206, 225, 233, 249, 250, 266
Marcus Aurelius, Roman emperor 277, 278, 279
Mardonius 116, 117, 118
Marius, Gaius, Roman consul (107 BC) 229, 231, 232
Marshall Plan 255
Mark Antony *see* Antonius, Marcus
marriage
    Etruscan 98
    forced 102
    Macedonians with Persians 172
    mixed 185
    Roman 250
    wife-sharing 129
martyrs 294–5
mask, ancestral 197
mask, theatrical
    Ai-Khanoum 6, 180
    Athens 151
    Nero and 254
    Sparta 132
Maxim's, Paris restaurant 108
Maximinus, Roman emperor 280–1
Maximus, late Roman philosopher 310
Medea 332–3
Medes 105–6, 112
medical research, Greek 185 *see also* Asclepius; vivisection
medical students, modern, and Alexander III of Macedon 171
Medina 328
Mediterranean Sea, *mare nostrum* 302
Megara Hyblaea, Sicilian Greek settlement 78–9
Megara, mainland Greece 78

Meiji, Japanese emperor 11, 288
Meilichius, cultic name 84
Melos, Cycladic island 18, 141–2, 143, 145
memory, social 111
men *see* males; women
Menelaus, wife of Helen 45, 46
mercenaries
    Greek 67, 68, 181
    Italian 217
merchants
    Greek 69, 73
    Phoenician 85
    Roman 261, 311
    see also businessmen; trade
Mercury, Roman god 291
merit, meritocracy 126, 166, 202
Mesopotamia, Mesopotamians 67–8, 169, 172, 308, 328
    Parthians and 237
    Seleucids and 179, 182
    see also Sasanian Persians
Messenia, Messenians 129, 147
metallurgy 21 *see also* bronze; copper; gold; iron; lead; mines; silver; tin; zinc
Metelli *see* Caecilii Metelli
metics (foreign residents in Greek cities) 127, 139
Metropolitan Museum, New York 70, 247
Michelangelo 149
migrants, migration 5, 33, 67, 74, 75, 78–9, 80
    'chain' migration 80
    Germanic 277
    Hellenistic 181, 183
    later Roman Empire and 282, 311–12, 317–18, 319–21, 323–4, 327
    see also colonisation; barbarian; diaspora; metics
Miletus, Ionian Greek city 52, 53, 54, 67, 72, 113
militarism, Roman 222
military recruitment, Roman 210, 226, 229, 278, 314–15, 320, 323
military training *see* discipline
Miltiades 121
Minerva, Roman goddess 268
mines, mining, Athenian 144
Minoans, Minoan 24–7, 29, 59
Minos, mythical Cretan king 23, 24
miracles, ancient 278, 297–8
misogyny, ancient 102, 283
Mitford, Nancy 119
Mithradates VI, king of Pontus 231, 232, 233
Mohammed *see* Muhammad, prophet

Molek, Moloch 84
monarchy
    Macedonian 164, 223
    Minoan 26
    modern 240
    Mycenaean 29
    Roman 200
    Roman imperial 238–9, 249
    see also 'bread and circuses'; courts;
        emperors; kings, kingship; worship of
        rulers
monks 328–9, 330
Monmouthshire 264
Morgantina 80–1, 190–1
Morocco 319
mosaics 187, 189, 267, 279, 322
Moses 103
Mosul 169, 191
Motya 85, 91–2
Muhammad, prophet 288, 327–8
Museum, Alexandria 184
Muslim, Muslims 328, 329
music
    Greek 71, 145
    Greek drama and 151
    Nero and 254
    Roman drama and 148
Mycenae 28, 30
Mycenaeans, Mycenaean 28–31, 36, 38, 42,
    59
mythology, myths, Greek 248 see also
    Danaus; drama; Medea; poems;
    Stesichorus; Trojan War; Vaux-le-
    Vicomte

Naevius, Roman playwright 200
names, personal
    Greek 196
    Celtic 267
    Germanic 314
    Roman 196, 221
Naples 322
    Archaeological Museum 151
    Bay of 100, 212, 243, 292
Naqš-i Rustam, Iran 107–8
National Archaeological Museum, Athens
    28, 30, 39, 123, 332
Naucratis 69, 70, 71
navy
    Athenian 114
    Carthaginian 95
    Spartan 145
    see also galleys; triremes
Nazis 277
Nefertiti, Egyptian queen 30

Neolithic 20, 21, 22, 24, 33, 66
    'mind' 20
    Neolithic Revolution 15
Neptune 268
Nereid Monument 149
Nero, Roman emperor 253–5, 259–60, 261
    Christians and 291–2
Neronian Games 254
Nestor, king of Pylos 77
    'Nestor's Cup' 77
New Testament 286–7
Newcastle upon Tyne 161
Newcastle University, England 272
Nicaea, modern Iznik 306
Nicene Creed 306
Nicias, Athenian general 143–4
Nightingale, Florence 263
Nile, River 24, 68, 69, 70, 182, 230, 236,
    255
Nisibis, modern Nusaybin 311
nobiles 199, 257, 258–9 see also aristocracy,
    aristocrats
nomads 283, 311
novel, historical, modern see Vidal, Gore;
    Waugh, Evelyn
novel, Roman 247
Novi Sad, Serbia 303
nudity
    female 22, 98, 149, 324–5
    Greek male 56–7, 70, 72, 87

obelisk 316–17
obsidian 18
Octavian 236–9 see also Augustus
Odoacer, king of Italy 323, 324
Odysseus 38
Odyssey see Homer
Oedipus, mythical Greek king 28
Old English 330
Old Testament 65
olive, olive oil, olive trees 24, 26, 128, 183,
    247
    trade 25, 82, 92
Olympia 40, 42–4, 100, 146, 313
Olympiads 254, 313
Olympic games 32, 40, 146, 254, 313
Olympus, Mt 164
Olynthus 166–7, 174
omens 99, 144 see divination; haruspices
oracles, Greek 114, 306–7
oral performance, orality 38, 40, 111
Oration, Funeral, of 'Pericles' 125–7
orators, oratory
    Greek 160–1, 246–7
    Roman 227, 245–7

see also Attici; Demosthenes; rhetoric
orientalism 106, 283 *see also* Attici; Persia
'orientalizing' 64
Origen, Christian writer 295
Orthia, Spartan goddess 131–2
Oscan dialect 232–3
ostracism 121, 122
Ostrogoths 323, 324, 327
Ovid 206, 253
Oxyrhynchus, Egypt 295

Paestum 322
paganism, late Roman 306, 307, 308, 309
  see also Didyma; Julian; Maximus
Pakistan 106, 170, 273
palaces
  Alexandria 184
  Attila's palace 321
  Macedonian 164
  Minoan 24
  Mycenaean 29, 30, 32
  Pergamum 187
  Sasanian 304
Palermo 88, 190
Palestine 10, 331
Palmyra 282–3
pankration 313
Pantalica, Sicily 80
papyrus 69, 110, 120, 132, 151, 185, 243,
  269–70, 290
Paris 98
Parry, Milman, American scholar 38
Parthenon *see* Athens
Parthian Empire, Parthians 237, 273
  Parthian shot 273
Patara 261–4
Patmos 307–8
patricians *see* Romans
Patroclus 38, 42, 49
patronage, Roman 202, 243, 253, 259, 263
Paul of Tarsus 287
Pausanias, Spartan regent 105, 116, 118,
  135
pax Romana *see* peace
peace, Roman imperial ideology and
  271–2, 273
peasants 181, 226 *see also* farmers; serfs
pederasty, boy love *see* homosexuality
Peloponnese, Peloponnesians 73–4, 115,
  116, 127, 139, 147, 158
Peloponnesian War 139–45, 153, 168
performance artists, erotic 325
Pergamum 184, 187–9, 251
Pericles 124–7, 130, 137, 139, 140, 141, 142,
  165, 281

persecution, of Christians 291–7, 299,
  306–7 *see also* homosexuality;
  paganism, late Roman
Persepolis 108, 137
Perseus, Macedonian king 223
Persia, Persians 3, 4, 88–9, 105–18,
  134–7, 167
  barter and 182
  decadence, supposed 167
  Greek stereotype of 174
  Macedon and 167–76
  Spartan alliance 145
  see also Achaemenids; Sasanian Persians
Persian language (Old Persian) 110, 113
Persian Wars 105–18, 145, 174, 282
  Pergamum and 189
  Rome and 246, 250
Persians, play by Aeschylus 3–4
Peter, apostle 299
Peter the Great 165
petitions 269–70
Phalaris, tyrant of Acragas 82–3
Pharsalus, battle of (48 BC) 235
Pheidias, Athenian artist 125, 149
Philip II of Macedon 162, 163–8, 175, 181,
  232 *see also* Alexander III of Macedon
Philip V of Macedon 219, 220, 248, 249
Philip, Roman emperor 270
Philippopolis, modern Plovdiv 181
Philistis, Queen 190
Philodemus, Greek philosopher 243
philosophers, philosophy
  Greek 52–4, 67, 113
  late Roman 309–10
  Roman 244
  see also Anaximander; Aristotle; Cicero;
    Delphi; dialectic; Epicurus; Maximus;
    Philodemus; Plato; Socrates; Stoa;
    Stoics
Phoenicians, Phoenician 30, 64, 90
  and Greek alphabet 5, 39, 64
  Persian subjects 113, 169
  Sicily and 84–5
  see also Carthage
Piacenza, Italy 99
Piazza Armerina, villa 332
piracy, pirates 95, 226
Piraeus 115, 138, 140
Pisistratus, Athenian tyrant 50–1, 56
Piso *see* Calpurnius Piso Caesoninus,
    Lucius; Calpurnius Piso Frugi
    Licinianus, Lucius
Pithecusae, modern Ischia 77, 96
Pizarro 173
plague *see* epidemic

Plataea 117
    battle of (479 BC) 88, 116–17, 121, 134, 135
Plato, Athenian philosopher 87, 124, 156–8, 310, 331
Platonic love 156
plebeians, plebs, Roman *see* Romans
Pliny the Elder 292
Pliny the Younger 292–3
plunder *see* booty
Plutarch, Greek writer 227, 232
Po, River 212, 322
poems, poetry
    drama and 151
    Greek 39, 58, 77, 87, 132, 244, 252, 328, 329
    Roman 251–3
    see also drama; Homer; Horace; Nestor, Nestor's Cup; Ovid; Sophronius; Virgil
Poeni 85 *see also* Carthage
poison 156, 171, 260
polis see city-state
Polybius, Greek historian 94
    First Punic War and 216–18
    Roman army and 211, 219
    Roman imperialism and 217, 218–19, 224
    Roman religion and 206–7
    Roman republican constitution and 200–1
Polycrates, Samian tyrant 72
Pompadour, Madame de 125
Pompeii 232–3
Pompeius, Gnaeus, Pompey 233–5
    descendants 257–8
pontifex maximus 289
pontiffs, Roman 208
Pontius Pilate 286
Pope Francis 282
population
    Archaic Greece 46
    Athenian citizen body 124
    Greek overseas settlements 78
    Megara Hyblaea 79
    Roman 214, 226
    Rome (city) 238
    Spartan citizen body 129–30, 147
Populonia 96
Pope, Alexander 37, 252
Poppaea Sabina 254
porphyry 284–5, 304
portraiture, Roman 197–8, 233–4, 257, 247, 257–8, 304–5
Poseidon 124, 140

potters, pottery, pots, potsherds 20, 26, 34, 81, 94, 104
    Athenian 55–7, 119–20, 121, 151, 164, 174
    'Etruscan' 95–6
    Geometric 35, 61
    Phoenician 64
power, Greek ideas about 141
Praeneste, modern Palestrina 229–30, 248
praetorians 259
Predjama, Slovenia 210
priest, priestess, pagan 24, 26, 91, 99, 208, 212, 277, 289, 293, 307 *see also fetialis*; pontiffs; Vera; Vestal Virgins
princeps 257 *see also* Augustus; emperors; monarchy
Priscus, Roman diplomat 321, 323
Procopius, eastern Roman writer 324–5
prodigies, Roman 207–9
proscriptions, Roman 232, 237
prostitutes, female 72, 98, 325 *see also* courtesans; women
Proust, Marcel 258
provinces, Roman 219, 257–70 *see also* Asia; Britain; Egypt; Gaul; Greece; Judaea; Lycia; Sardinia; Sicily; Syria
provincial governors, Roman 262–9
provincials
    as local benefactors 263
    Roman provincial ideology 276
    Roman support for rich 262, 266–8
Psammetichus, Egyptian pharoah 68
psyche see soul
Ptolemies, Macedonian dynasty 179, 183–7, 190, 230, 237
    as pharaohs 185, 236
    see also Arsinoe II; Cleopatra VII
Ptolemy I 179, 186
Ptolemy II 186
Ptolemy III 182
Punes 85 *see also* Carthage
Punic Wars, First (264–241 BC) and Second (218–201 BC) 216–18
puns, in the New Testament 287
purple dye 72
Pygmalion, mythical Cypriot king 66
Pylos 28–9, 30, 77
Pyrrhus, Epirot king 212, 215–16

queens, queenship
    Hellenistic 186–7, 190
    see also Arsinoe II; Cleopatra VII
Quinctius Flamininus, Titus, Roman consul (198 BC) 219–20, 222
    Greek worship of 288

racism, ancient 185 *see also* barbarian, orientalism
Ramesses II 68
rape 79, 102, 103, 115, 248, 318
Ravenna 322, 323
Raqqa 191
recruitment *see* military
refugees *see* exiles; migrants
religion, ancient 279, 309
    Aristophanes and 154
    Etruscan 99
    Greek 41–2, 154–6
    Greek Sicily 84
    manipulation of 51, 208–9
    nature of 54–5
    Roman 206–9, 287–90, 293, 295, 309–10
    Socrates and 155–6
    see also Christianity; ghosts; haruspices; magic; miracles; omens; oracles; paganism, late Roman; priest, priestess; sacrifice; soul; temples; worship of rulers
religion, Jewish 65–6, 274–5
Renaissance 11, 85, 148, 331, 332
Remus *see* Romulus
republic, Roman *see* Romans
Res gestae, political testament of Augustus 238–9, 250
rhetoric 143, 231
    Aristotle and 160
    Demosthenes and 160–1
    Greek teachers of 154, 245
    Rome and 245–7, 249
    see also orators
Rhine, River 234, 276, 280, 318, 321, 324
Rhodes 243
Rhodopis, Greek courtesan 69–70
roads, road-building, Roman 228, 262
Romania 253
Romanovs 253
Romans
    constitution, republican 200–2
    dictatorship 232, 239
    electioneering, elections 201–2, 222, 227, 231
    good faith and 221
    Greece, attitudes to 33, 265, 308
    Greek civilisation and 240, 241–55
    Greeks view as barbarians 216
    imperial-period identity as 270, 276, 296
    knights 205–6, 228, 259, 306
    morality, morals 239–40, 244, 245, 246, 248, 249–50, 255, 308–9, 327
    'new man' 202

patricians 198–9, 234
plebs 198–9, 222, 254
racism and 185
republic 195–235, 238
revolts against *see* Boudicca; Jews
Senate 200, 205, 222, 248, 257, 261, 318
tribunes of the people 198, 227, 232, 233, 234
triumph 222–3, 247
Trojan ancestry 215–16, 253
unconditional surrender and 220–1
see also Aeneas; aristocracy; armies; assemblies; booty; citizens, citizenship; consulate; divination; emperors; Punic Wars, First; imperialism; law, Roman; *nobiles*; patronage; provinces; religion, Roman; Romulus and Remus; slavery; wolf
Rome (ancient city) 94
    Alaric's sack 318–19
    Augustan building programme 249–51
    cattle market 206, 249
    Column of Marcus Aurelius 278–9
    foundation 8, 103
    Forum Augustum 250
    Forum Romanum 249
    Greek culture, capital of 245
    Hercules, temple of 206, 249
    'hut of Romulus' 101
    Palatine Hill 101, 249
    population 238
    St Peter's basilica 299
    Senate house 318
    stadium 254–5
    theatres 248
    via Appia 195
Rome (modern)
    Centrale Montemartini museum 197
    Palazzo dei Conservatori 304–5
    Piazza Navona 254
    Roman National Museum 258
Romulus Augustulus, Roman emperor 324–5
Romulus and Remus 8, 101–2, 103, 326
Rowling, J. K., writer 290
Roxane, marriage to Alexander III of Macedon 170
Russell, Bertram 52–3
Russia 165

Sabini, Sabines 102, 212
sacrifice, animal
    Etruscan 99
    Greek 65–6, 84, 175
    Jewish 65–6
    late Roman 308, 313

Roman 207–8
sacrifice, human 152
    child 91–2
sailing 25, 138–9
Salaambô, novel 90–1
Salamis 115
    battle of (480 BC) 3, 115–16, 117, 189
Samnites 212–14, 226
Samos, East Aegean island 51–2, 55, 69, 72
San Giovanni di Ruoti, Italy 322
sanitation 264
Santorini, Cycladic island 25, 89
Sappho, Greek poet 69, 71
Sardinia 92, 93, 94
    Roman province 219
Sardis, Lydian capital 72
Sarmatians 283
Sasanian Persians 283, 303–4, 308, 310–11,
    321, 324, 328
Satyricon, Roman novel 247
Saxons, Saxon 284, 321, 330
Scandinavia 282
Schliemann, Heinrich 28, 32
science, ancient 191 *see also* Aristotle;
    astronomy; botany; medical research;
    zoology
Scipio family 222 *see also* Cornelius Scipio
    Africanus, Publius; Cornelius Scipio
    Barbatus, Lucius
Scotland 265
sculptors, Greek 139
sculpture
    Athenian 149 *see also* Pheidias
    booty 223, 241, 249
    Egyptian influence on 70
    Greek 72, 80, 332
    late Roman 316–17
    Pergamene 187–8
    Persian 106, 107–8
    Ptolemaic 185–6, 236
    Roman 197, 223, 249–51, 273, 278–9
    Roman Sparta 280
    see also Cyclades; Delphic Charioteer;
        Neolithic; portraiture
seafaring, ancient
    Archaic Greece 61, 70
    capes and 73
    Greek Bronze Age 21–2, 23
    Greek Stone Age 19
    Hellenistic 190
    Minoan 25
    Phoenician 64
    see also galleys; lighthouses; merchants;
        navy; sea-power; shipping; trade;
        triremes

seals, Minoan 25
sea-power 23, 25
    Athenian 138
    Etruscan 99
    Persian 169
    Spartan 145
    Roman 217
    see also empire; navy; seafaring
Segesta 7, 142
Seleucid dynasty 179, 233 *see also*
    Antiochus I; Antiochus III
Seleucus I, Macedonian king 179, 180
Selinus 81, 83–5, 291
Sempronius Gracchus, Gaius 197, 227–9,
    232, 233
Sempronius Gracchus, Tiberius, Roman
    consul 177 BC, husband of Cornelia
    199
Sempronius Gracchus, Tiberius, brother of
    Gaius 226–7, 232, 233
Seneca, Nero's tutor 259–60
Septimius Severus, Roman emperor 280
Serbia 277, 303, 321
serfs 181 *see also* Helots
Sesklo, Neolithic site 19, 20, 21
sexual love, Greek *see* courtesans; *erōs*;
    homosexuality; marriage; prostitutes;
    rape
Shakespeare, William 87, 186
sheep and goats 19, 93, 99
shields
    Macedonian 215, 223
    Roman 223
shipping, ships 86, 112
    Isthmian haulage 73
    Minoan 25
    Phoenician 92
    see also galleys; triremes
Sicani 82
Sicels 80
Sicily, Sicilians 5, 93, 149–50, 332
    Archaic Greek settlements on
        77–89
    Athenian expedition against 142–4
    Hellenistic 189–92
    pupils of Plato 158
    Roman province 219, 320, 327
    see also Carthage; Romans
Silchester, Roman 268
silver 96, 109–10, 218
    coins 71, 182–3
    see also mines
skyscraper envy 55
slavery, slaves 57, 69, 83, 333
    agricultural 128, 226

Athenian democracy and 127, 139, 142, 144
revolts 129, 132, 204–5
Roman 204–5, 218, 225–6, 247, 28
see also Helots; freedmen, freedwomen; mines, mining; piracy; serfs
Socrates 125, 148, 154–8, 260 see also Aristophanes; Plato; Seneca
Solon 49–50, 53
Soluntum 190
Sophocles, Athenian playwright 2, 148
Sophronius, bishop 329
soul, belief in 156
Spain, 9, 64, 75, 92, 319
Carthage and 217, 218
Roman province 219
Sparta, Spartans 45–6, 75, 89, 102, 106, 127–33, 134–5, 150, 189
Athenians, contrasted with 139–40
'decline' 145–7
Peloponnesian War and 139–41, 143–5
Persian Wars and 113–18
Roman 279–81
Roman ideas about 246
Taras, overseas settlement 215
see also Caryae
Spartacus, film 204
Spartacus, slave leader 204–5
Sparti, modern Sparta 130, 280
speeches see Cicero; Demosthenes; Thucydides
spices 171
sport see athletes; pankration; wrestling
status anxiety, Roman 206
Stesichorus, Sicilian Greek poet 87
Stoa, Stoics, philosophical sect 259–60
Stone Age 15, 18
see also Neolithic
storage jars, 25, 26, 69, 128 see also amphora
Successor wars 179
suicide 237, 254
Sulla see Cornelius Sulla, Lucius
Sunium 116, 124
Susa 170
Swallow Islands 136
symposium, Greek drinking party 57–9, 77, 156
Athenian democracy and 122
convivium and 244
Symposium, Plato's dialogue 156–7
Syracuse 77, 100, 145, 242, 298
Apollo, temple of 70
Athenian expedition against 142–4, 149–50

Euryalus 191
Hellenistic 190–2
Roman capture 219
theatre 190
Syria 66, 169, 270
Roman province 233, 280, 282, 324
Seleucids and 179, 182–3
Syro-Canaanites 30

Tacitus, Roman historian 258–9, 264, 266, 267, 277
Christians and 292
Tajikistan 170, 180
Taras, Tarentum, modern Taranto 212, 215–16
Tarquin the Proud, Roman king 103
Tarquinii 97–8, 100, 103
Tarsus 287
tattoos 22
tax, taxation 50, 123, 169, 182, 190–1, 228, 263, 265, 306, 315 see also tribute
Taygetus, Mt 128, 129
temples, temple-building
Greek 41, 52, 55, 66, 70, 71, 82, 84, 87, 89
see also Athens, Acropolis; Athens, Parthenon
Roman 267
Tertullian, Christian writer 279
Tetrarchy 284–5, 304
Thales, Greek philosopher 54, 67
Thasos 136
Thatcher, Margaret 182, 218
theatres
Greek 150, 164
Roman 248, 261, 263
see also drama; Athens, Theatre of Dionysus
Thebes, central Greece 28, 30, 161, 168 see also Boeotia
Thebes, Egypt 26
Themistocles 114, 115, 281
Theodora, Roman empress 324–5
Theodosius I, Roman emperor 313–14, 316–17, 318, 322
Thera 89 see also Santorini
Thermopylae 114
battle of (480 BC) 114–15
Thespiae, central Greece 278
Thessalonice, modern Thessaloniki 166, 313
Thessaly 19
Thompson, Homer A., archaeologist 119
Thucydides, Athenian historian 23, 33, 34, 124, 125–7, 129, 292, 331
Peloponnesian War and 140–4

Tiber, River 100, 102, 103, 299
Tiberius, Roman emperor 238
Tigris, River 171, 311
tin 30, 31
Tiryns, southern Greece 30
Titus, Roman emperor 279
toga, Roman 204, 205, 266, 276
Togidubnus *see* Claudius Togidubnus,
    Tiberius
Tomis, modern Constantsa) 253
Topkapi Palace 327–8
town planning 78, 249, 261
trade, traders 29, 31
    Alexander III of Macedon and 171,
        183
    Archaic Greece 61, 68, 69, 72–3, 77
    Archaic Sicily 82
    Carthaginian 92–4
    Etruscan 96–7
    Phoenician 85, 92
    Roman 225–6, 261, 282
    see also businessmen; merchants;
        Palmyra
tragedy, Greek 164
    Athenian 150–2
Trajan, Roman emperor 288
    Christians and 293–4
translation, translators, post-antique 330–1
    see also Pope, Alexander
transvestism *see* cross-dressing
treaty, treaties 94, 104, 145, 214, 312
tribute 71
    late Roman 321
    Persian 110
    Roman 219
    see also Athens, naval alliance; tax
Trimalchio 247
tripods 42, 88, 117
Triptolemus, Greek demi-god 19
triremes, Athenian 138–9
triumph *see* Romans
triumvirs 237
Trojan War 32–3, 37, 45–6, 140, 168
Troy 32, 38, 102, 104, 169, 215 *see also*
    Aeneas of Troy; Romans
Trump, Donald 176, 218
Tullius *see* Cicero, Marcus Tullius
Tunis 93
Tunisia 85
Turin, Museo di Antichità 197–8
Turkmenistan 174
Tuscany 96
Tussaud, Madam 197
Tutankhamun 164, 186
Twelve Tables *see* law, Roman

tyrant, tyranny 50–1, 82, 92, 121 *see also*
    Gelon; Phalaris; Pisistratus

Uluburun, Cape, southern Turkey
    29–30, 73
urbanisation
    Hellenistic 182
    see also cities; drainage; houses; town
        planning; Rome (ancient city); Patara;
        Pergamum
utopia 157

Valens, Roman emperor 311–12
Valentinian III, Roman emperor 323
Vandals 319–20, 327, 328
Vaux-le-Vicomte, French château 331–2
Venice 284–5
Ventris, Michael, linguist 28, 29
Venus, Roman goddess 253
Vera, priestess of Patmian Artemis 307–8,
    309
Verania, wife of Piso Licinianus 260–1
Veranius, Quintus, Roman governor 261–4
Vergina, Macedonia, ancient Aegae 163–4
Vestal Virgins 290
Vesuvius, Mt 242, 243, 292
Victoria, Roman goddess 216
Victorian, Victorians 11, 23
Vidal, Gore 308
Vienna 276, 282
Vilia Procla 263–4, 265
Villa of the Papyri 243
villas, Roman 242–3, 272
    lifestyle 247
    villa estates 284
    see also Fishbourne; Piazza Armerina
vines, vineyards 93 *see* wine
Virgil 251–2, 330
    Carausius and 284
Visigoths 318, 319, 321, 322 *see also* Alaric
vivisection 185
Volsci, Italic people 202, 212
Vulci 103–4

Wagner, Richard 254
Wales 264, 265
war, warriors 30, 49, 87–8
    Etruscan 97
    Greeks and Sicilians 81–4
    Hellenistic 183
    Macedonian 166
    Roman 212
    see also armies; booty; empire; males;
        Peloponnesian War; Persian Wars;
        Punic Wars

warmongering
  Macedonian 167
  see also militarism, Roman
water supply 56–7, 261, 264
Waugh, Evelyn 299
weaponry, weapons 27, 30, 49, 87, 97
  Macedonian 161, 164–5, 219
  Roman 210, 219
Wedgwood, Josiah 95
Wheatley, Dennis, writer 84
wine, wine-drinking, wine-making
  Alexander III of Macedon and 171–2
  Archaic Greek 57–9, 69
  Chian 244
  Etruscan 98
  Italian diaspora and 225
  Minoan 25, 26, 27
  Morgantina 81
  Mycenaean 28–9
  trade 82, 92
wolf, Roman 8, 101, 230
women 115
  ancient ideas about 102, 127, 333
  Augustan art and 249–50
  enslavement of 142
  Etruscan 98
  Neolithic Greece 20
  public places and 155
  pupils of Plato 158
  Roman 196–7, 201
  Roman law and 270
  Spartan 129, 132

see also children; courtesans; Cycladic
  figurines; fertility; males; marriage;
  misogyny; performance artists;
  prostitutes; rape
worship of rulers 164
  Alexander III of Macedon and 174–6
  Greek ideas about 175–6
  Japanese 288
  Roman 239, 288–9
wrestling 43, 313
writing
  Carthaginian 90
  Minoan 25–6
  Greek 39–40, 47
  see also alphabet; graffiti; inscriptions;
    Linear A; Linear B; literature
Wyoming, University of 325

Xenophanes, Greek poet 58
Xenophon, Athenian writer 144–7
Xerxes I, Persian king 88, 106, 110, 114–18,
  134, 145, 165, 189

Yannina 215
Yauna 108 *see also* Ionia
York 330

Zama, battle of (202 BC) 218, 221
Zenobia 283, 284
Zeus 42, 44, 87, 91, 188, 215, 313, 332
zinc 96
zoology, Greek 158